'In recovering what he can of the near-vanished histories of Britain's lost realms, Williams has done an admirable job, evoking the spirit of an age that was both chaotic and creative, from the ferment of which England and ultimately Britain emerged. It is a gift indeed to be reminded that Dumnonia, Lindsey, Fortriu, Hwicce, Elmet and Rheged – faint ghosts of places though they may now seem – made their own contributions to what we are today'   *Literary Review*

'Thomas Williams's *Lost Realms* offers an imaginative alternative to [the] standard historical narrative. Under Williams's pen, the traditional story of seven large kingdoms – the so-called heptarchy – makes way for one of nine "minor" kingdoms … Rich and captivating'
Times Literary Supplement

'Williams has a fine command of the literary, administrative, religious and archaeological sources of early medieval Britain. He is a diligent scholar and a likeable writer'   *The Times*

'The book is beautifully written, pushing at the very limits of our ability to understand the early medieval world'
British Archaeology

LOST REALMS

*Histories of Britain from
the Romans to the Vikings*

THOMAS WILLIAMS

WILLIAM
COLLINS

William Collins
An imprint of HarperCollins*Publishers*
1 London Bridge Street
London SE1 9GF

WilliamCollinsBooks.com

HarperCollins*Publishers*
Macken House, 39/40 Mayor Street Upper
Dublin 1, D01 C9W8, Ireland

First published in Great Britain in 2022 by William Collins
This William Collins paperback edition published in 2023

1

Maps and illustrations by Martin Brown

A catalogue record for this book is
available from the British Library

ISBN 978-0-00-817198-8

Extracts from *Farmer Giles of Ham* by J.R.R. Tolkien (1949)
reprinted with permission of HarperCollins*Publishers* Ltd

Extracts from 'Remains of Elmet' by Ted Hughes
reprinted with permission of Faber and Faber Ltd

Set in Minion Pro
Printed and bound in the UK using 100%
renewable electricity at CPI Group (UK) Ltd

For my parents

+
MATER OPTIMA MAXIMA
PATER OPTIMVS MAXIMVS
+

Since Brutus came to Britain many kings and realms have come and gone [...] What with the love of petty independence on the one hand, and on the other the greed of kings for wider realms, the years were filled with swift alternations of war and peace, of mirth and woe, as historians of the reign of Arthur tell us: a time of unsettled frontiers, when men might rise or fall suddenly, and song-writers had abundant material and eager audiences.

J. R. R. Tolkien, *Farmer Giles of Ham* (1949)[1]

The natural vice of historians is to claim to know about the past. Nowhere is this claim more dangerous than when it is staked in Britain between 400 and 600. We can identify some events and movements: make a fair guess at others; try to imagine the whole as a picture in the fire [...] But what really happened will never be known.

James Campbell, *The Anglo-Saxons* (1982)[2]

Where now the horse? Where now the men?
Where now the benefactor?
Where now the seat at the feast? Where the hall-joys?
Alas, bright beaker! Alas, burnished warrior!
Alas proud prince! How that time has gone,
dark under night's helm, as if it had never been.

Anon., *The Wanderer*[3]

It is the middle of the Dark Ages – ages darker
than anyone had ever expected.

Jabberwocky (1977)[4]

CONTENTS

A JOURNEY IN THE DARK

– *Prologue* –

Night is falling. Your land and mine goes down into a
darkness now; and I, and all the other guardians of her
flame, are driven from our homes, up out into the wolf's jaw.
But the flame still flickers in the fen. You are marked
down to cherish that. Cherish the flame, till we can
safely wake again.[1]

David Rudkin, *Penda's Fen* (1974)

What happens when the rug is pulled, when all the certainties
melt away and when what had yesterday felt permanent,
unchanging, unchangeable, collapses at breakneck speed? And
what comes after?

All ages of the past are dark because the past is a grave. It is a
void that historians and archaeologists seek to fill with knowledge
– with things made by long-dead hands and the ghosts of buildings
long demolished, the uncanny traces of people and their lost lives,
poignant in their mundanity: a used bowl, a broken glass, a clay
pipe, a worn shoe, the pieces of a game scattered and abandoned. It

1

whispers with the words captured on the skins of animals or fragments of birch bark and lines breathed by poets in fire-lit halls, frozen in ink, repeating again and again across the generations, as the bones of their authors crumble in the cold, dark earth. The more we find to fill that void, the better illuminated the past appears. It takes on three-dimensional form in standing buildings and tangible artefacts, detailed reconstructions of costume and paraphernalia. Film and television provide illusory glimpses of the irrecoverable; historical fiction and immersive histories promise time travel to places we feel we might inhabit – regardless of their many distortions and omissions. And, by and large, the further away a historical period sits relative to our own lives, the less vital and vibrant it feels – the colour footage turns to black and white and then to sepia, it freezes into still photography and then mutates into artist-mediated renderings of life: oil paintings, frescoes, manuscript illuminations, scratches on rock. Eventually it recedes altogether into darkness.

It has become fashionable in recent decades to argue that the trauma of the collapse of the Roman Empire has often been overstated, that for many people life changed little if at all, that the tales told of devastation, plague, poverty and violence were exaggerations, that the archaeological evidence for widespread and rapid civic collapse has been misinterpreted. Historians have always seen the past through the prism of their own age, in the shadow of recent memory, and the last period of relative peace experienced in the West has been remarkable for its overall stability and prosperity.* For those in Europe and North America who lived through the world wars and endured the omnipresent spectre of nuclear obliteration, however, the idea that civilizations could be annihilated, that human savagery was limitless and that the lives of individuals

---

* This chapter was written in 2020, well before Vladimir Putin visited sweeping horror on the eastern marches of Europe. War in the Balkans in the 1990s notwithstanding, the war in Ukraine – with its origins in 2014 and its obscene flowering in 2022 – has raised a fresh phalanx of morbid visions to stalk the Western imagination.

and of whole societies could be plunged into existential crisis in a matter of months (or even minutes) was not in doubt. For people in many other parts of the world, the proximity of trauma has seldom been out of sight. And for those who lived through the Middle Ages, death and misfortune were constant companions.

The events of the very recent past, however, have demonstrated with stunning brutality that in the blink of an eye the world can change for ever. What comes afterwards is always unknowable, but the actions and decisions of individuals and societies – sometimes spontaneous and sometimes after a prolonged period of anxiety and introspection – will set the stage for what will follow: nothing is inevitable about the path the world will take. The clarity with which that is felt in the third decade of the twenty-first century adds a complexion to this book that it did not possess at the outset; some chapters – those written later – perhaps reflect this more fully that those written earlier, though all are coloured by it to a certain degree. The kingdoms that emerged in Britain in the shadow cast by failing Empire were social experiments in responding to trauma, to the pulling of the rug, and this book is, in part, about how societies facing crisis can find very different paths through and out of it. What emerges more clearly than I had envisaged is the tension between forces that might be imperfectly described as conservative and progressive – between those who seek solace and security in the symbols and structures of the past and those who, for good or ill, see potential in the strange and the foreign, abandoning the solidity of stone walls and civilization for something as yet unmade, risking the eradication of older ways of being. Those paths may ultimately converge, but the pain of walking them leaves scars that never fully heal.

The term 'Dark Ages' – used vaguely for the period between the end of Roman Imperial government in Britain in c.400 and, normally, an ill-defined point between the years 600 and 800 – is widely disowned by most modern scholars. Objections are frequently raised that to single this period out as 'dark' is to downplay the accomplishments of the age and exoticize its mystery, while casting unwarranted shade on aspects of its social, cultural or economic history.* To me, however, the assumption that 'darkness' necessarily equates to 'badness' is lazy and a little ugly. And it is clear – in fact one of the only things that actually is clear about the period – that the most heavily Romanized parts of Britain underwent a socio-economic collapse of unusual suddenness and severity in the period when Roman rule in Britain was coming to an end. That this was accompanied by war and a long period of chronic instability is almost certain. For the people who lived through this and were affected by it, these must have been grim days indeed. The fact that other periods may have been more unpleasant (and therefore more deserving of the adjective 'dark') is neither here nor there – nobody wants to play 'bad times' poker ('I'll see your so-called Dark Ages and raise you a Black Death').

In any case, I have always rather liked the mystery that the term 'Dark Ages' implies. Just as blank spaces on the map tug on the imagination of the explorer, so the darker spaces of history hold an allure that speaks to hidden facets of the human psyche. This, I think, is one of the reasons why early medieval history captured me as an undergraduate and has held me ever since. The struggle to understand the scattered and difficult sources, the possibility of genuine discovery in a world where nothing can be taken for granted, represent an endless quest where everything is on the table to be interpreted afresh and the deepest secrets still lie locked within the earth.

---

* In 2016, the adoption of the term 'Dark Ages' by English Heritage for the whole of the period between 410 and 1066 sparked a furious backlash from academic historians and archaeologists. Despite some notable dissenters, the orthodox view – and one which seems now to have been adopted by English Heritage (at least online) – is that the terms 'early medieval' and 'early Middle Ages' are adequate to describe the 650 years or so prior to the Norman Conquest. There is no need, the argument runs, to insult the public intelligence by supposing that people are incapable of differentiating the 'early' from the 'late' medieval period. That, I suppose, is fair enough (though the supposed simplicity of this argument is undermined a little by the fact that medieval historians frequently distinguish the 'Late Middle Ages' – the period between c.1300 and c.1500 – from the 'High' or 'Central' Middle Ages – the period between c.1000 and c.1300).

This book is for those who understand that the glimmer of gold in torchlight can be worth a thousand sun-drenched spires; it is a book that tells the stories of the most obscure kingdoms to have risen in Britain in the dim post-Roman dawn. Some of them died in near darkness, never to fully experience the wan light shed by the slow accumulation of historical record. Their brief lives can only be told from scraps of legend and ambiguous archaeological traces, and the writings of men who lived centuries after the history they recorded. Other realms lived long enough to experience the relative illumination of later centuries, falling into obscurity amid the tumults of the Viking Age. In all of them, however, the surviving traces of life can be related to fragments of history, the archaeology brought into a relationship with a people and the stories they told. The halls of farmer-lords can still be found as ghost marks in the earth, patches of dark soil where curling ribbons of smoke once climbed the great pillars to the roof beams they shouldered; the hill-forts of warlords and sea-lords and kings of the trade winds yet cling to the peaks of rocky outcrop and mountain fastness. The grave-fields and barrow-mounds still hold their bodies just as weathered grey stone and brittle yellow parchment bear their names – tying the landscape back to a past where lives were lived with as much vigour and joy as in any other age, where people fought and loved and toiled and suffered grief and disappointment just as cutting as our own.

Out there amid heath and hedgerow the tombs of unknown kings lie forgotten beneath stands of ash and birch – the graves of heroes whose names once rang beside hall-fires, whose horns once echoed in the hills; swords rusted, gold torn by the plough, treasure scattered over fields. Bones are dislodged from resting places, gnawed by foxes, badgers, rats; tossed and broken by grey roots questing among the dead.

And still the lords of the lost realms slumber on.*

* Parts of this prologue, in rather different form, appeared previously in an article for *BBC History Magazine* (March 2020).

BRITAIN

C. 600 AD

Atlantic
Ocean

North
Sea

FORTRIU

DAL RIATA

ALT
CLUT

RHEGED

NORTHUMBRIA

Irish
Sea

ELMET

LINDSEY

GWYNEDD

POWYS

MERCIA

EAST
ANGLIA

DYFED

HWICCE

ESSEX

Southern
Bight

WESSEX

SUSSEX

KENT

DUMNONIA

English Channel

LITTLE
KINGDOMS

– *Introduction* –

The face of the land has changed since that time, and
kingdoms have come and gone; woods have fallen, and
rivers have shifted, and only the hills remain, and they
are worn by the rain and the wind.

J. R. R. Tolkien, *Farmer Giles of Ham* (1949)[1]

In 1949, Allen & Unwin published a short book by Professor
J. R. R. Tolkien titled *Farmer Giles of Ham*. It was, at surface
level, a children's story, and its genesis was in a tale of the 1930s
devised for Tolkien's own children. But it was also a story packed
with knowing asides and philological in-jokes, a pseudo-
medieval legend that lightly satirized the work of Anglo-Norman
writers like Geoffrey of Monmouth (whose *Historia Regum
Britanniae* – the 'History of the Kings of Britain' – of 1135, stuffed
with tall tales and ripping yarns, laid the groundwork for the
great medieval boom in Arthurian literature).[2] Unlike Tolkien's
other works of fiction – the juggernauts of fantasy literature that
ensured his lasting reputation – *Farmer Giles* was not set in

7

Middle Earth.* Instead it was set in a place that Tolkien called the Little Kingdom, a place he situated with great specificity in Oxfordshire and Buckinghamshire.[3]

The contours of the Little Kingdom were intimately familiar to Tolkien. All of the locations mentioned in *Farmer Giles* and its abandoned sequel – Ham (Thame), Worminghall, Oxenford (Oxford), Oakley, Farthingho(e), Islip, Otmoor – are real places in the vicinity of Oxford where the Tolkien family lived. In hair-raising journeys of the 1930s, the Professor would propel his wife and children through the landscapes of the Little Kingdom in a Morris Cowley, blundering into dry stone walls and ploughing across lanes of Oxford traffic with the resounding battle cry of 'Charge 'em and they scatter!'[4] These were also the places that studded and described a landscape in which Farmer Giles ('Ægidius Ahenobarbus Julius Agricola de Hammo' to use his proper name) was deeply rooted; they surrounded and defined the fields where he kept his sheep and raised his crops, where he pastured his ill-fated cow Galathea; they joined the paths where he walked Garm (his dog) and took his goods to market, a countryside threatened by the depredations of giant and dragon.

In contrast to the book's concrete geographical setting, Tolkien insisted that *Farmer Giles* was set in a 'no-time' – that it was a fantasy of the past: a real place that existed in an imaginary epoch.[5] His antiquarian instincts, however, evidently compelled him to place the story in a vague – but carefully chosen – time frame. In his Foreword, Tolkien indicated that the Little Kingdom thrived 'after the days of King Coel maybe, but before Arthur or the Seven Kingdoms of the English', i.e. between the fourth and seventh centuries.†[6] This places the story firmly in the 'Dark Ages' – albeit

* 'Middle Earth', a straightforward translation from the Old English term *middengeard* that Tolkien encountered in his reading of early medieval poetry, is the setting of *The Hobbit* (1937), *The Lord of the Rings* trilogy (1954–5) and the posthumously published *The Silmarillion* (1977) among other minor works.

† 'King Coel' refers to the figure of *Coel Hen* ('Coel the Old'; sometimes known as *Coel Godebog* or 'Coel the Protector'), a legendary figure who

8

Tolkien's Little Kingdom, as drawn by Pauline Baynes.

a wilfully anachronistic Dark Age resplendent, like the legends of Arthur and the Knights of the Round Table, in the chivalric colour of the medieval world (and crucially augmented by a blunderbuss). And what Tolkien also knew, and what his story hints at, is that the land occupied by the Little Kingdom had – in those 'years […] filled with swift alternations of war and peace, of mirth and woe, as historians of the reign of Arthur tell us' – been home to a people whose lives and stories were real, vital and utterly obscure.

*   *   *

stands at the head of a number of medieval Welsh genealogies. If he lived at all, he seems to have been a figure of the late fourth century. The 'Seven Kingdoms of the English' is a reference to the so-called 'Anglo-Saxon Heptarchy' (see below).

If ever an age could be rightly described as 'dark' it would be the two centuries that followed the collapse of Roman authority in Britain at the beginning of the fifth century. To those who study late antiquity and the beginning of the early Middle Ages, the period between c.400 and c.600 is a time when not only historical narrative fails, but also the ability to interpret with conviction the archaeological remains. Fundamental questions about the end of Roman governance, the nature and scale of migration into Britain, the origins of kingdoms, the continuity of Christian belief and organization, even the fate and whereabouts of the Romano-British population remain largely unanswerable.

The region of the Upper Thames Valley – Tolkien's Little Kingdom – is not the most benighted area of the Dark Age map, but it lingers nonetheless in a deep penumbra. In common with most of Britain, the written sources that purport to describe the doing of kings and warlords in these years are either silent or useless. The archaeology presents, by contrast, a glittering record – a portrait of a people who – from the fifth century onwards – buried their dead in elaborate fashion, interring their loved ones with swords, spears and shields, and with jewellery that linked their modes of self-expression with those of communities that originated in northern Germany between the rivers Weser and Elbe.* And yet, without the written word as guide, who these people were, who they believed themselves to be (which is not at all the same thing), where they came from and how they organized themselves are matters that remain opaque.

At the end of the sixth and beginning of the seventh century elaborate – so-called 'princely' – burials were sprouting up along the valley of the Thames at places like Asthall and Cuddesdon (Oxfordshire) and (on the eastern side of the Chilterns) at Taplow (Buckinghamshire). These were barrow-burials, Beowulfian in their splendour, earthen mounds raised over corpses richly arrayed with weapons and glassware, drinking horns and gaming pieces,

* See **ESSEX**.

Byzantine treasures and garnet-encrusted jewellery. It was the occupants of these barrows who, presumably, wielded power among the still pagan people of the Upper Thames, exercising a measure of authority among the barrow-downs and standing stones and little rivers, along the banks of the Thames and the Windrush and the Cherwell. Evidence of great timber halls at Sutton Courtenay and Long Wittenham in Oxfordshire demonstrates the power and ostentation of the region's wealthiest inhabitants, holding court in a landscape densely threaded with the traces of settlement and burial.[7]

The end of the sixth century was also the period in which the region emerges in halfway credible historical sources as a kingdom: a single realm ruled over by a man named Ceawlin, the king of a people called the *Gewissae*.*[8] In time, the Thames Valley kingdom ruled by Ceawlin and his successors would expand, its borders would shift and its centres of power move south – to Hampshire and to Dorset. Its first bishopric – at Dorchester-on-Thames, only a few miles from Sutton Courtenay and Long Wittenham – would cede its role to Winchester in the 660s. Ultimately the kingdom's name would also change. By the reign of King Cædwalla (r.685/6–688), the realm of the *Gewissae* came increasingly to be known as the kingdom of the 'West Saxons': the kingdom of Wessex. In the two centuries that followed, the history of the West Saxon realm was dominated by struggles with its neighbours and a steady, though not linear, accumulation of power and territory in southwest England, a process accelerated and complicated by the irruption of Viking armies into Britain from the end of the eighth century onwards.† By the late ninth century, Alfred king of Wessex (r.871–899) was the only repre-

---

* Ceawlin's regnal dates are confused: different sources attribute to him a reign of seven, seventeen or thirty-two years; historians tend to accept a short chronology and the suggestion that he ruled between 581 and 588.

† The story of Britain's experience in the Viking Age is the subject of my earlier book *Viking Britain* (HarperCollins, 2017).

sentative of an original English dynasty to have survived the Viking wars of the preceding decades; his heirs would go on to unify all of the territory that now comprises England under their rule.* To this day the British monarchy traces its descent to Alfred and, through him, to Ceawlin of the *Gewissae* and thence to Cerdic, the legendary founder of the West Saxon dynasty.

It is tempting to imagine that Tolkien had all this in mind when he was writing *Farmer Giles*; that when the eponymous hero ended his days as monarch of the Little Kingdom, a fictional seed was being planted in the Oxfordshire soil from which the English nation might grow. In truth, however, it is unlikely that Tolkien made the connection: in 1945 – four years before the book was published – he wrote to his son Christopher to describe how he had stayed up late reading Frank Stenton's monumental *Anglo-Saxon England* and expressed his interest in 'the origins of our peculiar people'.†[9] Stenton, however, clearly subscribed to the then orthodox position that the origins of the West Saxon kingdom and the *Gewissae* lay further to the south and west.[10] Tolkien did, however, seem to have had in mind another kingdom of the Dark Ages when framing the geography of *Farmer Giles*. To the north of his Little Kingdom, the author placed another realm that he called the 'Middle Kingdom'. The choice of name is a not particularly veiled reference to a kingdom that eventually encompassed the lands of both the 'Middle Angles' and the 'Middle Saxons' and which was situated squarely in what is today referred to as the English 'Midlands': the kingdom of Mercia (lit. 'people of the marches' or 'the border dwellers'). The capital of Tolkien's Middle Kingdom was said by him to have been situated 'some twenty leagues' to the north of Ham' (i.e. around sixty miles). And as Tom Shippey has pointed

* For my use of the term 'Anglo-Saxon' and related issues see **A Note on Terminology**.

† That he thought about this in terms that would now be found troubling ('things of racial […] significance') marks Tolkien as a typically conservative scholar of his time; see **A Note on Terminology**.

out, sixty-eight miles from Thame (Ham) lies the ancient settle-ment of Tamworth, a place which, by the reign of King Offa at the latest (r.757–796), was, alongside Lichfield and Repton, the royal heart of the Mercian realm.*[11]

From the later seventh century and on into the ninth, the king-dom of Mercia was in frequent conflict with Wessex in the Upper Thames Valley, and the region of Tolkien's 'Little Kingdom' became a disputed borderland ravaged by raids and reprisals. There was no room in the midst of this for any little kingdom to survive. Tolkien knew that well enough and, with characteristic affection for the parochial and the small, crafted an alternative history for the area – giving it the briefest glimpse of glory in an age of darkness.† In doing so he produced a fable that is knowingly mischievous, teas-ing the reader with perversely false etymologies for place-names (despite knowing full well that the accurate derivation of toponymy provides one of the only means of accessing the first glimpses of post-Roman settlement in Britain). Nevertheless, for all its donnish whimsy, *Farmer Giles* gets at a greater truth; for as Tolkien also knew, the 'Dark Age' history of Britain is replete with half-forgotten kingdoms and tribal groups whose history – if not entirely absent – is threadbare to the point of vanishment. Some left barely a mark or a trace of themselves behind, not even a name by which to know them. Others whose names have somehow survived – like the *Noxgaga* or the *Ohtgaga* or the *Hendrica* or the *Unecungaga* – are so obscure that they resist attempts to place them on a map. But others have stories that can be told: of saints and gods and miracles, of giants and battles and the ruin of cities.

This is a book about these little kingdoms, about the places whose histories followed unique trajectories all their own before they flamed out or faded away, appearing in the footnotes of

---

* See **HWICCE**.

† It was this same region, along with the west Midlands countryside of his childhood, which inspired the gently rolling landscapes of the Shire in Tolkien's depictions of Middle Earth.

regional surveys, or as short paragraphs in the histories of longer-lived domains; a book about the lands and peoples who fell beside the wayside, blotted out by their rivals, identities absorbed and names erased: the lost realms of early medieval Britain.

This book started life with the idea that I might tell the story of how and why Britain changed between the end of functioning Roman government in Britain – an event conventionally dated to the year 410 when an appeal for aid by British communities was rejected by the Emperor Honorius – and the turmoil of the ninth century when Viking armies irrevocably scrambled the political geography of the island. It would be a sort of prequel to *Viking Britain*, a rollicking series of anecdotes about kings, saints and battles, thrumming with the miracles and magic that saturate poetry and saints' lives, animated by the violence of the chronicles. I imagined a broadly chronological narrative that would travel the long road through post-Roman collapse, continental migration, Christian conversion and war before finally arriving at the fateful day when the West Saxon reeve Beaduheard confronted a Viking crew on the Portland Strand – the place where Viking Britain – and *Viking Britain* – began. It quickly became apparent, however, that this was a story unusually resistant to being told.

Roman rule in Britain lasted around three hundred and fifty years and affected every corner of the island, even those places where Roman writ did not run. The essential territorial division was the *civitas*, an administrative unit based on Iron Age tribal territories and named after the groups that inhabited them: the *Dobunni*, *Iceni*, *Brigantes* and so on.* The tribal centres of these civitates generally came to be developed as regional foci of Roman administration known as civitas capitals – Britain's first proper towns, built on the Roman model. In the lowland regions of the island (broadly speak-

* The 'Iron Age' is generally considered to encompass the period *c*.800 BC–AD 100.

ing, England south of the Pennines, excluding Cornwall and Devon west of Exeter), Roman Britain was governed by a civilian administration based in these and other urban centres, supported by an established, educated, countryside elite who inhabited elaborate countryside villas set in an intensively managed agricultural landscape. The towns – the largest of which were complete with stone walls, large public buildings and luxurious town-houses – hosted markets, industries and a wide variety of craft specialists. They (and the wider Empire through exports) depended on the local countryside and an exploited peasantry for produce and taxation.

Elsewhere, the island was managed more or less actively by a military occupation which, at its greatest extent, extended as far north as the Antonine Wall – an earthwork frontier begun in AD 142 that spanned the bottleneck between the Forth and the Clyde. Beyond that point, independent tribal communities continued to exist independent of Roman rule (though not free from Roman influence). The Antonine Wall was manned for less than a decade. Long before Roman rule was withdrawn from Britain the Imperial frontier line had withdrawn to the more permanent and substantial defences of Hadrian's Wall (begun in AD 122), a series of forts and defensible towers joined by a masonry wall that extended for seventy-three miles – from Newcastle in the east to Carlisle in the west and beyond. By the end of the Roman period, the forts of the wall had, like other forts of the militarized north and west, acquired a permanency that was reinforced by the development of subsidiary market-settlements (Latin *vici*) that supplied them with goods and services supplied by local communities.

Throughout the island, Roman towns, forts and other economic and military infrastructure were connected by an extensive and well-maintained system of roads – although in the most remote parts of nominally Roman Britain, as beyond its northern boundaries, life continued much as it had in prior centuries, the people dwelling in traditional circular roundhouses in autonomous tribal communities. And, despite having gained a footing among the wealthiest of lowland Britain's townhouse and villa-owning class, there is little evidence to suggest that Christianity had penetrated the rest of the island to any meaningful degree. This, in very broad terms, was the shape of Roman Britain as it approached the crises of the late fourth century and beyond.

By the time that Viking armies began reshaping British political geography in the ninth century, Britain had changed out of all recognition. Though many of the towns of Roman Britain were still physically present in the landscape, they were – for the most part – deserted and derelict, with only pockets of habitation in towns like London (*Londinium*) and Lincoln (*Lindum Colonia*) clustered around churches built within (and from) the Roman ruins. The villas had crumbled, the walls and forts had been abandoned or repurposed. The roads remained in use but had not been maintained for centuries. Britain had become essentially an island without proper towns or systematically organized infrastructure where evidence for settlement of any kind is sparse across large areas: particularly in Wales, Scotland, northern England and the extreme southwest. Nevertheless, though the focal points of power and wealth had shifted, Britain remained vital, with evidence – particularly in lowland Britain – of settlements ranging in size from small farmsteads comprising a handful of timber houses to monasteries and trading centres comprising homes and warehouses, churches and workshops, markets and riverside embankments.* A handful of defended settlements – Hereford, Tamworth, Winchcombe – had appeared in Mercia during the eighth century, and many more of these 'proto-towns' would appear over the course of the Viking Age, some of them making use of Roman ruins, marking the re-emergence of widespread urban life.

In the four and a half centuries before the coming of the Vikings,

---

* These trading centres, or 'emporia', were known in Old English as *wics* (from the Latin *vicus*, an unplanned settlement, often attached to a Roman fort); some were located in the vicinity, but not within the walls, of old Roman towns – exploiting locations that were already poised to access communication by road, river and sea (e.g. *Lundenwic* was situated beside, but separate from, Roman *Londinium*).

an enormous number of political entities appeared, re-emerged, flourished, dwindled, vanished or – in a very few cases – emerged as enduring geo-political units. Some were defined by territory and others by group or family identity. In England, a few traces of the old tribal-administrative geography survived.* But for the most part, a patchwork of new territories divided up a land that had been overwritten – Roman and Celtic place-names superseded by Old English words that described the topography or named the dwellers on the land: the owners, the families, the kin-groups. The south-western shires together formed the kingdom of Wessex – the kingdom of the West Saxons – whose heartlands lay in Dorset and Hampshire, but whose lands extended roughly to include Wiltshire, Berkshire, Somerset, Devon and (from the ninth century) Cornwall. Mercia, the great Midland realm, occupied the whole central portion of England from the Welsh borders to the Wash and from the Humber to the Thames. Northumbria – literally 'the land north of the [River] Humber' – exercised lordship over all of northern England and parts of lowland Scotland. East Anglia comprised the shires of Norfolk and Suffolk; the ancient kingdoms of Kent, Sussex and Essex still retained a vestigial independence despite genera-tions of shifting subordination to their larger neighbours.

In Wales a complex arrangement of kingdoms had emerged, some of which seem to have arisen from ancient tribal and terri-torial identities that stretched back into the Iron Age. The largest of these, as they existed in the ninth century, were Gwynedd in the north and northwest (the *Ordovices*), Dyfed in the southwest (the *Demetae*), Gwent in the southeast (the *Silures*) and Powys in the northeastern regions (the *Cornovii*); others, however, bore little or no relation whatsoever to Roman administrative geography and presented a shifting and apparently quite fluid pattern of overlord-ship and group affiliation, particularly in the region between the Wye and the Severn. All of these kingdoms, however, were 'British'

---

* Kent is a notable example – the kingdom's name and boundaries mirror the old tribal territory of the *Cantii*.

in both a cultural and a linguistic sense and distinguished themselves in their own writings sharply from the 'English' realms of lowland Britain. They maintained the use of a Brittonic Celtic language and seem to have also fostered a sense of continuity with the Romano-British past in ways that the English speakers of the east did not.

British kingdoms and peoples survived to the ninth century elsewhere in the island: in Cornwall, the descendants of the *Cornovii* (not to be confused with their namesakes in eastern Wales) maintained their independence until the mid-ninth century and their language for much longer.* In Scotland the Brittonic-speaking people of Alt Clut controlled the region bordering the Clyde from their fortress at Dumbarton Rock. Elsewhere in Scotland, however, territory was divided between the Pictish kingdoms that dominated the north and east and Dál Riata, a Gaelic-speaking kingdom that ruled the fractured western fringes of Scotland's Atlantic edge and at one time spanned the Irish Sea to include the northeastern part of Ulster as well as Argyll and Lochobar. Both the Picts and the Gaels of Dál Riata spoke Celtic languages, though they were distinct from each other as well as from the language spoken by the Britons of Alt Clut and elsewhere.†

Without exception, all of the kingdoms that would ultimately face the storms of the Viking Age were, by the ninth century, Christian realms. They possessed churches and monasteries, bishops and abbesses: men and women who laboured over manuscripts

---

* Cornish died out in the eighteenth century but was revived in the early twentieth century. Since 2002 it has been recognized by the UK government as a minority language under the terms of the Council of Europe's Charter for Regional or Minority Languages.

† Celtic languages are divided into two groups. Goidelic (or 'Q-Celtic') and Brittonic (or 'P-Celtic'). Gaelic (the language of the Gaels in Ireland and western Scotland) is a Goidelic language related to Manx, whereas Pictish (so far as it can be understood given the extreme scarcity of known Pictish words) is probably closer to the Brittonic languages spoken elsewhere in Britain (Welsh, Cornish, Cumbric) than it is to Gaelic, though its origin(s) are still in dispute.

and venerated the lives of local saints who had baptized the faithful in familiar rivers and enacted miracles that illumined familiar hillsides. They were also territories ruled over by kings – rulers with a heightened sense of legitimacy that derived partly from historic and dynastic claims and partly from the sanction provided by religious ritual, their temporal claims validated by a divine seal of approval and supported by the infrastructure of the Church. Monasticism – protected by royal patronage – had given the technology of the written word to the rulers of Britain, granting them efficient new tools: law codes, legal documents, written lineages, chronicles. These attributes, alongside the protoplasmic urban spaces that were beginning to appear in some areas, lend the impression that Britain by the ninth century was on the cusp of becoming recognizably 'medieval' in its outward characteristics, utterly transformed from the late antique world of the fifth century.

Finding a coherent way to explain these profound transformations is deeply challenging. Many of the developments that occurred during these crucial centuries were complex, drawn out and profoundly difficult to understand in the light of surviving historical and archaeological evidence. Several of them remain the most hotly contested and vigorously debated problems of early British history and any one of them could form the thematic heart of a book seeking a path through these centuries: the nature, effect and aftermath of the collapse of Roman governance; the scale of migration and the means by which new 'English' ethno-linguistic communities in Britain were formed; the progress and process of Christian conversion and the nature of the belief systems that were replaced; the construction (and disappearance) of new political entities across the island; the survival of overseas contact and the precise political/economic nature of that contact; the appearance of dynastic kingship; the introduction of monasticism, law and literacy; the emergence of new literatures, art styles and identities; profound linguistic change; the social, political and economic drivers of endemic militarism, warfare, conquest and subjugation. And so on.

That is not to say that no 'traditional' history of early medieval Britain exists. There is, in fact, a common narrative that can be found in many older and popular treatments of the period. In broad terms, this tells how English-speaking settlers came to Britain from continental northern Europe and carved out new lands for themselves among a degenerate British population and the ruins of vestigial Roman antiquity. The newcomers established themselves in tribal groups that, over time, coalesced into pagan 'Anglo-Saxon' kingdoms covering much of the area that is now England, all the while happily slaughtering the native Britons and chasing the survivors into the wild margins of the land – to Wales and Scotland and Cornwall.* Through a process of quasi-Darwinian selection, these Anglo-Saxons warred against the Britons and among themselves until only the mightiest kingdoms remained: Wessex, Mercia, Northumbria, East Anglia, Kent, Sussex and Essex – an Anglo-Saxon 'Heptarchy' of nations.† The pagan kings of these realms, having been exposed to the Christian faith of Rome by the missionary work of evangelists sent to Britain by Pope Gregory the Great (a process that began in 597 with the arrival of Augustine in Kent), led their communities in conversion, endowing churches and fostering monasticism. In the process, the Anglo-Saxons were revealed to be a 'chosen people' – the vehicle of divine providence (in contrast to the Britons, whose wrong-headed 'Celtic' Christianity was justly suppressed). Although rivalry between the Anglo-Saxon realms continued, it was the Viking cataclysm of the

* For the people of those regions their resistance to the English – sometimes glorious but always fleeting – became a narrative of long defeat and noble sacrifice, of dispossession and stubborn resilience, thronged with the heroes of poetry and folklore.

† This term – literally the 'rule of seven' – was coined by the sixteenth-century antiquarian William Lambarde (1536–1601) and derived from the work of twelfth-century historians like William of Malmesbury and Henry of Huntingdon. It is actually rather unhelpful since at almost no time was the territory of England administered by precisely seven independent 'Anglo-Saxon' realms.

ninth century that ultimately destroyed the Heptarchy. During the 860s and 870s, marauding Viking barbarians left only the West Saxons and their king, Alfred, still in possession of their ancestral lands. On the plus side, however, this meant that the surviving Anglo-Saxons became a single nation under a single king – a king, moreover, possessed of such an extraordinary range of qualities that he was in fact 'the most perfect character in history'.[12] It was thanks to Alfred's far-sighted wisdom, alongside the martial heroism of his son Edward and grandson Athelstan, that the heathen Viking menace was defeated throughout the former Anglo-Saxon lands. Finally in 937, a triumphant and unified kingdom of England was forged – united under the house of Wessex.

This is the standard version of early English and British history: an Anglo-centric account of unfolding national greatness that congealed in the nineteenth century, stuffed full of familiar and outdated themes of English Christian nationalism. And, despite being factually incorrect in a number of ways and deeply questionable in others, it has exercised a powerful grip. Promoted in British schools and universities and through popular poetry and history it became a sustaining narrative for those who laboured to expand, preserve and justify Britain's Empire in the nineteenth and twentieth centuries.[13] Its subtext – that the 'Anglo-Saxon' English were chosen by God, that they were inherently superior to the native British people whom they displaced, that their Christianity elevated their morality, that their violence against others was justified by the providential ends it served – provided a template to excuse and even celebrate the brutal treatment of both 'Celtic' and non-Christian people and their cultures wherever they were encountered across the globe. E. A. Freeman, the famous nineteenth-century historian of the Norman Conquest whose assessment of Alfred's character is quoted above, wrote of America that 'This would be a grand land if only every Irishman would kill a negro, and be hanged for it'.[14] The enduring currency of attitudes like these within British colonies abroad fed easily into notions of racial superiority and Manifest Destiny – ideas which drove the genocidal expansion of

European settlement in North America and elsewhere and bred a toxic legacy of white supremacy that has lasted to the present day.[15]

Early British history, polluted by nationalist myth and racialized attitudes, has long been in obvious need of reframing. Scholars of the past half-century have worked hard to apply more critical standards to the assessment of sources and interpretative frameworks through which the period has been viewed. It is no longer justifiable to see this period through the prism of Christian progress or Britain's imperial project. Replacing the traditional narrative with something truthful and nuanced yet easily grasped has not, however, proved easy – partly because more simplistic views of history continue to hold a powerful appeal for those who seek to make political use of them.* The problem is probably a fundamental one: perhaps the whole premise of a grand narrative is fatally flawed.

All too often history – especially national history – becomes a narrative imposed from above, a map-maker's view, an artificial imposition of order. I began to wonder how the processes that transformed Britain in the early Middle Ages might appear when observed from the ground – like a landscape experienced by foot rather than by air, feeling the gradient and beholding the view, walking beneath the canopy of the trees to find the places that the aerial observer cannot see. What might look from the air like jumble and disorder might, at ground level, appear rational and explicable in its earthbound context, when rooted in its place. Perhaps the 'big picture' is just the accidental accumulation of myriad local flowerings; maybe there is no easy way to explain why the picture turned out the way it did. The phenomena that defined Dark Age Britain were experienced by different people in different places in different ways at different times; their consequences were felt unequally and responded to in markedly

* See **A Note on Terminology**.

divergent fashion. Dozens of kingdoms rose in the post-Roman political vacuum – some flourished and others fell, some undoubtedly left no trace whatsoever. In circumstances such as these, whose triumphs and tragedies are deserving of narrative focus, whose story worth the telling?

The natural tendency, even in the most sophisticated approaches to the period, has been to focus attention on the larger kingdoms of early medieval Britain at the expense of many others. In England in particular, four kingdoms dominate the pre-Viking history of Britain, sucking up all the early medieval oxygen: Wessex, Northumbria, Mercia and East Anglia. This dominance is partly because these kingdoms gave rise to some of the most iconic characters, objects, monuments and manuscripts of the age: the Staffordshire Hoard and Offa's Dyke (Mercia), Bede, the Lindisfarne Gospels and the tomb of St Cuthbert (Northumbria), the Sutton Hoo barrow cemetery (East Anglia), King Alfred and the *Anglo-Saxon Chronicle* (Wessex). But it also stems from the fact that three of these kingdoms – Wessex, Mercia and Northumbria – ultimately devoured many of their smaller neighbours and rivals over the course of the period, subsuming them within growing super-regional realms, stifling them before they had a chance to reach their potential.

I decided early on that these were not the stories I wanted to tell, at least not from the perspectives of the bullies and the victors. Instead, it was the small fry of early medieval power politics that fascinated me – the little kingdoms that failed to survive the period in any meaningful, independent form; those realms whose struggles and failures, I felt, better represent early medieval Britain in all its diversity of place and experience. I allowed myself the conceit of imagining the book as a cabinet of curiosities – a wooden grid divided into nine equal square compartments, each compartment holding its own specimen, each one unique and precious and deserving of its space. Every chapter – every kingdom – would appear as an object to be taken in the hand and considered in the round, self-contained, as detailed and textured and fascinating as the next. *Lost Realms* is the result. By turning the history of early medieval Britain inside out I have written something very different from *Viking Britain*. This book does not tell 'a story', because there is no one story that can be told. It does not follow the progress of a single phenomenon as it irrupted into Britain; there were many seismic events and transformational processes that afflicted and roiled the island. It does not – it cannot – take a linear path through the chronology of its period; the chronology is everywhere muddied and confused by invention and reinvention, retelling and reordering. Certain questions, however, echo over and over through the biographies of these lost realms. How are kingdoms formed and why do they fail? How do communities adapt to change and how do they insulate themselves from it? How do they construct the past? How do they deal with loss? There is no single answer to these questions – and sometimes there are no answers to be found. But by looking for them through the lens of the little kingdoms, something can be seen that is more truthful than any nationalist fantasy.

The nine kingdoms that are represented in the following chapters are a personal selection. They are not, however, a random selection, and in making the list I was guided by a few general principles. The first was to exclude the most obvious candidates. Consequently, the Big Beasts of Anglo-Saxon England – Wessex, Northumbria, Mercia, East Anglia – are not the subject of this book, even though their kings and prelates, wars and ambitions figure prominently throughout. A handful of other realms with a disproportionate prominence in early medieval historiography – the kingdom of Kent, for example, thanks to the richness of its archaeology and its role in the history of conversion and migration, and the Welsh kingdom of Gwynedd, the realm that would come to dominate Wales in the later Middles Ages and which still embodies ideas of ancient Welsh resistance to English rule – do not feature here. After those initial decisions, however, determining which kingdoms to exclude became more difficult. I knew that

I wanted to represent the whole island of Britain so far as was possible. I also wanted to satisfy a sense of cultural balance by giving equal weight to regions traditionally regarded as 'Anglo-Saxon', 'British' or something else. There also had to be enough to say to warrant a substantial and sustained chapter; but not *too* much. As I have come to discover, these considerations are not easily balanced.

One place to start is with the so-called 'Tribal Hidage'. This is a list (preserved in an eleventh-century manuscript but believed to originate in the seventh or eighth century) of some of the formative kingdoms and tribal groups of lowland Britain – a document fundamental for understanding the political and economic geography of seventh-century Britain east of the River Wye and south of the River Wharfe.[16] The document lists territories alongside the number of 'hides' each territory encompassed, a 'hide' being a unit of land that notionally supported a single homestead. The size of a hide could, therefore, vary considerably depending on the economic potential of the land and the number of hides therefore cannot be treated as a straightforward calculus for determining the size of a territory. Though the origins, purpose and accuracy of the Tribal Hidage are disputed, it was evidently an assessment of the economic value of various regions – possibly for the purpose of calculating the amount of tribute that could theoretically be extracted. Mercia (which appears at the head of the document and is known to have dominated southern Britain for long periods during these centuries) or Northumbria (whose two major constituent kingdoms – *Deira* and *Bernicia* – are conspicuously absent) are the places where the list most likely originated: both kingdoms wielded some form of arching authority over all or most of the territories named in the Hidage at one time or another.

Leaving aside questions of purpose and authorship, the Tribal Hidage provides an invaluable – if crude and questionable – tool for identifying and mapping the political units that comprised central and southern England and ordering them roughly by their heft. The top four kingdoms are Wessex (100,000 hides), Mercia (30,000 hides), East Anglia (30,000 hides) and Kent (15,000 hides). Beneath them are seven others that were assessed at 7,000 hides each: the *Weocansaetne* ('Wreocansaete'; roughly Cheshire and Shropshire), the *Westerna* (Herefordshire; elsewhere known as 'Magonsaete'), the East Saxons (Essex plus Middlesex and parts of Hertfordshire and Surrey), the South Saxons (Sussex), *Hwince* ('Hwicce'; mainly Gloucestershire and Worcestershire) and *Lindesfarona* ('Lindsey'; northern Lincolnshire). Then there are the seven whose size varies between 1,200 and 5,000 hides: territories like those of the *Ciltern sætna* (4,000) and the *Herefinna* (1,200). Finally comes the mass of tribal groups – seventeen in all – whose hidage was assessed at less than a thousand apiece, including five – like the people of *Hicca* or *East Wixna* – whose territory supported only 300 notional homesteads.

Four of the five territories from the Tribal Hidage that appear in this book – Hwicce, Lindsey, Essex and Sussex – were valued at 7,000 hides, a group of kingdoms whose one-time size and influence left enough to write about even though their status as independent kingdoms is often glossed over.*[17] All of them are typically considered to be 'Anglo-Saxon' kingdoms although, as we shall see, this label has very little explanatory value. Between them they represent the two peoples whom Bede in the eighth century described as comprising the bulk of the migrants from continental Europe who settled in Britain – the Angles (Hwicce and Lindsey) and the Saxons (Essex and Sussex) – though this, too, is deeply problematic.† (The Jutes, whom Bede mentions as the third migrant

---

* In the Old English poem *Beowulf*, the eponymous hero is given (among other treasures) *seofan þûsendo* ('seven thousand') by Hygelac, king of the Geats. It is generally assumed by modern scholars that this is a reference to land and is normally translated as 'seven thousand hides'; it may well be that 7,000 hides had a special significance as the measure of a substantial realm, albeit one that remained subservient to a more powerful overlord (the significance of which the following chapters will, I hope, make plain).

† See, in particular, **LINDSEY** and **ESSEX**.

group to settle in large numbers, sadly do not get a look in; neither place where Bede situated Jutish settlement features in this book.*)

The only other chapter which takes as its subject a group listed in the Tribal Hidage, however, is that devoted to Elmet – the land of the *Elmed sætna* – a kingdom whose land in West Yorkshire was valued at a feeble 600 hides. It is perhaps true to say that Elmet is the most obscure of all the realms written about in this book. But it is also an important reminder that the Tribal Hidage is no secure guide to the historical significance of any of the territories it includes. Elmet, for example, had been subsumed by its neighbours before the Tribal Hidage was compiled and its diminished status there does not reflect its prior history as an independent British kingdom. The same may well be true of other minor groups listed in the Hidage, though for the most part any view of their former reach and power is, in comparison with Elmet, even more occluded.

The remaining four kingdoms that are covered in this book do not appear in the Tribal Hidage at all. In three cases – Dumnonia, Powys and Fortriu – this is for the simple reason that they remained outside the limits of 'Anglo-Saxon' dominion until long after the Tribal Hidage was compiled (and, in the case of Powys and Fortriu, enduringly so). Dumnonia, in Britain's southwestern peninsula, retained its independence until its absorption into Wessex in the mid-ninth century. Powys in northeastern and central Wales, though the kingdom seems to have periodically endured Mercian overlordship, ultimately lost its independence to the Welsh kingdom of Gwynedd at some point during the ninth century. Fortriu – the kingdom of the northern Picts centred on Moray, north of the Cairngorms – vanished with the creation of the kingdom of Alba in *c.*900, though its regional identity had already been subsumed into the wider Pictish realm. Lastly Rheged, like Elmet, is a kingdom whose origins remain deeply obscure. Even its location – traditionally Cumbria and Galloway – is far from certain. It is included here

---

* The kingdom of Kent (too big) and the kingdom of the *Wihtwara* on the Isle of Wight (too small).

because its afterlife in Welsh medieval literature, in particular the reputation of its most famous king, Urien, elevates it above other comparable realms of what became known in Welsh as the *Hen Ogledd* (the 'Old North') and because the archaeology of the region with which it is traditionally associated speaks to important post-Roman developments.*[18]

In each case I have tried to give a sense – so far as can be known – of the circumstances in which these kingdoms came into being, the historical events that shaped them, their geography and archaeology and how they ceased to exist as independent realms. In several instances the latter point is difficult to define. While in some cases the end of a kingdom was decisive, elsewhere it was far from clear-cut. (The kingdom of Powys, for example, its original line of kings extinguished, was resurrected in the eleventh century as an appendage of the kingdom of Gwynedd and lasted as a principality until the late thirteenth century.) How I have understood the 'end' of a kingdom has therefore varied considerably. It is also important to recognize that knowledge of this period – whether derived from texts or objects or place-names – is often hard won and frequently remains contingent on new discoveries and the reinterpretation of evidence. Very few areas of the field are uncontested.

What this means in practice is that the text of this book is beset by legions of qualifiers: words like 'probably', 'conceivably', 'possibly', 'might', 'could' and 'may have' advance over the page with alarming frequency. As do multiple frank admissions of total ignorance. If you prefer certainty in historical writing, ground that doesn't shift beneath your feet, an unimpeachable record of dry facts and narrative churn, then this is not the book you're looking for. What this also means, however, is that I have felt able to linger over material that is sometimes dismissed in books about the history of the early Middle Ages, taking time over legends and folk-

---

* The other obvious candidate to represent this part of the island – Alt Clut – was treated at length by Norman Davies in his book *Vanished Kingdoms* (Penguin, 2010) and I had no desire to re-tread the same ground.

lore, the fabrications and the embroideries, the many ways that people constructed memory and dealt with loss. Over and over again these chapters touch on the ways in which people reacted to notions of their own pasts and to the pasts of others, and how they forged a sense of belonging to landscapes from which they were alienated by cultural dislocation, dispossession and time. That, to my mind, is a subject worth exploring – however dark the road.

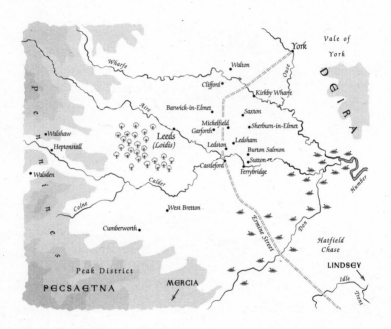

ELMET

– *West Yorkshire* –

Time sweetens
The melting corpses of farms
The hills' skulls peeled by the dragging climate –
The arthritic remains
Of what had been a single strength
Tumbled apart, forgetting each other –

Ted Hughes, 'The Sheep Went on Being Dead', *Remains of Elmet* (1979)[1]

I n 2011 I attended the International Medieval Congress (IMC) at Bodington Hall, a complex of student accommodation owned by the University of Leeds on the outskirts of that city in West Yorkshire. The event – an annual gathering of medievalists from all over the world – had been held there since 1994 and over nearly twenty years the unique atmosphere of the venue became inextricably woven into the personal memories and career biographies of innumerable historians, archaeologists and literary scholars. My own overriding memory is of sitting alone by the back door of my ground-floor student cell, drinking a pint of very average beer from a plastic cup and listening to the distant, unsettling sounds of serious academics dancing to Dire Straits at the notorious IMC disco.

In truth it would be hard to conceive of a place less conducive to a week-long immersion in the medieval past. Opened in 1961 to architectural acclaim, Bodington Hall was a model village of post-war modernism – a rash of green-panelled windows and orange brick, of squat rectilinear blocks and flat roofs, of metal-framed windows backed by brown patterned curtains, of chipped veneer and herringbone parquet and doors glazed with wire-inset safety glass – all set in a sea of anodyne parkland and sports fields.* Its removal from any sort of recognizable context left Bodington out of place and out of time – like the setting for a forgotten Cronenberg movie, an uncanny relic of a modernity that had come and gone.

The last time the IMC was held at Bodington was in 2012. The site had been sold to developers and the entire complex was oblite-rated over the years that followed. There is now no trace of the halls of residence that once stood here, and the refectory – a temple of polished wooden floors and titanic mechanical drapes that once protected the modesty of its angular glazed flanks – was levelled in 2013. With it there vanished a world that can never be recovered, a complex locus of memory for the transient generations who inhab-ited its melancholy corridors and time-stranded halls. Most of the people who have come to inhabit the estate of tidy new housing on roads like Bodington Way and Woodsley View live their lives in ignorance of the shades of shabby student life that haunt their shrubberies, the post-modern critiques of *Beowulf* that susurrate behind their garages. Even fewer will pay any mind to the lost king-dom that lies even deeper below their feet.

All places have their ghosts; with such a deep history of human habitation, an island as crowded as Britain is thick with them, the pasts of many ages layered one on top of the other like a pancake stack. West Yorkshire is as crowded as any other corner of the island, a region punctuated by the spectres of decommissioned power stations and ruined Methodist churches, girded by the relics

* In 1964, the architect Denis Mason-Jones won the Leeds Gold Medal for his work on Bodington Hall.

of Stone Age hunters and the cairns of the prehistoric dead, a land of faded industrial power and aching pastoral subsistence. It was also – for one brief moment in the period that followed the end of Roman Britain – home to a little kingdom of surpassing obscurity: the kingdom of Elmet.

In many ways, Elmet serves as an ideal introduction to the range of problematic sources faced during any exploration of Britain's lost realms. Diverse, difficult and scarce as it as, the surviving record – whether historical, artefactual or onomastic – is forever accompanied by chronic uncertainty, ambiguity and falsehood. No one even knows exactly where the borders of the kingdom were drawn, only that it lay somewhere between the marshland of the Vale of York and the Pennines to the west. Nor can anything much be said of Elmet's origin, and many of the most basic historical facts concerning the kingdom can never be uncovered. The reach of its power, the strength of its arms, the line of its kings, the lives of its people – all lie in shadow. Only a few glimpses of its heroes and warlords survive: Aliortus the wanderer, Madog the warrior, Gwallog whose deeds shook the mountains, Ceredig who lost his throne.

Slender evidence suggests that the people of Elmet – like their British neighbours to the north and west – spoke a Celtic tongue and worshipped the Christian god. And, of course, the name of the kingdom endures.*[2] But by the time anyone wrote of Elmet it was

---

* Although it cannot be proven definitively, it seems likely that the name is derived from a conjectural Celtic word *met meaning 'cut' or 'reap'. (Note: an asterisk placed in front of an italicized word as here indicates that the term is unattested in historical documents and has been reconstructed on the basis of philological reasoning). The first element (el) means 'many' in the archaic Brittonic tongue, and it may be that the people of Elmet were known – or knew themselves – as the 'people of great reaping', a name that probably referred more to their imagined battlefield prowess than their crop-harvesting skills. Other Celtic tribal names provide examples of a bellicose self-image: the tribe inhabiting modern Hertfordshire, Bedfordshire and south Cambridgeshire had a name meaning something like 'battle-masters' (Catuvellauni) and the tribal name Ancelites (?Berkshire/Middlesex) means 'the very hard ones'.

already gone. The Venerable Bede knew a little in the eighth century; the author of the ninth-century 'History of the Britons' (*Historia Brittonum*) may have known a little more. There are a few place-names, an inscription on a standing stone, a seventh-century ethnonym preserved in an eleventh-century miscellany. But the inescapable fact remains that the certain history of the kingdom of Elmet could be carved on a shin bone. It is a lost world, irrecoverable really, a whisper in the moorland grass; yet it was once a real place of people and things, of daily lives and a thousand tragedies and hopes – long since blown away like dandelion seeds, to land and grow or rot in patches far removed, in ways unrecognized and unmarked. What follows is all that remains.

For the poet Ted Hughes (1930–98), Elmet was an area centred on Hepstonstall on the western edge of Yorkshire's West Riding, 'the deep valley of the upper Calder and its watershed of Pennine moorland […] territory roughly encircled by a line drawn through Halifax (on the east), Keighley (on the northeast), Colne (on the northwest), Burnley (on the west), and Littleborough (on the southwest): an "island" straddling the Yorks-Lancs border, though mainly in Yorkshire, and centred […] on Heptonstall'.[3] Hughes imagines that the kingdom had shrunk under pressure from the 'Anglo-Saxon' east, the last partisans of Celtic independence fleeing west to the hills, holding out in this 'narrow cleft and its side-ginnels, under the glaciated moors'.[4] It is an idiosyncratic vision, but there is no one who can refute it. The simple truth remains that, though determining the kingdom's general whereabouts is relatively straightforward, locating its heart and inscribing its borders remains almost impossible.

What may be the earliest reference to a place and a people known by the name Elmet is found in the Tribal Hidage.* Here the *Elmedsætna* ('the people of Elmet') constitute a very small realm of

* See **LITTLE KINGDOMS**.

only 600 hides (the same, in fact, as the figure given for the Isle of Wight). They are listed between the *Pecsætna* who inhabited the Peak District (and who gave their name to it, or vice versa), and the *Lindes farona* – the people of Lindsey – in what is now northern Lincolnshire (whose territory, by contrast, was numbered at 7,000 hides).* Since both of these regions can be safely located, and the list also seems to be organized in geographical sequence, Elmet should occupy a position between them: i.e. in an area between the Pennines and the Vale of York, encompassing Leeds.

Given the apparent location of Elmet, it is generally assumed that the kingdom of Elmet fractured from the remains of the Brigantian tribal confederacy that encompassed much of what is now northeast England. Though it can be little more than conjecture, it is possible that the withdrawal of Roman military units from what is now northern Britain at the end of the fourth century allowed pockets of British self-government to develop around former tribal centres and Roman garrison towns: one such – in the West Yorkshire region – may have formed the nucleus of the kingdom of Elmet. Skeletal remains recovered from sites at Garforth, Ferrybridge and the former Roman fortress at Castleford (all in West Yorkshire) have provided radiocarbon dates consistent with the fifth/sixth centuries. These burials bring us face-to-face with people who dwelt within the likely footprint of Elmet before its apparent disappearance, and tentatively suggest a previously unrecognized continuity with the Romano-British settlements, burial culture and infrastructure that gave birth to the kingdom.[5] There are no historical records, however, that can shed any light on how exactly these people and places became organized into an independent realm.

The earliest figure who can be associated with Elmet is a sixth-century character named Gwallog *ap* ('son of') Leenog. Legends of Gwallog largely survive in fables and fragments, almost all of them first written down centuries after his death, and these

* See **LINDSEY**.

can play only a limited role in understanding the real world in which he lived. It was said, for example, in traditions preserved in the early ninth century, that Gwallog was one of four British warlords who, in the sixth century, fought against the English (and probably among themselves) for control of what would come to be referred to in Welsh literature as the *Hen Ogledd* (the 'Old North'): a broad swathe of northern Britain south of Stirling and north of the Humber.* Later still, in the Welsh *Trioedd Ynys Prydein* – the 'Triads of the Island of Britain' – Gwallog was named variously as one of the 'Three Pillars of Battle', one of the 'Three Bull-Protectors' and one of the 'Three Battle-Rulers' of Britain; in later medieval Welsh prose he was called a companion of Arthur.†[6] All of which, though it reveals nothing about the real man or his doings, is at least evidence that the name 'Gwallog' had made a memorable impression and retained powerful associations for centuries among the Britons of Wales.

Gwallog, however, was also the subject of two poems which, in part at least, may be roughly contemporary with the man they describe.[7] These are preserved in the famous 'Book of Taliesin' (*Llyfr Taliesin*), a compendium of verse that purports to be the collected poetry of the legendary eponymous bard (who must have lived, if he lived at all, in the second half of the sixth century). Although *Llyfr Taliesin* was compiled in its present form in the later Middle Ages, it does contain a number of poems which some scholars of Welsh literature believe might have originated in the

---

* The other British warlords are named as Morcant, Rhydderch of Alt Clut and Urien of Rheged.

† The Triads are a long series of poetic three-line stanzas preserved in a number of medieval Welsh manuscripts. They recount traditional British lore by grouping three related things or persons together under a single heading: a mnemonic manual for bards. The material they contain is undoubtedly older than the manuscripts, and perhaps very old indeed; it is, however, impossible to date any of it with confidence before the twelfth century. Nevertheless, it does provide evidence of the sort of legendary material that once circulated about the heroes of Britain in the courts of Welsh princes.

late sixth century, even though they were written down by a four-teenth-century hand.* In one of these poems Gwallog was remembered as *ygnad ar Elvet*: 'the law-giver of Elmet'.[8] On the face of it, little Elmet – at only 600 hides – was hardly equipped to sustain the reputation of mighty Gwallog 'who made armies feeble'.[9] However, the information that the Tribal Hidage contains was not recorded before the late seventh century.† By that time (as we shall see), Elmet seems already to have vanished as an independent realm and there is no knowing the true extent and power of Elmet in Gwallog's day. It is also possible that Gwallog may have been the ruler of a large swathe of territory of which Elmet was only part: *ygnad* literally means 'judge', but it seems also to have had the sense of 'overlord'.

Certainly, the poetic celebration of Gwallog's exploits saw him rampaging widely across northern Britain. 'They tell me of feats in Pictland,' the poet recalls, 'and the region of Manaw and Edinburgh. [...] He made provocation for York' and 'a hundred armies would tremble in Aeron'. Gwallog laid low his enemies 'at Bathgate [...] before Gwydawl [...] on the Winster [...] by Snow Hill [...] at Pen Coed of the long knives' where linger the 'carrion crows everywhere'.‡ In the poetic imagination this Gwallog was a warrior of terrible effectiveness, 'a warlike king, acrimonious', who 'made armies feeble', a proponent of direct action who 'preferred a pile of

---

* Whether they can truly be ascribed to the legendary poet Taliesin is another matter.

† The Tribal Hidage is problematic evidence in a number of ways. It has proved difficult to date and is only preserved in copied form in a manuscript of the eleventh century. Although the information it contains could have been compiled in the late seventh century, it is impossible to know what changes or errors might have crept into its text over the centuries; nor can any definitive explanation of its purpose be given. Without knowing what the Hidage was *for*, it is hard to be confident about the significance of its data; see **LITTLE KINGDOMS**.

‡ Not all of these places can be identified, but see **RHEGED**; Aeron is probably Ayrshire.

the slaughtered to trickery'. He was a warlord of whom it was said that 'He who has not seen Gwallog, has not seen a real man', a macho reputation that long outlived him.[10]

Of all the references to Gwallog's warlike deeds in early Welsh verse, however, one stands out: a snatched memory (in a possibly seventh-century poem commemorating Cadwallon of Gwynedd) of 'brave Gwallog [who] wrought the desolation of brave and noble Catraeth'.[11] Quite what Gwallog was doing at Catraeth (apart from wreaking desolation) is a mystery, but for anyone with any knowledge of early Welsh literature this place-name echoes loudly in the imagination. One battle that was famously fought there, probably sometime in the later sixth century, became the subject of the longest, and perhaps one of the oldest, of all British poems: *Y Gododdin*. This poem, contained in the manuscript *Llyfr Aneirin* (the 'Book of Aneirin'), is purportedly the work of the poet Aneirin, another legendary bard of the sixth century.* It describes a campaign organized by Mynyddog Mwynfawr of Gododdin, a kingdom of the eastern Scottish lowlands. Its objective was apparently to wrest control of a place called Catraeth from the heathen English-speaking people of Deira and, possibly, Bernicia in what is now northeastern England, although theories have been advanced that place British protagonists on both sides of the conflict (one version of the poem also lists Picts and Irish as adversaries and, in truth, the precise circumstances are impossible to reconstruct).†[12]

Whatever its relationship to the true history of Dark Age northern Britain, *Y Gododdin* is a poem of vivid imagery and pathos, a collage of commemorative vignettes for heroes who fell in battle and the great and bloody deeds they performed. Much of

---

* See **RHEGED**.

† *Y Gododdin* is preserved in two manuscripts; the later of the two is the only one to specifically mention Bernicians as being among the enemies of Gododdin; *Saesson* ('Saxon') is the word the poet uses to describe the English; for the location of Catreath see **RHEGED**; for Picts see **FORTRIU**.

its power is derived from brief but repeated recollections of the year-long feast at the court of Mynyddog in *Dun Eidyn* (Edinburgh) that preceded the hopeless venture: images of mirth and drinking, of joyful heroes and warbands gathered from many realms, of gift-giving and swift horses and mead beside the hall-fire. In the end, however, the price of mead was death, and it was a price the lords of Gododdin and their allies were forced to pay in full:

> Men went to Catraeth, keen their warband.
> Pale mead their portion, it was poison.
> Three hundred under orders to fight.
> And after celebration, silence.
> Though they went to churches for shriving,
> True is the tale, death confronted them.[13]

The story that *Y Gododdin* tells is of a military debacle that resulted in the almost total annihilation of the host of northern Britons.* And, although the poet sought to gild the sacrifice of the the 'laughter-loving' young men who went to Catraeth, ultimately it is clear that they gave their lives for nothing but a brief mention in verse, finding none of the greater lasting fame that was attached to other heroes of Welsh tradition.†[14] Most of these warriors had come, apparently, from the land of Gododdin itself; but there were a number who joined the host of Mynyddog who had made longer journeys to the mead-hall at *Dun Eidyn*. Whether Gwallog of Elmet was among them is unclear – although *Llyfr Taliesin* connects him with Catraeth, *Y Gododdin* makes no mention of him at all. But the

---

* The two versions of the poem that are preserved number the survivors, including the poet himself, at either two or four from a host that originally numbered either 300 or 363.

† Indeed, the fact that the eighty or so men named in *Y Gododdin* go otherwise unmentioned in the substantial corpus of medieval Welsh literature suggests that the core of the poem may well be a genuine product of the sixth or seventh centuries.

poem does name one warrior from Elmet who fought on the
battlefield of Catraeth:

When he butchered with blades, unbudging,
He was no sorry sight in combat.
He was no wretch, safeguarding spectre,
Baneful shield-bearing Madawg Elfed
   [Madog of Elmet].[15]

There is no way of telling who Madog was or his relationship to
Gwallog: whether he was a ruler of Elmet, an exile or a champion.
All the poet tells us, as in almost every other paean for the slain, is
that he was a fearsome killer of men. But it does at least hint that
Elmet belonged – or was thought by the poet to belong – to a patchwork of British kingdoms which at times sought common cause
against English-speaking peoples: the poem mentions a number of
warriors who, like Madog, had supposedly travelled from Pictland
(northern Scotland), from Gwynedd (northwest Wales), from
Ayrshire (southwest Scotland) and, perhaps, from Lindsey (north
Lincolnshire).*[16] These inclusions have sometimes been taken
alongside later poetry and chronicles to imply a sense of brotherhood among the people of the Old North and their kin in Wales, an
ethnic solidarity forged in opposition to the hated English. In truth,
this impression is almost certainly a poetic construct, a wish-fulfill-
ing dream magnified by the romantic politics of later centuries.
Nevertheless, real connections between the British kingdoms can
sometimes be discovered. A stone monolith, inscribed in Latin of
the fifth to sixth century and found near the church of Llanaelhaearn
in Gwynedd, reads ALIORTVS ELMETIACO[S] HIC IACET –

---

* These included Cyndilig, Cynri, Cynon and Cynrein of Aeron (probably
Ayrshire in southwest Scotland); Cadwal and Cadafwy of Gwynedd; Llif
'from beyond *Bannauc*' (i.e. from Scotland north of Stirling); and, from
'beyond the sea of *Iodeo*' (probably the Firth of Forth) came 'Bubon [...]
mighty in wrath'.

The Aliortus stone at Llanaelhaearn (© Gilli Allan 2022).

'Aliortus of Elmet lies here' – a memorial, perhaps, to a man who died far from home.*[17]

Nothing more is known for certain about the reign of Gwallog 'the law-giver of Elmet', and even less about Elmet itself. Quasi-reliable and intelligible written sources only speak of the kingdom at the very end of its existence, and then only retrospectively of a

---

* It should be noted that there is a cantref named 'Elvet' [Elmet] in Carmarthenshire which might be the place referred to in the inscription. There is, however, no evidence that this other Elmet was territorially or politically significant enough to warrant this sort of memorialization. The stone is also atypical in its Latin, and this has been taken as additional evidence of its relative exoticism, although – however foreign Aliortus may have been to Gwynedd – he is unlikely to have carved his own memorial stone.

realm that had already passed into memory. Yet while Gwallog's life is shrouded in mystery and embroidered with legend, it was in the reign of his son that Elmet stumbled, however briefly, into the half-light of history.

The comprehensible history of Elmet resides entirely in the person of the kingdom's last known ruler: *Keredic ap Gvallavc* – 'Ceredig, son of Gwallog'. Like his father, Ceredig was also remembered in the accreted matter of Welsh legend though sadly, in his case, that memory is spectacularly unhelpful: in the Triads, Ceredig is referred to as the owner of *Gwelwgan Gohoywgain* ('Silver-White, Proud and Fair'), one of the 'Three Lovers' Horses' of the Isle of Britain.*[18] The words may still flow like an incantation – a spell to conjure the warm breath of horses and the dampened thump of hooves on sweet-perfumed turf – but the legend they invoke is utterly forgotten. Instead, to gain any sense of what happened to Elmet and to Ceredig, it is necessary to turn – as historians of this period so often must – to the work of an English monk named Bede (*c*.673–735).

Bede lived and worked at the monastery of Monkwearmouth-Jarrow in what is now Tyne and Wear from around 680 (when he was sent there as a child novice at the age of 7) until his death on 26 May 735. In around 701, when he was ordained as priest, Bede completed his first books and embarked on a scholarly career that ultimately resulted in around sixty works of translation, theology, hagiography, history, natural philosophy and astronomy, as well as works intended to educate young monks in grammar, rhetoric and orthography. He was a hugely influential figure in western Christian thought and remains the only British ecclesiastic – and one of only

---

* The same reference to Ceredig appears in closely related versions of *Trioedd Ynys Prydein* that appear in two medieval compendia of Welsh poetry: the 'White Book of Rhydderch' (*Llyfr Gwyn Rhydderch*) and the 'Red Book of Hergest' (*Llyfr Coch Hergest*), dated to *c*.1350 and *c*.1400 respectively.

thirty-six individuals in the history of Roman (Catholic) Christianity – to be recognized as a Doctor of the Church. Nevertheless, despite Bede's great importance to the development of early medieval science and theology, his most widely cited work – and the one on which his modern reputation in Britain is largely founded – is his *Historia Ecclesiastica Gentis Anglorum* ('Ecclesiastical History of the English People'), completed around the year 731. As a guide to the general course of historical events (particularly in northern Britain), Bede's testimony in the *Historia Ecclesiastica* is invaluable and often unique; much of the history of Britain in the seventh and early eighth century simply could not be written without it.

The *Historia Ecclesiastica* tells the story of how a new people came to Britain from what is now northern Germany, Denmark and the Low Countries and ultimately adopted the Christianity of the Roman Church. By the standards of his time, Bede was an unusually careful and conscientious historian, mindful of perceptions 'as to the accuracy of what I have written' and the good opinion of posterity. He evidently worried about the credibility of his information: in his preface to the *Historia Ecclesiastica* and throughout the text he identified his sources and pointed out where his knowledge was based on hearsay.[19] Nevertheless, it cannot be stressed enough that Bede – like all historians – was a prisoner of his own biases and world-view. In particular, he was animated by a very clear purpose: the desire to present the English-speaking people of his own time, and in particular the kings and ecclesiastics of his home kingdom of Northumbria, as God-chosen standard-bearers of Christian progress on this island. As a result, not only do the other inhabitants of Britain (the Britons, Picts and Scots) get short and frankly hostile shrift, there are a great many things that he glossed over or left unsaid because they did not serve his agenda. And although it is true that much of the narrative is apparently founded on reliable first-hand testimony and, perhaps, written records of the seventh century, Bede's analysis of causation and his record of direct speech are frequently dubious. He remains, however, for long stretches of our treacherous journey into Britain's seventh-century history, the only guide we have.

Bede was born, lived and died in Northumbria, a kingdom that was in those days a political and cultural powerhouse among the many realms of Britain. It was originally comprised of two smaller kingdoms: Deira and Bernicia. Deira, the land that lay between the Humber and the Tees, was centred on the ancient Roman city of *Eboracum* – the town that English speakers came to know as *Eoforwic* and which today is known as York (by way of the Old Norse form of the name: *Jórvík*). The earliest king of Deira mentioned by Bede was a character called Ælle, who reigned in the second half of the sixth century.* His background, his regnal dates and his inter-familial relationships are notoriously nebulous, but his name would suggest that his cultural affiliations were 'English'. This is entirely in accord with Bede's belief that the Northumbrians were descended from the Angles – a people who originally inhabited what is today a region of northern Germany south of the Jutland peninsula. And indeed, a number of cemeteries in East Yorkshire support the notion that the culture and political identity of the kingdom formed around an immigrant community of northern European origin in the region between York and the North Sea coast, before later expanding – after adopting Christianity in the years around 627 – to religious communities in, among other places, Whitby, Lastingham, Beverley and Ripon.

Bernicia, by contrast, seems to have received rather less migration from continental northern Europe than more southerly parts of eastern Britain, including Deira, and it is difficult, in Bernicia, to square the surviving archaeology with Bede's insistence that 'all the Northumbrians (that is those, people living north of the River Humber)' were descended from Anglian migrants.[20] Stretching north from the borders of Deira to Lothian, Bernicia encompassed

---

* Not to be confused with Ælle of Sussex (see **SUSSEX**); the *Anglo-Saxon Chronicle* marks the beginning of his reign in 560; the *Chronicle*, however, is not a reliable source for sixth-century Deira.

a former militarized hinterland of the Roman Empire and possessed relatively little in the way of Roman infrastructure north of Hadrian's Wall (which was close to, and may have formed part of, the Deiran border). It was, however, a realm possessed of impressive native power-centres. A remarkable complex of structures assembled within a massive earthwork enclosure and incorporating a number of prehistoric monuments was excavated at Yeavering (Northumberland) in the 1950s. Despite the broadly 'Anglo-Saxon' style of its buildings and evidence of pagan religious expression, the whole site has wider affinities with British and Pictish elite settlements of northern Britain.* Another site with royal associations, Bamburgh Castle on the Northumberland coast, was – according to legends recorded in a Welsh source of the ninth century – a fortress of the Britons named in Brittonic *Din Guairoi* that was acquired by conquest in the mid-sixth century by Ida, the progenitor (according to Bede) of the Bernician royal line.†[21]

Ida supposedly became king of Bernicia in 547, and nothing – or, at least, nothing reliable – is known about him or several generations of his successors. It is generally assumed that if he existed he and his people were, like their Deiran counterparts, migrants from northern Europe or, perhaps, transplants from an English-speaking community in southern Britain. (Welsh poetry – some of which may or may not have its origins in this period – characterizes the Bernicians as pagan and 'Saxon'.) But, in reality, there is remarkably little evidence to indicate the true origins of Bernician culture, and it seems probable that it was a largely British realm, overlain with a fairly thin veneer of English language and identity. The name Yeavering, for example, derives from the

---

* See **FORTRIU**.

† Recent archaeological investigation of the site has confirmed that the rock on which the medieval castle is perched has served as the foundation of a fortress since the Iron Age. After the Viking capture of York in 867, Bamburgh (from the Old English *Bebbanburh* – 'the fortress of Bebba') served as the base of the surviving 'Anglo-Saxon' nobility of northern Northumbria.

Brittonic *Gefrin* ('hill of goats') and the name of the kingdom – from the Brittonic *Bryneich* – is itself of British origin.

The first Bernician king of whom anything much can be said is Æthelfrith, a contemporary of the Deiran king Ælle. Although the chronology of his reign is extremely confused, Æthelfrith apparently seized the throne of Deira around 604, becoming the first king to rule both Bernicia and Deira simultaneously – the originating moment for a future kingdom of all the Northumbrians. According to Bede, Æthelfrith's usurpation of the Deiran throne drove both Ælle's son Edwin and Edwin's nephew Hereric into exile.*²² Edwin fled first to Mercia (possibly via the British kingdom of Gwynedd in what is now northwest Wales) and then to the court of Rædwald, king of East Anglia. Hereric, meanwhile, fled to the court of Ceredig – the man named in Welsh sources as the son of Gwallog and king of Elmet. It was thus that the dynastic history of Northumbria intersected with the fate of that obscure little kingdom, and the result for Elmet ultimately proved disastrous.

Both Edwin and Hereric constituted an obvious threat to Æthelfrith's power. As close relatives of the deposed Deiran kings, either man could potentially press a dynastic claim to the Deiran throne. As such, they were individuals around whom resistance to Æthelfrith's new regime could easily coalesce, and – irrespective of the personal satisfaction they might have derived from it – both would have stood to gain by Æthelfrith's downfall. As a result, it is unsurprising that Æthelfrith seems to have been anxious to have the fugitive princes returned or otherwise neutralized. According

---

* Bede mentions that Hereric was Edwin's nephew and the *Anglo-Saxon Chronicle* states that Æthelfrith replaced Æthelric as king in Northumbria. No other siblings of Edwin are mentioned with the exception of a sister, Acha, who was apparently married to Æthelfrith swiftly after the latter's seizure of the Northumbrian throne. The situation is further confused by the fact that Æthelfrith's father also seems to have been named Æthelric.

to Bede, when Æthelfrith learned that Edwin was at the court of the East Anglian king Rædwald, he sent messengers three times demanding that the Deiran prince be bound over to him or killed. Faced with the threat of war and increasingly large bribes, Rædwald was apparently on the brink of caving in to Æthelfrith's ultimatums when – again according to Bede – he was dissuaded by his wife. (She supposedly suggested – and it is best to take this with a little salt – that 'it was unworthy in a great king to sell his best friend in the hour of need for gold, and worse still to sacrifice his royal honour, the most valuable of possessions, for love of money.')[23] Whatever its inspiration, Rædwald's change of heart was dramatic; not only did he choose to resist Æthelfrith's demands, but he also invested his considerable military strength into a military campaign in support of the exiled prince Edwin.*[24]

The fate of Edwin's nephew Hereric played out very differently. Bede does not reveal whether Æthelfrith brought the same pressure to bear on Ceredig of Elmet as he applied to Rædwald, but it seems to be a reasonable assumption: Hereric, 'died from poison' while 'living in banishment under the protection of the British king Cerdic [Ceredig]'.[25] Though Bede does not directly implicate anyone in Hereric's murder, or even indicate precisely when he died, it seems likely that the Deiran prince was killed at Æthelfrith's instigation – with the connivance (or at best indifference) of Ceredig.

Elmet was much closer to Northumbrian territory than East Anglia (which was buffered by the kingdoms of Lindsey and Mercia), and was therefore extremely vulnerable to Æthelfrith's threats. It is very likely that Ceredig decided that either gold was indeed worth more than royal honour, or that his kingdom would

---

* It was then, according to Bede, at the time of greatest danger, that Edwin had a nocturnal visitor, a stranger who promised – in return for pledges of obedience and acceptance of future guidance – 'to persuade Rædwald not to harm you or betray you to death […] that you should become king, crush your enemies, and enjoy greater power than any of your forebears'; the cost was bitter – Rædwald's son Rægenhere died in the fighting.

not withstand an invasion. If so, Ceredig's choice may have sealed his kingdom's fate.

In 616, King Rædwald of East Anglia rode north with his army, Edwin of Deira by his side. They encountered the Northumbrians on the eastern bank of the River Idle, at the border between the kingdoms of Mercia and Northumbria. The river, a stream that winds its way through the flat, green countryside of Nottinghamshire, is placid and meandering, a fat, reflective ribbon beneath wide and heavy skies. The name 'Idle' is probably derived from the Old English word *Idel* meaning lazy and slow. There is little purchase for the mind in this landscape; sleepy and sluggish like the river, flat and hard to compass, a dreaming land riddled by dykes and ditches. The river itself can be stumbled on almost unawares. But it is also a landscape bedevilled by flooding, by bloated outgrowths of brown water that modern drainage is not always able to contain. In the seventh century, without the benefits of agricultural engineering, this was a marshy and waterlogged world, part of a wide region south of York and east of Leeds riddled with the many tributaries of the Humber, where travel was difficult and dangerous.

In this sort of country, travellers – and warbands – would have made use of well-established lines of communication. Roman roads remained the primary transport network in Britain throughout the Middle Ages and up to the eighteenth century; it is very likely that Ermine Street – the Roman thoroughfare that carves north from London to York via Lincoln – was the route used by Rædwald and Edwin on their ride north. If so, somewhere near Bawtry (Nottinghamshire) – the place where Ermine Street meets the Idle – is the most likely place that the East Anglians met Æthelfrith's army in battle. Apparently taken by surprise, the Northumbrians were overwhelmed by the much larger forces commanded by King Rædwald. A scrap of Old English poetry, preserved in Latin in the twelfth-century *Historia Anglorum* by the Anglo-Norman writer Henry of Huntingdon, relates how *Amnis Idle Anglorum sanguine sorduit* – 'The River Idle was befouled with English blood'.[26] King

Æthelfrith was killed in the fighting alongside his warriors, his blood joining that sordid stream, reddening the lazy river, seeping out with the floodwaters to saturate the soil.

In the aftermath of battle, and with Rædwald's backing, Edwin son of Ælle became king of all Northumbria: the joint realm of Deira and Bernicia. For his part in the bloody business, Rædwald found himself in a commanding position. Edwin owed everything to his East Anglian benefactor: his life, his crown and his continued grip on power. It was a debt that ultimately enabled Rædwald to eclipse all his rivals in influence and to wield – in Bede's eyes – *imperium* over all other 'English' kingdoms south of the Humber and probably considerable power in Northumbria as well.[27] In 624, when Rædwald died, the mantle of *imperium* would settle on Edwin's shoulders. For these players in the drama the events of 616 had been a triumph; Edwin's arrival as an exile at the East Anglian court had offered Rædwald a chance to seize more power than he could otherwise have hoped to accumulate (it may well have been a calculation to this effect, rather than any moral awakening, that had caused the East Anglian king to rebuff the Æthelfrith's threats and bribes and to turn with such ferocity against him).

For Hereric and Ceredig, however, their choices had led them down a more dismal path – a lesson in how brutally fortune's wheel could turn in the early Middle Ages and a glimpse of those it ground into dust.[28] Hereric's arrival in Elmet had heralded disaster – for him, certainly, but also for Ceredig. If, as seems likely, Ceredig had facilitated Hereric's death under pressure from Æthelfrith, it would suggest that Elmet had been effectively subordinated to Northumbria power. This put Ceredig firmly on the wrong side of events as they unfolded. When the conflict of 616 resulted in the defeat and death of Æthelfrith and the transfer of Northumbrian power into the hands of Edwin, Ceredig found himself in an unenviable spot. Not only had he lost the protection that Æthelfrith's overlordship might have afforded, but he also had now to reckon with a powerful neighbour who was the close kinsman of the Deiran prince whose murder Ceredig had overseen. No one knows whether Ceredig and the people of Elmet played an active role in the violence of 616. But it is reasonable to imagine that when the warriors of Edwin and Rædwald massed at the borders of Northumbria, when their banners flew beside the Idle and their spear-points glimmered bloody in the dawn, Ceredig felt their coming like the tramp of doom.

If that is so, it was justified. In the early part of his reign, King Edwin invaded Elmet, driving Ceredig into exile. Within a year, the last known king of Elmet was dead: snuffed, along with the kingdom itself, out of existence.

The paragraphs above present what might be described as the standard history behind the fall of Elmet. It is in many ways a deceptively straightforward narrative: a story of revenge and betrayal, conquest and defeat that satisfies the primal demands of storytelling. As such it is seductive – and, despite all the following caveats, it could easily be true. However, it cannot be denied that the story (and in particular its ending) is, in many ways, an exercise in rationalization that may or may not be justified: of papering over cracks, dismissing and ignoring problems with the sources. Consider, for example, that Bede nowhere states that Hereric was poisoned on Æthelfrith's instruction – this is merely, in context, a plausible inference and possibly one that Bede is steering the reader towards. However, the fact that he doesn't actually provide a timeline of these events leaves open the possibility that Hereric was poisoned not at Æthelfrith's instigation, but at Edwin's, in a move to eliminate potential dynastic rivals to the Deiran throne (a scenario that would put rather a different complexion on the whole narrative and the motivations of its key actors). In fact, although Bede confirms the existence of a British king called Ceredig (Anglicized to 'Cerdic' in Bede's text) and mentions a region called 'Elmet', nowhere does he actually connect the two. Nor is there any mention in Bede's text of Edwin's decisive campaign against his British neighbour. Both of these ideas – that Ceredig was king of Elmet and that Elmet was conquered by King Edwin – have their origins in a single statement contained in a work entitled the *Historia Brittonum* (the 'History of the Britons'), a bald and unambiguous assertion that 'Edwin, son of Ælle, occupied Elmet and expelled Cerdic [Ceredig], king of that country'.[29]

The *Historia Brittonum* was written, or rather cobbled together, in the late 820s, from (in the words of its compiler), 'a heap of all that I have found, both from the Annals of the Romans and from the Chronicles of the Holy Fathers, and from the writings of the Irish and the English, and out of the traditions of our elders'.[30] It reads much as one might expect from such a pungent description: an apparently incoherent amalgam of disparate matter, that piles together royal genealogies and snippets of genuine history alongside miracles, marvels, legends and the doings of wizards and saints.*[31] This makes it hard to evaluate as a historical source at the best of times, but when it comes to assessing what the compiler knew about Elmet, there are only two things we can be pretty sure of. The first is that he or she didn't know very much at all: no other surviving source makes any mention of Elmet in the years that elapsed between the writing of Bede's *Historia Ecclesiastica* and the construction of the *Historia Brittonum*, and reliable knowledge of the kingdom itself (which had vanished from the political scene long before the latter was put together) is very unlikely to have survived in communal memory.† The second is that the compiler of the *Historia Brittonum* had read Bede. Given these two likelihoods, historians are apt to wonder whether the idea that Edwin invaded Elmet, as recorded in the *Historia Brittonum*, was based on anything more than rational extrapolation from Bede's narrative (just like the idea that Æthelfrith and Ceredig were responsible for Hereric's

* This impression is in some ways misleading, for – as the historian David Dumville has pointed out – the *Historia Brittonum* may have been carefully constructed to serve quite specific ends.

† Which is not to say that other sources that mentioned Elmet never existed – just that if they did, they haven't survived the centuries and we don't know anything about them.

poisoning). And while the *Historia Brittonum*'s testimony could have been based on folk tradition or oral history or – just perhaps – a lost chronicle, there is no evidence to prove this either way.

The statement apparently acknowledging Ceredig's death – *Ceretic obiit* – is even more problematic. It is recorded in the *Annales Cambriae* (the 'Welsh Annals') which are probably a product of the later tenth century and therefore even more recent than the *Historia Brittonum*. Once again, while the Welsh Annals could be based in part on older oral or written traditions, such sources, if they exist, cannot be identified. The authors of the *Annales* did, however, have access to the *Historia Brittonum* and to Bede's history, and so it is entirely possible that the date, the name, or perhaps the entire entry was manipulated or fabricated in the tenth century (or later) to fit the established narrative of Elmet's demise.*
Perhaps the best that can be said with conviction about Ceredig's career is that, by the early ninth century at the latest, a tradition had developed that associated the fall of Elmet's last known king with aggression from King Edwin's Northumbria – a tradition that may or may not be true.

I raise these issues not to be a curmudgeon, but simply to convey some of the difficulties encountered when attempting to write the history of this period. It can sometimes be tempting to construct a version of the post-Roman past that, while it may give every impression of a well-researched and plausible narrative, is conveyed with a surety and conviction utterly unwarranted given the flimsy foundations on which it is built. John Morris' *The Age of Arthur* (1973) is a famous example of where this road can lead. An enor-

---

* Also problematic is the fact that in the *Annales* the death of Ceredig is dated to 616 and precedes an entry for 617 noting the beginning of Edwin's reign. This makes a mess of the chronology (Edwin was already king when he is supposed to have conquered Elmet), and suggests that either the *Annales* dated these events in error or that the *Ceretic* mentioned here is not Ceredig of Elmet at all. Or perhaps the *Annales* are right and the *Historia Brittonum* is wrong: perhaps King Ceredig fought and died at the battle of the River Idle, not living long enough to see his kingdom overrun.

mously popular work by a well-regarded historian of his day, *The Age of Arthur* wove a compelling narrative of Britain in the Dark Ages that has beguiled a vast readership in the decades since its publication. However, even at the time it was regarded by other professional historians as little more than clever creative embroidery: fiction-with-footnotes that succeeded with great panache and very little ethical justification to weave an illusory lost 'history' from difficult and disparate material. The result was a work that shackled an abject failure of scholarly judgement to an almost Tolkienian ambition. Morris' reputation as an academic was seriously damaged; generations of readers were seriously misled. In the end, nobody won (except, perhaps, the publisher).

Whatever truth lies behind references in the Welsh sources to Ceredig, it is probably fair to say that the upheavals which beset Northumbria in the early seventh century precipitated the terminal decline of an independent Elmet. Certainly by Bede's day there was no kingdom of Elmet to speak of: it evidently did not exist at all at the time he was writing in the early eighth century, and he only mentioned Elmet once (and then only as the name of a forest, not a kingdom). But in reality, the route that the kingdom took towards oblivion was almost certainly bumpier and more complex than the compressed Welsh sources imply. Bede relates how King Edwin himself died in battle in 633, cut down at Hatfield Chase (Yorkshire, near the borders of Elmet) by the pagan Mercian king Penda and his ally Cadwallon of Gwynedd. Elmet must have been affected in some way by this crisis, even if there is no way of knowing how. Cadwallon was described by Bede 'not as a victorious king, but as a savage tyrant' who, 'although he professed to call himself a Christian, was utterly barbarous in temperament and behaviour' and 'had no respect for the newly established religion of Christ'.[32] But whether Cadwallon was really worse than any other warlord of his day is moot (Bede is rarely able to conceal his anti-British bigotry). It is perhaps reasonable to speculate whether, for the Christian Britons of Elmet, rule by Cadwallon might not have been more appealing than subjugation to Edwin's Northumbria.

Did the people of Elmet make common cause with the British-Mercian alliance? Did they attempt to reclaim their independence amid the turmoil? Alas, it is impossible to say. Within a year of Edwin's death, Northumbrian power was restored by King (and later Saint) Oswald (r.634–641/2), son of King Æthelfrith who was killed at the battle of the Idle in 616. No other sovereign realm – named 'Elmet' or anything else for that matter – ever played a role in this part of England again. Yet there can be little doubt that, for the people who inhabited the region, these crises must have prolonged and complicated the disintegration of their identity. Myriad tales of resistance and cruelty, of bravery and endurance and despair must have accumulated by the crags and dales and falling rivers, pooling uncounted, unremarked and ultimately forgotten. For Elmet, oblivion arrived cloaked in darkness, and the end was probably protracted, silent darkness.

In his collection *Remains of Elmet*, Ted Hughes is preoccupied with the industrial heritage of the Calder Valley and the bleak land and skyscapes of the moors; hollow valleys and blasted heaths, outcrops of rock that stand sentinel on the wind-wracked edges of highland sheep pasture, ruined farmsteads and crumbling walls standing as metaphors for the winnowing away of a rural, Methodist mill culture that was already gone – slipping past his pen even as he tried to write it. Of the ancient kingdom that stood behind that world, a dark mountain looming beyond it, Hughes understandably had little to say. He imagined it shrinking away into the Calder Valley, a place of diminishing refuge from the changes that time wrought, a place of bandits, outlaws and rebels.* Of more recent

* This was the Elmet depicted in Benjamin Myers' *Gallows Pole*, an untamed corner of Britain that squirmed uncomfortably in the strictures of Hanoverian England, that threw up men like 'King' David Hartley whose coin-clipping enterprise challenged the authority of king and excise man and exposed the brutality that impregnates the rock and moss and squamous undercarriage of the West Riding.

history, however, Hughes wrote vividly: he paints a terrifying picture of Parson William Grimshaw's eighteenth-century evangelism and of how his 'heavenly fire, straight out of Blake's Prophetic Books, shattered the terrain into biblical landmarks: quarries burst open like craters, and chapels – the bedrock transfigured – materialized in them. The crumpled map of horizons became a mirage of the Holy Land'.[33]

For his part, Bede offers no sense whatsoever of Elmetian identity and only very little of Elmet's geography. He only mentions the name once, with no reference to the people that the Tribal Hideage called *Elmedsætna*. He does, however, offer a tiny window into the landscape of Elmet as he experienced it – a world, like Parson Grimshaw's, of almost wholly religious significance, reordered by spasms of violence and upheaval. Describing a church that was built for King Edwin after his conversion to Christianity in 627, Bede recalled that it stood at a royal hall in a place called *Campodunum* that was burned by the armies of Penda and Cadwallon in 633. After its destruction, the hall was rebuilt *in regio quæ vocatur Loidis* ('in the region which is called Leeds').[34] The church's stone altar, however, which had survived the burning, was preserved in a monastery that in Bede's time was run by an abbot named Thrymwulf. This monastery lay *in silva Elmete* – in the wood of Elmet.[35]

Bede doesn't really explain where exactly this forest lay. *Campodunum*, the site of the original church and royal hall, was almost certainly the same place listed as *Camboduno* in the third-century list of Roman routes and destinations known as the *Itinerarium Antonini Augusti* ('the Itinerary of the Emperor Antoninus', or 'Antonine Itinerary' for short). Unfortunately, however, no one knows where *Camboduno* is either, except that it lay somewhere between Tadcaster and Manchester. In any case, even if the precise location of *Camboduno* could be established, it wouldn't help very much with defining the boundaries of Elmet. Bede is not entirely clear about the relationship between *Campodunum* and the altar's subsequent home *in silva Elmete*, or how close either of those places were to Leeds (although, given the practical difficulties that would presumably attend lugging a stone altar around the countryside, historians tend to assume that these places were all reasonably proximate. This is far from certain, however, and plenty of people before the modern era are known to have shifted more impractical objects over more improbable distances.)*

Taken alone, Bede only gets us so far: to a region accessible from Northumbria, and probably not a million miles from Leeds. Thankfully, however, other evidence clarifies the situation considerably and brings us a little closer to the region's inhabitants. Old English place-names that indicate trees and clearings proliferate to the south and west of Leeds: a possible signpost to the location of Bede's *silva Elmete*. More substantive evidence, however, can be found in a group of eight place-names in the West Riding wapentakes of Barkston Ash and Skyrack.† All of these have at one time contained the name Elmet since first being recorded in the Middle Ages. In Barkston Ash they are: Sherburn-in-Elmet (*Schirburn in Elmett*), Clifford (*Clyfford in Elmette*), Saxton (*Saxtun in Elmet*), Mickelfield (*Mikelfeld in Elmet*), Kirkby Wharfe (*Kyrkby in Elmete*), Burton Salmon (*Burton in Elmett*) and Sutton (*Sutton in Elmett*); in the wapentake of Skyrack there is Barwick-in-Elmet (*Berewyke in Elmet*).‡[36]

All of these places lie to the east of Leeds, between the valleys of the Aire and Wharfe, in a broad corridor either side of Ermine Street. It is possible that these names preserve the approximate eastern boundary of Elmet. They are names of Old English origin, applied by people who spoke a different language from that which

---

* Bede makes a clear distinction between *silva Elmete* and *regio Loidis*, implying that he regarded them as geographically distinct places.

† 'Wapentakes' (from the Old Norse *vápnatak*: 'weapon-taking') are territorial units beneath the county level equivalent to the 'hundreds' of southern Britain; they typically comprise a varying number of individual parishes.

‡ The place-names given in parentheses are the oldest recorded versions of these place-names and date back to the medieval period.

was native to the original post-Roman inhabitants. The designation of a settlement as being 'in such-and-such-a-place' is only really likely to occur where there is some probability of confusion or dispute over the matter: i.e. at a notable break in linguistic, political or ethnic continuity. In this case, the naming in English of a number of places as being specifically 'in Elmet' is good evidence that places further to the east were 'not in Elmet'. In other words, it is very likely that these place-names demarcate the boundary of Elmet with Deira. These were presumably the places that it was useful for Deirans to remember lay outside or liminal to their own sphere of influence. (The distribution of a growing corpus of 'Anglo-Saxon' archaeology, discovered through metal detecting along the same north–south axis, reinforces the impression of the Roman road as a border region.[37])

This sense of separation between the Britons of Elmet and their 'English' neighbours is also present in a range of Old English place-names that include the elements *Walh* ('foreigner' [i.e. Briton]), *Brettas* ('Briton') and *Cumbra* (from Brittonic *Cymry*, the British self-designation – later adapted as an Old English personal name, possibly for someone of British heritage). All of these imply the presence of notable British communities in West Yorkshire – notable, that is, from the perspective of English speakers busy renaming the land in their own tongue. In the generations that followed the digestion of Elmet in the belly of Northumbria, new names were coined that directly acknowledged these linguistic and cultural fault-lines: Walsden ('valley of foreigners'), Walshaw ('copse of foreigners'), two places called Walton (both 'foreigner town'), West Bretton ('Briton town'), Bretland ('Briton land'), Cumberworth ('Briton-man's enclosure').

Elsewhere within Elmet, a few other clues survive. Leeds, for example, is a Celtic-derived place-name (*Loidis*), and other places which include the same name element (Ledsham, Ledston) perhaps indicate the wider *regio Loidis* that Bede referred to. Their survival might suggest the tenacity of Celtic language-speakers in a world increasingly dominated by Anglophones. If so, it represented a transient resistance to cultural annihilation: the vast majority of place-names in West Yorkshire are of English (or later Norse) origin. In a more important way, however, names offer a window onto a matter of profound significance in the lives of the *Elmedsætna*. A remarkable cluster of place names containing the element 'eccles' survives in the West Riding: at Eccles (Stanbury), Eccles Parlour (Soyland), Ecclesall, Ecclesdo (Kirkheaton), Ecclesfield, Ecclesgrass Head (Horsforth), Eccleshill (Baildon), Exley (Southowram), Exley Gate (Penistone) and Exley Head (Keighley). 'Eccles' – an Anglicization of the Latin word *ecclesia* transmitted via Brittonic – means 'church', and it is generally accepted that the word was used by English speakers to indicate the presence of native British sites of Christian religious observance. The substantial clutch of 'eccles' names in West Yorkshire therefore constitutes powerful evidence for an established Christian community within the presumed boundaries of Elmet, a community that must have predated the period of English linguistic and cultural dominance.

The total absence of historical or archaeological evidence for Elmetian religious preferences makes the 'eccles' place-names of West Yorkshire enormously significant. These place names signify a preserved tradition of late Romano-British Christianity in Elmet, a cultural hold-out that may have survived the collapse of Empire and lingered long enough to be met by the encroachment of new forms of expression and a new vocabulary of power, culture and religious convention: of what would become 'Englishness'. No other trace of the Elmetian church has ever been found. Only the place-names survive, labels applied by English speakers, badges of alienation in a landscape that no longer spoke the language of its people.

Hughes' Calder Valley is a dark place; a paradise lost. It is a haunted, blasted world – all weeping sores and bones exposed beneath the heavens, where:

[…] the millstone of sky
Grinds light and shadow so purple-fine
And has ground it so long
Grinding the skin off earth
Earth bleeds her raw true darkness
A land naked now as a wound
That the sun swabs and dabs
Where the miles of agony are numbness
And harebell and heather a euphoria.[38]

Remains of Elmet is shot through with the imagery of pain and decay, of death and dementia: it is a portrait of a world forgetting itself as it physically falls away – a palimpsest of loss, played out over the corpse of one of the most forgotten of Britain's forgotten realms. Like Hughes, the people of early medieval Britain also dwelt deeply on lost pasts, siting their churches within the tumbled walls of Roman cities, burying their own in the grass-grown tombs of people millennia dead. They spun tales of tarnished treasures and broken swords, of the world they knew and the pasts they imagined. But the people of Elmet left almost nothing behind, forgetting themselves in the cultural displacement that erased their language and their landmarks, leaving no memory of their world to those who came after. Their fate engenders both unease and sadness, an uncanny absence that bleeds into a mournful cry of loss.

Ultimately all ghost stories end this way; disquiet giving way to pity, to grief for the dead and for our own mortality, and the knowledge that one day we too will all be dust: our voices lost out on the moor, our bodies annihilated, our names forgotten.

HWICCE

– *Gloucestershire and Worcestershire* –

Well-wrought this wall-stone, weird broke it;
Bastions busted, burst is giant's work.
Roofs are ruined, ruptured turrets,
Ring-gate broken, rime on lime-work,
Cloven shower-shields, sheered, fallen,
Age ate under them. Earth-grasp holds fast
The noble workers, decayed, departed
In earth's hard-grip, while a hundred times
The generations pass.

Anon., *The Ruin*[1]

From the edge, beyond the miles of farmland that cover the vale, the great river basks in the sunlight, its dull and silty coils burnished to silver as they wind into the far distance. Clouds rush from the west, towering grey leviathans that thunder across vast skies and fracture the sunlight into splintered rays or smear its golden stain across their dark underbellies; colours of overboiled egg yolk. At other times the rain comes hard, chasing the light down from the Welsh mountains, across the distant forest and the river, across the plain. It comes close to terror – watching that tide of shadow race over green and yellow fields, the edge of the storm approaching like a cavalry charge, the world beyond veiled in a murky swirl of broken light and muddled vison. Then it hits with a howl of rage and sudden gloom, lances of rain battering the limestone bulwarks and the human figures foolish enough to have remained to face it, scattering them back towards the shelter of the woods.

I was born in London, but I grew up in the Cotswolds. Since early childhood I walked the wooded edges of the limestone hills, taking the paths that trace the escarpment between Randwick and Haresfield. Sometimes I forged straight lines across the hills, burrowing through undergrowth and over barbed wire, into ditches and fields full of cows, seeking the barrows and the trig points and the shattering sight of the world falling into the Severn plain. From up there I would sometimes imagine an invasion: distant ships dark on the river, columns of smoke rising, armed horsemen swarming like ants over the flood-plain. I would imagine lighting signal fires and gathering weapons, waiting to defend my little kingdom from its enemies. It was a long time before I learned that my kingdom had a name – that between the beginning of the seventh century (or even earlier) and the end of the eighth, all of Gloucestershire east of the Severn, most of Worcestershire and parts of Warwickshire, a bit of Oxfordshire, the city of Bath and a few small bites of Wiltshire formed a single realm: claimed, at one time or another, by the kings and bishops of the Hwicce.

Gloucestershire, my adopted county, fits awkwardly into the regional scheme of Britain. Since 1994, the shire has officially been defined as part of the South West Region, the only county so described that lies beyond the northern reaches of Hardy's Wessex. At other times the county is described as belonging to the 'south Midlands', or sometimes the 'west of England', but these labels carry little conviction. And, though the Thames may rise near Cirencester, the regattas and the rowers of the lower river feel a world away from the angry, ugly bull-rush of the Severn, the knots and knuckles of the limestone hills and highlands. In local terms, the region is defined more by its geology than arbitrary labels. The Cotswolds, a range of hills rising at points to over 1,000 feet, run through six counties, though the vast bulk lies within Gloucestershire. The slope rises gently, just west of Oxford. It ascends steadily, smoothly, crowned with thick remnants of ancient woodland, before ending abruptly in a high escarpment – a broken edge of oolitic limestone that rises from the Severn plain like a pie crust snapped and forced upward by the downward pressure of a knife at its eastern edge. The bedrock formed more than 150 million years ago, the floor of a Jurassic ocean that teemed with creatures whose fossils infest the rock and whose shattered shells formed the egg-shaped (oolitic) beads that give the rock its name and granular texture.

The Cotswolds sit uncomfortably astride modern administrative boundaries. The counties that the range touches to the north – Worcestershire and Warwickshire – are, unlike Gloucestershire, part of the West Midlands Region of England. But it is in the south – in the territory around Bath where the southern thrust of the hills gives way and the last bastions of the limestone scarp hem Bristol against the Severn – that the greatest geographical anxiety can be experienced. It is a region of perennial identity crisis, its status spasmodically redefined in a bewildering succession of obsolete counties and bureaucratic fudges. When the county of Avon (created 1974) was abolished in 1996, the region was divided into four 'extraordinary unitary authorities': 'South Gloucestershire', including several suburbs of Bristol, falls within the ceremonial county of Gloucestershire; 'Bath and North East Somerset', along with 'North Somerset', belong to their eponymous ceremonial county. Bristol itself, however, has constituted a 'county' in its own right since 1373 and boasts its own High Sheriff. To make matters even more confusing, since 2017 three of these authorities (excluding North Somerset which refused to take part) are grouped together as the 'West of England Combined Authority'.

Despite any regional anxieties, however, the shires of the west remain certain of what they are not. From the Cotswold edge, beyond the Forest of Dean and the Malvern Hills, the Black Mountains rise spectral in the pale distance – a shadow of estrangement against the horizon. Despite (or perhaps because of) the proximity, there is rarely a mention of Wales in Gloucestershire that fails to provoke an outburst of puerile chauvinism and affected disdain. As a teenager, a rugby excursion to Monmouth – through the wooded crags and boar-haunted thickets of the Wye Valley – was made to feel like Marlow's journey up the Congo. This is not the way things have always been; the sharply delineated identities of Wales and England have been centuries in the making. Their origins lie in the early medieval past when contested boundaries and muddled loyalties produced a zone of confrontation and compromise between the British and the English, between the Church of Rome and the Christianity of the Britons, between Wessex and Mercia. And yet, despite the tensions, the spectre of an older community of the Cotswolds and the Severn still hangs over the region: the ghost of the Hwicce, dispelling attempts by medieval warlords and modern bureaucrats alike to overwrite the deep geology, the buried history.

In the year 577, according to the *Anglo-Saxon Chronicle*, an army came into the west. It was led by two Saxon warlords – Ceawlin of the *Gewissae* and his son Cuthwine. They, in the words of the anonymous monk who inscribed the annal into the oldest manuscript of the *Anglo-Saxon Chronicle*, 'fought against the Britons and slew three kings – Coinmail, Condidan and Farinmail – at the place which is called Deorham [probably Dyrham, near Bath]; and they took three of their cities: Gloucester, Cirencester and Bath'.[2] By the twelfth century, an elaborated version of the same story entered the written record. Geoffrey Gaimar's *Estoire des Engleis*, a chronicle of English history composed in Anglo-Norman rhyming verse, recounts how Cirencester, besieged on all sides, was overcome.

'Through negligence on the part of the Britons, the town was set alight by sparrows which brought fire and sulphur into it and set fire to many of the houses. And the people outside besieging the town launched their attack with particular ferocity. The town was then captured, and in its turn Gloucester was taken. They pursued their conquest right up to the Severn, killing all the most prominent Britons, and from the sea where they had originally landed they took possession of the whole country and the kingdom as far as the Severn, and they drove the Britons out.'[3]

Gaimar's folklore-inflected story is pure legend, but the *Chronicle* account on which it builds is harder to discount. On the face of it, the story is seductively simple – a tale of how the Saxons had come from the east to drive the Britons from the old Roman cities in which they dwelt, a microcosm of the myth of English origins. The three towns it mentions – Gloucester, Cirencester and Bath – were among the most prosperous and well-established Roman towns in Britain. The *Chronicle* narrative implies that these three cities of the Britons were, in the late sixth century, still thriving: bastions of Romano-British authority in territories administered by kings who, for what it's worth, were apparently possessed of entirely credible Celtic names. Serious doubts, however, both general and specific in nature, can be raised about the reliability of the *Anglo-Saxon Chronicle* entries for the sixth century. In this case, the particular circumstances of the *Chronicle's* origin – in the later years of the reign of the West Saxon king Alfred (r.871–899) – allow for the suspicion that the story of the conquest of Gloucester, Cirencester and Bath by Ceawlin and Cuthwine (a pair of figures claimed as ancestors in the genealogies of the later West Saxon dynasty) was concocted to provide historical justification for the West Saxon annexation of this region in the reign of King Alfred.*

---

* The absorption of western Mercia, including the region of the former kingdom of Hwicce, occurred in the years after the West Saxon victory over the Vikings in 878 at Edington (Wiltshire) and the diplomatic arrangements that followed.

That the region was utterly transformed between the beginning of the fifth century and the end of the sixth is beyond doubt. But alluring though it may be, the *Anglo-Saxon Chronicle*'s story of Ceawlin and Cuthwine's conquest is probably a mirage. In truth, the precise mechanisms that caused one of the most prosperous regions of the former Roman province of Britannia to mutate into the kingdom of Hwicce are painfully obscure and complex in ways that we can barely begin to understand, an era constructed from a flimsy wattle of slender facts thickly daubed with an abundance of speculation, half-truths, tall tales and other accretions. The historical record, as for the whole of Britain, is practically non-existent. The best surviving source is an excoriating polemic, *De Excidio Britanniae* ('On the Ruin of Britain'), written by the British monk Gildas sometime between the late fifth century and *c.*530, lamenting the political, moral and religious failings of the fifth and sixth centuries and the calamities that these had unleashed on the island. It is not a historical work, but a rhetorical barracking of Romano-British leaders – both prior to and in Gildas' own time – whom he blamed for the unhappy fate of Britain in the twilight of Roman rule. Most of the few places Gildas mentioned cannot be identified. Most of the people he lambasted cannot be named. The dates of the events he described – even the date at which he wrote – remain controversial.[4] Nevertheless, it is the best we have, and it provides the traditional narrative of post-Roman Britain from which all others are ultimately derived.

Gildas describes a world that had spun rapidly out of control. As the western Roman Empire fell into disorder, Britain was left exposed and vulnerable. Militarily depleted and politically mismanaged, weakened by famine and plague, the British elites – led 'by a proud tyrant' (*superbo tyranno*) named later as *Guarthigirn* ('Vortigern') – devised a strategy. They would invite Saxons from continental Europe ('let into the island like wolves into the fold') to act as a shield against raids by Scots (from Ireland) and Picts (from Scotland). This plan ('How desperate and crass the stupidity!') swiftly backfired.[5] The Saxons, using disputes over pay and rations as a pretext, turned against the Britons and began to wreak havoc. Britain was left in ruins, a place where 'in the middle of the squares the foundation-stones of high walls and towers that had been torn from their lofty bases, holy altars, fragments of corpses, covered (as it were) with a purple crust of congealed blood, looked as though they had been mixed up in some dreadful wine-press'. In this land of nightmares there 'was no burial to be had except in the ruins of houses or the bellies of beasts and birds'.[6]

This had all happened before Gildas' birth, before the Britons had pulled themselves together under the leadership of a Romano-British aristocrat named Ambrosius Aurelianus and before the invading Saxons from continental Europe had suffered a resounding defeat at the siege of *Badonicus Mons* – 'Mount Badon' (a battle in which the Britons were led, according to the ninth-century *Historia Brittonum*, by a warlord named Arthur).[7] The location of Mount Badon is unknown. The medieval writer Geoffrey of Monmouth, synthesizing, elaborating and substantially inventing the legend of King Arthur in the twelfth century, imagined that Badon was Bath. There is no good reason for thinking that he was right about this. The modern place-name comes from the Old English word *bæð* (lit. 'bath'), but the Roman name for the city was *Aquae Sulis* ('the waters of [the goddess] Sulis [-Minerva]'). It is hard to understand why Gildas, writing in Latin, would choose to Latinize a Germanic word (mangling its pronunciation in the process) to describe a place with a perfectly good Latin name already. In any case, it is extremely unlikely that anywhere in western Britain had come to be commonly known by an English name at the time Gildas was writing (probably in the first decades of the sixth century).

There are other, more convincing, contenders for the location of Mount Badon.* But wherever the battle was fought, the victory was not a panacea for all the ills spawned by Britain's post-Imperial

---

* E.g. Badbury Rings (Dorset), Liddington Castle, near Badbury (Wiltshire).

decline. 'External wars may have stopped,' Gildas explains, 'but not civil ones' and 'the cities […] are not populated even now as they once were: right to the present they are deserted, in ruins and unkempt'.[8] If Gildas is to be believed, it is hard to imagine what sort of power Coinmail, Condidan and Farinmail strove vainly to preserve at the battle of Deorham in 577, what manner of urban life they sought to protect in their cities of Bath, Gloucester and Cirencester from the barbarian onslaught, what exactly remained of Roman Britain to be expunged by Saxon conquest.

The end of Roman Britain is among the most controversial and hotly debated subjects in British archaeology. The evidence is slight and the chronologies are vague: the same data have been used to support widely divergent views of what happened as the institutions of Roman Imperial rule fell away.[9] But if one looks only at the evidence from Gloucestershire, it is hard to escape the impression of a world that had – at least for the inhabitants and patrons of some of the grandest buildings in late Roman Britain – gone badly awry. This does not necessarily reflect what was happening elsewhere in the former provinces of Britannia, something that will become increasingly clear in later chapters. But in this particular corner of the Empire, in the lives of some of the richest and most 'Roman' of Roman Britons, the formal end of Empire appears to have rolled in like a thunderhead of doom.

Cirencester, on the eastern slopes of the Gloucestershire Cotswolds, is a handsome old market town. It is a place that feels well settled into its historic wealth: a town that grew rich on the late medieval and Tudor wool trade, its church a masterpiece of swaggering provincial gothic. It remains genteel, well-to-do and liberal, in a Waitrose, National Trust, Radio 4 sort of way. That it is underpinned by a girding of classical urbanity feels somehow appropriate. By the second century, Cirencester (Roman *Corinium Dobunnorum*) was, at c.240 acres within the walls, the second largest city in Britain (after London) and, from the end of the third century, the presumed capital of the province of *Britannia Prima*.* It had developed from a legionary fort into the tribal capital of the *Dobunni*, the native British tribe that inhabited modern Gloucestershire and parts of the surrounding counties. In its Imperial heyday, *Corinium* was a conspicuously wealthy place with a basilica, forum and amphitheatre that rivalled those of *Londinium* in scale. The town's richest citizens dwelt in stone houses decorated with wall-paintings and elaborate mosaic floors. They patronized top-flight mosaicists and stonecutters, glassmakers and bakers, and they watched in delight as men and beasts tore each other apart for their pleasure, cheering from stone tiers rising twenty-five feet from the blood-soaked arena floor.[10]

By the later decades of the fourth century, at a time when public buildings were falling into disuse in other towns, *Corinium* seems to have been wealthier than ever. New private dwellings were being built – impressive complexes, complete with bathhouses, courtyards and lavish mosaic floors. Roads were regularly maintained until the early fifth century and major investment in public buildings continued: the backrooms of the basilica were given over to metalworking shops at some point after 364, and the inner portico enclosed and floored with mosaic. The forum piazza, meanwhile, was resurfaced with flagstones, and the amphitheatre adapted for use as a marketplace. The city defences had been enhanced around the same time: the ramparts were heightened and external towers added to the already impressive circuit of masonry walls. The latest archaeologically visible alterations were to the street that passed beneath the Verulamium Gate, the imposing portal through which the long road to St Albans (Akeman Street) ran. It was resurfaced, twice, in the decades after 388.[11] These were the last improvements of any kind made to the city's defences and infrastructure.

---

* *Britannia Prima* was, along with *Britannia Secunda*, *Maxima Caesariensis*, *Flavia Caesariensis* and *Valentia*, one of the five probable provinces of Britain that were established after reforms of the late third century in the reign of Emperor Diocletian (r.284–305); their precise locations, boundaries and origins remain debatable.

Within a single lifespan, all the vitality of *Corinium* would pass away.

An old woman lies dying in a single bare room, the last habitable corner of her former home. It is AD 435 and she is 65 years old. She thinks of her childhood in the 370s – a little girl playing games in the wide, swept spaces of the forum, running between the shadows cast by the colonnades; she remembers tracing the lines of dolphins and hares on the mosaic floors, learning the names and deeds of gods and heroes: Venus, Silenus, Actaeon, Orpheus. She gazes at the meagre possessions she has saved – an old coin, a repaired ceramic jug, a few beads: the things that remind her of a better time. She remembers gazing as a child at the faces of the distant Emperors on coins of silver and bronze – imported from distant mints in Italy and Gaul ... now she doesn't know who the Emperor is, or even if there is one; no one brings news to the city any more, hardly anyone passes through. The last Imperial silver she had seen was issued by Emperors Arcadius and Honorius between 397 and 402, and the supply of bronze coins dried up even earlier, as the mints of the western Empire wound down their operations.

Already at that time the city was dying, once thriving industries failing, the population melting away. Grand homes and public buildings were abandoned, rubble and junk accumulating in houses and courtyards: the kipple of Empire piling up or rotting away to form layers of debris and dark earth, empty of anything that might signify urban life of the type that had gone before. Grass began to grow in streets already crumbling under the onslaught of weeds and weather. Organic matter – leaves, earth, shit – filled up the roadside ditches, leaving more dark earth in place of the grey silt that had once been thrown up by wheels and hooves on well-maintained and surfaced roads. She wondered if anyone would bury her, would care enough to do it properly. Perhaps she would remain here, left among the remnants of her hollowed life; or else she might be dragged out and dumped by the roadside, a corpse left to rot in a ditch, snails crawling in the empty caverns of her skull.*[12]

In comparison with the region's other Roman towns, the archaeology from Cirencester (*Corinium*) is the most comprehensively published, but the evidence from Bath (*Aquae Sulis*) and Gloucester (*Glevum*) is consistent with the same vision of civic collapse. At Gloucester, the forum became buried in the fifth century beneath more than a foot of sludge ('40 cm [...] of stoneless grey loam of silty appearance') – the result of waterlogging and abandonment; other parts of the city were similarly affected and subsequently used as rubbish dumps (evidence that, despite the foetor and neglect, life of some kind carried on in some quarters).[13] At Bath, the monumental temple complex that surrounded the hot springs began to fall into disrepair around 350; the great altar was destroyed later in the century and, as time wore on, activity dwindled and the signs of entropy multiplied. Votive deposits (including a large hoard of late Roman silver) were still being left at the fountain-head until the end of the fourth century and possibly later, but the buildings seem to have been brought down in around 450.[14] (The temple to Mercury at Uley in Gloucestershire likewise fell into ruin in the late fourth century, the degraded rump of the temple building remaining in some sort of use until the whole thing was completely demolished in the early fifth century.†[15])

The falling away of urban life would – one imagines – have been most pronounced in those urban spaces that were particularly

* The picture presented in the foregoing paragraphs is consistent with the extensively published archaeological record. For example, the number of rooms occupied in the town declined dramatically from over 140 in 375, to around ten by 425; the cemeteries fell out of use over the same period, but bodies have been discovered that were buried in roadside ditches.

† There are religious implications to the demolitions at Bath and Uley, perhaps indicating a shift away from Roman civic paganism towards other beliefs; whether those other beliefs were Christian or not is harder to establish.

dependent on links to the Roman army and Imperial bureaucracy and access to the wealth, prestige and symbolic capital of Rome. A place like *Corinium* – a civitas and probable provincial capital – would have been affected particularly badly. To judge from the surviving fragments of late Imperial metalwork, a military presence persisted in *Corinium* until the end of the fourth century – as it did elsewhere in the Dobunnic civitas and more widely across lowland Britain.* But this evidence vanishes from the record around the same time as the coins. The historical sources – meagre though they are – indicate that the vast bulk of the Roman field army units (*comitatenses*) and many border garrisons (*limitanei*) were deliberately withdrawn between 388 (by the usurper Magnus Maximus) and 407 (by the usurper Constantine III). There is no evidence that any Imperial army was ever dispatched to Britain thereafter. Given that it was the army who acted as a police force, the army who enforced the collection of taxes and the army who maintained civic defences, it becomes hard to imagine how the economy, the security and the very fabric of Roman towns could have been effectively maintained. At the same time, the civilians who might have been expected to organize things like markets, taxes and public building work also began to disappear. This collapse of high-status occupation suggests that the aristocratic administrator class either suffered a precipitous downturn in their fortunes or otherwise moved out: not only from their lavish town houses, but from their country estates as well.

The Cotswolds were home to some of the largest and most luxurious private dwellings anywhere on the island during the Roman occupation. At places like Woodchester, Frocester, Great Witcombe and Chedworth (all in Gloucestershire), the late Roman aristocracy expressed their wealth and power over the agricultural landscape with sprawling stone dwellings, long ranges of domestic building enclosing immaculate swept courtyards, interiors decorated with

---

* This is in stark contrast to the hitherto more militarized northern and western highland zones.

lavish mosaics and warmed with under-floor heating. By the early fifth century, however, these – like the towns – were decaying and partially abandoned: roofs fell in, earth banks collapsed to swamp the walls and buildings, rubbish and rubble accumulated, trees and vegetation broke through the mosaic floors. Sometimes the buildings continued to be occupied, but nowhere were they maintained to the same standard, and never in their entirety. At Frocester, for example, habitation by the end of the fourth century retreated into two rooms that had formerly been workshops, and fires were lit directly on the concrete floors. One of the larger domestic rooms became a home for animals. The decay was hastened by the destruction of the main buildings by fire at the beginning of the fifth century, and the villa was eventually abandoned. The perimeter walls collapsed and the bodies of the last inhabitants were buried in shallow graves around the villa grounds. One of them was buried face down; one had suffered a serious injury from a bladed implement; one was buried in a ditch; one was abandoned among the rubble of a collapsed building.

Some have described the fifth century as an Armageddon;[16] but the fate Roman Britain faced was not the biological or nuclear annihilation of late modernity's apocalyptic nightmares; sub-Roman *Corinium* was not Hiroshima, or even Pripyat after the Chernobyl disaster. The bees buzzed and the cats meowed and for many a peasant life in the fields carried on pretty much as it always had. Nevertheless, the total collapse of the Roman elite lifestyle indicates something frightening had indeed happened at the socio-economic level; frightening, at least, for the wealthiest members of society, and for those who depended on them for patronage and protection. It is perhaps more helpful to think of places like *Corinium* as the rust-belt towns of post-Roman Britain: places where capital flight, the collapse of industry and the absence of functioning markets had led to a fatal downward turn in the economy, leaving behind abandonment, poverty, decay and ruin.

For others, however, those who had always lived outside the urban bubble, these changes may have represented opportunity. No longer required to produce the agricultural surplus that Roman taxation demanded, the collapse of the Imperial system may have been a welcome relief for those at the labouring end of the economy. At the same time, the loosening grip of Empire gave some room for more radical elements to seek societal change and/or personal aggrandizement. The idea that, in the absence of Imperial coercive power, native peasants, deserting soldiery and social outsiders might have become disobedient to the point of civil unrest should be seriously entertained. Resentment against the established ruling class had simmered within the Empire since the third century, bubbling over into popular uprisings in Gaul and Spain against taxation and exploitation; it is not hard to imagine something similar happening in Britain in the years around 400. At the end of the fifth century, the Greek historian Zosimus described how, in 409, Roman administrators were ejected from Britain as the natives took power into their own hands.[17] If he was right about this, any subsequent attempt to internally administer the province may never have been particularly coherent or centralized and, in the absence of the incentives that the Imperial hierarchy could offer, those with the will would have sought to exercise control over resources in new ways, to find new models for wielding power.

In the decades after the end of the fourth century, the amphitheatre at Cirencester was adapted to new uses. It had already ceased to function as a venue for entertainment. Around the middle of the fourth century, the walls were roughly repaired and the stone-built entrance block on the northeast side was demolished. Access to the arena was widened: deep wheel-ruts and frequent resurfacing have been taken to imply that the space was converted for use as a market area. In the first part of the fifth century, however, this activity ceased, and the northeast entrance was partially blocked with a wooden palisade and blocks of masonry; timber buildings were erected on the arena floor.[18] By analogy with the amphitheatre at Chester and others in Roman Gaul, it seems likely that these changes were intended to make the structure defensible; to turn it into a fortress while the streets and plazas and bastions of the city beyond fell into ruin. It is possible to imagine this place as a make-shift stronghold – the militarized compound of some local hard-man, perhaps, or the refuge of a fearful and denuded popu-lace, no longer able to maintain the defences that had once shielded them: a post-apocalyptic township of the sub-Roman world. It wasn't the only such place.

Thousands of years before the Romans ever came to Britain, people had lived on the Crickley Hill promontory, a triangular spear-point thrusting westwards from the Cotswold Edge. A Neolithic settlement, enclosed by a bank, palisade and ditch had once commanded the hill's sweeping views of the Severn Vale; centuries later an Iron Age hill-fort had twice been raised and burned before being abandoned in the fifth century BC, the wooden defences wrecked and the earthen rampart that cut off access to the promontory slumping into ruin. But about a thousand years later, in the decades that followed the end of the fifth century, people returned to Crickley Hill. A large rectangular wooden building, equipped with several hearths and perhaps a stone-built chimney, was erected within the Neolithic camp – a structure, possibly with a porch, that may have superficially resembled the dwellings of the late Roman urban elite. It was accompanied by a number of other substantial buildings including a grain store, and various well-made structures of circular plan. All were enclosed within a wall of timber and wattle. At the same time, beyond the wall (though still within the Iron Age enclosure), another settle-ment grew up. Its buildings were smaller and shoddier, more diverse and some with few parallels anywhere else in Britain; almost as though a group of people of differing backgrounds had come together to try to start a life in this place, bringing with them a variety of building traditions. The people who lived here laboured: they processed grain and worked iron, bronze and precious metal. Spindle whorls and a copper needle suggest the working of textiles; local pottery was used and possibly produced.

Though not yet fully published, the archaeology of Crickley Hill parallels the large and growing body of evidence for the reoccupation of long-defunct and defensible locations across the west of Britain: at Dinas Powys (Wales), South Cadbury (Somerset), Cadbury Congresbury (Somerset) and elsewhere.[19] It suggests a socially stratified settlement, a place where the inhabitants of a defended enclosure profited from and controlled agricultural supply and the provision of skilled labour. It is hard to know how to describe whoever was in charge at Crickley Hill; they may well have thought of themselves as Roman and bestowed upon themselves the Latin administrative titles – *protector*, *magistratus*, *rector* – that others in the British west would come to adopt. Perhaps they styled themselves with greater pomposity as *rex* or *princeps* or *dux*. Or it is just possible that these were people who did not, or no longer wanted, to see themselves as Roman – that they had rejected or emerged from outside the Empire's traditional ruling classes and sought new (or very old) ways to express their power. Perhaps they named themselves in the British tongue: *arbennig* ('headman') or *gwledig* ('supreme ruler'), *iud* ('warrior') or *tywysog* ('leader').[20]

Whoever they were and however they thought of themselves, they were making their way in an unstable and increasingly unfamiliar world. On one level the reoccupation of hill-forts speaks of insecurity and the threat of violence, of competition for resources among communities and a growing fear of predatory gangs roaming the roads, the forests, the hills. On another level this retreat to the hills may have been an escape to the comfort of the deep past, a search for stability in a half-forgotten age before the triumph of *Romanitas* with its villas and its townhouses. But however much this settlement represented an attempt to build something new, its inhabitants were yet unwilling or unable to shake off the trappings of Rome. Among the finds from Crickley Hill are a much-worn late Roman military buckle and a sherd of Samian-ware repaired with a rivet. Both objects hint at an attachment to ideas of institutional hierarchy and luxury in a world that could no longer easily provide either: their curation and repair suggests that they were recognized as repositories of symbolic value – precious things.

Stepping out from their home on Crickley Hill, onto the limestone edge, the inhabitants could look to the northwest and catch a glimpse of *Glevum* (Gloucester) rising from the plain, its walls catching rose-gold in the setting sun, the River Severn a wide silver ribbon beside the walls. It would have been impossible to see the splits in the masonry and the collapsing roofs of buildings, too far to see the weeds cracking the mosaics and the river slime pooling in the forum. It was a mirage, a distant dream of the world that had receded, a honeyed smear before the misty blue hills of the horizon. But closer to home, down below the edge to the southwest, the people of Crickley Hill would have looked down on the reality of the change that had outstripped them. The palatial villa of Great Witcombe had been abandoned at roughly the same time that Crickley Hill was reoccupied. It squatted in the valley below in clear view of the occupants of the new settlement's principal dwelling – people who might well have known the place before the fall, perhaps even have been acquainted with the dying villa aristocracy. From the hill they would have watched these old lives and identities crumbling slowly into ruin: an ever-present reminder of what had been lost and what could never be reclaimed.

The hill-fort settlement at Crickley Hill was burned on two occasions. After the first fire, the settlement was rebuilt; the second time it was abandoned, smouldering into oblivion. On both occasions both the inner and outer settlements were destroyed. This seems improbable if the fires were not deliberate, but who started them – and why – will always remain a mystery. Nor is there any good evidence that can be used to precisely date the destruction and abandonment, though it seems likely to have occurred in the late fifth or early sixth century. If one wishes to believe Gildas, we should look for the doom of communities such as these in the coming of the Saxons and other pirates, the barbarian scourge wielded by the Almighty's red right hand, lashing the life from the iniquitous Britons in the Roman half-light. But at the time Crickley Hill burned and the Cirencester amphitheatre was abandoned, 'Saxons' – as an archaeologically identifiable presence – were a marginal presence in western Britain.

Foreigners there were to be sure. An early fifth-century grave, cut through the concrete floor of a Roman mausoleum at Kingsholm, Gloucester, was found in 1972 to contain the remains of a 40-year-old man buried with silver belt fittings and a knife with silver inlaid handle. The burial rite itself is Roman, but the objects are typical of those worn by Goths, Huns, Alans and other ethnic groups of the Black Sea region.[21] The suggestion that this individual might have been an 'exotic' presence in sub-Roman Britain has met with a certain degree of scorn, but analysis of isotopes in the man's teeth has recently revealed that he did, indeed, grow up in the cold climate of Europe's eastern reaches (eastern Poland, western Romania, Hungary) and may have been born even further east or north (in what is now Russia, Ukraine or Belarus).[22] In many ways, however, his foreignness was the least significant thing about him.

The man buried at Kingsholm, wherever he was originally from, was one of the last of his kind – a man who owed his power and probably his place in Britain to the wealth, structures and hierarchies of the Roman Empire. For all his otherness in the minds of those who buried him – a lingering sense of overseas origins, expressed through the objects that he was given in death – he still belonged to the world of Empire: he was buried with the Roman symbols of his rank, in the Roman fashion, in a Roman mausoleum, in a Roman cemetery, at the edge of a Roman town. If we are looking for a 'barbarian' – for someone who identified with a world beyond the Imperial *limes* (wherever he may have actually come from) – the 'Gloucester Goth' is not our man. Instead, we should instead be looking for the expression of cultural difference, rather than geographical origins: for the communities who chose to treat the dead in ways (like cremation) that were manifestly non-Christian (and therefore, by the fifth century, non-Roman), to the settlements that grew up in places and in forms consciously separate from the Roman built environment, to the religious and ritual practices that stood at odds with the official religion of the late Empire.

Evidence of such self-consciously non-Christian, non-Roman people starts to appear in the archaeological record of the region from the middle of the fifth century and, by the middle of the sixth century, a number of new cemeteries had come into use in the southern and eastern parts of Gloucestershire – particularly around Cirencester and on the gently rising eastern slopes of the Cotswolds. These cemeteries included both cremations and inhumations, the latter accompanied by grave goods that spoke to identities shared with those whose ancestry lay beyond the bounds of the Roman Empire in northern Germania. The settlements that these grave-yards served remain largely invisible to archaeology, with an important exception at Lechlade, but the material culture and the nature of the funerary rite indicates the presence of living communities of people who, in cultural terms, archaeologists have come to broadly describe as 'Anglo-Saxon'. More specifically, in this case they seem to have formed part of the 'Saxon' culture of the *Gewissae* that had been developing around the valley of the upper Thames since the mid-fifth century and which would, in time, form the nucleus of the West Saxon kingdom.

To the north, however, a different cultural community was establishing itself. In Worcestershire and west Warwickshire, a string of cemeteries extends along the valley of the Avon and spreads across the plains west of the Cotswolds towards Worcester. As elsewhere, settlements themselves have been harder to find; a group of 'sunken-featured buildings' (SFBs or *Grubenhäuser*) at Ryall Quarry (Worcestershire) currently represent the most westerly example of typical early 'Anglo-Saxon' building remains discovered in Britain. The communities that these sites represent were thriving in landscapes that were far less overtly dominated by Roman heritage. Worcester itself had been a small and undistinguished settlement during the Roman period, boasting none of the great public build-ings that distinguished Bath, Cirencester and Gloucester; the county at large was on the whole empty of villas, in extreme contrast to the region to the south. When the people of Worcestershire looked to reorient their communities in the centuries that followed the withdrawal of Empire they were, perhaps, less inclined than those further south to perpetuate a self-consciously Roman iden-tity. The people of the west Midlands would, ultimately, find political expression within the kingdom of Mercia, part of a much broader 'Anglian' identity that was spread across the middle of England to East Anglia and the lands north of the River Humber (east of the Pennines).

It is not known whether any of the individuals buried in the 'Saxon' cemeteries at Lechlade, Hampnett, Fairford and Kemble in Gloucestershire or in the 'Anglian' cemeteries of Beckford, Broadway and Upper Snodsbury in Worcestershire were them-selves migrants or the descendants of migrants from beyond the North Sea or whether they were simply the descendants of the local Romano-British population. What the evidence does suggest, however, is that a number of communities had – from the late fifth, throughout the sixth and into the seventh century – begun express-ing themselves in ways that set them apart from the habits of the old Romano-British. Their dead, buried or cremated or inserted into ancient Bronze Age and Neolithic barrows, indicate a people experimenting with new ways of disposing of the dead, with new fashions in dress and the appropriate way to prepare bodies for the grave, with new locations in which to situate their burials. The communities who were open to these processes – to what we might regard as a progressive attitude to cultural change – were estab-lished fairly early in the post-Roman dawn: the earliest burials from Lechlade, Fairford and Hampnett have been dated to the mid-fifth century, likewise those from Broadway and Beckford in the valley of the Worcestershire Avon.[23]

But in the heart of Gloucestershire – along the south spine of the Cotswolds and across the wide plains of the Severn – no 'Anglo-

Saxon' presence emerged.* Nor, to judge from the archaeology of the region, did anything much else. The living can be seen only through scatters of grass-tempered pottery and a few ephemeral traces of occupation. At Frocester, for example, the villa that had burned and been abandoned in the early fifth century was partially reoccupied; a corridor was converted into a domestic dwelling and partitioned for the stabling of animals. Their hooves pulverized the buried mosaic floors and their shit submerged it further. In the grounds of the villa new timber buildings rose. From the footing of two of them the skulls of oxen have been recovered – the beasts had been slaughtered, decapitated and their remains interred at the birth of new dwellings, their flesh consumed, perhaps, in feasts to celebrate new beginnings built upon the ruins of the past. These remains provide the only evidence for when this settlement came into use, carbon analysis suggesting a date somewhere between 430 and 660 (the probability curve peaks around 590). The human dead, however, are almost nowhere to be found.[24]

Maps of fifth-, sixth- and seventh-century burial data exhibit weird blank areas. The southern Cotswolds and the Severn Vale account for one of them and there are different theories to explain this apparent lack of mortality. One is that, in the absence of Roman civilization, the Britons returned to (or maintained) the prevailing burial rites of their Iron Age forebears, which have likewise left little archaeological trace. These practices seem to have involved a

---

* An exception to this pattern – at Bishop's Cleeve, just north of Cheltenham with the Cotswold scarp rising to the east – has plausibly been interpreted as the cemetery of a single family or small community who buried their dead over a period of around fifty years in the second half of the sixth century. The dead were interred with a relatively unglamorous range of artefacts including jewellery ('Saxon'-style copper-alloy saucer brooches of a type that seems to have originated in the valley of the upper Thames; amber beads) and simple weaponry (spears and knives). It is possible that this cemetery is a relatively late outlier of the group of Avon Valley communities and might represent the adoption of 'Anglo-Saxon' burial traditions by a community on the southern fringe of Anglian influence.

A typical 'Saxon' saucer brooch (© Gilli Allan 2022).

variety of means of disposing of and treating the dead, including excarnation (leaving bodies to decay in the open air), cremation without burial, disposal in water and exhumation followed by dismemberment and the subsequent distribution of body parts.[25] It seems just as likely, however, that a habit of labelling all Roman-style burials as 'late Roman' has had the effect of imposing insupportably early dates on many cemeteries – cemeteries which might well have continued in use for a considerable time beyond the early fifth century.[26]

Whichever way one looks at the problem, it seems as though – in the heavily Romanized territories around Gloucester and Bath – a conservative attitude endured, a desire to maintain stronger connections with the Roman, or even pre-Roman, past coupled with a rejection of newer, more foreign habits. Like the inhabitants of Crickley Hill, however, such communities were trying to negotiate their way in a world that had changed utterly. Their solution was, perhaps, to seek security and identity in the rites of the past, to build their homes on the ruins of Rome, to seek out the hill-forts of their distant ancestors. But at the margins of this little Britannia, a new world was being born; the rise of English-speaking kingdoms – of Wessex to the southeast, of Mercia to the north – would prove decisive in determining the shape of things to come.

The boundaries of the Hwiccian realm as they are now broadly understood were preserved by the medieval diocese of Worcester. Those bounds describe a land that stretched from just north of Bath to the edge of the Birmingham plateau, from the western eaves of the Wychwood forest (the *Huiccewudu* – the 'wood of the Hwicce-folk') to the eastern eaves of the Forest of Dean; a rich and varied land, marbled and bounded by rivers – the many tributaries of the Tame, Wye, Avon and Severn fed from streams that descended from the Malvern Hills and the Cotswolds. Below the limestone highlands the wide and fertile vales of Gloucester and Evesham spread themselves, a vast natural basin enclosed by hills and forests.

Place-names and later charters recording land grants augment this map, adding territory and clarifying borders. The name of the kingdom is itself preserved in place-names. At the further reaches of the diocese, Whichford (Warwickshire) and Wichenford (Worcestershire) both compound the name of the Hwicce-folk with 'ford', suggesting that rivers demarcated the boundaries of Hwiccian territory. Most striking is the *mons Hwicciorum*, the 'mountain (or hill) of the Hwicce', that is mentioned in a charter by which King Offa of Mercia granted – among other things – ten hides of land at a place called *Codeswellan* to St Peter's minster at Bredon (Worcestershire). The precise location of this *mons* is uncertain, but three miles to the northeast of Cutsdean – a village in the likely vicinity of *Codeswellan* – the Cotswold edge rises to a height of over 1,040 feet. Situated on the shire boundary between Gloucestershire and Worcestershire, it is the highest point in the northern Cotswolds. It is not what anyone would call a 'mons' – as part of the escarpment it is largely undifferentiated from the long sweep of the hills – but perhaps for those travelling southwards this place marked the passage into the core of Hwiccian territory.[27]

Probably the earliest mention of Hwicce – as the name of a people and their territory – is found in the Tribal Hidage, where the *Hwince* (sic) are assessed at a respectable 7,000 hides: equivalent to the territory occupied by the South Saxons, the East Saxons or the people of Lindsey. Its name has long puzzled historians: the celebrated place-name scholar Margaret Gelling believed that the name of the people was identical with the Old English noun (*hwicce*), which means 'box' or 'ark', and suggested that the topographical cradle in which the kingdom sat was envisaged as an open container, its sides formed by the Cotswold and Malvern Hills.[28] More convincing, to my mind at any rate, is the suggestion that the name derives from an ancestor of the otherwise unattested Welsh term **Hywych*. This word – a hypothetical compound of the Welsh word *gwych* ('excellent') with the superlative prefix '*hy-*' – produces a fairly typical Celtic epithet meaning 'the most excellent [ones]', a name entirely in keeping with several other tribal names including those of the *Brigantes* ('the high ones'), *Catuvellauni* ('the battle-masters') or even, perhaps, the Elmetians ('the people of great reaping').[29]

If this is correct, it would imply that the people of Hwicce were more closely associated with the British traditions of the west than with any nascent 'Anglo-Saxonness'. Bede in fact strongly implies as much in his description of a meeting at a place known (retrospectively one imagines) as 'Augustine's Oak' in 602 or 603. It was an opportunity for British church leaders to meet with the mission to the pagan English that had arrived from Rome in 597, a mission led by a monk and bishop named Augustine. The Roman missionaries had come to evangelize heathen barbarians, but had encountered in Britain a form of Christianity that had been officially practised in Britain since the fourth century, and which had developed by the sixth century into the dominant insular faith. Although the degree to which the British church deviated from Roman orthodoxy has been much exaggerated, insular Christianity differed outwardly in ways that were provocative to continentally trained ecclesiarchs and their disciples. Most painful to Bede were the (to his eyes) erroneous haircuts of British monks and – even more controversial – the way that they calculated the date of Easter.

Roman practice when it came to tonsures was to go for the classic shaved-on-top, hairy-round-the-sides look – the familiar image of the medieval monk that was believed to have been pioneered by St Peter in emulation of Christ's crown of thorns. British and Irish monks, by contrast, shaved the head in a way that was, in the words of Bede's mentor St Ceolfrith, 'abominable and detestable' because it reminded him of the hated biblical figure of Simon Magus and other disreputable wizards.*[30] What the insular tonsure actually looked like, however, is hard to determine.[31] The shaved area seems most likely to have resembled a D shape from above, with the straight edge running from ear to ear so that, from the front, it had a 'superficial resemblance to a crown'. Only on going around the back would the full horror be revealed, 'the apparent crown cut short' a cursed 'characteristic of simoniacs and not of Christians'. (One can almost hear the collective gasp of shock should a visiting brother have turned around to reveal himself as a surprise disciple of 'simoniacal wickedness'.[32])

The Easter controversy, by contrast, was a much more technical issue. Calculating the date on which Christians celebrated the resurrection of Christ, the most important date in the liturgical year, had long been problematic. The provisions of the Council of Nicaea in 325 had rejected reliance on the Hebrew calendar and stipulated that Easter must be celebrated on a Sunday. However, since Sundays fall on different dates in different years, deciding which Sunday was the right Sunday became difficult to determine, a problem made even more complicated by a variety of different calendrical systems that had to be reconciled. The whole subject was, and remains, frankly bewildering. In the Middle Ages it gave

---

* Ceolfrith, c.642–715, was Bede's guardian, friend and colleague; he was abbot of Bede's monastery at Monkwearmouth-Jarrow.

rise to a science all of its own – *computus* – that was dedicated to the calculation of the Easter date and, through the close observation of solar and lunar (and, by extension, celestial and planetary) motion that it entailed, helped to advance the cause of mathematics and astronomy in western thought throughout a period wrongly caricatured as a scientific vacuum. Bede himself wrote a series of treatises on these subjects – *De Natura Rerum* ('On the Nature of Things'), *De Temporibus* ('On Times') and, especially, *De Temporum Ratione* ('On Reckoning Time') – which became standard manuals throughout the Middle Ages.

Unfortunately, the Council of Nicaea failed to determine a universal method, leaving churches in different parts of Christendom to find slightly different ways of working it all out. It wasn't until 664 that an ecclesiastical council held at Whitby in Northumbria determined that practice in Britain and Ireland should henceforth follow Roman conventions by adopting a 532-year cycle of Easter dates, replacing the insular tradition that followed an eighty-four-year cycle. But, although agreed in Northumbria, it took longer to implement in practice everywhere else, and British churches in Wales were still using the eighty-four-year cycle as late as 768. These persistent differences allowed 'English' culture warriors to characterize the Britons as backward and backsliding, wallowing in errors that were more pernicious than simple ignorance. To Bede the Britons were 'obdurate and crippled by their errors', and he condemned them not only for 'going about with their heads improperly tonsured', and for maintaining 'bad customs against the true Easter of the Catholic Church' but also with rather unfair retrospection, for failing to 'share their own knowledge of the Christian Faith with the English'.[33]

The meeting that took place at Augustine's Oak in 602 or 603 was the first, abortive, attempt to straighten all this out. Wielding the delegated authority of Pope Gregory and a high-handed manner, Augustine urged the British clergy to assist in evangelizing the heathen and to reconcile their erroneous customs with Roman practices. Bede, hardly an impartial chronicler in this regard, described the obduracy of the Britons – in particular their refusal to reckon the date of Easter 'correctly' – and recounts a story of how the British Christians insisted that 'they could not abandon their ancient customs without the consent and approval of their own people, and therefore asked that a second and fuller conference might be held'.[34]*

Augustine's Oak, Bede explained, was a place 'which lies on the border between the Hwicce-folk and the West Saxons [*in confinio Huicciorum et Occidentalium Saxonum*]' and that it was to this place that Augustine summoned 'the bishops and teachers of the nearest British province'.[35] It would be perverse to insist that Augustine called a meeting with British clergy at a place that was out of touch with British territory, and it seems very probable that the people of Hwicce were considered by Bede to have been culturally 'British' (i.e. 'Welsh') in the early seventh century. If that is so, it would explain why Bede seems to have had so little interest in them. The most significant detail that he does convey, however, even if only in passing, regards their faith – a faith that they seem not to have needed Augustine's help to find. Bede explains that the Hwiccian princess Eafe 'had already received baptism in her own province of the Hwiccas' before her marriage to Æthelwealh, the recently pagan king of Sussex, in 661. He notes too that her father and uncle were also Christians, 'as were their people'.[36]

Eafe was the first member of the Hwiccian royal dynasty to be mentioned by name. She was, Bede explains, the daughter of a chap called Eanfrith and niece to his brother Eanhere.† It seems likely that Eafe's marriage to Æthelwealh took place in Mercia as part of a ritual that included Æthelwealh's conversion and acceptance of the

---

* The outcome of that second conference would turn out to be an even greater disaster; see **POWYS**.

† This could imply that Eanfrith and/or Eanhere had at one time been kings in Hwicce, although nothing more concrete can be said on the matter.

Mercian king, Wulfhere, as his 'Godfather'. These proceedings sealed a lopsided alliance between the Mercians and the South Saxons – an arrangement that allowed King Wulfhere (r.658–675) to extend his influence all the way to the south coast and threaten West Saxon authority in the region. Bede seems to imply that Æthelwealh's mariage to Eafe was part of this deal and it is likely that neither she, nor her family, had much say in an arrangement that has every appearance of diplomatic convenience. The implication, of course, is that Hwiccian independence was already by the 660s an illusory concept. And since many historians believe that the Tribal Hidage – the place where the Hwicce first appear – originated as a means of assessing the tribute due to the kings of Mercia, it would seem likely that political domination from the north was a feature of Hwiccian politics from the moment the kingdom's name was first recorded.

The people of Mercia had their origins somewhere in the English midlands. The name itself – from OE *mierce* – means 'boundary', and the people who bore the name were presumably considered a border-folk, although precisely which border rather depends on where they dwelt when their name first came into use and who gave it to them. Wherever they originated, by Bede's day the Mercians were a people whose heartland was situated either side of the River Trent in the western Midlands but whose authority stretched east as far as the River Idle and south to the Thames and Avon. The main royal centre was at Tamworth with a royal mausoleum downstream at Repton. When the Mercians adopted Christianity in the 650s, their principal bishopric was established at Lichfield. Yet for all their evident power and dominion over a huge swathe of English territory, Mercia is a poorly documented and misunderstood kingdom. In the form that Bede knew it in the early eighth century, the kingdom had taken on the characteristics of an empire or a confederacy, a swollen realm that encompassed a large number of smaller kingdoms and tribal groups whose distinctive identities had been subsumed to a greater or lesser degree: the Middle Saxons (London and Middlesex), the *Magonsæte* (Herefordshire and Shropshire), the *Wreocansaete* (the 'Wrekin-dwellers' of Shropshire), the *Pecsætan* (the people of the Peak district), the various tribes of the Middle Angles and – in due course – the kingdoms of Sussex, Lindsey and Hwicce. This so-called 'Mercian Supremacy' was the work of many hands, but it was King Penda (d.655) who really got the ball rolling. Penda cuts a fearsome figure in Bede's history, a committed heathen who terrorized his neighbours and was responsible for the death and humiliation of numerous rival kings.* (He was, in Bede's eyes, *strenuissimus* – 'most energetic'.[37])

In 628, according to the *Anglo-Saxon Chronicle*, it was the turn of a pair of Saxon warlords – King Cynegils of the *Gewissae* and his son (or close kinsman) Cwichelm – to fall foul of King Penda. Though there is no way of really knowing how the politics of the region had developed over the long sixth century, it seems very likely that regional tensions had been building, part of a broader rivalry between the neighbouring kingdoms. It seems possible that longstanding claims of the *Gewissae* over the historically 'Saxon' communities of the Cirencester region and Mercian influence over the 'Anglian' people of Worcestershire and the northern Cotswolds led to friction that ultimately only war would resolve. Cynegils and Cwichelm led an army to Cirencester, just as their ancestors Ceawlin and Cuthwine were supposed to have done half a century earlier, and were met there in battle by Penda's forces. The exact place of conflict is unknown, and the scale of the fighting is unrecorded. The *Chronicle* doesn't even bother to report who won. All that the tight-lipped annalist saw fit to relate was that the protagonists 'afterwards came to terms', without bothering to reveal what those terms were.[38]

This reticence would in itself be reason to suspect that the outcome was not at all favourable to the kings of the *Gewissae*. The *Anglo-Saxon Chronicle* was a ninth-century product of the West

---

* Edwin and Oswald of Northumbria and Ecgric and Anna of East Anglia were killed in battle by Penda's armies; Cenwealh of Wessex was driven from his own kingdom; see **LINDSEY** on the fate of King Oswald.

Saxon court (as the *Gewissae* rebranded themselves in the later seventh century), and conspicuously biased towards its interests. Had Cynegils and Cwichelm carried the day at Cirencester, the *Chronicle* would have been sure to make their victory plain. The fact that it does no such thing is pretty good evidence to suggest that Penda emerged, as he so often did, as master of the battlefield and in command of subsequent negotiations. What can also be said with some certainty is that, if the campaign had been an attempt by the *Gewissae* to exert dominion over the wider region, it failed utterly. Although the kings of both Wessex and Mercia continued to claim rights over the extreme southeast of the Hwiccian region (what is now northwest Wiltshire) deep into the eighth century, after 628 it was Mercia alone that would dominate the lion's share of Hwicce.*[39]

The deal Penda struck after the battle of Cirencester in 628 was a turning point, perhaps even a formative moment, for the kingdom of Hwicce: it was only after this statement of Mercian dominance that the first members of Hwicce's ruling dynasty (Eafe, Eanfrith and Eanhere aside) appeared in written sources. The names of eight, possibly ten, kings of the Hwicce have survived, spread across six (or seven) generations. But unlike the dynasties of many other British kingdoms, no genealogical lists are preserved to aid understanding of their relationships or their claims to power. There is no foundational hero or deity from whom they believed themselves sprung. Instead, the names and succession of the Hwiccian kings have to be pieced together from passing references in the histories of other places, or from the charters in which they appear as signatories, subservient to a Mercian over-king.

---

* Where Wessex ended and Hwicce began was long a matter of dispute and unsatisfactory compromise. As late as 802, after the line of Hwicce's kings had already failed, 'Ealdorman Æthelmund rode from *Hwiccium* over Cynemær's ford [Kempsford] where he was met by Ealdorman Weohstan with the Wiltshire folk [*Wilsætan*]; there a great battle was fought, and both ealdormen were slain, and the *Wilsætan* had victory' (an ealdorman was, by the ninth century, an aristocrat in control of a shire – frequently, but not necessarily, related to royalty).

It has, in fact, long been suspected that the Hwiccian royal house was implanted (or at least propped up) by the kings of Mercia after 628 and controlled by them thereafter.*[40] The family seems likely to have emerged from the area of Anglian culture that had developed in northern Gloucestershire in the sixth century. Winchcombe in particular, and the surrounding area, seems to have been a place of special importance to them. A number of churches were founded in the region by members of the Hwiccian dynasty – significantly without any interference from the Mercian kings – and it may well be that Winchcombe once lay at the centre of the family's hereditary lands. It is notable that Winchcombe lies only a few miles from Cutsdean and the probable location of the *mons Hwicciorum* that may have been the topographical gatepost to the kingdom's heartlands.†[41] How these people with their English names and Anglian sympathies related to the general population of the wider territory remains utterly obscure; the political and cultural direction of the kingdom over the following 150 years, however, is clear enough.

The first ruler of Hwicce whose deeds and power can be reconstructed to any degree is King Osric (r.670s). Osric's energy and faith were transformational, and two acts of generosity towards the Church left a legacy that endured long after his death. The first was an endowment of 100 hides of land made in 676 to Abbess Bertana for the purpose of founding a convent adjoining the place known to English speakers as *hat Bathu* – 'Hot Baths' – the English name for the Roman city of *Aquae Sulis*.[42] Although Bath was excluded from the later bounds of the Worcester diocese, it is likely that the city was originally part of Hwicce. The bishops of Worcester

---

* It is not even certain that the Hwiccian dynasty originated within the kingdom – a number of strikingly coincidental names has led some historians to suspect a link with dissident members of the Northumbrian royal houses.

† Indeed, the region maintained a distinct identity for centuries, with Winchcombe eventually forming the nucleus of a short-lived county – Winchcombeshire – which lasted from the 920s for around a century until its dissolution.

claimed authority over the city until 781 (when King Offa of Mercia (r.757–796) claimed the land as rightfully his), and in the 820s Bath was still considered to lie within Hwiccian territory by outsiders.*
The compiler of the *Historia Brittonum*, in his description of the manifold wonders of Britain, described 'the hot lake, in the country of the Hwicce [*in regione Huiche*]. It is surrounded by a wall, made of brick and stone, and men may go to bathe at any time, and every man can have the kind of bath he likes. If he wants, it will be a cold bath; and if he wants a hot bath, it will be hot.'[43]

Elsewhere, Osric was to make an even more extravagant religious endowment. In around 679, King Æthelred of Mercia made a huge grant of 300 hides at Gloucester to King Osric. This land, according to the charter, was granted by Æthelred in order that Osric could found a monastic church (a minster) in the city: the origin of the church (later cathedral) of St Peter.[44] What stands out most about this second endowment, however, is the degree to which Osric appears to have been subordinate to the Mercian king. The land that Osric required to found his church at Gloucester – a huge swathe of territory apparently in the gift of King Æthelred – was land in the heart of Osric's own kingdom. It may well be that this whole convoluted arrangement was more symbolic than practical, a legal fiction designed to emphasize Æthelred's ultimate superiority. If so, it did its job, underscoring with humiliating clarity Osric's lack of independent sovereignty: he had lost the right to give away his own possessions without permission from the Mercian king.†[45]

---

* Nothing has been found of the earliest incarnation of Bath Abbey apart from a cemetery of the eighth or ninth century and some later Anglo-Saxon stone carvings. But the Abbey itself has endured and been rebuilt and reimagined throughout the centuries, still dominating the centre of the old Roman spa town.

† Osric's grant of land in Bath, though made in Osric's name, was also made with 'Æthelred's permission'; to compound matters, King Æthelred also made grants of Hwiccian land to the Bishop of Worcester with no reference to the kingdom's nominal rulers.

This unequal relationship was emphasized during the reign of Osric's brother and successor Oshere (r.690s). The latter, described plainly as Oshere *rex Huicciorum* ('Oshere, king of the Hwicce') in a charter of 693 by which he granted land for a convent at Inkberrow (Worcestershire), is listed as merely *comes* ('count') or *subregulus* ('under-kinglet') in charters of the Mercian king Æthelred (documents in which Oshere appeared merely as a witness).[46] Similar indignities were shouldered by Oshere's son and successor Æthelric in 736, during the reign of the Mercian king Æthelbald.[47] From the moment that a Hwiccian dynasty becomes visible, it seems to have been firmly under the Mercian thumb. The last rulers of the Hwicce to be named as kings were three brothers who ruled jointly from 757: Eanbehrt, Uhtred and Ealdred. Each appears in charters as *regulus* ('kinglet') or *subregulus* ('under-kinglet'), but by this point their status was so diminished that even these humiliating epithets required further qualification. To Offa, Ealdred was 'my little under-king, that is to say ealdorman of his own people the Hwicce'.[48] Uhtred, meanwhile, was grudgingly accorded 'a certain degree of rule over his own people'; even the mirage of independence had come to stick in Offa's throat.[49] By the time of Offa's successor, Coenwulf (r.796–821), no little king was suffered to reign in Hwicce at all. When Coenwulf died in 821, he was laid to rest in Winchcombe Abbey, any symbolic power that resided in the ancestral homelands of the Hwiccian kings absorbed into the person of the Mercian king: a final act of domination.

The ecclesiastical hierarchy is even more likely to have been controlled by outside interests. The first known bishop of the Hwicce – Bosel – was invested between 675 and 680.[50] The diocese was one of a number to be created by the Archbishop of Canterbury, Theodore of Tarsus, in the 670s, imposing a new ecclesiastical structure and conventions. If there had ever been British bishops in, or with jurisdiction over, the lands of the Hwicce, nothing is known of them. But it is reasonable to assume that invasive religious reform from Canterbury marched in lockstep with political intrusion from Mercia. This impression is supported by the choice of a new diocesan capital. It might have been expected that the seat of the bishop would have been fixed at Gloucester, Cirencester or Bath, capitalizing on the symbolic associations of Roman Imperial authority; this was, after all, what happened at other major Roman cities – at London (*Londinium*), York (*Eboracum*) and Lincoln (*Lindum Colonia*). Instead, however, in this once most Roman corner of Britain, the head of the diocese was to be located at a small Roman town on the road from Gloucester (*Glevum*) to Wroxeter (*Viroconium*) that was so insignificant that no reliable record of its Latin name has survived. In Old English, however, it was known as *Weorgona-caester* and in modern English as Worcester.[*][51] Unlike the great Imperial cities that had been over-looked, Worcester was far from the heavily Romanized regions of southern Hwicce, and much closer to the 'Anglian' cultural zone that had developed in the sixth century. It had evidently been determined that the seat of Hwiccian bishops was to lie deep in the shadow of Mercia, the political and military power that sustained and protected the developing identity of the realm.

Nevertheless, the grants made by the Hwiccian kings to Gloucester and Bath demonstrate that the old Roman centres retained their symbolic potency. In the establishment of a new Christian geography, it was still to the legacy of Rome that English kings looked, tying their power and their faith to the visible remains of a lost Empire. To the British Christians of the Cotswolds and the Severn Vale, this may have felt like a usurpation – an unwanted intrusion of Anglian influence and 'Roman' Christianity into the charged centres of Romano-British memory: a colonial act that trampled and obscured whatever paths the people of the Severn and the Cotswolds had followed in the long years that followed the collapse of Roman rule.

---

* Although sixth-century burials have been found below the Norman cathedral, the suggestion that Worcester housed an early British church remains unproven.

The political and religious Anglicization of the Hwiccian realm was, in the end, total. As for the people of Elmet so for the Hwicce: there was no going back – a cultural shift had occurred that permanently changed the self-identity of the region. When English-speaking people came to rename the landscape and describe in poems the ruins that surrounded them – shattered wall-stones jutting like broken teeth from earthy gums, the bones of the earth extruded, shaped and tumbled, crumbling in the hoarfrost; mossy ramparts and stagnant ditch-works; broken towers and rime-scoured mortar – they saw only alienation: *enta geweorc* – 'the work of giants', or of powers inscrutable, gods and devils, their works weed-choked and time-wracked and doomed by fate.[52] The broken villas of Frocester and Woodchester were not their heritage, nor were the shattered mosaic floors of Cirencester and Gloucester and Bath. The abandoned hill-forts of the Cotswold edge were never their homes; the bones they stumbled upon in ditches or found hidden beneath scavenged masonry were not their ancestors. The people of Hwicce no longer remembered who they were, where they had come from, whose past they inhabited. Instead they lived in a world subsumed by the created identities and mythologies of Englishness, by a sad belief in their estrangement from the land they inhabited.

LINDSEY

– *North Lincolnshire* –

I was with Huns and with Glory-Goths,
With Swedes and with Geats and with South-Danes.
With Vendels I was and with Varni and with Vikings.
With Gepids I was and with Wends and with Gefflegs.
With Angles I was and with Suebi and with Ænenes.
With Saxons I was and with Sycgan and with Swordmen [...]
With Franks I was and with Frisians and with Frumtings.
With Rugians I was and with Gloms and with Rome-Welsh [...]
With Scots I was and with Picts and with Sliding-Finns.

Anon., *Widsith*[1]

'There is in the midland district of Britain,' wrote the monk Felix in the 730s, 'a most dismal fen of immense size, which begins at the banks of the river Granta not far from the camp which is called Cambridge, and stretches from the south as far north as the sea. It is a very long tract, consisting now of marshes, now of bogs, sometimes of black waters overhung by fog, sometimes studded with wooded islands and traversed by the windings of tortuous streams.'[2] Almost nothing of this landscape survives: a waterlogged wilderness that once dominated eastern England. From Cambridge to Peterborough, Lincoln to Skegness, the wetlands ran unchecked, continuing north in a belt of coastal salt marsh that connected the Wash to the Humber. In Lincolnshire, as almost everywhere else, the fens have long since been drained and managed and turned over to agriculture, the flatlands banked and dyked to reclaim the soil and preserve it from the water that once encroached from the North Sea or seeped from thickly braided rivers. In only a few places do fragments still survive – restored or preserved as havens for the declining fauna and flora that once thrived in Britain's lost wetlands.

The diversity of fenland wildlife had little value to Felix. For him, as for many in the early Middle Ages, such places were dreary and threatening environments, unproductive for growing cereal crops, useless as pasture, dangerous to travellers. And yet it was these very qualities – the bleakness, the harshness – that made landscapes like these appealing to certain religious-minded men and women.

From the third century onwards, a tradition had developed among the most motivated Christians to seek out punishing habitats in which they might – through isolation and self-mortifying deprivation – seek spiritual enlightenment. In this they were inspired by the example of Christ's own desert wandering, but also and more approachably through the example of St Anthony who had supposedly endured torment at the hands of the devils of the Egyptian desert. Many others followed his example and these so-called 'Desert Fathers' (and Mothers) exerted an enormous influence on the development of Christian monasticism. The 'Life of St Anthony', written in c.360 by Bishop Athanasius of Alexandria, helped to spread the ascetic example far beyond its desert origins. British and Irish monks, however, denied the dusty hells of the Holy Land by an accident of latitude, were forced to be creative in their search for devils, misery and isolation.

Felix's evocation of the dismal wetland landscapes of the eastern Midlands were a part of this tradition, forming an integral part of his biography of the hermit-saint Guthlac: the *Vita Sancti Guthlaci* ('Life of St Guthlac'). According to Felix, his hero Guthlac had spent his youth engaged in the warlike pursuits expected of someone of his aristocratic class and gender, 'gathering together companions from various races and from all directions' and devastating 'the towns and residences of his foes, their villages and fortresses with fire and sword'. He evidently did quite well out of it, amassing 'immense booty'.[3] Nevertheless, after a few years of this sort of thing Guthlac seems to have experienced a spiritual awakening, abruptly wandering off in search of maximum discomfort. His quest 'through trackless bogs within the confines of the dismal marsh' led him to Crowland, an 'island in the more remote and hidden parts of that desert', deep in what is now the south Lincolnshire fens.[4]

What Felix's *Vita* really required for its didactic and theological purpose to be realized was a world that spoke of alienation, threat and bodily mortification – a place as far removed from the comforts of early medieval life as it was possible to get, a world that Felix's audience (including King Ælfwald of the East Angles who reigned from *c.*713 to 749 and commissioned the work) would easily be able to contrast with the aristocratic pleasures that Guthlac had purposefully left behind. The Old English poem *The Seafarer* expresses these contrasts directly. The meditations of a traveller willingly adrift on the ocean, 'pinched by the cold, shackled by the frost [...] bereft of kinsfolk, hung about by ice spikes', the poem is steeped in the same early Christian traditions of earthly sacrifice in pursuit of spiritual fulfilment. 'Sometimes I would take the song of the swan as my entertainment, the cry of the gannet and the call of the curlew in place of human laughter, the sea-mew's singing in place of mead-drinking', the poet-narrator ruefully recounts; 'there is no one on earth so confident [...] that he never worries about his seafaring, as to what the Lord will send him; he will have no thought for the harp, nor for the ring-receiving ceremonial, nor for the pleasure of a woman nor for trust in that which is of this world, nor for anything else [...] the fellow blessed with affluence does not understand this – what those individuals endure who follow the ways of alienation to their furthest extent.'[5]

Guthlac apparently found alienation aplenty at Crowland. It was a place which, according to Felix, others had rejected on account of the 'unknown portents of the desert and its terrors of various shapes' and 'the phantoms of demons that haunted it'. On reaching this happily inauspicious terminus, 'Guthlac, the man of God, despising the enemy, began by divine aid to dwell alone among the shady groves of this solitude' – or, to use the version later rendered into Old English: *betwyx ða fenlícan gewrido ðæs wídgillan wéstenes* – 'amongst the fenny thickets of the wide-spreading waste'. There he found an old tomb to sleep in and a host of the devil's minions with whom he was able to test his dedication to a hard life.

Crowland, halfway between Peterborough and Spalding in modern Lincolnshire, lay within territory inhabited in Guthlac's day by people known in Old English as the *Gyrwe* ('the mud people' or 'marsh dwellers'). It is unclear whose (if anyone else's) authority they felt themselves subject to when Guthlac pitched up: the *Gyrwe*, alongside their neighbours the *Spaldingas* and *Billingas*, were one of a number of fenland people (listed in the Tribal Hidage or identifiable from groups of place-names) whose political affiliations and ethnic identities are almost entirely opaque before the eighth century. (In one possibly revealing anecdote recounted by Felix, Guthlac's demonic tormentors appeared in the guise of dastardly Britons – an episode entitled in its Old English translation, *hu tha deofla on brytisc spræcon* ('how the devils spoke in Brittonic') – a detail which has been taken to imply a tenacious native presence in the fens.[6]) In time, the marshy hinterlands south of the Roman city of *Lindum Colonia* (Lincoln) would be drawn into the competing orbits of the Mercian and East Anglian realms; but in earlier days they had likely been subject to the influence of – if not direct control from – the city that lay to the north and the territory that developed around it: the enigmatic kingdom of Lindsey or, more correctly, *Lindissi*, which may itself have had its origins in a Romano-British realm of enduring vitality.*

The world that Felix describes – a world of monks and marshes, of the perpetual tension between the island realms of men and the watery outlands that surrounded them – was one which helped to shape and define the land of Lindsey. The core of the territory was effectively isolated by water, bounded on all sides by rivers, marshland and sea. It was an island realm, Crowland writ large, a dry and habitable oasis formed from two unequal areas of relatively high chalk upland separated along a north–south axis by Barlings Eau (a tributary of the Witham) in the south and the Ancholme Valley in the north. Indeed, the later Old English rendering of the name *Lindissi* as *Lindesig* probably represents a rationalization of the name to one meaning 'island of the Lindon-folk' (**Lindes* + OE *īg/ēg*: 'island'). Between them they formed the Isle of Lindsey, the nucleus of a kingdom whose name is retained by the northern division of the modern county of Lincolnshire, and whose boundaries were preserved in the Lindsey Survey of 1115–18. The eastern zone – the Lincolnshire Wolds – was and is by far the broader and higher of the two, spreading out with the bulge of the coastline into a trapezoidal island of gently rolling hills. The high ground to the west, a long, narrow limestone escarpment that runs south to north, is bounded to the west by the River Trent as it flows north to meet the Humber Estuary. In the south this ridge is cut by the eastward flow of the River Witham and it is here, rising above the eastern fens and the river valleys of the south and west, that the city of Lincoln sprawls, its low hill crowned by cathedral spires that rise like fairytale pinnacles above the flood-plain.

* *Lindissi* is derived from Brittonic **Lindes*, 'the people of Lindon'; i.e. the people of the territory centred on *Lindum Colonia* (Lincoln).

It is hard now to get any real sense of how the traveller, arriving from the south in around the year 500, might have experienced an encounter with *Lindum Colonia*. Now the approach is buried under concrete, the river channelled and controlled, the road elevated above the contours of the land. Like the hinterland of so many ancient towns, the approach to modern Lincoln is a sprawl of edge-lands and bypasses, self-storage and supermarkets, the warehouses and retail parks jostling uncomfortably with Victorian housing estates and a handful of churches and older buildings, cut from their moorings by road widenings and roundabouts and set to drift in a sea of urban sprawl. There are only occasional glimpses of the cathedral that crowns the city, the perimeter of the old town lost among centuries of development.

Fifteen hundred years ago the walls of the city would have been visible for miles. The old roads – the Roman roads – rutted and unmaintained, but hard and firm and set above the dampest ground, would have cut through a bleak and empty landscape, tracing the spine of the tapering chalk and limestone ridge that sweeps north, dividing the fens in the east from the valley of the Trent to the west. The road dips where that ridge is bisected by the Witham. The river was wider and slower than it appears today, prone to fanning out in heavy weather to saturate the land around, filthy brown water lapping at the walls of the city and spilling into the lower streets, forcing endless detours to the west.* On drier days, the approaching traveller would have gazed across the river valley and into the confines of *Lindum Colonia* spreading up the hillside. It would have appeared, from a distance, as a great metropolis of towering walls and mighty gatehouses, its upper precincts dark against the vastness of the northern sky, a fearsome testament to the might of its builders.

Safely across the river, however, the traveller finds instead a haunted and broken citadel, all brooding silence and decay. Weeds

---

* A sense of the sort of flooding that can bedevil the Witham Valley was provided by Storm Dennis in 2020.

cover the cracked and broken surface of the road, silted ditches overflow with stagnant water. Tumbled blocks of stone lie scattered at the foot of ivy-mantled walls, split by frost, lichen-shrouded. An owl screeches from a deserted gate-tower, surfaces smeared with generations of birdshit, black windows lifeless – the sockets of a skull. Inside the walls some buildings still stand, roofs sunken, collapsed, open to the sky. In the interior spaces where people once lived, bramble and thorn have forced their way through blankets of rubble, nourished by rotting timber and refuse. Elsewhere, where the walls have fallen and the stone been taken away, only moss-grown mounds mark out the lines of homes and workshops, whole urban districts reverting to scrub or flooded with foul water. A stray dog howls in the distance.

But as he climbs higher up through the town, up the long incline from the river towards the inner city on the hill's crest, the traveller finds the precincts of the original walled fortress. And inside those internal walls, in the inner sanctum of the crumbling city, he finds God.

Lincoln, like Cirencester (*Corinium*), had in all likelihood been a Roman provincial capital. As *Lindum Colonia*, the city is thought likely to have been the capital of the province of *Flavia Caesariensis*, a region that encompassed a substantial portion of central Britain.[7] It was a large place, its walls enclosing around a hundred acres, and it sat at the junction of the Fosse Way (the Roman road that ran northeast from Exeter) and Ermine Street, the Roman road that ran from London to York and passed along Lindsey's Liassic ridge of limestone, chalk and clay. Although excavations at Lincoln have not been as extensive as those at Cirencester, it is clear that by the end of the fourth century Lincoln possessed substantial (and substantially repaired and reinforced) masonry walls, gate-towers, major public buildings and an extensive ditch and rampart. The city was also served by an aqueduct, and there is evidence of large and well-appointed private dwellings.[8]

Some of these substantial Roman masonry structures endured long beyond the end of Empire. The Mint Wall, for example, probably part of the Roman basilica, still stands to a height of around twenty feet just off West Bight. The building of which it once formed part must have remained a hugely impressive architectural landmark for centuries. Nor is there any evidence that the defences or gates were seriously compromised before the early fifth century. But, as in so many other places, the decades approaching the year 400 marked a terminal decline in most observable aspects of urban life and economy. The improvement and maintenance of roads and defences came to an end. Private dwellings were abandoned and then demolished, stones taken elsewhere, rubbish pits dug through their floors. Dead dogs were dumped in the ruins. Nesting birds colonized crumbling gate-towers and owl pellets were regurgitated amid the rubble. A once thriving meat-processing industry failed and vanished, the link between countryside and urban market broken. The kilns were abandoned. Nowhere did meaningful habitation apparently survive. As a town in the Roman sense – in any familiar sense – Lincoln died at the end of the fourth century.[9]

Perhaps the only area of civic life that experienced some vitality in this Imperial twilight was Christian worship. In the late Roman period the city may have possessed its own bishop (if the Adelfius who attended the Council of Arles in 314 was indeed the delegate from Lincoln),* and by the late fourth century there is archaeological evidence for organized Christian worship within the walls.

In the 1970s, excavations in the Roman forum uncovered the traces of a sequence of structures erected within this former public space. The earliest of these, aligned west to east, was probably constructed in the fifth century, and no earlier than the late fourth:

* This is by no means a certainty; it rests on an argument that a scribal error produced 'de civitate Colonia Londenensium' from the assumed original 'Colonia Lindensium' (the Bishop of London, Restitutus, had already been listed separately as the delegate from 'de civitate Londenensi'; London, unlike Lincoln, was not a colonia).

a coin of the Emperor Arcadius (r.388–402) was sealed beneath the internal floor area of the building, implying that the construction must have post-dated its loss (the layout of the building is consist-ent with Roman ground plans of the late fourth century). It was carefully constructed to respect the lines and monuments of the forum: its western end may have been entered from the colonnade between standing stone columns. This structure was subsequently replaced by a timber building on the same alignment – large enough to accommodate around a hundred people – that boasted an apse at its eastern end. There can be very little doubt that this second building – and quite possibly its predecessor as well – was a church.[10]

The forum itself ultimately became a graveyard. Radiocarbon dates taken from the burials strongly suggest that the dead were interred around the year 600. Since some of the graves overlay the original position of the church walls, they clearly post-date the demolition of the building (it would have been impossible to dig them had the church walls still been standing). It can therefore be said with reasonable confidence that the second forum church was destroyed before the year 600 and that the evidence suggests the continuous presence of churches on that site during a period between c.400 and the date of the second church's destruction. This is stunningly early evidence for organized Christian worship in post-Roman Britain. It clearly implies that a form of late Roman Christianity – unrelated to any imported missionary activity – continued to thrive within the walls of *Lindum Colonia* through the fifth and probably into the sixth century, even as the city lost its economic purpose and otherwise fell into disrepair.*

Beyond the walls of Lincoln, however, lay a very different world – a world of communities ripe for missionary zeal. Out there in the

---

* This is not the only evidence for late Roman Christianity in Lindsey: for example, the remains of a fourth-century cylindrical lead font embossed with the Chi-Rho monogram – the unambiguous symbol of early Christianity – were found in Walesby in the Wolds; X ('Chi') and P ('Rho') are the two first letters of the Greek Χριστός ('Christos').

countryside dwelt people who burned their dead on funeral pyres and buried the charred remains with objects that spoke to a world far beyond the borders of the Roman Empire and to beliefs that had no part of Christ.

Beyond Lincoln the archaeology of early Lindsey is dominated by (though not limited to) four large cemeteries – at West Keal, Cleatham, Elsham and South Elkington, with another major cemetery at Loveden Hill to the south of Lincoln in the southern portion of Lincolnshire.* These are overwhelmingly cemeteries of the cremated dead, the burned remains interred inside pottery urns decorated, like those from across eastern England, with a wide variety of decorative and geometric motifs. From these urns other items were recovered – jewellery and grooming items, spindle whorls and gaming pieces, knives and whetstones, animal bones and cowrie shells. Some of these objects – animal bones, brooches and beads, combs and other personal items – were found to have been burned. These had presumably accompanied the dead to the funeral pyre: the corpse dressed for death, surrounded by the remains of animals slain for the funeral feast. Other objects – tweezers, razors, shears and comb fragments – were found undamaged, placed in the urn by the living during rituals that followed the burning of the body. These things, the urns in which the burned remains were gathered and the rite of cremation itself, precisely parallel the centuries-old death rituals practised by communities in what are now northern Germany, southern Scandinavia and the Low Countries – the places which are often referred to as the 'Anglo-Saxon' homelands.[11]

* Of these, Loveden Hill is the largest, with *c*.1700 individual cremation urns excavated. Cleatham is the second largest and most recently excavated and contained an estimated 1,528 cremation and inhumation burials. South Lincolnshire – constituting today Holland and Kesteven – is not normally counted as part of the kingdom of Lindsey, though it is not entirely clear that this should be the case.

Bede, in his foundational narrative of where the English people – the *gens Anglorum* – originally came from, provides essential context that has provided the basic historical framework and starting point for all subsequent attempts to understand the emergence of 'Anglo-Saxon' England. Building on the tale that Gildas told in *De Excidio Britanniae* of the arrival of the *Saxones* – first as mercenaries, then as invaders and colonists – Bede drilled into the specifics. He explained that the 'newcomers were from the three most formidable races of Germany, the Saxons, Angles and Jutes. From the Jutes', Bede clarifies, 'are descended the people of Kent and the Isle of Wight who are called Jutes to this day. From the Saxons – that is, the country now known as the land of the Old Saxons – came the East, South and West Saxons. And from the Angles – that is, the country known as Angulus, which lies between the provinces of the Jutes and Saxons and is said to remain unpopulated to this day – are descended the East and Middle Angles, the Mercians, all the Northumbrian stock (that is, the people living north of the Humber), and the other English peoples.'[12]

With this in view, the narrative of Lindsey's formation seems relatively simple to reconstruct. Though Lindsey was not named specifically by Bede among the destinations of his Angles, Saxons and Jutes, it was hemmed in by Anglian realms to the north (Deira), west (Middle Anglia) and south (East Anglia) and by the North Sea to the east, its waters a gateway to the people, ideas and Germanic languages of northern Europe and Scandinavia. The Old English name bestowed on the people of Lindsey in the Tribal Hidage and elsewhere – *Lindisfaran* – means something like the '*Lindés*-farers', or 'the people who went to *Lindissi*', a name that rather implies an external origin (or, at least, a later belief in one).[13] A simple reading of the cemeteries likewise reveals a people whose mode of dress was foreign (and entirely consistent with other 'Anglian' cemeteries in East Anglia and Deira) and their rites pagan: cremation was an explicitly non-Christian mode of disposing of the dead, and there is no positive evidence of Christian belief from these cemeteries at all. Specific objects are particularly forceful. One cremation urn found at Loveden Hill and dated to the late fifth century was inscribed with words that seem to spell out a Germanic personal name – *sīþæbæd* – and an indeterminate phrase including, possibly, the Old English word for tomb (*hlæw*). The inscription, however, is not only English in language, but is carved in the runic alphabet, a script that seems to have its origins in southern Scandinavia (the oldest known runic inscriptions, inscribed on portable objects and deposited in bogs, date to the mid–late second century) and which appears in Britain for the first time (that we know of) in the fifth century.*[14]

Thus, on the face of it, it seems obvious that these cemeteries should indicate immigrant communities of Anglian heathens who had taken over the Lindsey countryside in the vacuum left after the collapse of Roman power. The apparent absence of distinctively Romano-British settlement and burial likewise lends support to Gildas' view of these newcomers as a horde of hostile migrants, slaughtering or enslaving the natives or driving them to 'lands beyond the sea … singing a psalm that took the place of a shanty: "You have given us like sheep for eating and scattered us among the heathen".[15]

It is true that Bede's origin story agrees with the archaeology of the early medieval north in ways which are difficult to argue with. It is undeniable, for instance, that broad differences in pre-seventh-century burial practice and artefact preferences can be identified that largely conform to Bede's sense of ethnic geography. The people south of the Thames and the Stour (including the 'Saxon' inhabitants of Essex, Sussex and Wessex) preferred to bury their dead entire; those to the north of the Thames and east of the Pennines (including the denizens of Mercia, East Anglia, 'Middle Anglia' and Northumbria) tended to cremate their dead. 'Jutish'

---

* During the seventh century, the runic alphabet would become widespread in English-speaking parts of Britain and was elaborated to include a number of new characters. A seventh-century woman's grave from Cleatham contained a bronze hanging bowl scratched with what seems to include the runic characters ᛗᚾᛉᛁᚻ ('EDIH', which may well always have been meaningless).

objects have, indeed, been found in Kentish graves. Most dramatically, there is considerable evidence to demonstrate the abandonment of a number of settlements in coastal northern Europe during the fifth century due to rising sea levels, a plausible context for migration across the North Sea.[16]

Nevertheless, however beguiling Bede's confidence and knowledge appear to be, it is also evident that there were very many things he seems not to have known, to have simplified or to have suppressed. For example, it is pretty clear from the archaeology of southern Britain that influence from Gaul (modern northern France) was considerable and that migration from that direction is very likely; likewise from Scandinavia into eastern Britain. Similarities between Old English and Old Frisian dialects also suggest that close cultural ties to Frisia (the modern Low Countries) and, in fact, the Byzantine historian Procopius – who died around 570 and was therefore writing much closer in time to the migration (though, in the eastern Mediterranean, further away in space) – listed the Britons, Angles and Frisians as the principal peoples of Britain.[17] Even Bede complicates matters by suggesting elsewhere in his *Historia Ecclesiastica* that the 'Angles' and 'Saxons' were derived from a cornucopia of other 'German' peoples that included 'Frisians, Rugians, Danes, Huns, Old Saxons, and Bructerians besides many other races in that region who still observe pagan rites'.*The cultural climate of lowland Britain from the time of Bede onwards seems in fact to have promoted a sense of, and belief in, an ever-widening continental community among people of widely dispersed geographical origins. Thus Old English poems like *Widsith* and *Deor* demonstrate a deep and detailed knowledge of the myriad peoples of (mostly northern) Europe, their legends and their storytelling; knowledge that reveals a richer and more complex heritage than any monolithic 'Anglo-Saxon' identity could possibly encompass.[18]

---

* The Rugians were one-time inhabitants of the Middle Danube region; the Bructerians were a tribe associated with the Ruhr Valley.

In particular, however, Bede was most careful to hide (though not always completely successfully) any hint of the contribution made by the existing inhabitants of Britain to the 'Anglo-Saxon' kingdoms of his own day. Aside from their role as 'bad Christians' singled out for a divine hiding, there was little room for the Britons. They are, for the most part, simply and implausibly absent. Apart from a doctrinal animus towards what Bede regarded as wrong-headed British ideas about the date of Easter and proper tonsures, this was largely due to a biblically inspired sense of history that equated the 'English' (as he names them) with a God-chosen people: first wielded as a scourge against the backsliding Britons (an idea that he cribbed from Gildas) and then chosen as a vessel to receive the true and unsullied faith as brought by Roman missionaries and institutionalized through the power of newly Christian kings (especially those of his own kingdom, Northumbria). It is also important to recognize that Bede was describing and explaining the world as he found it in his own day (he died in his early sixties in 735), when many of the differences in custom, dialect and belief that existed between the people of Britain had crystallized into broad groups who identified politically as Saxons, Angles, Britons, Picts or Scots, regardless of their actually ancestry; his migration story, in other words, was back-projection, not history.

Broader political changes played their part in the simplification of identity that seems to have been occurring at the outset of the seventh century. As the fate of kingdoms like Elmet, Hwicce and others makes plain, complex regional identities were increasingly considered unhelpful by the great players of seventh- and eighth-century power-politics: men for whom broad supra-regional ethnicities were more useful to the pursuit of their ambitions. As Northumbrian, Mercian or West Saxon kings flexed their muscles and expanded their borders, memories of cultural accommodation, of compromise between incomers and natives, slipped away. It was a loss accelerated by deliberate forgetting, the silent omission of people and their deeds in the selective histories written by people like Bede and, later, the authors of the *Anglo-Saxon Chronicle* – writers who depended on the patronage and protection of self-serving dynastic warlords.

In truth, however, the evidence for the continuity of British communities, religion and even power can frequently be identified. In Lindsey the survival of late Roman Christianity at Lincoln is of particular importance, and it has been suggested that the respectful distance of the cremation cemeteries from Lincoln (the closest, Loveden Hill, is seventeen miles south of the city; Cleatham is nineteen miles away to the north) implies the survival of a distinct British authority centred on the city and its hinterland, controlling and 'managing' the settlement of Anglian incomers out in the countryside – migrant reservations held at arm's length through whatever coercive force the people of Lincoln yet wielded.[19] As to who in fifth- and sixth-century Lindsey might have possessed that sort of power, the sources offer only very slender clues.

It was in the ninth-century *Historia Brittonum* that a warlord named Arthur was first explicitly associated with the strife that beset post-Roman Britain. He appears there as a superhuman figure, Arthur *dux bellorum* ('war-leader'), who led the Britons in a sequence of battles against the heathen *Saxones* that culminated in the battle of Mount Badon – a battle which Gildas, writing several centuries earlier, had referred to as an epoch defining victory for the British:

> The first battle was at the mouth of the river which is called *Glein*. The second, the third, the fourth and the fifth were on another river, called *Dubglas*, which is in the land of *Linnuis*. The sixth battle was on the river called *Bassas*. The seventh was the battle in the forest of *Celidon*, that is *Cat Coit Celidon*. The eighth battle was in the fort of *Guinnion*, and in it Arthur carried the image of

the holy Mary, the everlasting Virgin, on his shield* and the heathen were put to flight on that day, and there was a great slaughter upon them, through the power of Our Lord Jesus Christ and the power of the holy Virgin Mary, his mother. The ninth battle was in the City of the Legion [*Urbe Legionis*]. The tenth battle was fought on the bank of the river called *Tribruit*. The eleventh battle was on the hill called *Agned*. The twelfth battle was on the hill of Badon [*monte Badonis*] and in it nine hundred and sixty men fell in one day, from a single charge of Arthur's, and no one laid them low save he alone; and he was victorious in all his campaigns.[20]

There is no doubt that Arthur's 'battle list' is a compelling and evocative prose portrait of a lost and bloody age. While its apparent specificity confers an aura of authenticity to the places and events to which it refers, its very brevity – the broad-brush strokes with which its author worked – leaves wide spaces to be filled with invention and speculation; and it is ripe with the heady stuff of legend, thick with landscape and religion and violence. As a result, very many writers have been seduced over the years into reading it as a genuine relic of the Dark Ages: one of the true fragments of ancient tradition from which the *Historia Brittonum* was bodged together, despite it having been repeatedly demonstrated that there are historical, formal and textual reasons why the list, in the shape it survives, is unlikely to predate the ninth century. (In fairness, it is not entirely impossible that the battle list does preserve elements that somehow date back uncorrupted to the fifth century. However, even if this were the case and it were possible to determine which bits were more reliable than others (it isn't), this would still not be reason in itself to trust its testimony – a historian would still wish to know who preserved these elements, how they did so (in writing or orally), and for what purpose. All of which leads to the frustratingly familiar conclu-

---

* Or possibly 'shoulder'.

sion that none of it (with the exception of the battle at Badon) can be considered reliable information.*)

Nevertheless, the list does at least indicate that by the time the *Historia Brittonum* was compiled certain places were remembered as appropriate settings for ethnic conflict of the fifth and sixth centuries. From an early ninth-century perspective, if Arthur of the Britons had fought the Saxons anywhere, these were the places he would have done it. What exactly that memory reflects – a preserved folk history of real battles, a residual sense of late Roman power centres, enduring pockets of ethnic 'Britishness' – is likely to remain impossible to establish. But what can be said with some certainty is that of all the places where Arthur was imagined to have fought the heathen, one stands out as a venue for repeated strife: the river *Dubglas* in the land of *Linnuis* where Arthur fought the 'second, the third, the fourth and the fifth' battles of his career.[21]

Linnuis, with very little doubt, was intended to mean the region around Lincoln. The name is simply the Welsh development of the same Romano-British root *Lindēs* that gave rise to *Lindissi* and *Lindesige* (Lindsey). The river *Dubglas* ('black water') is unidentifiable, but Lindsey certainly has its fair share of rivers. Indeed, Arthur's 'first battle was at the mouth of the river which is called *Glein*' and it is possible that this too can be located in Lindsey.† A case can in fact be made that some of Arthur's other battles can be found in what is now Lincolnshire and that Arthur himself should be envisaged as a Lincoln man – a warlord of the Wolds. Given the

* As mentioned previously, Gildas referred to a battle at Badon but did not specify the protagonists and did not mention 'Arthur' at all. Thus the association of Arthur with Badon may have occurred at any point in the intervening three-plus centuries between Gildas' *De Excidio Britanniae* and the *Historia Brittonum*.

† There are two rivers named Glen in Britain: one in Northumberland and one, perhaps significantly, in Lincolnshire; there is no reason, however, to assume that the Celtic word *glein* – derived from a root meaning 'clean' or 'pure' – was not at one time applied to many more rivers and streams in Britain.

deficiencies of the evidence, not to mention the tenuous basis for a historical Arthur of any stripe, this is not a subject that can be pursued too far without getting ensnared in all sorts of pitfalls and circular detours. Nevertheless, as the archaeology of the region indicates, the idea that Lindsey was in some sense on the front line of post-Roman ethnic conflict and accommodation rings true.[22]

In a more general sense, this memory of Lindsey as a home to the British warriors of a heroic age may have been deeply rooted in the poetic imagination. The following lines constitute the fifteenth stanza of *Y Gododdin* in the translation published by Joseph Clancy in 1970; they were, in the opinion of John T. Kock (one of the most influential scholars of the poem and its language), derived from a text written as early as the beginning of the seventh century:

> Of the battle of Catraeth the tale
> Is of fallen men, long lamented.
> In hosts, in hordes, they fought for the land
> With Godebawg's sons, savage folk.
> On long biers were borne men drenched in blood.[23]

In Clancy's translation, the phrase 'men drenched in blood' is, quite acceptably, a translation of *lynwyssawr*. The word *lynwyssawr*, however, is not a straightforward one to interpret. Derived from the reconstructed archaic Celtic construction **linuissaur*, the term can also be rendered as 'men of Lindsey' – slender and contestable evidence that, like their near neighbours in Elmet, the people of this lost kingdom might at times have found themselves (in the minds of poets at any rate) in company with other realms of the *Hen Ogledd*, taking war to the English. Although the brotherhood of the Old North was always a fantasy, it is by no means inconceivable that the people of Lindsey (some of them at least) might at times have found common cause with other northern kingdoms.*

* Lindsey and Elmet were separated only by the marshlands of Hatfield that lay between the Idle and the Ouse.

114

If that is so, it raises a number of questions about politics, ethnicity and social organization within Lindsey. Far from being an ethnically homogenous enclave, evidence suggests that the region played host to a complex relationship between immigrant and native: scattered traces of accommodation and burgeoning identity that resist the application of tidy ethnic labels and notions of cultural apartheid or regional genocide. As in so many other corners of the island, Britain's politics and ethnic fault-lines were far more complex than Gildas, Bede or the medieval bards were ever willing to recognize.

The graveyard that was established in place of the apsidal church that was demolished in the Lincoln forum contained one grave that was more impressive than the rest – a 'cist' (a sunken grave lined with stones and covered with stone slabs) in which someone had been buried alongside an elaborate bronze hanging bowl. Whoever made it and for whom, the presence of this bowl in the grave indicates that the person buried with it was thought to possess an unusually high status. At some later date, the bones and any other grave goods were carefully removed (the hanging bowl was left behind, apparently by accident). Such careful removal of human remains from a grave was not normal; in fact, it is only documented in cases that involved the relics of the holy dead – those shreds of mortality which were believed to retain their power after death. The position of the grave reinforces the impression of a particularly important or holy burial: it was sunk into the forum on a precise central alignment with the floor of the old apsidal church, laid out west to east before the high altar; or, rather, where the altar had once stood, for by the time the grave was cut, the church had been pulled down to make way for the cemetery that grew up around that central burial. Above the cist, a small timber building was later erected – a shrine, perhaps, to honour the sanctified dead. Both the grave and the building that covered it are products of the early seventh century.

The bronze hanging bowl that was recovered is a fine example of one of the most recognizable and characteristic objects of the early Middle Ages in Britain. Thin bronze rounded vessels, hanging bowls are named on account of the three or four equally spaced hooks (sometimes shaped to resemble long-necked animals) and escutcheons that were attached to the upper rim of the vessel. Sometimes with a ring attached, these fittings were intended to enable the suspension of the bowl from above. No one really knows what their purpose was, but the degree of skilled craftsmanship and their presence in elaborate burials indicates that they were prized objects (the famous Sutton Hoo mound 1 burial contained three of them). They were often beautifully decorated, with intricate red enamel designs – spirals and triskeles predominate – applied to both the escutcheons and to decorative plaques that were attached to the upper outer surface of the bowls.[24]

Of 117 bronze hanging bowls found in England whose details have been published, at least twelve were discovered in the tiny former kingdom of Lindsey.[25] This stands in contrast to the seven found in Scotland and seventeen in Ireland. Not a single example has been recovered from Wales or Cornwall.* Differences in prevailing burial practice across Britain undoubtedly skew this picture. Burial with grave goods became the most widely practised burial rite in southern and eastern Britain during the sixth and seventh centuries. As a result, there is in those regions a plethora of objects that are routinely discovered in the course of modern archaeological excavation – from hanging bowls to beads, from weaponry to animal remains, and much else besides. As a result, it has become much easier to picture the appearance and lifestyle of those people who buried their dead with grave goods than less archaeologically visible communities. The impression has thus been generated that the 'English' people of lowland Britain were

* Interestingly, twenty-nine (more than those from Ireland and Scotland combined) have been found in Scandinavia where inhumation with grave goods was practised for much longer than it was in Britain (prior to the Scandinavian immigration of the ninth century).

both richer than their British neighbours in material possessions and fundamentally distinct from them in their manner of dress. Neither premise is well founded.

Bronze hanging bowls are generally referred to as 'Celtic' in their form, decoration and manufacture and thus attributed to 'British' craftspeople. However, because these 'Celtic' bowls are found over-whelmingly in the east of England (and in Scandinavia), scholars have felt compelled to seek explanations to account for this perceived problem in their distribution: either some sort of exchange mechanism must have transferred these objects from manufacturers in the 'Celtic' west of Britain to consumers in the 'Anglo-Saxon' east, or cadres of self-consciously 'Celtic' craftspeople must have survived to labour – perhaps under duress – to produce fancy treasures for their 'Germanic' overlords. To me these theories seem unnecessarily complicated; it seems more straightforward to assume that these bowls were objects that continued to be produced by people working in traditional ways, in places that they had never left. In other words – regardless of the collapse in urban life, the influx of foreigners and foreign fashions, the changes in religion and burial practice – a resilient conservative native artisanal tradi-tion endured alongside local consumers who valued its products, no matter where their fathers or grandfathers may have been born.

Why hanging bowls were so valued is another matter, however. They were certainly prestige items – the result of considerable skill and labour and investment in valuable metals – and as such they imply the wealth and power of their owners. On a simple level, this is undoubtedly one of the reasons why they accompanied some individuals to the grave. And in some cases this may be the only reason. But the fact that there continued to be a market for such objects, produced to a markedly conventional design, implies that there was something specific about hanging bowls that made them particularly desirable for people of a certain social status to own. For those who self-consciously identified as immigrants, that appeal may have lain in the suggestion of dominance over local cultural forms – a quasi-colonial appropriation of the trappings of a supplanted ruling class. For other newcomers, the appeal may have resided in the appearance of legitimacy such objects conveyed, a sense that to wield status in Britain required the adoption of those trappings of power that retained currency among the natives. And then there must also have been those whose self-identity, regardless of the advent of new people, fashions and customs, remained rooted in a distinctively British tradition – those who saw themselves not as 'Angles', but as 'Britons' or maybe 'Anglo-Britons', the heirs to an increasingly distant Romano-British heritage. One such figure, a man named Cædbæd, can perhaps be glimpsed in a genealogy of the later kings of Lindsey. The name is an English transliteration of the Brittonic name *Cadbodu* (literally 'battle-crow'). Nothing more than this can be known about him, but it is perhaps significant that, from the perspective of later generations, the line of Lindsey's kings contained an ancestor whose Celtic name implies that his identity – or at least the sympathy of his parents – was in part 'British'.

The British heritage of Lindsey did not survive only in high-status objects like bronze hanging bowls. Penannular brooches, a broken circle of metal with a pin that is rotated to 'lock' it in place after the clothing to which the pin is attached has been secured, were an accessory of British and Irish dress manufactured, designed and worn in the British Isles from the third century BC. Though their popularity waxed and waned and varied by region, penannular brooches were remarkably consistent in their basic form and function, remaining in use in parts of Britain until the end of the first millennium. They are, like the hanging bowls, distinct from the continental style of metalwork that began to appear from the fifth century in Britain, and in Lindsey nine examples have been found in fifth- and sixth-century graves at Cleatham, Mount Pleasant Farm, Sheffield's Hill and Kirmington – all in graves which, in traditional archaeological terms, would normally be considered 'Anglo-Saxon'.[26] Likewise, at Cleatham, a number of the cremated dead were interred during the fifth century in pottery urns of Roman style, an indication of a continued engagement with the

Reconstructed escutcheon from a Lincolnshire hanging bowl.

cultural forms and symbolism of the Romano-British world (as well as the surviving technical knowledge of Roman pottery production which is otherwise assumed to have fizzled out).

The presence of 'Celtic' metalwork or 'Roman' pottery in a grave does not redefine the ethnicity of the dead – most of the people who worked the land would most likely have been bemused by modern angst over their identity and the puzzlement with which we regard their jewellery choices. For them, in the words of the archaeologist Kevin Leahy, 'the view of the ox's backside remained depressingly familiar'; Roman, Briton, Angle or Saxon, life's daily grind carried on much as it always had.[27] But taken altogether, these few aspects of Romano-British culture – the bowls, the brooches, the hints of a tenacious late Roman Christianity – represent a slender thread of continuity, the weak stitching by which the old Britain remained connected to the new. They raise questions about how individuals thought about themselves and their relationship to the current and former inhabitants of the land that became Lindsey.

Eastern Britain was a world that was shifting decisively away from fading memories of Romanitas, absorbing new people, languages and gods. Yet at the end of the sixth century a feeble flame still burned for the old ways, dancing from surfaces of burnished bronze and spirals of blood-red enamel; it would not be long before it finally guttered out.

The royal genealogy for Lindsey in which Cædbæd is named is one of several such genealogies recorded together in a group known to scholarship as the 'Anglian collection'. These are preserved in a number of different manuscript versions that have their origins in a lost original that was probably compiled in Mercia in the late eighth century.[28] Royal genealogies are not king-lists, but, rather, an expression of patrilineal descent arranged in reverse order (i.e. they begin with the current or most recent entry) and designed to bolster the claims of the ruler or rulers for whom they were produced. The genealogies typically follow a conventional format in which each person entered onto the list is qualified by relation to his father. The repetition of the suffix *ing* which is appended to the father's name (i.e. 'progeny of') and the frequent alliteration of names lends the genealogies a poetic, hypnotic quality which rather implies that they were designed to be memorized and declaimed in public.* The royal genealogy for Lindsey runs as follows:

Aldfrið Eatting
Eatta Eanferðing
Eanferð Biscoping

---

* Old English genealogies, with their distinctive 'so-and-so *son of* so-and-so *son of* son-and-so' format provided the model for the lists of antecedents frequently encountered in Tolkien's fiction: e.g. Thorin son of Thrain son of Thror. Tolkien's genealogies also pick up on the frequent alliteration of names across generations found both in the Old English genealogies and widely in English dynastic history (e.g. Edward son of Edgar son of Edmund son of Edward).

Biscop Beding
Beda Bubbing
Bubba Cædbæding
Cædbæd Cueldgilsing
Cueldgils Cretting
Cretta Winting
Winta Uoding
Uoden Frealafing
Frealaf Frioðulfing
Frioðulf Finning
Finn Goduulfing
Godulf Geoting
Geot

All of the royal genealogies that have survived are in some measure difficult to understand and typically feature legendary figures whose very existence cannot be substantiated. The list for Lindsey is no exception and is in fact particularly intractable. This is largely because none of the individuals named above *Uoden* (Woden) in the list are mentioned anywhere else. Indeed, it is something of a puzzle as to why anyone bothered to record them at all given the apparent lack of interest taken in the kingdom's affairs by Bede and others. What this means in practice is that while Aldfrið is the first named and therefore the *latest* king of Lindsey to be known by name, he was not necessarily the *last* king of Lindsey; nor do we know *when* he reigned. None of the others were necessarily kings of Lindsey at all, though a number of them might well have been.

It should be clear by now that any attempt to recover the history of fifth- and sixth-century Lindsey is likely to be a struggle. Sources which purport to say something of this period invariably tell us a great deal more about the preoccupations of the eighth or ninth centuries than they do about the Dark Ages. And in the case of Lindsey, the problems are deepened by the fact that every surviving scrap of information reflects the perspective of outsiders. Nevertheless, the genealogy of the Lindsey kings provides one further insight: that Lindsey was once accounted among those realms whose kings boasted descent from a god – from Woden – and that in this they were considered the peers in pedigree and prestige of the royal families of Deira, Bernicia, Mercia, East Anglia, Kent and Wessex.*

Woden is how English speakers referred to a god who answered to a number of different names across Scandinavia and northern Europe: *Woden* in Old English, *Oðinn* (Odin) in Old Norse, *Wotan* in Old High German – all of which derive from the lost proto-Germanic name **Wodanaz*. Despite being one of the few Germanic deities whose name was recorded at a reasonably early date, very little is known directly about how his power was imagined to operate before the thirteenth century in Iceland where parts of his mythology were first systematically recorded.† Nevertheless, valiant attempts have been mounted to reconstruct his character, based largely on comparison between the evidence of first-century Roman writers and that of the thirteenth-century Icelandic scribes. Twelve hundred years, however, is a daunting chasm of time to bridge and the disparate geographical origins of the data from which that bridge is built leaves the whole edifice dangerously deficient in structural integrity. Unfortunately, the Woden of the English lives slap bang in the middle of it, and venturing out there to look for him often feels like a pretty terrible idea – especially since the chasm beneath flows with torrents of toxic balderdash.

In any case, what Woden meant in sixth- or seventh-century Lindsey is entirely impossible to know. The kingdom's royal geneal-

---

* The genealogy of Lindsey is actually notable for the five additional generations that appear before Woden, although it is generally thought that these were added to standardize the length of the lists that appear in the Anglian collection. Two of the figures in these later generations – Finn and Geat (*Geot*)– also appear in elongated versions of the West Saxon genealogy, and both are figures who appear elsewhere in northern legend.

† The earliest mention of Woden dates to between 550 and 650 and appears in a runic inscription scratched onto the back of a brooch found in Nordendorf, Bavaria.

ogy was written down in Northumbria in the late eighth century – a century or more after Lindsey's independence was lost. No one can say with any confidence what political purpose it may have served to assign this common ancestor to the major realms of England, or who Woden was to the Christian scribes who recorded his name, but it is fairly certain that the genealogies were contrived for purposes other than preserving the pagan religious and folk customs of Lindsey. The antiquity of the genealogies and the information they contain cannot be established. Nor can it be known what the people of Lindsey themselves thought about the ancestry of their kings – or who, indeed, they believed their kings to have been. What it does seem to reflect, however, is the culmination of cultural changes that took place during the seventh century: changes that saw a decisive break not only with vestiges of the Romano-British past, but with more local and particular identities as well.

Over the course of the period from the late sixth to the early eighth century, cremation of the dead gradually came to an end and burial became the norm. These burials were in some cases still well furnished with grave goods, but the quantity of material buried declined for the majority, and the most distinctive features of local identity disappeared across England to be replaced by a widespread and relatively uniform 'Anglo-Saxon' repertoire of metalwork styles and dress-fittings that took cues from Scandinavia, continental Europe and the Byzantine world. At the same time, the richest graves grew in visibility and opulence: the wealthy dead were interred in prehistoric burial mounds or in newly built structures that emulated them. These linked phenomena – the stratification of society and the birth of a more homogenous identity – gave rise to both kingship and 'Englishness', as Bede understood these concepts in his own lifetime. To be descended from Woden could function as a marker of both: part of the justification by which an elite class wielded power and a distinctive point of common origin for themselves in the British lands over which they ruled.

That origin was self-consciously sought in a temporally imprecise 'Germanic Golden Age' of heroes and kings whose doings were already receding into legend. Among the other ancestors included in the Lindsey genealogy is a character named Finn, a man almost certainly to be identified with the protagonist of two episodes preserved in Old English poetry: the *Finnesburg Fragment* and the 'Finnsburh' episode in *Beowulf* which both tell the same story (with some variance) of the violent goings-on at the hall of Finn, king of Frisia, who was killed in bloody and tragic circumstances as a result of a long-running beef with his Danish hostage-cum-vassal Hengest (very probably the same Hengest who was imagined to have founded the Kentish dynasty).[29] For the kings of Lindsey, descent from such a figure lent a potent sense of belonging to a transmarine community of hero-sprung warlords, whatever the prosaic nature of their true origins. In the words of the distinguished literary scholar Roberta Frank, such texts 'conjured up for their contemporaries a magnificent, aristocratic descent, a proud history embodying current hopes and fears, a pleasant dream transmuting the desert of daily existence into a landscape rare and strange'.[30]

In 1849, the Reverend Edwin Jarvis took a team of workmen to a barrow at a place called Caenby, roughly ten miles north of Lincoln and not far from Ermine Street. The mound was huge – 110 feet across and 8 feet high at the centre. Over the course of several days that autumn, Jarvis and his men dug down through the pine-grown barrow and recorded what they found. The first day was disappointing. Despite initial excitement at the discovery of burning and stone, their 'ardour was quickly damped by finding small pieces of coal amongst the debris'; they had found the remains of a lime kiln. Undeterred, however, the excavation continued. On 9 October, after extending their trench to the centre of the barrow, 'two portions of bones were brought to view'; these were to be the first finds of an extraordinary discovery. 'One of the workmen handed me a small green lump; it proved to be a buckle; the tongue was quite distinct. From this moment small thin pieces of copper were continually turning up; then a bit of whitish-purple metal, subsequently ascertained to be silver, with interlaced ornament. The workmen had plenty of room, and used their tools as cautiously as possible. In the N. E. corner of the trench there appeared a deposit of bones; we cleared them gently, and found that it was a human skeleton, in a sitting position, but very much crushed together by the weight of superincumbent soil.'[31]

Jarvis had discovered a burial of the seventh century, its occupant sealed in a chamber, buried in a seated position. All that remained of the grave goods were fragments – the scraps left behind when the barrow was robbed of its treasures: silver fittings, chased with tightly wound interlace, still adhering to the timber fragments of a shield; the bones of a horse and parts, perhaps, of its bridle; a fragment of embossed metal foil. This last is the most intriguing of all the objects retrieved from the Caenby barrow. The image it bears depicts part of a figure with two avian heads sprouting from his hat. This figure is known from many other archaeological contexts where he appears naked and shaking a spear, attributes that have led to him being widely known as the 'weapon-dancer'. The most famous examples from England are found on a sixth-century belt buckle found in a grave at Finglesham (Kent) and on relief panels that adorned the seventh-century helmet at Sutton Hoo. The motif had an extraordinarily long and geographically widespread life across the northern world, and it has long been suggested via a complex (and in places strained) chain of argument that this is an image of Woden. That may well be correct; it may equally well not be. There is no way of knowing definitively either way. What is very likely, however, is that the Caenby weapon-dancer once decorated a helmet.[32]

Only seven helmets, the Caenby fragment aside, survive from early medieval Britain and, of these, two others share the same style of decoration: the helmet discovered at Sutton Hoo (also on Britain's eastern littoral) and the disassembled helmet components found in the Staffordshire Hoard (origin uncertain), both of which feature the weapon-dancer. Whatever the motif itself meant to the people who made or owned these objects, its presence in the Caenby burial mound indicates that the owner of this helmet belonged to a select group – one of only a few individuals who ever owned (or whose family wanted, and could afford, to bury) such an impressive object. The precise reasons why the kin of the deceased would choose to dispose of such costly and elaborate objects in the ground were undoubtedly complex and probably reflective of local concerns; but it seems pretty clear that the dramatic potential of this (presumed) man's funeral, along with the scale of the monument raised above him, was designed to convey an image of power and lordship that would be remembered far and wide for many years – generations even – to come.*

What is also significant is that helmets of this type find their closest parallels not in Britain but in Sweden, where a number of elite graves in the cemeteries at Valsgärde and Vendel contained remarkable, ornate and strikingly similar examples – several of which also featured the horned weapon-dancer. This prompts the recognition that, whatever the internal ethnic and religious dynamics of Lindsey itself, the cultural world to which the occupant of the Caenby barrow wished to belong was evidently not preoccupied by insular navel gazing, but instead disposed to looking outwards (or perhaps backwards?) towards a greater sea and more distant shores – to neighbouring coastal realms and to the tribes and chiefdoms of pagan Scandinavia and northern Europe with whom he (and perhaps his people) shared converging cultural priorities: an island lord of the North Sea rim, not merely the backwater prince of a soggy British province.

How true this vision was is hard to gauge. But we should picture him in death as his people wished him to be seen: seated upon his throne, a great helm upon his knee, his horse beside him in the chamber, awaiting the mound to be raised above him. One of the first and last great lords of Lindsey, preparing for eternity.

*   *   *

* The mound itself stood at the crossroads of Ermine Street and an important local trackway: it was clearly intended to be seen, commented on and remembered by everyone who passed its imposing flanks.

In 628, no more than a single generation after the demolition of the apsidal church at Lincoln and the burial at Caenby, Bishop Paulinus of York, evangelist of Northumbria, turned his attention to the land south of the Humber. The land of Lindsey had been marked for 'conversion'.

Bede's information regarding the Northumbrian conversion of Lindsey was relayed by a priest named Deda. He was, according to Bede, 'a most reliable authority when relating the story of the Faith in this province'.[*][33] Deda was the abbot of Partney, a monastery in the east of Lindsey at the southern end of the Wolds. It is from him that we learn – via Bede – that the conversion of Lindsey began with a man named Blaecca, described as *praefectus Lindocolinae civitatis* – 'Prefect of the city of Lincoln'.[†] Bede also describes how Paulinus raised a stone church within the city, a building of 'fine workmanship'. According to Bede it was, in his day, already ruinous, having lost its roof 'either through neglect or enemy damage', though the walls yet stood and provided a venue for miraculous cures to be sought.[34]

In light of evidence for the long continuity of Christian worship at Lincoln, this story is a bit odd. For one thing, Paulinus' church has proved difficult to square with archaeology – no trace of such a

---

[*] Whether or not this is true, we have Deda to thank for one of the only verbal portraits to have survived from the early Middle Ages. According to Deda, Paulinus cut a somewhat sinister, vulpine figure: 'a tall man with a slight stoop, black hair, an ascetic face, a thin hooked nose, and a venerable and terrifying presence'.

[†] In Imperial terminology, the word 'Prefect' was used fairly widely to qualify a range of official administrative and military titles. In seventh- and eighth-century Britain, however, its meaning is rather harder to pin down. In eighth-century West Saxon and Mercian charters, *praefectus* was selected as the appropriate translation of the Old English term 'ealdorman'. The ninth-century translation of Bede into Old English, however, renders Blaecca's title as 'reeve' – a subordinate administrative role that was more elastic in application than the heavyweight title of ealdorman. In truth, the best we can do with Deda's information is to say that Blaecca was somehow, in a secular sense, 'in charge'.

structure of the correct date has ever been identified in Lincoln – and it seems surprising that a brand-new stone church (if it ever existed) would have survived for only a century before falling into ruin.* Even more puzzling is why Blaecca, the *praefectus Lindocolinae civitatis*, was in need of conversion in the first place – let alone instruction from an outsider. Bede in general seems to have had no conception that Lincoln already possessed an established Romano-British Christian community (or, if he did, he suppressed it). A sceptical reader might therefore consider the possibility that Bede (or Deda) didn't actually know anything much about early seventh-century Lincoln, and that the whole story was an anecdote designed to bolster the reputation of Paulinus (in particular) and Northumbria (in general).

The broader conversion of the Lindsey-folk apparently took place at the River Trent, on the western edge of the kingdom. According to 'one of the oldest inhabitants' of Lindsey whose words were reported by Bede, 'he and many others had been baptized by Paulinus in the presence of King Edwin [of Northumbria]'.[35] The baptism occurred near a place known to Bede as *Tiowulfingacaester*.†\n*Tiowulfingacaester* could be an old name for the Roman town of *Segelocum* (Littleborough in Nottinghamshire), though this is far from certain, and nothing is otherwise known about the place. Perhaps the most notable thing about *Tiowulfingacaester*, however, is where it wasn't. One might have thought that Lincoln, with its topographical prominence and Imperial past, might have provided a more suitable and effective setting for the Northumbrian prelate and king to put on a show.

---

* My suspicion is that Bede – ever anxious to embiggen the reputations of his Northumbrian antecedents – deliberately associated a ruined and suitably impressive Roman building with the bishop's legacy in Lindsey. If so, the Roman basilica – a building of such scale and technical achievement that it would likely have appealed to Bede's sense of Northumbrian ecclesiastical grandeur – makes a plausible candidate.

† The *caester* (OE 'fortified Roman settlement') of the *Tiowulfingas* (the 'people of Tiowulf').

Elsewhere in his *Historia*, Bede is pretty clear in his view that the adoption of Christianity was a top-down process: when kings changed their faith, the people were expected to follow suit. There was no real model for king-free conversion. But in this case, as Bede tells it, there was no king of Lindsey on hand to lead his people to the river. Indeed, Bede nowhere makes mention of any royal ruler in Lindsey at all: the only leader referred to by him is the aforementioned Blaecca, the Lincoln 'prefect' (whose presence at the Trent is in any case not specified).* Nevertheless, royal gravitas was not entirely absent. Indeed, King Edwin of Northumbria is conspicuous by his presence: a watchful and intimidating actor whose involvement changes the complexion of the moment considerably, transforming what was ostensibly a religious moment into an event with heavy political overtones. It seems almost certain that the event at *Tiowulfingacaester* was conceived as a symbolic gesture designed to project an image of Northumbrian power. For just as baptism signalled the spiritual supremacy of Bishop Paulinus and the see of York, so the presence of King Edwin signified the extension of Northumbrian political dominance: a carefully stage-managed spectacle intended to dramatize the subordination of Lindsey to its larger northern neighbour.† What is harder to perceive is the degree to which the projected image reflected any sort of political reality.

---

* It is possible that Blaecca was in fact a king – or at least a member of the royal dynasty – but was not afforded the honour of this title by Bede. This is not impossible, as Bede was mostly concerned with the prestige of Northumbria and clearly had nothing but contempt for 'British' Christianity and anything connected with it.

† If, in fact, the whole thing was orchestrated entirely for propaganda purposes, there is no reason to believe that it was a well-attended event: all that Bede actually provides is the second-hand testimony of an old man who claims he was there 'with many others': it hardly sounds like Woodstock. One can easily imagine the Northumbrian king, shuffling impatiently beside the river on a chilly Nottinghamshire morning, as he watched his bishop flick baptismal water at a dozen befuddled peasants before pronouncing some grandiose claim of overlordship to the four winds, getting back on his horse and riding back to York post haste.

Given the choice of location, Bede's reticence regarding the situation and status of Lincoln and its 'prefect', the absence of Lindsey's own rulers and the presence of the Northumbrian king, it becomes hard to take the 'conversion' of Lindsey at face value. There were doubtless very many Lindsey-folk who, in 628, were still pagan. It is hard to imagine they were all baptized in one go in the River Trent, however, and presumably a lot of the hard and unglamorous work of conversion and instruction happened at a local level over an extended period, well after the initial spectacle of stage-managed baptism had concluded. The evidence for a Christian community at Lincoln (which Bede pointedly and predictably ignores) also suggests that there were at least some people in Lindsey who already considered themselves to be Christians. For them, baptism would not have been an induction into the Christian faith in general, but into a Northumbrian communion, an acknowledgement of the political 'protection' they were now subject to and not really a religious ritual at all.

Whatever the precise nature of Northumbrian interference, however, it was the beginning of the end for Lindsey as an independent realm and probably, too, as a place for pagan beliefs to survive unchallenged. For most of the rest of the century, Lindsey pinballed between Northumbrian and Mercian domination, a disputed hinterland caught between the ambitions of greater powers and newer religious hierarchies. In 633, Edwin of Northumbria was killed at Hatfield Chase, the sparse and desolate marshland, bisected by Ermine Street, that separated northwest Lindsey from southeast Elmet. His death left control of Lindsey open once more to dispute, as Penda of Mercia and his ally, Cadwallon of Gwynedd, asserted their authority in Northumbria's southern marches. In the following year, however, Cadwallon and his army were destroyed by Oswald of Bernicia, whose victory restored the royal house of his father, Æthelfrith (who had been killed by Edwin of Deira at the Idle in 616). It seems likely that his victory also returned Northumbrian rule to Lindsey.

King Oswald died in 642. He met his end at a place known to Bede as Maserfelth, killed in battle by the forces of King Penda of Mercia.[36] After the fighting, Penda had the fallen king dismembered, hacking his head and arms from his body. The severed parts were hoisted on wooden stakes: a foul *tropaion* hung, not with the weapons and armour of the vanquished in the manner of the ancient Greeks, but with corpse-fragments. It was a dark memorial of Penda's victory, a dedication to his gods perhaps, or a warning to his enemies. Bede, on whose account we rely for the story, does not specify where the head and arms of Oswald were displayed – whether they marked the battlefield, or were erected in some other place where Penda's savage power could be celebrated. But wherever they were, by Bede's day in the early eighth century, both the ground where Oswald fell and the timber on which his remains were displayed had become sources of miraculous healing – repositories for the holy power that resided in the blood of martyrs. Oswald had been sanctified in death, the first warrior-saint of English Christianity.

Penda's *tropaion* remained standing until the following year, when Oswald's brother and successor Oswy led an army to reclaim the detached segments of the corpse, returning them to Northumbria. The arms went to the royal fortress at Bamburgh. The head was taken to the monastery at Lindisfarne that Oswald himself had founded in 635. Situated on an island connected to the Bernician mainland by a tidal causeway, Lindisfarne was destined to become one of the premier religious locations of seventh-century England. The rest of Oswald's body, however, remained wherever it was. It was only much later, at some point between 679 and 697, that Oswy's daughter Osthryth, then queen of Mercia, had the bones of her uncle raised and moved.* She had them taken to a

---

* Osthryth had married Penda's son Æthelred, king of Mercia from 675 to 704, and wielded considerable power and influence within her husband's kingdom – enough, in fact, for her eventually to rouse the ire of the Mercian nobility and to be murdered by them in 697.

monastery that was situated on the isle of Bardney, near the city of Lincoln, in the land of Lindsey.

The wheels of the wooden cart sink slowly into the rutted mud of the causeway. Up ahead, at the gate that closes the island off from the profane world outside, the driver remonstrates with a gatekeeper, their words lost on the wind. His companion at the cart sighs, turns to glance at the load behind him, a sepulchral cargo wrapped and covered. Turning back, he pulls the hood of his cloak closer around his head, shielding himself from the wind that blows unceasing across the marshes, twisting the willow and the alder, a dry simmer through the reed beds. He feels the weight of the sky above him, the grinding motion of titan clouds that fill the vastness; grey cliffs towering above a pale sea, grasses roiled and rippled in the breeze. Close to the road, patches of tarnished silver water gleam among peat-black shadows, drawing down the darkening heavens: reflections of unfathomed vastness, an illusion of eternity flickering on the fen.

Oswald's mortal parts were not welcomed with unbridled joy by the inmates of Bardney. According to Bede, 'when the wagon carrying the bones arrived towards evening at the abbey, the monks were reluctant to admit it; for although they acknowledged Oswald's holiness, they were influenced by old prejudices against him even after his death, because he originally came from a different province [Northumbria] and had ruled them as an alien king'.[37] Being ruled by alien kings, however, had, by the late seventh century, become *de rigueur* for the people of Lindsey. Between Oswald's death in 642 and his body parts pitching up at Bardney, control of Lindsey had changed hands with absurd frequency. After the battle of Maserfelth in 642 it first reverted (probably) to Penda's Mercian overlordship, before being made subject to Northumbria again when Penda was finally slain in battle by Oswald's brother and successor Oswy at the battle of the Winwaed in 655. Oswy subsequently divided Mercia between Peada (Penda's son and Oswy's son-in-law) and himself. Peada received the southern half of the kingdom; the northern portion – including, presumably, Lindsey – was ruled directly from Northumbria. Oswy's power in Mercia and Lindsey was ended, however, with the rise of Penda's son Wulfhere, who became king of a restored Mercia in 658. Wulfhere is known to have made a grant of land within Lindsey (at Barrow upon Humber) to the Mercian bishop Chad (d.672), and so it seems at that point that the kingdom had once more reverted to Mercian control.

This was not the end of the ping-pong. In 674, Wulfhere mounted an attack on Northumbria but was defeated by Oswy's son and successor Ecgfrith (r.670–685). According to the Northumbrian monk Stephen of Ripon (writing in the early eighth century), 'countless numbers were slaughtered, their king routed, and the kingdom of Mercia itself put under tribute. Later Wulfhere died (I do not know the exact cause) and Ecgfrith ruled a wider realm in peace.'[38] That Ecgfrith's realm included Lindsey is specifically confirmed by Bede who noted that the province had been annexed to Northumbria after Wulfhere was defeated and driven out.[39] It was at this time that Lindsey received its first bishop: an individual called Eadhaed who was consecrated to his see at York. Once again, however, this new dispensation was not to last; in 679 the new king of Mercia, Wulfhere's son Æthelred, 'recovered the province of Lindsey'.[40] This was to be the last time that Lindsey changed hands before the Vikings upended the gaming table in the 860s.

The monastery at Bardney was itself probably a Mercian venture: when Osthryth died in 697, her remains were interred there. A few years later, when Osthryth's husband King Æthelred retired from royal life in 704, he took monastic vows and became abbot of Bardney; when he died a few years later, he, too, was buried there.* There were few more unequivocal ways of marking territorial

---

* Both Osthryth and Æthelred were later remembered as saints in their own right.

claims in the early Middle Ages than by planting royal corpses in the soil.* The burials of Osthryth and Æthelred at Bardney sent a clear message that this land was, after all, Mercian land. What had upset the monks was not so much Oswald's foreignness to Lindsey, but specifically his Northumbrian heritage. At Bardney, Mercian identity was no reason to feel alienated: whether everyone in Lindsey felt the same way is impossible now to know.

Hidden among bewildering channels of the dank and spreading Witham Valley, Bardney was an outpost of hermetic monasticism on the borders of the kingdom, a last homely house before the wide wilderness began. When Oswald's remains arrived there in the late seventh century, the monastery was probably not very old. The precise date and circumstances of its founding are unknown, although it is often assumed that Osthryth and Æthelred were the guiding force behind its establishment. Bardney itself was once an island (its Old English name means 'Bearda's island'), a feeble prominence near the banks of the Witham at the southern edge of a vast wetland zone. The original monastery probably had no single focus, with churches and chapels dispersed across the long, narrow strip of land it occupied. A narrow isthmus connected the island to the drier land to the northeast, cut by a ditch called Scotgrove Dyke which, though apparently modern, may well have been cut on the line of a much older boundary that separated the monastic enclave from the secular landscape that lay beyond. The abbey buildings are long gone; even the late medieval buildings – abandoned when the monastery was dissolved by Henry VIII in 1538 – are reduced to mere outlines in the grass and a few persistent stone footings for long tumbled pillars.

Bardney was probably the first of a number of monasteries that would develop in the region, all of them situated at the margins of the land – at the places where high ground gave way to marshes – the liminal zone, at the edge of things: Partney in the upper valley of the River Lymn where the wolds of the southeast give way to the

* See **HWICCE** for the burial of Coenwulf at Winchcombe in 821.

salt marsh, Flixborough on the edge of the Trent floodplain, Barrow beside the Humber. They appear like bulwarks against the encroaching night, like the hall of Heorot in *Beowulf*, a beacon of life and light, bright beside the monster-infested wastes beyond; or, like the sanctified hermitage of Guthlac's Crowland, a lonely outpost amongst the dark, spreading waters. But these monasteries were in many ways intrusions into the old land of Lindsey, sponsored by foreign powers and stocked by monks from elsewhere. It was an overwriting of the landscape with new mythologies, the absorption of Lindsey into the Mercian sphere and the thorough-going Christianization of its hills and valleys. But beneath it an older world still brims and rises in the floodwaters – a world of halls and warriors and grim-faced kings under mounds; a world of Frisians, Danes, Finn and Woden and, deeper yet, of ancient chapels rising amid ruin, of Arthur perhaps and Cædbæd Battle-crow and of torchlight glinting on bronze.

Having initially left Oswald's holy relics outside the gates of the monastery, the monks were eventually persuaded to take custody of them by a column of supernatural light that burst skyward from the bones during the night. It was, writes Bede, 'a light that was seen by nearly all the inhabitants of the province of *Lindissi*', illuminating for one last radiant moment the lost kingdom of Lindsey – a forgotten island realm sinking back in slumber to dream betwixt the marshes and the salt flats and the swollen, spilling rivers.*[41] By the eighth century the independence of the Lindsey-folk was fading in memory – had been waning for a hundred years. And yet a thriving realm had quietly risen and fallen in the softly rolling land between the Humber and the Wash, an Anglo-British realm

---

* Abashed at their erstwhile reluctance, the monks of Bardney 'began to pray earnestly' and hurried to accommodate the evidently holy bones, washing them, placing them in a purpose-built casket (one they had conveniently made earlier) and hanging Oswald's purple and gold banner above their resting place in the church.

that blended traditions of deep antiquity with the new preoccupations of a maritime North Sea world, whose kings were counted among the sons of Woden. No single moment brought down the kingdom of Lindsey, no moment of conquest or heroic death in battle – not even the sad demotion of a once proud ruler to a 'kinglet' or 'ealdorman'. Only in the obstinacy of the Bardney monks can the last breath of Lindsey's independence be heard, susurrating in the reed beds, lost upon the wolds.

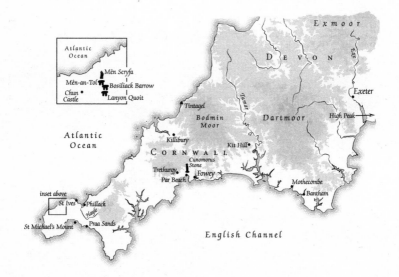

D'UMNONIA

– *Devon and Cornwall* –

Then from the castle gateway by the chasm
Descending thro' the dismal night – a night
In which the bounds of heaven and earth were lost –
Beheld, so high upon the dreary deeps
It seem'd in heaven, a ship, the shape thereof
A dragon wing'd, and all from stem to stern
Bright with a shining people on the decks,
And gone as soon as seen.

Alfred Lord Tennyson, *Idylls of the King* (1859)[1]

I n the second century AD, the Greek geographer Ptolemy referred to a people called the *Dumnonii*. He indicated that they lived west of the *Durotriges* – the people of the Dorset region – and gave no suggestion that there was anyone living further west than they did. The Dumnonii, in other words, were the people of Devon and Cornwall. Their capital was at Exeter or, as it was known in its Latinized form, *Isca Dumnoniorum*: 'the water of the Dumnonii' (*isca* being a Latinization of the Brittonic word for flowing water).* Exeter has never been subject to the sort of extensive archaeological autopsy that towns like Cirencester have benefited from, but it is clear that in its Imperial phase it was a city on the typical Roman model – with public buildings and stone walls and civil engineering and mosaic floors and all the rest of it. And, like other cities on the Roman model, it went into the same spiral of economic decline and abandonment at the end of the fourth century – possibly with a hint of ongoing small-scale occupation in a very limited area (analogous, perhaps, to the church community at Lincoln).[2] Elsewhere in the region, however, evidence for wealthy Roman lifestyles is not much in evidence. The few villas that have been found are mostly confined to the east of Dartmoor and these fell into ruin along with the collapse of urban life.† In Cornwall, aside from a few apparently temporary forts, there is almost no trace of anything that might be called Roman at all.‡

The first mention of a post-Roman kingdom of Dumnonia occurs in Gildas' *De Excidio Britanniae* and, taken at face value, the name seems to reflect straightforward continuity with the Romano-British tribal group referred to by Ptolemy. First impressions are of a people whose origins and identity lay deep in prehistory: a realm in which the trappings of Imperial membership were only ever the flimsiest and patchiest of veneers, easily and willingly shed. And, in some respects, the extreme conservatism observable in Dumnonian archaeology would appear to bear this characterization out. Many of the distinctive fortified settlements of the region – the circular enclosed villages known as 'rounds', and the greater hill-forts and defended coastal promontories – were constructed in the pre-Roman Iron Age

---

* The city was later renamed, in English as *Exanceaster*, 'the Roman fortified town [*ceaster*] on [the River] *Exe* [Isca]'.

† The one exception to the absence of 'Roman' buildings in Cornwall is the villa at Magor which, though not a very impressively executed example of its type, was certainly designed with Roman ideas of domestic planning in mind.

‡ The forts are located at Nanstallon, Restormel Castle and Calstock – all in the east of Cornwall.

and endured through the centuries of Roman rule to emerge the other side remarkably unaltered in basic form, function and location.

And yet a paradox confronts those archaeologists who search for the post-Roman kingdom of Dumnonia. For all the apparent continuity of the ancient British west – its Iron Age ambience and its severance from the mainstream of Romano-British life – it is in Cornwall that some of the most spectacular evidence for a lingering and meaningful British attachment to Mediterranean culture has been found. The story of Dumnonia is the story of how a dream of civilization was manifested at the farthest fringes of a fading Empire: a determined effort to reach towards the fading light in a place that had barely felt the sun. It tells of how the grey surf that pounds the Cornish coast once washed the traces of a brighter sea against the slate and granite, gilding gloomy citadels rosy-gold in the dimming Imperial afterglow.

And seen from a distance, in that haze of light and spray, there appeared the phantoms of Britain's oldest and most potent legends: shining indistinct, immaterial as the rainbow.

In around 1136, a scholar and churchman called Geoffrey produced a manuscript that he titled *Historia Regum Britanniae*: a 'history of the kings of Britain' from the fall of Troy (in the twelfth or thirteenth century BC) to the wars of Northumbria in the seventh century AD. Geoffrey – *Galfridus Monemutensis* as he called himself ('Geoffrey of Monmouth') – was quite possibly born in Wales (he later became Bishop of St Asaph) and by virtue of his geographical origins was likely well acquainted with the stories that circulated in the west of Britain: with the folk tales and poems and pseudo-histories, the genealogies of once prominent families and the defiant boasts of a people whose land and identity were slowly being eroded by the inexorable Anglo-Norman tide.* He was also,

---

* It is also likely that Geoffrey was, by education and upbringing, more Norman or Breton than he was British, part of a community who dominated the ecclesiastical and aristocratic life of the Welsh borders in a region that had been heavily settled by the beneficiaries of the Conquest.

however (or so he claimed), the recipient of 'a certain very ancient book written in the British language' which had been given to him by his good friend Walter, archdeacon of Oxford. This book, Geoffrey wished it to be believed, had furnished much of the material contained in his *Historia*.

There is no knowing if such a book ever existed; or, if it did, what exactly it contained; or how old it was; or who wrote it. Under normal circumstances, such matters would generally be considered the esoteric province of a vanishingly small number of academic specialists, and not something that the general public should be expected to worry about unduly. In this case, however, the nature of Geoffrey's source material has implications that have inspired endless spirals of controversy and consternation. And that is because the central figure of Geoffrey's manuscript was a British king named Arthur.

Before Geoffrey, Arthur was primarily a concern of Welsh and Breton bards, one of a number of semi- or pseudo-historical characters who became the subject of embellishment and embroidery in tall tales and manipulated pedigrees. Gwallog of Elmet was one such, Urien of Rheged another, two among the host whose names litter the Triads of the Island of Britain (*Trioedd Ynys Prydein*) and poems of early Welsh literature (some, as in *Y Gododdin*, survive as names severed from their stories, floating in a sea of forgotten heroic legend). Arthur was one of these figures – albeit one with a weaker claim to historicity than many others – a warlord who supposedly lived around the turn of the fifth century, but who seems to have gone unmentioned until a dramatic ninth-century debut in the *Historia Brittonum*.[*3] After Geoffrey's book appeared,

---

* See **LINDSEY**; a line in the B text of *Y Gododdin* which refers to a fellow called Gwawrddur who, although 'he fed black ravens on the rampart of a fortress', was nevertheless 'no Arthur', may conceivably predate the *Historia Brittonum*. However, it is unclear how old this line in this version of the poem actually is. Moreover, it is not certain whether the poem is referring to the same Arthur as the figure referred to by the *Historia Brittonum* (though on balance that seems likely). Quite what Gwawrddur had done to deserve being undermined in this way is, of course, equally unknowable.

however, this was to change profoundly. It established at a stroke the image of Arthur the King: a Christian paragon who, with a host of noble companions and a magic sword, put the world to rights with a blaze of godly triumphalism and mountains of slaughtered foreigners and immigrants.

Geoffrey's *Historia* was the equivalent of a bestseller in its day. In England, its popularity can best be explained by considering how Geoffrey's Arthur provided the model for a king who not only brought all of Britain under his rule, but who also sought and won vast dominions beyond the sea – an attractive idea for ambitious Norman kings and barons who were actively seeking to maintain and extend their dynastic lands in England, Wales, Scotland, Ireland and France. Most importantly, the expansion of Arthur's realm was not the product of dull diplomacy or clever marriage, but of the violent exploits that most stimulated the chivalric impulses of England's knightly class. As Geoffrey told it, Arthur's was an empire won by derring-do – carved from history with a sword like a royal effigy cut from an alabaster block.

The appeal to knightly tastes was plainly intentional on Geoffrey's part. His *Historia* was stuffed to the guts with ripping yarns; written, as he makes explicit, in a pacey, unpretentious Latin that could be read for pleasure by the sort of no-nonsense fellow who would best appreciate bluff stories of battles, sieges, giants, sorcerous seduction and more battles – men, in fact, like Robert, Earl of Gloucester (d.1147), the illegitimate son of Henry I, to whom the book was dedicated. Geoffrey appears to have had a canny sense of Robert's intellectual limits. 'If I had adorned my page with high-flown rhetorical figures,' he explains in the dedication, 'I should have bored my readers, for they would have been forced to spend more time in discovering the meaning of my words than in following the story.' Men like Robert, Geoffrey was implying, couldn't be expected to think too hard: it might make their brains hurt.[4]

Partly as a result of Geoffrey's keen sense of his audience's tastes, King Arthur and his companions gradually became ubiquitous in poetry and prose – not only in Britain but throughout Europe.

Vastly embellished in French and German writing of the later twelfth and thirteenth centuries – most influentially in the romances of the French troubadour Chrétien de Troyes (*fl.*1160–90) – stories about the king and his knights became knotted into a vast tangle of interconnected legends and lays that became known as the 'Matter of Britain'.*[5] So popular did these stories become that several were even adapted into medieval Old Norse, including *Merlínússpá*, a translation by the Icelandic monk Gunnlaugr Leifsson (died *c.*1218) of the Prophecy of Merlin contained in Geoffrey's *Historia*.†[6] For anyone growing up in the aristocratic milieu of the late twelfth and early thirteenth centuries, the 'Matter of Britain' would have been deeply insinuated into the mental architecture.

In 1225, a 16-year-old boy named Richard was made 'Earl of Cornwall' by his brother King Henry III (r.1216–72). The title was not new – a number of Norman earls had preceded him – but neither was it ancient.‡ In all probability there had never been a native Earl of Cornwall; the title was an invention of William the Conqueror, a reward in land and honour for those who had partici-

---

* The popularity of the stories never died away. In 1485 William Caxton printed an edition of a prose version of the Arthurian legend by the Englishman Sir Thomas Malory (d.1471). It was accessible, widely available and written in English, and it codified and rationalized much of the accumulated lore that had built up in disparate sources over the preceding three centuries. Malory's *Le Morte d'Arthur* became the standard version of the legend for English readers, inspiring – amongst much else – the poems of Tennyson's *Idylls of the King* in the nineteenth century. All modern retellings of the Arthur legend run through Malory to Geoffrey of Monmouth (*Galfridus Monemutensis* has a great deal to answer for).

† In particular, the patronage of Norwegian king (and chivalry enthusiast) Hákon Hákonarson gave rise to a number of translations that included a version of the legend of Tristan and Yseult prepared in 1226 by the English monk 'Brother Robert' (*Tristrams saga ok Ísöndar*).

‡ Brian of Brittany (died *c.*1086), Robert, Count of Mortain (died *c.*1095) and Robert's son and successor William (d.1140), Alan 'the Black' (d.1146) and Reginald de Dunstanville (d.1175).

pated in the conquest of England. That is not to say, however, that the medieval lords of Britain did not imagine themselves as heirs to a deeper tradition. The young Richard, immersed in the swirl of Arthuriana that saturated the imaginative life of the English, would have taken for granted that, high on the savage cliffs of Cornwall's northern coast, a great castle once had stood: a castle, as Geoffrey of Monmouth described it, 'built high above the sea, which surrounds it on all sides, and there is no other way in except that offered by a narrow isthmus of rock. Three armed soldiers could hold it against you, even if you stood there with the whole kingdom of Britain at your side.'[7] It was the castle where – again according to Geoffrey – Gorlois, the fictional Duke of Cornwall, had secreted his wife Ygerna (Igraine) to protect her from the lustful advances of King Uther Pendragon – the castle where Arthur was conceived: the castle of Tintagel.

As Geoffrey tells it, the story goes that Uther, enflamed by ungovernable passion for Ygerna, had brought war to the land of Gorlois, besieging him in the fortress of Dimilioc. Not really having all that much interest in pursuing a beef with Gorlois, however, Uther swiftly turned his attention to his real objective at Tintagel. Knowing that the castle was impregnable, Uther summoned the prophet Merlin, who 'was ordered to suggest how the King could have his way with Ygerna.'[8] Merlin's cunning plan was to transform Uther into the likeness of Gorlois – and himself and Uther's friend Ulfin of Ridcaradoch into other members of Gorlois' household – through the use of magical concoctions or 'medicines' (*medicamina*). In this way they entered unsuspected through the gates of Tintagel, and Uther 'spent the night with Ygerna and satisfied his desire by making love to her. He had deceived her', Geoffrey elaborates, 'by the disguise which he had taken. He had deceived her, too, by the lying things that he said to her, things which he planned with great skill.'[9] This, it turns out, was all for the good because, that night, Ygerna 'conceived Arthur, the most famous of

145

men, who subsequently won great renown by his outstanding brav-ery.[10] It later transpired that Gorlois had been killed in the fighting at Dimilioc. Uther, we are told by Geoffrey with a wry smile, 'mourned for the death of Gorlois; but [...] he was happy, all the same, that Ygerna was freed from her marital obligations'.[11]

The story of Uther and Ygerna is, for modern readers, an uncom-fortable read. I remember finding it troubling as a child and it still leaves me feeling queasy. Not, I think, because the tale is in itself unusually unsettling (there are many, far more violent, sentiments expressed in older Welsh and English poetry), but more for the horny relish with which Geoffrey tells it and the enormous appeal he clearly expected it to have for its intended audience – men whose lives were measured by the castles, land and women they could seize through violence or trickery and the dynastic fame they could establish in the process. Whatever the base medieval drives it spoke to, however, the story of Arthur's conception had an impact that far outlived any erotic frisson it inspired in its readers. By romanticiz-ing its setting, the bare semi-detached headland of Tintagel became the Nazareth of the Arthur legend. There could be no better place for Richard, Earl of Cornwall to build a new castle.

I first saw Tintagel Castle as a 5-year-old boy. I have a dim memory, clouded by subsequent visits as a child and an adult, of a windswept headland and dark castle ramparts and a long and winding stair cut into the rock, a treacherous path that gave out onto deep chasms that plunged down to tearing rocks and the shiv-ering sea below. It felt endless, that stairway – like the steps that ascended to the pass of Cirith Ungol from the Morgul Vale in Tolkien's *The Two Towers*.[12] It thrilled and terrified me in equal measure. That path is now barely used, superseded by a slender bridge that spans the gap between the mainland and what is effec-tively now an island. It is a delicate design and seen from afar it resembles a filament of adhesive, stretched before breaking, that still clings to objects once conjoined, now pulled gingerly apart. The bridge has sometimes been presented as an example of bureau-cratic hubris – an incongruous modern intrusion into a timeless landscape. In reality, the filaments of steel support a path laid with Cornish slate that revives what was once a land bridge: Geoffrey's 'narrow isthmus of rock'. It was, even in the twelfth century when he wrote, little more than a membrane of land splitting wind and water. As the Middle Ages wore on, the elements did their work and the land bridge slowly gave way, tumbling boulders into the bay below. No one recorded the sundering of Tintagel and no one really cared; the people who lived nearby were indifferent, divorced in their daily lives from the foibles of medieval lords. When the Tudor antiquary John Leland visited the place in 1542 he found that access had been 'woren away with gulfyng yn of the se, yn so much that yt hathe made ther almost an isle, and no way ys to enter ynto hyt now but by long elme trees layde for a bryge'.*[13]

The castle that Richard Earl of Cornwall built at Tintagel was, in truth, unfit for much besides pageantry, to play Arthurian games with his friends and promote the idea of himself as the true successor to the lords of Cornwall's fabled past. A collection of flimsy walls, gate-towers and outbuildings, it hung precariously over the raging tide, suspended against the storm: slate stacks and arches, windows to frame the Atlantic, jagged teeth of black masonry for set dressing, a castle raised by a dream. In the end the dream was not enough to sustain it, and it fell into disrepair long before the land bridge failed. In 1337, when the Duchy of Cornwall was created and its assets listed, the buildings were described as decayed and ruinous. A combination of neglectful landlords and the relentless caress of Cornish weather had destabilized the walls of the great hall within only a few years of construction, as if it had never really been built to last.

Still it is easy to understand the magic that this place held for Richard, the sense, if ever the once-and-future king had been conceived, that this would have been the place for it. The roiling,

* 'worn away with gulfing in of the sea, in so much that it has made there almost an isle, and no way is [there] to enter into it now but by long elm trees laid for a bridge'.

cold water of the Atlantic thumps relentlessly into the great hunk of land to which the ruins cling like barnacles: the grey waves, frosted with foam, walloping with primordial force into the time-smoothed granite and sintering russet slate of the north Cornish coast. The coarse, stubby grass and thin soil barely hang on to the island's battered crown, an old broken skull tossed into the sea, enmossed and weather-worn. Down below, in the little sheltered bay that lies beside the headland's caves and boulders, the rocky base of Tintagel Island has been rounded into bulbous and aqueous forms by the endless attention of the pounding ocean. There, hidden among the scooped and striated waves of granite that mushroom beside the gaping mouth of 'Merlin's Cave', the wizard's bearded face – as imagined by the sculptor Peter Graham in 2016 – peers out across the strand. For all the controversy this addition to the landscape generated at the time of its carving, the artwork is entirely in keeping with the way this place has long reflected human preoccupations with the past. It is also just as transient. As it ages, the weather will work on it as thoroughly as it has worked on the rest of Tintagel, a ghost-face melting back into the bedrock, washed away by the tide.

Despite all the fantasy that has accrued to the place, Tintagel was indeed a fortress of the Dark Ages, long before Earl Richard's castle. Whether Geoffrey of Monmouth had any inkling of this truth is hard to say, but it is tempting to think – mysterious Welsh book notwithstanding – that some scrap of folklore attached to the place had survived to inspire his fictions.

The deeper antiquity of Tintagel has been uncovered slowly: first by Courtenay Ralegh Radford in the 1930s, then by a team led by Charles Thomas in the 1990s and most recently in a five-year programme of research and excavation begun in 2016 and carried out on behalf of English Heritage by the Cornwall Archaeological Unit (CAU).[14] Between them their work has revealed a fortified settlement, much older than the visible remnants of the medieval castle, dating to between the fifth and late seventh centuries. Today the visitor can see the outlines of small rectilinear buildings, low walls artificially laid by Ralegh Radford to suggest (not, it should be said, with a great commitment to accuracy) the floor plans of houses and workshops. Though not all of them were constructed or inhabited at the same time, there were hundreds of small slate-built structures: a settlement of far greater longevity and scale than the castle Earl Richard built on its ruins, extending across much of the island plateau as well as the areas later covered by the medieval castle's inner and outer wards. It was also stoutly defended: a massive ditch and bank – once surmounted by an imposing timber palisade – cuts the approach to the neck of land that separated the island from the coastal mainland. The very presence of a defensive structure on this scale is testament to either the coercive power of whoever commissioned it or the organizational sophistication of the community who constructed it.

It might be imagined that, in common with the haunts of other Dark Age tyrants whose timber halls have left their scattered traces on wind-scraped hilltops behind recut Iron Age ditches, or whose horn-gabled drinking dens are romanticized with such panache in the poetry of early medieval Britain, Tintagel was once the setting for some barbarian mead-hall. Indeed, it was long assumed that somewhere below the 'Great Hall' of Earl Richard's film-set castle lay precisely such a venue: 'mead-halls' are buildings so engrained in the imagination of archaeologists and historians of the period that their presence is only ever a short hop of the imagination away, their existence predicated on the strength of their archetype. This conjecture could still be correct, though it is likely that the later medieval castle utterly obliterated all traces of earlier buildings in this part of the island. Recent excavations in the southern part of the island's plateau, however, have instead revealed something quite different. Archaeologists working there from 2016 onward discovered a complex of stone buildings completely unexpected in their scale, elaboration and permanence, some with walls over three feet thick, with slate-tiled floors and stone stairways connecting them to the artificial terraces on which they sat.

Much of what is known about life at Tintagel has been revealed through fragments of pottery. Red Slip Ware is the term applied by archaeologists to the high-quality decorated red glazed pottery produced in the late Roman Empire, and is usually prefixed by the region in which it was produced: e.g. African Red Slip Ware or Cypriot Red Slip Ware or Egyptian Red Slip Ware. It was a luxury product – 'the good china' – and was a development from the earlier *Terra Sigillata* (also known as 'Samian Ware'): glossy terracotta-coloured bowls, dishes and flagons designed for the table, embossed with relief decoration and stamped designs that developed with the turning centuries and varied with the workshops that produced it. Two types of this pottery have been found at Tintagel in considerable quantity: Phocaean Red Slip Ware, which was produced in Asia Minor (in the vicinity of the ancient city of Phocaea) on the coast of the Aegean in what is now modern Turkey, and African Red Slip Ware, which was produced throughout North Africa west of Egypt. Both continued to be made as late as the seventh century, although the range of their distribution became increasingly limited to the eastern Mediterranean. Hundreds of fragments of this stuff have been found at Tintagel, with the height of imports into Britain dated between 475 and 550, although remnants of glass bowls and cups from Iberia and Frankish pottery from Gaul indicate that a diversifying trade in luxury tableware continued into the seventh century.*

In addition to all this, a huge number of sherds from cheap imported mass-produced pottery have also been found, the remains of vessels that were used for more mundane purposes. For the most part these vessels were amphorae, the distinctively shaped containers in which Mediterranean commodities such as wine and olive oil were stored and transported, and the evidence from Tintagel indi-

---

* The latest finds include fragments of 'E-Ware', a type of Roman-style coarse pottery produced in western Gaul and imported into Britain and Ireland throughout the seventh century. Finds of this stuff potentially extend the life of the settlement and its trade links to the end of the seventh century.

cates clearly that significant volumes of these goods were being imported and consumed. Alongside the higher-grade imports – the glass and the slipware – the amphorae offer a glimpse of a lifestyle: of wealthy, powerful, well-connected people who could afford to import some of the costliest manufactured products that the Mediterranean could produce and to indulge in its most refined luxuries. This battered knuckle of rock in the cold Atlantic spray was, for perhaps as long as two centuries after the collapse of Roman power in Britain, home to people who continued to dine from fancy Roman dishes, to quaff wine from delicate Iberian glassware, to drizzle olive oil upon their oysters.*

It is hard to overstate how extraordinary this all appears in the context of its time. Simply in terms of its size, Tintagel is one of the largest defended enclosures of its time in Britain.† Moreover, the existence, and number, of major stone buildings, and the complexity of their relationships to each other – alongside the profusion of high-quality imports – present an image of a place wealthier and better connected than perhaps any other in fifth- to seventh-century Britain. It was the discovery of literate inscriptions on slate, however, that suggests it was also one of the most sophisticated.

The first inscribed stone at Tintagel was found in 1998 and dated to the sixth century. It made quite an impression when it was first revealed to the press because the Latin inscription included the Celtic personal name *Artognou* – a name sufficiently similar to Arthur on a superficial level (despite being a completely different name) to get a lot of people all worked up.‡[15] The second stone,

---

* Excavated food remains included the bones of fish and pigs, as well as oyster shells.

† See **FORTRIU**, however, for the enclosed forts of the Picts in northern Britain.

‡ The full inscription is as follows: PATERN[--] | COLIAVIFICIT | ARTOGNOU | COL[.] | FICIT; this can be translated as '*Artognou descendant of Patern[us] Colus made (this). Colus made (this)*'.

found in 2017 during the CAU excavations led by Jacky Nowakowski and provisionally dated to 650–700, is less coherent in its message but is perhaps even more interesting. It seems to record, again in Latin, a gift from a man named Titus (a Roman name) to 'two men' (*viri duo*).* In classical inscriptions, 'viri duo' was commonly used to refer to the *aediles* – Roman officials responsible for, among other things, public buildings, festivals and markets – or to provincial officials in charge of weights and measures.[16] Either role could conceivably have been meaningful to the merchants of Tintagel. The inscription also mentions the son, or sons, of a certain 'Budic' (a Celtic name), and utilizes Greek characters alongside letters from the Roman alphabet, including a Christian monogram that has parallels in late Roman epigraphy. Like the first stone, the inscriptions are light and cursive – as if the scribe were practising his or her handwriting or working on a draft for a more formal inscription on stone or parchment. Together these slates constitute evidence for a world where people with a mixed Romano-British identity and a sophisticated knowledge of both the Latin and Greek alphabets were able to scribble casually on slates as if it were no big deal: members of a literate, Christian, cosmopolitan community.

Tintagel, in other words, was not merely the drinking den of some unreconstructed barbarian chief, tossing bones over his shoulder and philosophizing with an axe. Nor was it a sprinkling of squalid *Grubenhäuser* where shit-covered peasants lived out their short and brutish lives at the margins of the world. It was, rather, a citadel of stone: a haven for people with refined tastes, foreign connections and access to literate culture; people who probably considered themselves still to be, in all the ways that still mattered, part of an Empire that had never died.

* * *

* Or, just possibly, a man called 'Viridius'.

When Gildas sat down to compose his screed about everything that was wrong with Britain (*De Excidio Britanniae*) there were some particular issues that he wanted to get off his chest. A significant subset of these related to the British clergy. That Britain had a functioning church stocked with functionaries was not at issue – and in fact Gildas makes it very clear that he took Christianity for granted among the native British. It was the quality of the clergy that was the problem, and he furiously rebuked his contemporaries for what he saw as their stupidity, corruption, vice and greed. To Gildas, the priests and bishops of Britain were, by and large, a mob of oafs and lechers who 'yawn stupidly at the precepts of holy men [...] while they show alert interest in sports and the foolish stories of worldly fellows'.[17] They were, he complains bitterly, not really interested in saving the souls of the masses, but, rather, in seizing worldly power and wealth for themselves through the corrupt purchase of holy office. Having done so, Gildas explains, 'they remain in the same old unhappy slime of intolerable sin even after they have obtained the priestly seat of bishop or presbyter (they never sit, but wallow there disgracefully, like pigs)'.[18]

For all this self-righteous fury, however, Gildas made no reference to any of his colleagues by name (perhaps to avoid social awkwardness at the next British synod). In fact, very few individuals are identified anywhere in the *Excidio* – particularly in its chapters dealing with contemporary matters. He did, however, make some important exceptions when dealing with the other major target of his ire: Britain's political rulers. 'Britain has kings,' Gildas famously pronounced, 'but they are tyrants', guilty of a mountain of sin against God and humanity.[19] These men he was not afraid to name, and the first among the five bad kings of Britain was Constantine, 'tyrant whelp of the filthy lioness of Dumnonia'.[20]

Constantine's crimes were specific. Gildas charged him with fornicating in wedlock and mistreating his wife: 'for many years [...] overcome by the stench of frequent and successive adulteries, he put away his lawful wife against the ban of Christ.' There was a much worse stain on his reputation than this, however. Gildas also accused him of killing two youths in church before the holy dais, 'their arms outstretched not to weapons [...] but to God and the altar'. If that were not bad enough, Constantine himself was at the time apparently clothed 'in the habit of a holy abbot'.[21] The implication, no doubt, was that Constantine was not only a bad king but also a bad clergyman – one of those wretched simoniacs who had 'grabbed merely the name of priest – not the priestly way of life' and had 'received the apostolic dignity, without yet being suitable for entire faith and penitence for evil'.[22]

It is hard to pass judgement on the fairness of Gildas' criticisms – he undoubtedly had his own axe to grind – but there are a few incidental fragments of information that this broadside reveals. The first is that, in Gildas' own time (which is hard to precisely define, but is likely to have been the first half of the sixth century or perhaps slightly earlier), numerous British realms, including Dumnonia, were ruled by men who were referred to as kings (*reges*). The second is that, whatever his religious failings may have been, Constantine of Dumnonia was a Christian who, in externals at any rate, had adopted the trappings of a religious life (and that this, unusually, was not inconsistent with the direct exercise of royal power). He also presided over a realm where holy altars were, in themselves, unremarkable: it was being killed in front of them that was notable, rather than their absence or their presence. Just as significant, however, is the name that the king bore.

The Emperor Constantine I (r.306–337) was the archetype for every Christian king in early post-Roman Europe, the ruler whose edict of 313 (the 'Edict of Milan') definitively brought the official persecution of Christians to an end in the Roman Empire. And although the sincerity of Constantine's own conversion to the Christian faith is a little hard to assess (his personal observance was certainly unorthodox; he waited until he was on his death bed before accepting baptism), the transformative nature of his reign made him the first Christian Emperor of the Romans in the eyes of all who followed.* He was, in fact, a particularly potent figure in the British imagination because his elevation to the purple in 306 had taken place, not in Rome or some other sun-kissed Imperial resort, but in York (*Eboracum*). The fact that the king of Dumnonia was named after, or chose to be identified with, this towering figure of the late Roman world is instructive: it reveals something more of the character of the realm into which he was born – that it was a place whose rulers saw themselves as part of a tradition of muscular Christianity, of patrician Latinity, of domineering authority. In other words, he was precisely the sort of individual one might easily imagine enjoying the luxuries of Tintagel.

The end of the Roman Empire in the west is conventionally dated to AD 476. In that year a Roman general of barbarian origin named Odoacer deposed the adolescent Emperor reigning in the west – Romulus Augustulus – and was proclaimed by his troops *Rex Italiae* – 'King of Italy'. One of the first acts of the victorious new 'king' was to pack up the Imperial regalia and send it to the ruler of the eastern Empire in Constantinople. Odoacer did this not because he didn't want the Imperial regalia – we can be sure it was very nice – but because he needed the security and legitimacy that a still-reigning Emperor could bestow. The Emperor, Zeno, grudgingly recognized Odoacer as *de facto* ruler of Italy (in the continued absence of the long-exiled-but-still-hanging-around-like-a-bad-smell former western Emperor, Julius Nepos). Odoacer, for his part, recognized Zeno as Emperor of everywhere, east and west. This was perhaps a little hollow – the Roman Empire in the west

---

* This meant in part that the traditions of Imperial rule in which Constantine remained firmly grounded could be reinterpreted as *exempla* for future Christian rulers. His decisive victory in battle at the Milvian Bridge in 312, for example, was spun as a providential victory inspired by a vision of a fiery cross burning in the sky – a symbol of Christ with which the Emperor had his men mark their shields and which was carried before them on their standard (known thereafter as the *labarum*). For those warlords who found the pacifism of Christ's message indigestible, this sort of thing – alongside the example of the belligerent kings of the Old Testament – set a welcome precedent.

consisted at this time of only Italy and Provence, the rest of it having fallen to various barbarian regimes or otherwise in the process of devolving into a confusing mess (e.g. Britain) – and Odoacer wasted little time in consolidating his own power, particularly after Julius Nepos was murdered in 480. Nevertheless, the new King of Italy remained meticulous about trying not to aggravate Zeno too badly: the most prestigious coins that were issued in Italy during Odoacer's rule – heavy gold *solidi* featuring the bust of the diademed Emperor, spear nonchalantly cast over one shoulder on the obverse ('heads') and a winged victory on the reverse ('tails') – were struck with Zeno's name on them, not Odoacer's, a very public display of performative (if not necessarily effective) submission.* The point being that the people who ended up in positions of power after the western Empire came undone were painfully aware – even if it is sometimes forgotten in the modern west – that the eastern Empire was still strong like bull.

In modern historiography, the Roman Empire in the east has come to be known by a name derived from the small town of Byzantion on the western shore of the Bosphorus which Emperor Constantine chose in 324 to be the site of his new capital in the east (renamed in 330, after himself, as Constantinople). To modern historians the state centred on Constantinople is therefore referred to as Byzantium, or the Byzantine Empire.† The Byzantines themselves, however – despite their primary language being Greek rather than Latin – continued to refer to themselves, simply, as

* Odoacer did mint silver coins in his own name, although they do not use a regal or Imperial style, and depict him as characteristically barbarian with moustache and top knot.

† The adoption of 'Byzantine' as the adjective used to describe the eastern Empire was the result of the influence exerted on scholarship by the work of the sixteenth-century German humanist Hieronymus Wolf, a man whose pioneering study of ancient and medieval Greek manuscripts laid the foundations for modern Byzantine studies and, in the process, saved the world from the sesquipedalian horror of the 'Constantinopolitan Empire'.

'Romans'. They saw themselves, not as the heirs to a *fallen* Empire, but in straightforward continuity with it. From the perspective of Constantinople, the loss of Rome to a barbarian regime, though bitterly regretted, was never considered a fatal blow. These Romans of the east would not feel the hammer fall for another thousand years.*

At the time of Odoacer's capture of Italy in 476, the Byzantine Empire still controlled the territories of Greece, the eastern Balkans, Asia Minor (modern Turkey), Egypt, Libya and the Levant (modern Lebanon, Israel and Syria). A century later, at the end of the reign of the Emperor Justinian I (r.527–565), the Imperial borders once again encompassed Italy (including Sicily and Sardinia), the western Balkans, the remaining coastline of North Africa and southern Spain. For those living in coastal parts of southern Britain in the sixth century, the tide of the Roman Empire was rolling steadily back to a position of reasonable proximity and its products – including, presumably, its cultural and religious values – were readily available: either directly or through a series of intermediate trading networks along the Atlantic seaboard. Britain was not excluded from this ongoing commerce with the east – evidence for it has been found all along the south coast, into the Bristol Channel and as far as the Irish Sea. The most substantial beneficiary, however, seems to have been the Dumnonian peninsula.

Though Tintagel is the celebrity site in Dumnonia, it is not unique in boasting Mediterranean imports or substantial buildings. Fifth- and sixth-century amphorae have been excavated from a number of coastal locations in Devon and Cornwall, and some of these have been interpreted as coastal trading hubs – some of apparent scale and permanence. Traces of ovoid buildings at

---

* Although the borders of the Empire would contract as the centuries rolled by – most dramatically over the course of the seventh century when the armies of Islam swiftly conquered North Africa and most of the Near East – it would be 1453 before Constantinople finally fell, conquered by the Turkish Ottoman Empire.

Mothecombe (Devon), for example, are suggestive of exceptionally large dwellings and could well have been occupied by local bigwigs or itinerant rulers at various times.[23] Elsewhere, fortified settlements at Trethurgy, Killibury, St Michael's Mount and Chun (Cornwall) and High Peak (Devon) were all apparently occupied in the fifth to sixth centuries and all were locations where Mediterranean imports were consumed.[24] Other artefactual evidence of Byzantine influence in Dumnonia is ephemeral and/or controversial. Late Roman coins of the fourth century, for example from eastern mints rarely represented in British coin finds, have also turned up in this part of Cornwall, a trend that possibly implies a trading connection that predated the known influx of Mediterranean goods and pottery.

An inscribed stone that bears the late Roman 'Chi-Rho' Christogram – the monogram formed of the Greek letters X ('Chi') and P ('Rho'), the first two letters of the name of the Greek word for Christ (Χριστος; 'Christos') – was incorporated into the south end of Phillack church on the Hayle Estuary. It probably dates to the early fifth century and possibly suggests the ongoing influence of late antique religion in shaping the outward forms of British Christianity. Perhaps more suggestive is the dedication of a Cornish church to St Ia, the nucleus of the town of St Ives that grew up around it (St Ives is a corrupt form of St Ia). Although late medieval hagiography made Ia an Irish virgin who sailed to Cornwall on a miraculous expanding leaf, her real origins are almost certainly more exotic.[25] A woman of the same name was martyred in the fourth century by the Persian Emperor Shapur II (r.310–379), and her cult was promoted in the Byzantine Empire alongside a number of other Middle Eastern victims of persecution under the Zoroastrian regime. In the mid-sixth century, Procopius (c.500–c.565) described how the Emperor Justinian, 'found a martyr's shrine of St Ia, fallen in ruins, which he restored with all sumptuousness'.[26] The church was located in Constantinople 'on the left as one enters the gate which is known as the Golden Gate', a prime spot beside the massive triple-arched triumphal gateway that served as the main point of entry through the walls of the city. It was, in other words, a prestigious cult connected with lavish imperial patronage at exactly the time that the wave of Byzantine contact with Dumnonia was cresting. The appearance of a church in Cornwall dedicated to the same saint seems unlikely to be coincidental.

In truth, when seen against the glories of Byzantium, the architectural wonders of Dumnonia suffer a little. In 537, around the same time that Mediterranean imports to Tintagel were peaking, Emperor Justinian's Church of the Holy Wisdom in Constantinople – Hagia Sophia – was being completed. A thickset and bulbous profusion of heaped domes and rounded arches, the church was immediately a source of wonder, its gleaming white marble cladding (long since lost) returning the coral fire of the Thracian sunset out to the sapphire Sea of Marmara. The central dome covered a circle 108 feet in diameter and soared to 180 feet at its apex above the ground; the interior floors, walls and columns were a kaleidoscope of colours – veined and speckled marbles of purple, green, white, black and yellow, quarried from all over the Empire. The ceiling was a blaze of golden mosaic. Even Procopius, who wrote explicitly to magnify Justinian's many achievements, struggled to explain or adequately convey the scale, beauty and opulence of the church that had risen in the Imperial capital,

The Chi-Rho monogram at Phillack Church.

declaring it 'impossible accurately to describe the gold, and silver, and gems' with which its interior was smothered.[27] Nor was Hagia Sophia alone in its grandeur or ambition. Where Tintagel had a well, Constantinople had Justinian's Basilica Cistern, a vast subterranean water-tank whose thirty-foot-high ceiling is supported by 336 marble columns; where Tintagel had a defensive bank and ditch, Constantinople had a double line of stone walls behind a floodable moat that ran for four miles between the Sea of Marmara and the Golden Horn. These walls, constructed in the fifth century by the Emperor Theodosius, were punctuated by ninety-six towers that rose to a height of more than sixty feet above the approach to the city.

I make this comparison not to do the Dumnonians down, but to emphasize why it may have been that people living on the far fringes of the most far-flung provinces of the Roman Empire continued, despite the collapse of Roman rule, to look east for inspiration. Despite the changes that were roiling western Europe, for many communities – especially those more insulated by geography from the newer fashions and modes of social and political organization that were moving in from northern Germania and Scandinavia – the eastern Empire remained a shining beacon of learning, Christianity, power, kingship, wealth and artistic expression. It was perhaps inevitable that the potentates of southwest Britain would seek consciously to ape the culinary, religious and perhaps even 'urban' habits of the eastern Mediterranean – to model their own little realms on the glories of distant Byzantium.

What exactly the eastern Roman Empire or its intermediaries wanted with Britain's southwestern peninsula is another matter. The common assumption is that they were after tin. The rare metal is an essential component in bronze production, and Cornwall's natural deposits of it were exploited throughout the Roman period. Limited evidence suggests that it was still being mined as a commodity in the post-Roman period as well: ingots of the stuff have been found at Praa Sands and Par Beach in

Cornwall and the Erme Estuary in Devon – all in late/post-Roman settings. It is also possible, of course, that there were other reasons to perpetuate the relationship. Justinian in particular expended a great deal of energy on restoring Roman (Byzantine) rule in the western Mediterranean, and it is no great stretch to imagine that he envisaged an even wider Imperium. While it seems there was never any attempt to reimpose direct Roman rule in these former provinces, efforts to fold far-flung Christian communities into a dependent relationship with the resurgent Empire are entirely conceivable.

To imagine how this might have worked, it can be useful to think of how the cultural and economic heft of the USA was applied to further American interests around the world in the twentieth century. Where the Americans had Mickey Mouse and Coca-Cola, the Byzantines had Χριστος and olive oil. The sense that these things were important and desirable and marked out those who owned or understood them as more impressive than their peers might well have been similar. Such social and political advantage, however, can only be maintained through continued access to the cultural and economic products of the producer. For small states this generally means compliance with the wider agenda (whether political, economic or military) of the mightier empire, and there are many reasons why – one might speculate – a diplomatic toehold between northwest Gaul and the Irish Sea might have seemed appealing to an ambitious Byzantine regime. On the other side of the equation, the perception of being in communion with the distant Emperors of Constantinople would have done wonders for the standing of local Dumnonian elites, even if the reality of these relationships were transactional and decidedly unequal. Flaunting those connections by making devotion to exotic saints and feasting from African tableware was a way of turning long-distance trade and diplomacy into local prestige. Controlling the proceeds of that trade and access to its products, meanwhile, handed local rulers the levers of raw political power: patronage and exclusion, punishment and reward.

All of this, however, was precariously constructed; it was a Jenga tower of political arrangements and cultural aspirations built on exotic imports and contacts maintained over easily disrupted maritime trade routes – all at a time when the rest of Britain was busy transforming itself: culturally, linguistically, politically, economically. In the face of this reality, Byzantine *Romanitas* was always going to be difficult to sustain, and quite how 'Roman' the lords of Dumnonia might have appeared to the cosmopolitan elites of Constantinople is doubtful. This, in part, is what Gildas seems to have been getting at in his unflattering portrait of the Dumnonian king – that there was something still a bit provincial, a bit rough, about Constantine. He was a violent man who liked the company of other violent men – an image of those kings who, to Gildas' dismay, 'despise the harmless and humble, but exalt to the stars [...] their military companions, bloody, proud and murderous men'.*[28] Constantine may have aspired to Christ and nobility, Gildas seems to say, but at heart he was still just a warlord, still a barbarian.

With that said, it is unlikely that the opinions of men like Gildas did much to blunt the aspirations of the 'tyrant' Constantine. If the king allowed himself to dream, he dreamed of Rome and distant Constantinople. Whatever the distortions and limitations imposed by the reality of British life, in his own mind he was a Roman, and he hoped – expected even – that others would see him the same way. He was not alone.

Mên Scryfa stands alone on the high moorland above Penzance (Cornwall), one standing stone in a region thronged with standing stones – a monolith among megaliths. Within a radius of a few

---

* A brief cameo appearance from precisely such a figure features in the Breton life of St Samson of Dol who lived around the time of Gildas. The saint, travelling through Dumnonia on his way from Dyfed to Brittany, ran into a local tough called Vedianus (*Guedianus*) and his warband (*exercitus*) worshipping an idol of some kind on a hill in Trigg (northeast Cornwall).

Mên Scryfa, photographed in the late-nineteenth
or early twentieth-century.

hundred yards stand the Nine Maidens, a circle of stones that folklore claims was formed by women petrified for dancing on the
Sabbath. In the other direction there is the stone tripod of Lanyon
Quoit, sprouting from the ground like an alien mushroom – the
skeleton of a long defleshed burial chamber, now exposed to the
lichen and the scouring wind. There are the bared lithic guts of
Bosiliack Barrow, lying like an open sore on the moorland grass.
There is the fantastically strange Mên-an-Tol, a tumbled play-
ground for the children of giants. The weird, doughnut-shaped
Crick Stone at its heart was once used to pass goblin changelings
back to their kin in return for stolen human children, or to rid children of their ailments, or for women to climb through in a bid for
fertility, or to channel answers through a brass pin placed upon the
stone.

In such a setting, Mên Scryfa – a tall, solitary finger of undressed stone – is of no great consequence; just a lonely wanderer lost between the many little knots of other stones in friendly congress. Or, it would be, if it had not been picked out – probably in the sixth century – to be marked.* Running down its flank in degenerate Roman capitals is carved an inscription to the memory of Rialobranus son of Cunovalus: or, to give their names in their Brittonic, non-Romanized forms, *Rigalo-branos* ('kingly raven') son of *Cuno-ualos* ('valiant as a hound').[29] This is the only place where the names of these two men were recorded, incised into what is very probably a monument erected in deep prehistory – a way to bring the present of the stonemason into a dialogue with the unchanging bones of the Cornish landscape. It is one of hundreds of similarly inscribed stones, carved between 400 and 1100, that litter the Celtic-language regions of Britain. Of those found in England, the vast majority are located in the southwest peninsula – thirty-seven in Cornwall and eleven in Devon – and date to the years between 400 and 800. They bear witness to the obscure personnel who were considered worth remembering in the lost kingdom of Dumnonia.

They also bear witness to a determined tradition in the west of Britain to retain – or in many cases adopt – a way of commemorating individuals that has its roots in Roman funerary tradition. Some, at least, of these inscribed stones were grave markers, though many of them – if not most – have been moved from their original locations (though not, perhaps, Mên Scryfa). Some, in fact, contain the Latin formula *hic iacet* ('here lies') and around half are associated with churchyards – possibly indicating the seeds of early Christian sites.† They are also frequently associated with higher-status settle-

---

* Accurately dating the inscriptions made across Britain in the centuries between 400 and 1100 is a notoriously vexed process. In the case of Mên Scryfa, the two most widely cited authorities provide dates with very different confidence intervals: 533–566 (Charles Thomas); 500–800 (Elizabeth Okasha).

† Others, perhaps later, are sometimes positioned at territorial boundaries and may have been intended to mark land ownership.

ments that, like Tintagel, had their roots in prehistory and the Roman period but which continued in occupation through the fifth and sixth centuries: places like Killibury and Chun Castle in Cornwall and High Peak in Devon. In other words, beyond Tintagel, Dumnonia had an elite class who could sustain themselves in greater style and security than most – people for whom literacy, Christianity and Mediterranean imports were markers of their class.

Nevertheless, as elsewhere in Britain, the adopted *Romanitas* of the Dumnonians was superimposed on the traces of a deeper and older antiquity – onto the hill-forts of ages past, or behind the still impressive dry-stone walls of the 2,500-year-old Chun Castle, their names and symbols of faith scored into menhirs of the Bronze Age. Theirs was a sense of identity more complex than ethnic labels can compass, filtered through the prism of their lived experiences, the coarse grass and red-grey stone and choppy sea, and the received traditions of their ancestors. It was also an identity muddled by influences from elsewhere. Six of the inscribed stones of Cornwall and Devon carry legends written, not in debased Roman capitals, but in ogham: the curious vertical hatched alphabet of the Irish.

Thanks largely to the speculative reconstructions of Robert Graves in his imaginatively stimulating (but utterly discredited) book of 1948, *The White Goddess*, ogham has come to be viewed as a magical language of tree-signs and profound hidden lore: the cryptic preserve of bards and druids. Modern scholarship, however, though opinion remains divided regarding the antiquity of the script, has now pretty firmly settled on the view that ogham developed as an innovative but entirely practical means of expressing the sounds of the Irish language in written form – almost certainly inspired and influenced by the widespread use of the Roman alphabet in neighbouring Britain.

It was once believed that the presence of ogham inscriptions in Dumnonia – as in Dyfed on the opposite side of the Bristol Channel – was proof of an Irish colonial influence in parts of western Britain: part of a formerly prevailing view that novel cultural phenomena could only ever be accounted for by hordes of invading barbarians hoving into view and taking everything over. Such a scenario (known as 'invasion hypothesis') is no longer considered particularly likely in Cornwall given the long continuities of occupation generally observed at the archaeological level. What the presence of ogham does make plain, however, is that, in this – as in every other – period, people were moving freely between western Britain and Ireland, bringing their ideas and their innovations with them. Thus the Mediterranean was evidently not the only sea to which the Dumnonian realm was attuned: the Irish Sea in the early Middle Ages was a great crucible of art, religion and ethnicity. These contacts were not forgotten. As the case of St Ia illustrates, by the later Middle Ages the people of Cornwall had come to imagine their huge cast of local saints as migrants – from Ireland in particular – even though the stories that were told of their origins seem often to have been a product of the impressive medieval capacity for imaginative hogwash.

Ireland, however, was not the only – or even the most important – transmarine neighbour with whom the Dumnonians forged a connection. At the other end of Cornwall from Mên Scryfa, beside a quiet country road near the town of Fowey on Cornwall's southern coast, stands another inscribed monolith. It bears a Latin inscription of (probably) the sixth century, incised in worn capitals that run vertically down one face. The latter part of it reads '[…] HIC IACIT CVNOMORI FILIVS': a memorial to the son of Cunomorus.*[30] 'Cunomorus' is a name to conjure with. It is a

---

* Correctly interpreting the first part of the inscription – the name of the son of Cunomorus – is difficult and controversial. It has long been believed that the difficult to decipher name at the head of the inscription should be read as DRUSTANUS, an interpretation that depends on accepting the reversal of the first and seventh characters and the ligation of the latter with the preceding 'A'. 'Drustan' or 'Drust' is a Pictish name, shared by a number of Pictish kings and ecclesiastics (including St Drostan who supposedly lived around the year 600 and founded the monastery of Old Deer in Aberdeenshire). It is also the original form of the name 'Tristan', giving the stone its popular name (the 'Tristan Stone') and linking it via a complex

Latinized form of a native British name, a name rendered in Welsh as *Cynfawr* – the 'Great Hound' or 'Sea Dog'. A fellow called *Kynfa6r cat caduc* (Cynfawr 'battle-fog'), for example, is referred to in the Triads as one of the 'Three Bull-Protectors' of the island of Britain, and a number of Welsh genealogies also contain the same name.*[31] One particularly late genealogy that purportedly lists the descent of the Dumnonian kings includes a figure called *Kynwawr* (presumed to be a mangling of *Kynfa6r* – 'Cynfawr') who was imagined to be the son of the tyrant Constantine (the king so unbeloved by Gildas).

Aside from the person memorialized on the Cunomorus stone, the man bearing this name who has the greatest claim to historical reality is a sixth-century Breton count who was remembered in folklore as 'Conomor the Cursed'. His existence is attested to by Bishop Gregory of Tours (539–594) in his 'History of the Franks' (*Historia Francorum*), a dense accounting of the deeds of the kings, nobles and churchmen of Merovingian Gaul. There Conomor appears as a bit player in Breton power-politics, involved in an improbable story about hiding another Breton noble inside a tumulus in order to fool his relatives into thinking he was dead.[32] The story of Conomor was fleshed out and embellished, however, in a constellation of Breton hagiographies of the ninth century and later.† In these, and in later folklore derived from them, Conomor became a monster – a count of Carhaix with a penchant for murder and the brutalization of his wives.‡[33] In these fables he was defeated,

---

chain of literary and hagiographical coincidence to the legend of Tristan, Iseult and King Mark of Cornwall. This connection seems, however, to have now been exploded by the discovery through 3D imaging that the initial letter is not a reversed D, but a C and a separate letter I. The name thus transliterates as CIRVSINIVS, an otherwise unattested name of uncertain origin. So much for Tristan, but see p. 169 for King Mark.

* Both Urien and Gwallog were also named as 'Bull-Protectors'; see **ELMET**, and **RHEGED**.

† St Tugdal, St Samson of Dol, St Gildas, St Paul Aurelian.

‡ Conomor is the most likely candidate for the figure behind the Bluebeard legend.

ultimately, by saintly adversaries – led, in a neat twist, by our old friend Gildas (now St Gildas), who by this time had supposedly relocated from Wales to Brittany.

The saints' lives that established Conomor's bad reputation reveal a later tradition that saw the origins of Breton church culture in a migration of monks and evangelists like Gildas from western Britain in the fifth and sixth centuries. Some were explicitly connected to Dumnonia: St Winwaloe, for example, was thought by the ninth century to be the son of a Dumnonian prince named Fagan who had fled his native land in the fifth century to avoid the plague. According to Winwaloe's hagiographer, Wrdestin, the saint lived his life engaged in holy work throughout Brittany and died at the monastery he founded at Landévennec in 532.[34] His memory, however, transcended Brittany, and numerous church dedications to Winwaloe can be found across Cornwall and Devon.* Like the parallel Cornish tradition (which claimed Irish origins for Cornish saints) there are few good reasons to take the hagiography at face value. But, as also with the Cornish tradition, the memory of cultural discourse across the Celtic Sea may speak to a deeper truth. In the case of Brittany and Dumnonia, that truth is one of deep-rooted interconnection.

Brittany is, quite literally, the 'land of the Britons', and its language, place-names and religious traditions make it certain that Breton identity was formed as a result of substantial migration from southwest Britain into northwestern Gaul at some point in the early post-Roman period. Most tellingly, the Breton regions of 'Domnonée' and 'Cornouaille' are straightforward duplications of 'Dumnonia' and 'Cornwall'. The onomastic similarity is even more marked in their respective Celtic languages (for example, 'Cornouaille' in Breton is *Kerne* and 'Cornwall' in Cornish is *Kernow*); indeed, Cornish is the Celtic language to which Breton has the closest relationship. What is not known is how or why this

---

* At Gunwalloe, Landewednack, Poundstock and Tremaine (Cornwall) and East Portlemouth (Devon) as well as others in Wales, now lost.

situation came about or any detailed sense of the social, political or economic relationships between the two regions. The only sources that purport to shed any light on these matters are the later saints' lives and these – it bears repeating – are duff evidence for the fifth and sixth centuries, given to wild flights of the imagination.

That said, sometimes the hints they provide are tantalizing: the life of St Paul Aurelian, for example, written in 884 by a Breton monk from Landévennec called Wrmonoc, refers to a British ruler called 'Quonomorius' (Cunomorus), describing him as a mighty ruler with dominion over 'peoples of four languages'. It is tempting to imagine – as many have – that what Wrmonoc captured was the memory of a king identical with the Cunomorus of the Dumnonian inscription, the Cynfawr of Welsh tradition and the undoubtedly historical Count Conomor of the Breton coast: a 'Sea Dog' whose rule extended from the cliff tops of Cornwall to the forests of Cornouaille.* Sadly, in reality there is no good reason to assume that every instance of the name Cunomorus/Cynfawr/Conomor refers to the same sixth-century figure and it is, in any case, pretty unclear whom Wrmonoc thought he was talking about or where he imagined this Quonomorius ruled (it is also worth noting that the reference to 'peoples of four languages' is cribbed from Bede and may just be a learned shorthand for 'powerful dude').

Doubts will always linger about the various traditions of men named Cunomorus/Cynfawr/Conomor and their vexed relationship with historical reality. And, in many ways, trying to pin them down is a fool's errand. But opening the lid on this stuff does bring into (soft) focus something about Dumnonia that is worth emphasizing: that instead of thinking of the peninsula as a remote appendage to the backside of Britain, the kingdom might be better imagined as an island of its own, perched between the Irish Sea and

---

* Wrnmonoc's life of St Paul Aurelian also refers to a king called Marcus *quem alio nomine Quonomorium vocant* ('whom by another name they call Quonomorius'), a line that has led some to connect Conomor, Cunomorus and Cynfawr with the King Mark of Cornwall who appears in the legend of Tristan and Iseult.

the coastline of northern Gaul: a kingdom of the sea-lanes and the trade winds, set apart from the barbarian antics of the eastern lowlands from which it was severed by high moorlands and dense woodlands – a realm with far more in common with the people of Brittany and Wales and Ireland than with its English-speaking neighbours; and maybe, just possibly, however fleetingly, a little empire of its own.

Dumnonia faded from view in the seventh century, and almost nothing is known of its later kings. A great cornucopia of names survives in late genealogies and folklore, but assessing their historicity is largely impossible. All of them – including Cunomorus/Cynfawr/Conomor – are dubious. A stone inscribed to a man possibly named *Cumregnus* (roughly translatable as 'with royal power') may suggest someone with at least adjacency to kingship, as might Mên Scryfa, the stone dedicated to a chap called Ri(g)alobranus, whose name seems to incorporate a form of the Celtic word for 'king' (*ri/rig/rix*); another inscription, at Sourton in Devon, alludes to a *princeps* ('prince') called Iuriucus.[35] But who these people were or how their titles translated to real power or social status is unknowable. It is clear, however, that something was happening to Dumnonian society. For one thing, the importation of prestige goods dried up as the seventh century wore on, and by 700 the greater settlements – Tintagel included – had been abandoned. 'Rounds' – the distinctive defensible Cornish settlements – were in decline from the end of the sixth century and they, too, were largely abandoned over the course of the seventh century; in some places the farmland associated with them was abandoned, and new unenclosed settlements began to appear in different locations. (It was this period that saw the origin of the modern towns and villages of Cornwall and their characteristic *Tre-* names; *tre* meaning 'settlement'.)

The impression, overall, is of a society and an economy contracting, of an elite stratum that could no longer support itself in the style to which it had once been accustomed, nor maintain the economic surplus that large-scale defended settlements required. There were, it seems, fewer people in general – an increasingly impoverished realm with a greatly diminished capacity to resist the unwanted advances of its neighbours – whether these were cultural or military in nature. In the mid-seventh century, the *Anglo-Saxon Chronicle* records a series of assaults mounted by the kings of the *Gewissae* (the West Saxons) against their British neighbours to the west. In 658, King Cenwalh fought the Britons (*wealas*) at a place called *Peonnum* 'and drove them in flight as far as the [River] Parret' in Somerset.[36] Although Peonnum is not identifiable, it was very probably to the east of the Parret, and it seems likely that Cenwalh's advance involved a territorial annexation of land that had formerly fallen within the Dumnonian – or at least a 'British' – sphere of influence.* Three years later, Cenwalh fought the Britons again – this time at a place called Posent's stronghold *Posentesbyrig*).†[37] In 682, Cenwalh's successor Centwine was again putting Britons to flight, this time 'as far as the sea' (the *Anglo-Saxon Chronicle*, rather typically, fails to specify which one).[38] Geographical inexactitude aside, the broad picture is of a confident, expanding West Saxon realm that was banging – with increasing insistence though without any obvious agenda – against the Dumnonian back door.

Indeed, by the 680s it would seem that parts of Devon had already become Anglicized to a greater or lesser degree. Writing in around 765, the English missionary Willibald wrote a life of his predecessor, Wynfrith (aka St Boniface, *c.*675–754). According to

---

* *Peonnum* might be Penselwood, part of the great Selwood forest that once separated much of the territory that lay south of the Bristol Channel from the lands of the West Saxons to the east. Its significance as a boundary was preserved in the county lines that divide Somerset and Dorset from Wiltshire. However, Peonnum has also been associated with Pinhoe near Exeter and Penn near Yeovil. The name is derived from *Pen*, a Celtic word meaning 'head' – often in the context of a hill or headland.

† This could be Posbury in Devon, but equally well might be somewhere else.

Willibald, Wynfrith (which is an English name) was noviced in childhood to a monastery in Exeter that was at the time run by an abbot named Wulfheard (also an English name). Certain place-name forms in central and eastern Devon likewise suggest a degree of linguistic change around the same time. Nevertheless, Dumnonia as a political entity evidently still survived, as is made clear by two letters written by the West Saxon abbot Aldhelm at the end of the seventh century.

Aldhelm (*c.*639–709) was abbot of Malmesbury (Wiltshire) and, from 705, the first bishop 'west of the wood'. This 'wood' was Selwood forest and the episcopal see was Sherborne (Dorset) in the kingdom of the *Gewissae*. As such, he lived his life in a region that bordered on – and, in the case of his bishopric, was conceivably carved out of – the kingdom of Dumnonia. He is famous for his literary output, written in high-flown and difficult Latin, which included prose treatises, poetry, riddles (*enigmata*) and letters. He was a fascinating character – curious, learned, pompous and a brilliant writer; he was venerated as a saint after his death. He is also one of the only English writers to have directly concerned himself with the affairs of Britain's southwest peninsula in the early Middle Ages.

On one occasion Aldhelm wrote (in verse) to a fellow named Helmgisl about a miserable expedition he undertook to apparently 'dire Dumnonia' and through 'Cornubia' (Cornwall), a land 'lacking turves and prolific grasses'.[39] En route he experienced a devastating storm that tore the roof from the church in which he spent a night, describing his experience in apocalyptic terms ('Lightning bolts blaze, Widely through the heights of heaven, When their suspended jagged tips, Belch pallid flame'). On a separate occasion, while he was still abbot of Malmesbury, Aldhelm wrote to *Geruntius* (Geraint), king of Dumnonia, the only king other than the tyrant Constantine for whom any contemporary evidence exists. The content, for anyone already familiar with Bede's bugbears, follows a familiar track, consisting of a long and elaborately worded complaint about how the British clergy of the southwest don't do their tonsures properly and celebrate Easter on the wrong day.

What these letters reveal is that, whatever religious differences persisted, direct lines of high-level communication between Dumnonia and Wessex were open and that, on at least one occasion, a West Saxon abbot travelled as far as Cornwall on what may well have been a diplomatic errand. Certainly it seems that Aldhelm and Geraint had a personal rapport of some kind: the latter bestowed a grant of land at Maker in east Cornwall to the church at Sherborne – probably after 705 when Aldhelm became its first bishop. Nevertheless friction remained very much in the air. One year after Aldhelm's death in 709, Wessex and Dumnonia were at war again, the West Saxon king Ine taking the South Saxon king Nunna with him to fight 'against Geraint, king of the Britons [*wealas*]'.

King Ine of Wessex (r.688–726) is remembered as sponsor of the earliest English sets of laws to have survived outside Kent (appended to King Alfred's own law codes of the 890s). Among much else of interest, they reveal a society willing to discriminate directly on the basis of ethnicity. *Wergild* (lit. 'man-payment') was the price set by law as the level of compensation required to avoid a feud with a slain individual's family. Whilst the lowest free-born Englishman (the law code uses the terms *Englisc* and *Engliscmon*) had a wergild of 200 shillings, the lowest free-born *Wyliscmon* ('Briton', lit. 'Welshman') had a wergild of only 60 shillings. The lives of Britons in Wessex were literally worth less than their English neighbours of equivalent class. Nor was their word worth much more – the value of a Briton's oath (a measure of how much weight legal testimony carried) was only half as valuable as an Englishman's of comparable status. Ine's Wessex thus had the hallmarks of a segregated society, with all the injustice and degradation such arrangements imply. Under such circumstances, the pressure to jettison 'British' identity must have been intense and – unlike in the southern United States under Jim Crow – relatively easy to achieve outwardly.

One of the most tangible results of laws like these was linguistic. While Celtic place-names are ubiquitous west of the River

Tamar, the place-names of Devon (with the exception of a small pocket in the north of the county which probably reflects a historic change to the county boundary) are almost uniformly Old English in origin. It is an apparent ethnic watershed of unusual and startling definition – the product of centuries of linguistic attrition in a part of Dumnonia that found itself firmly and formally within the bounds of the 'English' West Saxon realm. The people of Devon were subject to direct political and cultural pressures to abandon old identities. In Cornwall, by contrast, that pressure was barely felt, and the region's landscape still resounds with *llan* ('church enclosure') and *bod* ('dwelling'), *pen* ('head') and *pol* ('creek').

Resistance to Englishness rumbled on in Cornwall. The Welsh annals record a battle of 722 at an unidentified place called *Hehil* 'amongst the Cornish' (*apud Cornuenses*),[40] and almost a century later the West Saxon king Ecgberht was moved to ravage the western Britons (presumably in Cornwall) *easteweardum op westewearde* ('from east to west'). Ten years later, in 825, the Cornish 'Britons' (*Weala*) were fighting the men of Devon (*Defna*) at *Gafulforda*, a conflict that neatly demonstrates how a century or more of cultural assimilation had sundered the kinship of *Defna* and *Weala* beyond repair.[41] The place-name means the 'ford of tribute' and it seems very likely that the conflict erupted at a border location established as a checkpoint or customs post – a place where tribute might be rendered by one side to the other: a natural location for trouble to break out. If so, it would undoubtedly have been the Cornish realm – not the increasingly mighty West Saxon kingdom – that found itself extorted and aggrieved.

Cornish resistance had one more throw of the dice – or, at least, one more than anyone saw fit to remember. In 838, a Viking fleet arrived in Cornwall and made common cause with the locals against the West Saxon king. Ecgberht met their combined army at a hill near the Tamar known (to English speakers) as *Hengestesdun* and put them to flight: the last known conflict between the English and the Cornish.*[42] Even this apparently decisive victory, however, did not lead to outright conquest of the peninsula. Indeed, as late as 875 the Cornish still had their own king. Dungarth, *rex Cerniu* ('king of Cornwall'), was drowned in 875 – punishment, according to the Irish Chronicles, for making further intrigues with the Vikings. Dungarth was the last Cornish king to be heard of. Thereafter West Saxon kings seemed able to act with unmitigated authority in Cornwall. Alfred (r.871–899) roamed around hunting in the region at some point before he became king, and he also owned estates in Trigg and elsewhere.[43] He also made his biographer Asser, Bishop of Exeter, 'with all the territory that belonged to it in England and in Cornwall'. Alfred's son, Edward, for his part, created the see of Crediton.[44] Its first bishop, Eadwulf, was instructed, every year, to 'visit the Cornish people, to stamp out their errors'.[45]

Nevertheless, although the political direction had been set, Cornwall never really lost its sense of difference, its vestigial independence, its ethnic alienation. In his letter to Helmgisl, Aldhelm wrote of the storm that harried his progress in terms that will feel recognizable to anyone who has ever been dealt a harsh hand of weather in the southwest: 'Thus did the sea swell with harsh, Blowings of winds, Dashing with blasts against, Rocky shores'.[46] The words presaged the fate of Dumnonia: a realm that was eroded, not conquered, worried away at until only the Cornish stump remained. The golden vision dimmed and the stormclouds rolled in, driving a hard tide that battered and stripped the mantle from the bone. But somehow, coded in folklore and swaddled in linguistic survival and revival, the memory remained.

---

* Probably Kit Hill near Callington in the valley of the River Tamar.

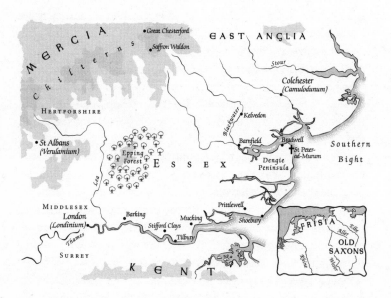

ESSEX

– *Essex and Middlesex* –

'… and I forsake all the Devil's works and words,
Thunor and Woden and Seaxnot and all those demons
who are their followers'

Anon., *Abrenuntiatio Diaboli* (eighth–ninth century)[1]

Grounded and earthed.

On the northern horn of the Dengie peninsula, between the Blackwater to the north and the southern most point of the North Sea as it tapers towards Southern Bight and the Strait of Dover, the decommissioned nuclear power station at Bradwell-on-Sea (1962–2002) lurks in quiescent malignity. Its brutal concrete aspect is now mummified in strange, corrugated cladding – the waste it generated entombed inside for a hundred years to come, shedding its lethal properties back to the earth and air and water as the unstable elements decay. In the meantime, a new and vastly expanded power station will (if ultimately authorized), rise beside it: 'Bradwell B' – a place, with its planned domes and plazas and pilastered basilicae, that will embody an oddly retro-futurist aesthetic, like the neo-Byzantine fantasies of the Trigan Empire or the streets of 'Germania', Albert Speer's unrealized Nazi utopia.* It threatens a social and environmental catastrophe with impacts that will long outlive anyone who sees it built.[2]

Just out of view, however, across the windswept flatlands of Dengie, at the end of a lane to nowhere, a very different building stands beside the sea, a rude and rectilinear stone hall, a simple pitched roof lidding a box of ancient masonry. It is a strangely forlorn place, the literal end of the road; only sea and sky lie beyond it. This is the church of St Peter-ad-Murum – St Peter-on-the-wall – a church that was first raised in the seventh century and which remains, albeit in mutilated form, one of the oldest standing buildings in Britain and one that, remarkably enough, still fulfils today the function for which it was originally intended. It was built upon the gatehouse foundations of a Roman fort called *Othona* that once stood here, most of which has since been claimed by the sea. Othona was one of the so-called 'Saxon Shore Forts', a chain of fortifications along the south and east coasts of England built in the fourth century – probably for the purpose of defending the Roman province against invasion, piracy or simple migration by (amongst others) a people whose origins were to be found in northern Germany, between the rivers Elbe and Weser – the land of the 'Old Saxons'.†

The fortresses of the coast ultimately failed to keep Saxon migrants away from Britain, to confine them beyond the limiting waves that chew year by year on the Saxon Shore. Indeed, they came in such numbers during the fourth, fifth and sixth centuries – or the weight of their cultural influence and communal memory was so strong – that they impressed themselves with forcible horror

---

* For those not familiar, *The Rise and Fall of the Trigan Empire* was a comic series published between 1965 and 1982. Its central premise revolved around a futuristic human/humanoid society set on the planet Elektron, whose dominant culture was directly modelled on the aesthetics and structures of the Roman Empire.

† See **SUSSEX** for fuller discussion of the 'Saxon Shore'.

on the imaginations of British writers like Gildas and ultimately renamed the very lands in which they settled in reference to their own identities: West Saxons, South Saxons, Middle Saxons and, in Essex, East Saxons. The local people who watched the church of St Peter rise were witnessing a new Christian chapter of their own history being constructed, quite literally, from the ruins of a system constructed to keep them out.

St Peter-ad-Murum has stood on the East Saxon coast for around 1,360 years, a witness to all the changes that this coastline has experienced over that vast span of time. It endures, squat and stalwart: a microcosm of all that the kingdom of Essex was – a realm built on the ruins of Roman civilization, whose Christianity was hard-won but lasting; a sentinel on the far shore of the sundering sea, looking back over its shoulder to the grey sea and the Old Saxon forests and a world left behind. This little church of St Peter saw 'Bradwell A' rise and will see it levelled. There is every chance that it will outlive its ill-begotten successor as well. It has changed over the centuries, its rounded apse shorn away, its side chapels amputated. And it has gone through a number of permutations of use that have weathered it to a thing of petrous solidity and gnarled longevity. In the words of Andrea-Renée Misler, writing about the lived experience of the nearby modern Christian community for whom St Peter's is the centre of worship, the church 'is simple, coarse, uncouth and rough. It was a monastery, a chapel-of-ease, a beacon, a lighthouse, a smuggler's hideaway for contraband, a barn and a billet. With this history one can assume that the Chapel is grounded and earthed.'[3]

At its greatest extent in the mid-seventh century, the East Saxon realm was far wider than the modern county that preserves its name. The county of Essex lay always at its heart, but at various times the kingdom also encompassed Middlesex (the land of the 'Middle Saxons'), the city of London, part of Surrey (*Sūþrīge* – the 'southern region' of the Middle Saxon land), and southeastern Hertfordshire. Even the kingdom of Kent lay, for a short time, under the shadow of East Saxon power. But although the kingdom at times verged on greatness, a contender for lasting stature among the realms of the English, the East Saxon kings were rarely free from interference, their strength waxing and waning with the fortunes of neighbouring powers and the fractures of internal division. Ultimately the kingdom of Essex dwindled, its people battered by war and pestilence, its lands carved off in great chunks by its neighbours, hemmed in by greed and the pounding waves of the grey ocean. But its legacy lives on – not least in London, the great city that East Saxon power kept on life support through the centuries of its dormancy. And somewhere behind it all dwells the dim memory of German forests and forsaken gods, receding into the impenetrable thickets of European prehistory.

The little church of St Peter long outlived the kingdom in which it was built. But it survives as a reminder, an anchor for the kingdom that was, and the land that remains; of a land stalked by proud ghosts.

Grounded and earthed.

'If any one of the race of the Saxons hereafter concealed among them shall have wished to hide himself unbaptized, and shall have scorned to come to baptism and shall have wished to remain a pagan, let him be punished by death.'[4]

This is the uncompromising message of Charlemagne's *Capitulatio de partibus Saxoniae*, a set of laws issued in the years between 782 and 785 at the height of the Frankish king's conflict against the pagan Saxons – a people who dwelt for the most part between the rivers Weser and Elbe. The context for this particular provision can be found in the exceptional violence that had accompanied Charlemagne's efforts to bring the Saxons into the Frankish Empire. In 782, a Frankish army had been defeated by Saxons led by the warlord Widukind and at least twenty-seven Frankish noblemen had been killed. 'When he heard this,' the *Royal Frankish Annals* explain, 'the Lord King Charles rushed to the place with all the Franks that he could gather on short notice and advanced to where the Aller flows into the Weser. Then all the Saxons came together again, submitted to the authority of the Lord King, and surrendered the evildoers who were chiefly responsible for this revolt to be put to death – four thousand and five hundred of them. This sentence was carried out.[5] For a people plainly reluctant to give up their independence and their traditional beliefs this was a bloody baptism.

Charlemagne's war had, from the outset, a markedly religious complexion. Resistance to his rule and resistance to his religion were inextricably bound. Although the brutality of the *Capitulatio* was alleviated to some degree at the end of the eighth century, once the Saxon wars were won, the pressure to convert and renounce the old ways remained. A remarkable set of vows which survived in a monastery at Mainz (Germany) is now preserved in the Vatican Library. Known as the 'Old Saxon Baptismal Vow', or *Abrenuntiatio Diaboli* ('the renunciation of the Devil'), the document records, in a ninth-century hand but an eighth-century voice, the words that the Saxon convert was required to utter in his initiation to Christian life. They are written in a mixture of Latin and a Low German dialect that has close affinities with Old Frisian, Old Low German and Old English. Clauses four to six deal with the things that the Saxons *should* believe in: God the Father (IV), Christ the Son of God (V), the Holy Spirit (VI). The first three, however, are more concerned with those entities that the convert should *not* have further dealings with:

I. *Forsachistu diobolae?*
('Do you forsake the devil?')

& respondeat. Ec forsacho diabolae.
('and he/she responds: I forsake the devil.')

II. *end allum diobolgelde?*
('and all devil-worship?')

respondeat. End ec forsacho allum diobolgeldae.

('he/she responds: and I forsake all devil-worship.')

III. *end allum dioboles uuercum?*
('and all the devil's works?')

respondeat. End ec forsacho allum dioboles uuercum and uuordum,
Thunaer ende Uoden ende Saxnote ende allum them unholdum, the
hira genotas sint.

('he/she responds: and I forsake all the Devil's works and words,
Thunor and Woden and Seaxnot and all those devils who are their
followers')

This document is chiefly remarkable for the fact that it preserves the
names of three gods who were known to the still pagan Saxons of
northern Germany at the moment of their conversion. That they
were recorded in words that undoubtedly originated from a native
speaker suggests that the vows were not anachronisms or learned
emanations from the mind of an educated ecclesiastic. They were
taken down by people who lived closer to the earth and the lived
experience of heathen folk, a record of names whispered in groves
and sanctuaries, invoked beneath the moon or in the first rays of the
sun, before the cutting of crops or the slaughter of livestock, at the
dawn of battle or at the birth of a child. Thunor and Woden are well
known in other texts of this and later ages, and across a fairly wide
geographical area; their names live with us in the days of the weeks
as Đunres-dæg ('Thursday') and *Wodnes-dæg* ('Wednesday'). And in
their Old Norse incarnations as Thor and Odin they have become an
ineradicable part of popular culture. Of the third god mentioned in
the *Abrenuntiatio*, however, there is nothing more to say except this:
of all the royal dynasties of the English-speaking realms of Britain,
only one claimed descent from a god other than Woden. That dynasty
ruled the kingdom of the East Saxons – the kingdom of Essex – and
the kings of Essex traced their line back to Seaxnot.[*6]

---

* The earliest surviving East Saxon genealogy probably dates to the late
ninth century.

Seaxnot (OE *Seaxnēat*) is a mysterious deity. All that can really be said of him is that his name implies a special significance to people who identified as 'Saxons' (OE *Seaxe*). Perhaps, as his appearance in genealogical lists implies, he was imagined to be a divine ancestor or tribal primogenitor. Both *Seaxnēat* and *Seaxe* are clearly derived from the same root – *Seax* – a word used to describe the long, single-bladed knife that was a distinctive accoutrement of the weapon-bearing dead in the early medieval inhumation graves of Britain and northern Europe. *Seax* probably has its origins in the ancient Indo-European term **sek* (meaning 'to cut'), and so the Saxons could be the 'people of the knife'. That would make Seaxnot an invented deity named after the people who worshipped him. On the other hand, the Saxons could be the 'people of Seaxnot', and Seaxnot could be a god whose name means something like 'knife-companion'. Interesting stuff, but not in itself very helpful; yet aside from his presence in the East Saxon genealogy, Seaxnot appears nowhere else in Old English literature or place-names – nowhere at all, in fact, before the *Abrenuntiatio* of *c*.800.

Whatever the exact nature of his role in the religious world-view of the East Saxons, Seaxnot's presence in the line of their kings demonstrates the migration of an idea. Somehow this obscure deity had made the North Sea crossing, arriving among the old Romano-British communities of the lower Thames. Nor was he the only god to do so: Woden and Thunor have both left their traces in the place-names of the Essex countryside. A 'field of Woden' (*Wodnesfeld*) near Widdington suggests an open space that was closely associated with that god, and four place-names are associated with Thunor, perhaps suggesting a more widespread cult of the thunder god in early Essex: *Thunreslau* (the 'tumulus of Thunor') at Bulmer, Thunderley and Thundersley (both 'the grove of Thunor') and, perhaps, Thurstable ('the pillar of Thunor').[7] Any of these might have been places of divine significance – the site of temples, perhaps, or features of the landscape where the god might be venerated somehow.

The presence of these names in Essex is just one strand of evidence that connects the early English communities of eastern Britain to an ancestral homeland in continental northern Europe. The apparent migration of gods and the vocabulary used to describe them implies that something of significance – some kernel of tradition – connected the Saxons of Britain to the Saxons of Germania; to the people who would ultimately be subjected to Charlemagne's rule and religion in the late eighth century. By that time, the East, West, South and Middle Saxons of Britain had been Christian for more than a century, and any sense of kinship between them and their distant ancestors had been stretched to breaking by time and distance and diverging custom. But the kings of Essex, at least, remembered Seaxnot; and the scribes of England – Bede first among them – preserved a tradition of descent from people who came to be known as the *Aldseaxe* – the 'Old Saxons' – in contradistinction to the pioneers of a new sort of British Saxondom.

Bede's view of immigration from continental Europe was – as we have seen – simplistic and schematic. Yet it is undeniable that migration was a major driver of social, cultural and linguistic change in many coastal regions of eastern Britain during the fifth and sixth centuries.[8] The people of Essex who may have remembered Woden, Thunor and Seaxnot in their fields, groves and family trees are in fact known to archaeology at a rare level of detail, and the hinterland of the Essex shore boasts some of the earliest evidence for substantial immigration in the early post-Roman period. Most famously, twin cemeteries that were in use between the late fifth and mid-seventh centuries – alongside a substantial settlement that remained in use until the eighth century – were discovered at a place called Mucking on the north bank of the Thames Estuary between 1965 and 1978. The excavations at Mucking remain the most extensive archaeological investigation ever conducted in Britain. By the time the dig concluded, the area surveyed covered almost 109 acres and the graves of more than 800 people and over 250 buildings had been found. Its many seasons of fieldwork provided a training ground for an entire generation of British archaeologists.[9]

The settlement at Mucking was composed of 203 sunken-featured buildings (SFBs), otherwise known as *Grubenhäuser*, and 53 'posthole buildings'. Sunken-featured buildings are slightly enigmatic structures whose characteristic mode of construction involved the digging of a shallow, flat-bottomed, excavation which was then covered with a gabled wooden roof supported on wooden posts. It seems most likely that they were used flexibly as store houses, ancillary dwellings and workshops and are a phenomenon found across northern Europe from the fifth century onwards. The other buildings are what in archaeological literature are sometimes referred to as 'halls': solidly constructed single-storey rectangular timber buildings whose walls bore the weight of the gabled roof (unlike SFBs, whose roofs rested on the ground, with pillars supporting the apex of the gable). The term hall implies something rather grand, but at Mucking these buildings were, for the most part, fairly modest. The largest measured a little over 40 feet in length, but the majority fell in a range between 25–35 feet – roughly analogous to the footprint of a medium-sized family home.

Of course, not all of the dwellings excavated at Mucking were inhabited simultaneously; the settlement appears to have been in use from the first half of the fifth century to around AD 700, and the settlement changed in extent, shape and location over this period. When considered in conjunction with the cemetery data, it would appear that the community at Mucking numbered only forty-five to fifty-six individuals per generation, inhabiting eight to ten 'posthole buildings' and making use of maybe fourteen SFBs at any one time. It was, in other words, a small hamlet of dwellings occupied by a handful of families who busied themselves working the land and engaging in small-scale craft production: exactly what one might imagine was a typical agrarian community of the lower Thames during the crucial period that followed the collapse of Roman authority in Britain; a place with the potential to reveal a great deal about who these people were – or at least who they thought they were.

Early medieval cemeteries are among the most exhaustively (and some might say exhaustingly) analysed resources in British archaeology. There are a number of reasons for this. The habit that some communities had between the fifth and eighth centuries of burying the dead with (and inside) material objects is chief among them, but the varied manner of burial and the location and organization of cemeteries are also major factors. The resulting complexity and variation in mortuary practice has created an enormously valuable and detailed body of data – data which, depending on how they are interrogated, can be asked to provide answers to a vast range of questions. The inferences that have been drawn, however, are not always: a) consistent with each other, b) susceptible to testing, or c) free from vigorous challenges from archaeologists invested in contradictory theoretical and methodological perspectives. In consequence, it can be hard to say anything at all about the archaeology of early medieval cemeteries that is neither controversial nor superficial.

Part of the problem is that dead people (accessed through their graves) and their communities (accessed through their cemeteries) embody all the same complexities and all the same tensions between the individual and the communal that define the lives and relationships of the living. Thus each grave is a unique construction that can be read as a profoundly individual statement: the presence (or absence) of 'grave goods' and the intent that lay behind the precise combination of objects in the grave and their treatment before burial, the decision made about the treatment of the body and the method of burial, the orientation of a grave, the presence (or absence) of above-ground structures and what that means; all of this says something about the specific deceased person and how he or she was regarded in the eyes of the living. Unpacking all of this can be enormously revealing about the human idiosyncrasy and agency that informed how the memory of an individual was constituted in the wake of his or her death.

At the same time, however, commonalities between different graves can show how, at a societal level, broader identities relating to age, gender, status, occupation and kinship were expressed in ways that could be commonly understood in local, regional and supra-regional terms. Classic examples include the ways in which the style of brooches worn by men and women seem to have indicated broad 'Anglian' or 'Saxon' identities that crossed the political boundaries of later kingdoms, or the way in which the presence of weapons functioned as an indicator of adulthood, gender and relative status within a community. The spatial relationship between graves can also indicate how kin-groups might have been organized and how status within them was publicly expressed. At the same time, the proximity of graves to other structures – contemporary, Roman, prehistoric – can reveal how people related to the past and the present and how a sense of community might extend in time as well as space, with the congregations of the dead acting as participants in communal life.[10]

Reconciling the personal with the communal dimensions of the dead is hard enough. But attempts to interpret cemetery data are made all the more difficult by the fact that the world of the dead acts as only the most imperfect mirror to the world of the living. A single grave may say something about how an individual was remembered by part of her community, but it may say very little about how the same person saw herself in life or how she was seen outside her own kin-group. Her burial in close proximity to others might imply membership of a particular community or association with a particular heritage, but it reveals nothing at all about the reality of private relationships or biological heredity – it only reveals the public claims staked by the living.

What was found at Mucking is typically puzzling. At first sight, the larger of the two cemeteries (Cemetery II) presents a relatively coherent picture of a thoroughly non-Christian community, suffused with foreign tastes and habits. Seven hundred and forty-five people were buried there, and 463 of them had been cremated. The bodies that were inhumed seem to have been positioned with little regard for their orientation. This is significant because it is typical in Christian burial practice to align bodies on a west–east axis, with head towards the west and feet towards the east.* Here, however, the dead (both cremated and buried) seem instead to have clustered around multiple focal graves – the oldest burials in the cemetery. These, presumably, were the founding graves of particular communities or kin-groups: ancestor figures for the families who made use of this burial ground beside the Thames. By contrast, the apparently smaller of the two cemeteries (Cemetery I) had been substantially destroyed by gravel digging and its original size can only be guessed at. It was found to be comprised exclusively of inhumation graves (sixty-four in total), carefully aligned (roughly west to east), although here, too, the graves seem to have clustered in what are likely kin-groups. The dead of both cemeteries were interred with grave goods.

The presence of two separate early cemeteries in the same place, with markedly different characteristics in their organization and composition, if not in their chronology and overall mix of inhumed grave goods, is not at all typical. Cremation, much more than burial with grave goods, can be construed as a demonstratively pagan and non-native manner of disposing of the dead, and the preponderance of cremation graves in Cemetery II implies the presence of significant numbers of non-Christians within the community – many of them likely migrants from northern Europe, judging by the nature of the cremation rite and the forms of pottery and jewellery interred with them. Identifying explicitly Christian burial is much harder, however. While west–east-oriented burial is consistent with Christian practice, it is not determinative: this way of organizing cemeteries had become customary across the late

---

* The reason for this was (and is) the belief that at Judgement Day – when the returning Christ appears in the east (Matthew 24:27) – the dead would exit their graves facing in the right direction.

Roman Empire and did not necessarily reveal much about the confessional preferences of the dead. Equally, the presence or absence of grave goods reveals nothing definite about the religion of the buried or the burier.* Thus the total absence of cremations from Cemetery I, and the orderly west–east orientation of graves, may say more about a divergent sense of communal origins than it does about divergent beliefs. It may be (and I stress that it really cannot be proven either way) that the people who used Cemetery I felt themselves heirs to a 'Romano-British' heritage (which may or may not have incorporated some element of Christian belief) in a way that the families who buried their dead in Cemetery II did not. The implications of this are made more interesting by the fact that the settlement at Mucking and its grave-fields were situated in close proximity to a Romano-British settlement complete with four cemeteries which, though in steep decline, may have continued in use into the fourth century.[11]

Attention has been drawn to two particular graves, notable for the quality of the artefacts present in them, their early date (420s–430s) and what they imply. Grave 117 in Cemetery I, for example, contained a famously elaborate example of a late Roman belt-set (*cingulum militare*) in the so-called 'quoit brooch style' – an early fifth-century flourish of a thoroughly late Roman artistic vocabulary. While the significance of the style itself is debatable, it is well established that belt-sets of this sort were a distinctive part of Roman military dress and carried connotation of elite authority ('look at my big belt'), coming to be associated with high-ranking civilian officials as well as soldiers. Their occurrence in graves of the

---

* Although burial with grave goods is often assumed to indicate pagan burial, it is actually from graves that much of the evidence for Christianity among seventh-century 'Anglo-Saxon' communities is drawn. The caveat to this, however, is that burial with objects of apparently Christian significance (crosses most obviously, but also fish motifs and settings of coins – Merovingian or Byzantine – displaying overtly Christian iconography) does not necessarily reveal very much about the deceased person's understanding of those objects and their meaning.

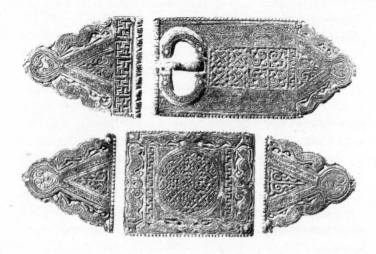

The belt-set from Grave 117, Mucking
(© The Trustees of the British Museum).

late fourth and fifth centuries – often outside the borders of the Empire – has sometimes been taken as an expression of male authority inculcated by proximity to the late Roman army (mainly by serving in it), or in emulation of its symbology.* Grave 979 in Cemetery II also contained a military belt-set (in plainer style) as well as a spear-head and a penannular brooch. None of this is specifically Saxon or even generically 'Germanic' – all of it is entirely consistent with expressions of late Roman military status across a broad region that encompassed parts of Britain and much of northern Gaul; the same is true of nearly all the inhumation graves dated to the fifth century.

* Graves containing these belt-sets are found in Britain, the Rhineland, in northern Gaul and in the Saxon homelands where they are sometimes found in association with female graves furnished in more typically local 'barbarian' style – leading to the suggestion that these men were returners from Roman military service, buried in proximity to their local wives and families. There are, however, numerous objections that can be made to this line of reasoning.

Since these are the earliest graves in the twin cemeteries, it is often assumed that their occupants were pioneers of the new settlement nearby and, therefore, that these men were leaders of an incoming community that no longer (or had never) followed the established practices of Roman Britain. Who they really were, however, is a matter of some debate. They might have been men, born overseas, who had adopted aspects of Roman militaria as a result of their own (or perhaps a family tradition of) military service before migrating to Britain – perhaps during the last knockings of Imperial rule. Or they could have been European mercenaries, hired by Romano-British rulers to help protect and police parts of the province in the absence of the legions (as Gildas described). Or – perhaps the most obvious solution – they might have been Romano-British locals (perhaps connected to the moribund local Romano-British community) who had struck out on a new course amid the collapse of urban and villa life. Their families perhaps felt the need to stress their status – and in particular their Roman military status – in a world that felt increasingly insecure and where very public displays were necessary to shore up local hierarchies and impress the neighbours.*[12]

Looking beyond these early graves, however, what is particularly striking about both cemeteries is the degree to which the fifth-century dead present a mixed and frankly confusing picture of communal identity during the Imperial hangover. There are people buried with objects that imply an attachment to late Roman status symbols interred in a late Roman manner; a few people buried in a more or less 'Roman' fashion but with decidedly non-Roman, northern European weapons and jewellery; and there are people buried with combinations of these or with nothing at all. Then, of

* In some individual circumstances it may be possible to identify a person's heredity or physical origins from their DNA or calcium isotopes (see, for example, **HWICCE** for the 'Gloucester Goth' and **SUSSEX** for isotope analysis). This, however, is not always possible, and frequently raises further imponderables. Ultimately, many of the questions which arise can only be answered by recourse to infinitely challengeable theoretical models.

course, there are those whose bodies were burned – incinerated on open-air funeral pyres in the manner typical of the non-Roman, pagan people of northwest Europe. The ashes of these people, alongside a range of both burned and unburned objects, were later interred inside the distinctive wheel-thrown pots so characteristic of early cremations in post-Roman Britain and whose earliest examples can be linked directly to methods of production and use in the Saxon homelands between the rivers Elbe and Weser. There can therefore be very little doubt that substantial numbers of those buried in the earliest generations of Cemetery II's use were migrants and the immediate descendants of migrants, even if many others were not. Perhaps the best that can be said overall is that the cemeteries at Mucking reflect a changing and changeable way of death among communities wrestling with the end of a dying social order, with an influx of foreign migrants, with disrupted religious and political certainties.

At one point in his *Historia Ecclesiastica*, Bede breaks off to tell a story about St Alban. Alban, who was a Roman citizen living in the British city of *Verulamium* (St Albans in Hertfordshire), is believed to have died in the third century. He was martyred, so it was said, for sheltering and then impersonating a Christian priest in order to shield him from persecution. Bede recorded the blackly comedic version that he was familiar with in the eighth century. According to this story, after decapitating the unfortunate Alban, the executioner's eyeballs plopped out of their sockets at the moment the martyr's severed head hit the turf. This was, Bede explains, a miracle intended to ensure the executioner would be disinclined to 'boast of his deed' (a divine intervention which, one imagines, was destined to be effective, at least in the short term).[13] More revealing is what Bede has to say about the later history of the site of Alban's death. 'Here,' Bede explained, 'when the peace of Christian times was restored, a beautiful church worthy of his martyrdom was built, where sick folk are healed and frequent miracles take place.'[14]

It is not entirely clear what Bede intended when he wrote that the church was built 'when the peace of Christian times was restored'. He might have meant when the Roman persecutions of Christians ended in the fourth century, or he might have meant after the conversions of pagan 'English' rulers in the seventh century. Happily, however, Bede is not the only source we have for the cult of Britain's first Christian martyr. The fifth-century *Vita Germani* (the life of St Germanus of Auxerre) describes a visit by St Germanus to the British 'shrine of the blessed martyr Alban', an episode which suggests (though not without some controversy among scholars) that a permanent memorial was already in existence by around 429.[15] It was apparently still there in the 730s when Bede was writing, though by that time Verulamium had come to be known as *Vaeclingacaestir* (the '[Roman] fortress of *Wæcla*'s people'). The archaeology of Roman Verulamium suggests that the Roman town was maintained to a standard that appears unusual in fifth-century Britain. Excavations there have found evidence for refurbished houses and piped water deep into that century – evidence consistent with an important place of pilgrimage and indicative of some limited continuity of life within the urban precinct.[16]

St Albans, in southern Hertfordshire, is at the outer limits of the region that would ultimately become the kingdom of Essex. It lay near the border of a region in which archaeological traces of settlement are sparse but place-name evidence implies the long-term survival of Celtic language speakers – prompting the suggestion that the *Cilternsaete* ('Chiltern-dwellers') recorded in the Tribal Hidage may reflect the survival of an independent and ethnically 'British' community until the late sixth century. It is not the only part of the region where these sorts of hold-outs have been suggested – similar Celtic place-name survival is recorded to the east of *Camulodunum* (Colchester, Essex).[17]

These pockets of possible ethnic separation aside, the geographical pattern of fifth-century settlement in Essex and Middlesex appears largely unchanged from the late Roman period, despite material changes in the archaeological record. Colchester did not apparently fall out of use until the mid-fifth century, with burials and stray finds suggesting that a fairly mixed community continued to inhabit the town until the point of its general abandonment, and its cemeteries remained in use for much longer. Most striking were a number of graves found near the site of the town's Roman Circus, a location used for burials since the second century. One particular group contained the remains of people cremated in the late fourth century, interred in ditched enclosures – probably former barrows. These graves have all the markers of non-Christian, non-Roman burial practice but predate the collapse of Roman government by some margin and could be interpreted as the graves of foreign-born soldiers from outside the Empire: either directly enlisted in the regular Roman army, or engaged as *foederati* (allied contingents). Moreover, they share some key characteristics of more typically 'Anglo-Saxon' graves on the same site that are dated to the fifth to seventh centuries, including the inhumed remains of men with spears by their sides, shields on their chests, knives at their waists and barrows raised over them.[18]

Here, at least, the presence of foreign funeral rites at Colchester seems to straddle the formal end of Roman Britain. It is a situation that might have any number of explanations, but certainly upsets any simple notion of a thriving Romano-British culture driven out by genocidal Saxon invaders. Instead, these and other burials from a number of locations around Colchester – as well as finds of late Roman military buckles, continental brooches and northern European pottery – suggest a culture that was becoming more militaristic and 'barbarian' in outward expression at the same time that the economy and urban life were becoming less and less 'Roman': a phenomenon that may have had less to do with immigration than it did with the increasing appeal of new way of life, better suited to the prevailing social conditions. If that is so, those social conditions were such that the signifiers of violent potential, and a familiarity with the barbarian culture of the North Sea, were seen as increasingly valuable. In other words, without the taxes and coinage to pay a professional military to provide security, the trappings of 'Saxon' warrior culture may have surged in popularity among people for whom the land between the Elbe and Weser was otherwise a truly foreign country.

By the late fifth and into the sixth century, the overtly 'Roman' elements of material culture in burial assemblages had dwindled. Instead, judging by prevailing jewellery styles, the dominant cultural references in both cremation and inhumation graves were to the Elbe–Weser region. In particular, archaeologists point to the prevalence of so-called 'saucer brooches' and their derivatives – an apparently diagnostically 'Saxon' style of jewellery. The decoration of metalwork may still have owed a great deal to Roman artistic conventions (as it also did on the Continent), but the way that this imagery was expressed seems to reflect a more uniformly 'Saxon' identity congealing among the people of the lower Thames – wherever their true origins and antecedents lay. Nevertheless, no matter how much the aesthetics may have moved on, the Roman past remained difficult to escape. Evidence for physical overlap between late Romano-British and early 'Anglo-Saxon' cemeteries and funerary rites is observable across the future kingdom of the East Saxons: at Mucking, Kelvedon, Stifford Clays (Thurrock), Saffron Waldon, Barnfield (Heybridge), Shoebury, Great Chesterford and around Colchester – all in the modern county of Essex. At Great Chesterford, a supposedly 'Anglo-Saxon' mixed-rite cemetery that was in use from the fifth to the seventh century occupied the same territory as a field of Romano-British burial mounds beyond the Roman town walls; excavated graves included several that, alongside their otherwise 'Saxon' characteristics, contained Roman jewellery and coins, some apparently placed upon the heads or in the mouths of the dead or clasped in lifeless hands.[19] The coins were part of an exceptionally long-lived tradition originally connected to the journey of the dead in the afterlife and the need to pay tolls to the gatekeepers encountered in the underworld.* Whether the

---

* In classical mythology, Charon the ferryman demanded payment of an obol (a low-value Greek coin) to provide passage across the subterranean waters of the afterlife – most commonly the rivers Styx and Acheron.

meaning of these traditions was remembered in fifth- and sixth-century Britain cannot be known, but the practices continued even among those who in most other outward ways had left the Roman past far behind.

In the autumn of 2003, archaeologists from MOLA (Museum of London Archaeology) were working to record any finds that might come to light as a result of a road-widening scheme just north of Southend, at a place called Prittlewell. They had been called in by the local council to survey the area because the land – at the edge of a twelfth-century priory – was already known to have yielded evidence suggestive of a substantial cemetery: graves containing swords, spears, shields and pendants of gold suggested burials dating to between 500 and 700. After a handful of minor discoveries that included a further three burials, the archaeologists unwittingly opened one of the finest tombs ever discovered in Britain.[20] It had originally contained a human body, presumed on the basis of the grave goods to be a man, laid out on his back in a wooden coffin.* The coffin was not buried in the earth, however, but was set within a timber-lined chamber roughly thirteen feet square and sunk five feet into the earth. Laid out around him, as though it were a bed-chamber rather than a grave, were the things that had given his life value and meaning in the eyes of the community who buried him: a great gold buckle and finely wrought weapons, a vast cauldron, a candelabrum and a folding stool, coloured glassware, a lyre decorated with garnets and copper and two Merovingian gold coins (known as *tremisses*) which the dead man may have held, like the dead of Great Chesterford, in his lifeless hands. As the *Beowulf* poet – mediated through the pen of Seamus Heaney – put it when describing a burial of an earlier era: 'far-fetched treasures were piled upon him, and precious gear [...] well furbished with battle-tackle, bladed weapons and coats of mail'.[21]

---

* The skeleton, all but a few scraps of tooth enamel, had been dissolved to nothing by the acidic Essex soil.

The other objects buried in the grave at Prittlewell hint at a wider sense of identity that reached out to horizons distant from the draughty halls of East Saxon lordship, far away from the mists and meres and hearth-fires of the North Sea diaspora – to Syria, North Africa and Byzantium and the Christian lands of the Mediterranean: a Byzantine flask, a bronze Coptic bowl, a silver spoon in a painted box and two delicate gold foil crosses where the skull had once lain. It is thought that the crosses were placed over the dead man's eyes – a strange ritual with few parallels, an attempt, perhaps, to incorporate the imagery of a new religion into an older way of death. 'Far-fetched treasures' indeed.

By combining the dates of the *tremisses* (*c.*580–*c.*620) with a range of radiocarbon dates derived from organic material in the grave-chamber, it has become possible for the burial to be dated with some confidence (an 83 per cent probability) to the final two decades of the sixth century. This was the period, not only in Essex but throughout lowland Britain, when everything began to change. The cremation of the dead came to an end and inhumation became the norm everywhere – not always necessarily Christian burial, but different from earlier inhumations in diversity and organization. Overall, fewer grave goods were buried, and frequently none at all, and the west–east orientation of graves became increasingly prevalent. However, whereas earlier cemeteries demonstrate remarkably little inequality between kin-group communities, the graves of the seventh century incorporate indications of a widening chasm between the common folk and a burgeoning elite.*

This was the age not only of Prittlewell, but of Caenby (Lincolnshire) and Sutton Hoo (Suffolk) and of other graves like them, the 'princely' burials of men and woman interred beneath barrows, surrounded by the treasures of the age. They were monuments to self-consciousness – to a sense of power, prestige and

---

* Inequalities were certainly present, but are observable within families and kin-groups along lines of age and gender; the evidence for markedly wealthy individuals and families is largely absent.

competition – and a reshaping of the trappings of barbaricum as the imagined panoply of emperors. They represent the working through of a social and religious landscape at a moment of critical inflexion; the ostentation, the superstition, the amalgam of Roman and barbarian, Christian and pagan, exotic and provincial all point to a desire to forge something grander, more durable and more symbolically literate and multivalent than what had gone before: a new image of power fit to rule in the Britain that was emerging. It was the birth, perhaps, of kingship as we might now recognize it. But it also seems to reflect a deliberate effort to bind divergent regional identities into coherent realms – forging a sense of common identity from the messy heritage of migration, economic upheaval and Imperial memory.

No one can say who was buried at Prittlewell: the grave was sealed before the written history of the East Saxon kingdom began. It is widely assumed, and the objects buried with him suggest, that the dead man was a Christian. This is not necessarily true; he was, after all, dead, and in no position to make decisions about what objects were deposited on his face, let alone what they meant to him. And while the crosses could well imply that the dead man's family and community were Christians, they could conceivably indicate only that the imagery of Christianity had gained desirable connotations of power, sophistication and wealth.* Nevertheless, regardless of personal faith, it is undeniable that the inmate of the Prittlewell tomb was buried at a moment in time when Christianity was on the verge of reshaping British politics and society.

In 597, on the opposite side of the Thames Estuary, an Italian bishop named Augustine arrived at Ebbsfleet on the Isle of Thanet. From there he went to the court of King Æthelberht of Kent and instituted a mission to the pagan people of England – an evangelical quest that was to meet with extraordinary success. Now there can be no doubt that many of the people of lowland Britain were

* It may also have been a local variant of the continental (Merovingian) habit of burying the affluent dead with gold crosses affixed to their clothes.

entirely familiar with Christian ideas already – the evidence for a shrine at St Albans, for example, or the provocative layout of Mucking's Cemetery I imply that Christian communities in the East Saxon and Middle Saxon lands had very likely been present for generations. But Augustine's mission was a sea-change inasmuch as it forged a powerful and enduring alliance between the increasingly assertive Church of Rome and the nascent institution of kingship, an institution that was just beginning to elbow its way forcefully into the picture, defining itself as it went along.

The first king of the East Saxons about whom anything much is known was called Sæberht.

Sæberht's mother was a Kentish princess called Ricula who had married Sæberht's father, Sledd. She was the sister of King Æthelberht of Kent, making Sæberht Æthelberht's nephew. Æthelberht had been converted to Christianity in 597 by Augustine's mission. He was also, according to Bede, master of 'all the English peoples as far north as the Humber' and was consequently Sæberht's overlord as well as his uncle.[22] Therefore, when Augustine dispatched the newly created Bishop Mellitus to evangelize the East Saxons, Sæberht would have had little option but to agree and accept the new religion on behalf of his people.* Nor could he do very much about it when King Æthelberht demanded that a church, dedicated to the apostle Paul, be built in the greatest Roman city under Sæberht's authority. That church was duly built, and Mellitus was installed as the first Bishop of St Paul's in London, a diocese that covered the territory of the East and Middle Saxons, and a metropolitan throne that sought to revive the most important centre of Roman *Britannia*.[23]

* This, of course, overlooks the possibility that many East Saxons may have already been familiar with Christianity – at least on a superficial level; the message of the mission to Essex may therefore have been as much political as it was religious, a way to make sure that it was Augustine's (and therefore Æthelberht's) authority that was promoted rather than any other.

In its heyday, *Londinium* had possessed an impressive array of Imperial trappings: a mighty set of walls, a vast basilica and forum complex, a governor's palace, a 7,000-seat amphitheatre, a temple to Mithras. But by the early seventh century, the archaeology of the city suggests that it had a lot of ground to recover. As early as the fourth century, London's public spaces slipped into a spiral of decline: the basilica was demolished in *c.*300, the amphitheatre abandoned in *c.*350, the Mithraeum in the 380s. Archaeology suggests that, by the second half of the century, the emphasis of city life had emphatically changed: fewer but larger private dwellings, public buildings converted to industrial uses, cemeteries intruding into sub-urban and intra-mural city-space (including within the open space of the amphitheatre), the construction of more liminal, possibly Christian, structures at the eastern edge of the city. *Londinium* remained occupied, but the evidence for neglect and population decline is everywhere to be found. The last public works involved the maintenance of the walls themselves. In the second half of the fourth century new projecting bastions were added to the eastern walls, and these were followed at the end of the century by a second line of defences in the south-eastern corner of the city. Their location implies the direction from which threats were expected to emerge – from the east, from the coast, from the sea, from the river. But whatever the intention behind these works, the impression is of investment in the shell of a hollow city, a city that would soon contain nothing worth preserving but its pride.

Mellitus was not the first Bishop of London – a Bishop Restitutus *de civitate Londenensi* attended the Council of Arles in 314 – but there is no evidence to suggest that the city retained its role as an episcopal seat beyond the end of the fourth century.[24] Nevertheless, the history of the city would have been remembered. Pope Gregory – the brains behind Augustine's mission – would have been well aware that *Londinium* was the most important city in Roman Britain and the probable capital of the late Roman *Diocesis Britanniarum* ('Diocese of the

Britains').* By seeking to install the first of his new bishops in London, the Pope seems to have envisaged the renewal of religion in Britain as conceptually linked to the revival of Empire – a new Imperium of faith to unite the former provinces in a shared spiritual destiny. The resuscitated bishopric, housed at the new church of St Paul's, would become the primary church for all the English, symbolizing the renaissance of Britannia's greatest city and the reinvigorated Empire of God.†[25]

By the beginning of the fifth century, however, in common with provincial capitals like Cirencester (*Corinium*) and Lincoln (*Lindum Colonia*), London had become a ghost-town, a place where alluvium and river water lay stagnant in flooded streets and open spaces, a city of ruins slowly being reclaimed by beasts and creeping vegetation, or submerged in the fetid overflow of the Thames and the Walbrook. In some places the desertion seems abrupt; at Poultry a dining table and set of glassware were left behind in the ruins of a home, a snapshot of domestic life interrupted. In others the intrusion of death and weird ritual suggest an existence that was lurching out of kilter in the hours before the post-Roman dawn: a decapitated body was interred in a drainage culvert, the headless corpse of a fawn was dumped down a well with a collection of pots and pans – as though someone were seal-

---

* The term diocese was used to describe an administrative territory above the provincial level comprising the five provinces of *Britannia Prima*, *Britannia Secunda*, *Maxima Caesariensis*, *Flavia Caesariensis* and *Valentia*.

† Pope Gregory was – at least according to Bede – specific about the 'English' (rather than any of the other inhabitants of Britain) being the target of conversion; the famous story goes that the Pope, on encountering some cherubic blond children for sale at a Roman slave-market, asked who these people were and received the answer that they were *Angli* ('Angles'). Gregory, wag that he was, responded with the pun: *non Angli sed Angeli* – 'not Angles, but Angels' – and immediately became determined to speedily convert them and all their kin in faraway Britain. The story, recorded in Northumbria 140 years later, is almost certainly hogwash dreamed up by Bede or one of his interlocutors; it does, however, provide some insight into what passed for witty banter in eighth-century Jarrow.

ing the abandonment of their former life with sacrifice. By the beginning of the fifth century, the impression is one of desertion, decay and brooding silences: of rubble, weeds and stagnation and the howling of wild dogs.

Outside the city walls, traces of small rural settlements have been discovered along the line of the Thames and its tributaries: at Clerkenwell (on the River Fleet), Whitehall, Chelsea, Battersea, Hammersmith, Brentford and Kingston; and there is tantalizing evidence from below the church of St Martin-in-the-Fields – a little to the west of the Roman Wall (now the east side of Trafalgar Square) – that 'Saxon' occupation took hold hard on the heels of the last Roman burials, suggesting, just perhaps, that, like the shrine of St Albans, the church of St. Martin retained a communal signifi-cance throughout this period of demographic upheaval. No one would suggest, however, that the evidence for meaningful settle-ment in and around London before the seventh century is anything other than thin. The construction of St Paul's in 604 represented the first sign of sustained investment within the walls after two centu-ries of neglect and decay, a dim light amid the ruin. (No trace of the original church has ever been found. It now lies buried, a deep-planted seed, somewhere, probably, beneath the bloated white carcass of Wren's mighty cathedral.) At the same time, a new settle-ment to the west of the old Roman city in the region of Covent Garden was beginning to appear: this place, known to contempo-raries as *Lundenwic* ('London trading emporium') was a new extra-mural commercial centre, built to capitalize on the opportu-nities for river traffic and access to coastal waters and the interior of southern England. It would go on to become a major economic hub during the later seventh and eighth centuries.[26]

On paper, therefore, the fledgling kingdom of Essex seemed to have the tools it needed to make a go of things as a major player in the early seventh century. It had proper kings; it had a powerful ally in Kent and it had access to a promising trading post on the Thames. It also had a new religious identity and all the adminis-trative advantages, diplomatic contacts and communal solidarity that the Church could provide. And yet, from the beginning, the realm never really managed to get its act together – not least because the East Saxons never really managed to agree with themselves about anything, never managed to stop hedging their bets until it was too late. The problem seems to have been in part that, for the Saxons of the lower Thames, the project of ethnogenesis – of forging a coherent community from the various people of the region – was ultimately a failure. The kingdom of Essex ended up with a split personality, the origins of which are observable as early as the bifurcated grave-fields of Mucking. As the kingdom's unfolding history implies, the East and Middle 'Saxons' seem to have felt an attachment to both the pagan forest groves of a lost Saxon homeland and to the Christian heritage of Rome with its Imperial glamour and martyrial shrines. This tension, inflected by residual ethnic identities and complicated by the interference of outside actors, was a flaw that would ultimately prove the kingdom's undoing.

Quite how difficult it would be for East Saxon kings to find lasting consensus would be revealed in the wake of King Sæberht's death in 616. The new kings of Essex – Sæberht's sons Sæward, Seaxred and Seaxbald – were apparently not enthusiastic about Jesus Christ or his earthly helpers and promptly booted Bishop Mellitus back to Kent.*[27] (They felt emboldened to take this stance because Great Uncle Æthelberht of Kent had died the same year and his son and successor, Eadbald (r.616–640), had much less clout than his father and was also a pagan with presumably little

---

* Bede offers the amusing, if not entirely believable, anecdote that the brothers took against Mellitus when he refused to give them any of the consecrated bread that the bishop reserved for his congregation: 'We refuse to enter that font,' the truculent siblings are alleged to have announced, 'and see no need for it; but we want to be strengthened with this bread.' If there is any truth to this (and if it's not just a way for Bede to make heathens appear a bit slow), it illustrates how, in the minds of those on the cusp of conversion, the barrier between religion and magic could appear non-existent.

interest in episcopal pride.*) The apostasy of Sæberht's sons was – in Bede's mind – righteously avenged by their annihilation in battle against the *Gewissae* (the West Saxons) very shortly afterwards (probably in 616).† But Bede was nevertheless forced to acknowledge that 'the fate of the instigators did not cause their people to abandon their evil practices, or to return to the simple faith and love to be found in Christ alone'.[28] When Bishop Mellitus attempted a return to London in around 619, he discovered that neither the backing of the recently converted King Eadbald nor the delegated authority of the Pope in Rome would convince the Londoners to let him back in. They preferred, in Bede's words, 'their own idolatrous priests'.[29]

That return of Christ to the East Saxons, when it came, arrived on a wind that blew from Northumbria and carried a whiff of unorthodoxy that Bede would doubtless have found disagreeable. In 653 the East Saxon king – Sigeberht II – was 'persuaded' by the Northumbrian king Oswy (r.642–670) to accept Christianity, almost forty years after the first abortive experiment. Bede describes the friendly theological discussions that Oswy and Sigeberht are supposed to have had on the latter's frequent visits to the Northumbrian court.‡ They were, in Bede's telling, somewhat one-sided. 'Oswy', we are told, 'used to reason with him [Sigeberht] how gods made by man's handiwork could not be gods, and how a god could not be made from a log or block of stone, the rest of which might be burned or made into articles of everyday use or possibly thrown away to be trampled underfoot and reduced to

---

* Mellitus had initially found an equally unwelcoming attitude at the court of the new Kentish king: Eadbald's paganism kept Mellitus out of Britain entirely until the king had a change of heart and embraced the new religion in 618/19.

† The cause of the fighting is not known, but control of Surrey seems a likely flashpoint between the two kingdoms.

‡ Although Bede describes Sigeberht as a 'friend' of Oswy, the most likely context for Sigeberht's repeated northward trips is to deliver tribute and re-emphasize Northumbrian overlordship.

dust.'[30] This religious kingsplaining apparently did the trick; Sigeberht was so impressed by Oswy's dubious logic that he forsook the construction of idols, inviting a Northumbrian mission to lead the (re)conversion of the East Saxons. This mission was led by a priest named Cedd, who had been brought up on Lindisfarne under the tutelage of the Irish monk and evangelist Aidan of Iona. As a result, some of the earliest churches of the East Saxons would undoubtedly have practised a form of Christianity disfigured, as Bede would have thought, by its Hiberno-British provenance (indeed, had Cedd not, in later life, accepted the Roman rite at the Synod of Whitby (664), Bede's attitude to the late evangel of Essex might have been very different).

Cedd founded a number of churches within the realm, including one at Tilbury (*Tilaburg*) on the Thames opposite Gravesend. He also founded a monastic church at a place that Bede called *Ythancaestir*. The Old English word *caester* (and its variant spellings) was used to describe Roman fortifications. It has survived as the suffix of a plethora of modern English place-names as '-caster', '-cester' and '-chester' (e.g. Colchester). *Ythancaestir* is therefore the Roman fortress of 'Ythan'. The only Roman fortress in the right part of the world that sounds a bit like 'Ythan' is the Saxon Shore Fort situated on the Dengie peninsula in Essex and named in the late fourth-century Latin document *Notitia Dignitatum* as 'Othona'. A little church, built in the 660s, still stands on the remains of the Roman fort: that stalwart chapel of St Peter-on-the-Wall.

Cedd became bishop of London, remaining in charge of the East Saxon diocese even after Sigeberht was murdered by his kinsmen in 660 and Northumbrian influence in the kingdom waned. Bede presents the killers as despising the king because he was 'too lenient towards his enemies and too readily forgave injuries when offenders asked pardon'.[31] It is a pretty obscure comment, although it has been taken as indicating the sort of tensions that might emerge when Christian ideas were introduced to a society habituated to rough justice. It is also likely, however, that profound disputes between rival branches of the family were at play, partly religious in nature, and no doubt stoked by the interference of outside powers – a new fracture emerging from the deep East Saxon fault-lines. The new king, Swithhelm (r.660–664), may well have been one of Sigeberht's murderers and took the throne as a pagan. When he eventually converted to Christianity in 662, it was Cedd who baptized him. But the baptism did not take place in Essex. Nor did it take place under the wing of the Northumbrians who had invested so much effort in his predecessor's spiritual wellbeing. Instead, Swithhelm took his baptismal vows at the court of the East Anglian king, Æthelwald. The East Saxons had apparently swapped one foreign overlord for another. It was a pattern that would ultimately tear the kingdom apart.

One minute things are going along as normal, the next – bang – a global pandemic shatters all the certainties on which life is built, throwing everything into confusion and the credulous into the embrace of all manner of weird prophets and outmoded ideas.

At ten o'clock in the morning on 1 May 664, the sky above Bede's monastery at Jarrow darkened, the heavens gloaming to a deeper blue, the horizon blazing spectral orange, a weird night falling in the east: an eclipse that darkened the sun. It would have been taken – as such things often were – as a bad omen. And, sure enough, shortly afterwards in that same year, a 'sudden pestilence [...] raging wide with fierce destruction laid low a great multitude of men'. It was to become a 'mortality which ravaged Britain and Ireland with cruel devastation', a 'pestilence which carried off many throughout the length and breadth of Britain'.[32] Modern scholars believe that the disease was probably bubonic plague, a resurgence of the same disease that had first blighted Europe and Asia in the mid-sixth century during the reign of the Byzantine Emperor Justinian (r.527–565).*[33]

* This first recorded outbreak of bubonic plague (541–549) is known to historians as the 'Justinianic Plague'.

For some, the onset of what several writers of the time described as 'the great mortality' may have strengthened their faith.[34] Bede recounts a story – relayed to him by Bishop Acca of Hexham who had it in turn from the missionary Willibrord – about an Irishman who feared for his soul: 'You can see,' the Irishman allegedly told Willibrord, 'how this disease has tightened its hold and brought me to the point of death. I have no doubt that after the death of my body I shall immediately be condemned to the eternal death of the soul and endure all the torments of hell; for although I have made a great study of the scriptures, I have for a long time devoted myself to evil-doing.' Lucky it was for him that Willibrord just happened to have a fragment of the stake to which the Northumbrian King Oswald's head was affixed after his death. A glass of blessed water, augmented with the aforementioned holy wood-chip, was just what the doctor ordered: 'the sick man [...] quickly began to feel better, and having recovered from his illness, he lived many years after.'[35]

For the people of Essex, however, it seems that relics and prayer were not the answer. For them, perhaps understandably, the pestilence that was tearing through their land was construed as a sign that the recent insistence on the inefficacy of 'gods made from logs' had been not only mistaken but downright dangerous. King Swithhelm died in 664, possibly from the plague, and was succeeded by his cousins Sigehere and Sæbbi who ruled jointly (just as the sons of Sæberht had done earlier in the century). Sigehere, Bede explains, 'together with many of the nobles and common folk', rejected his deceased predecessor's enthusiasm for the eternal afterlife (they 'even disbelieved in its existence', a wide-eyed Bede relates) and acted accordingly. 'Sigehere and his people abandoned the mysteries of the Christian Faith and relapsed into paganism', and set to work busily making as many graven images as they could: 'Hoping for protection against the plague [...] they therefore began to rebuild the ruined temples and restore the worship of idols.'[36]

Sigehere, however, was only half of the equation. His fellow king, Sæbbi, maintained his adherence to Christian teachings and started casting around for a new godfather. This time it was to the Mercians and their king, Wulfhere (r.658–675), that an East Saxon king turned. Wulfhere clearly saw an opportunity and promptly dispatched a new evangelist – Bishop Jaruman – to the pagan back-sliders of Essex with the sinister-sounding instruction to 'correct their error'.[37] Bede, perhaps unsurprisingly, does not concern himself with the internal dynamics of this new, Mercian, conver-sion of the East Saxons. He simply provides a sunny and uncomplicated assessment of mission accomplished.*

Whether the people of Essex were quite so quick 'to confess the name of Christ' having once again 'abandoned and destroyed the temples and altars they had erected' is actually rather unclear. Sigehere seems in fact to have canvassed external support of his own and may, in truth, have been a rather more potent force than Bede gives him credit for, and less amenable to 'correction' by Mercian bishops. During this period, Sigehere appeared as a witness to a char-ter issued by the West Saxon king Cædwalla (r.685/6–688). That charter appears to recognize Sigehere as king of Kent by conquest.[38] If that reflected any sort of reality, it may well be that the East Saxons had given their backing to Cædwalla's aggressive policies in Kent that the *Anglo-Saxon Chronicle* records for the years 686 and 687.†[39] In any case, the pagan faction within Essex was clearly capable of enlist-ing powerful allies of its own. It is hard to imagine that the situation within the East Saxon kingdom was not one of intense political and religious division – if not violent conflict.

* I find it hard not to imagine Bishop Jaruman returning to the Mercian court to report, with the delivery of *The Shining*'s Delbert Grady, that he had, indeed, '... *corrected* them, sir'.

† The charter in which this evidence appears seems to have been fabricated from a number of authentic seventh-century documents; if the passage relating to Sigehere is genuine, it would mean that Sigehere ruled jointly in Kent with a member of the West Saxon royal family named Mul who was described as a 'king of Kent' in a different charter; in 687, according to the *Anglo-Saxon Chronicle*, Mul and twelve of his supporters were burned to death by Kentish insurgents, provoking reprisals from Cædwalla in which Sigehere may well have participated.

When Sigehere died in 688 and King Cædwalla abdicated the same year, the situation once again changed rapidly. Sæbbi's son Swæfheard displaced the West Saxon influence in Kent, ruling there jointly with a member of the Kentish royal dynasty under the thumb of Sæbbi's Mercian ally.* What became of Sigehere's kin is unknown, but East Saxon paganism was never again to be a political force; Sæbbi became sole ruler of Essex, and continued to reign as a Christian king with Mercian backing, ushering in a period of apparent stability after nearly a century of political and religious flip-flopping. However, the chaotic progress of the East Saxon kingdom through the seventh century had demonstrated the fundamental instability of the realm's foundations. Weakened by the political fractures caused by long-standing cultural fissures and habitual joint-kingship and crippled by epidemic disease, the kingdom had been ruthlessly undermined and exploited by external forces. It would never truly recover.

Sæbbi died in 695. He was laid to rest in London in the church of St Paul, one of only two kings to have been buried there. For five centuries he slumbered undisturbed until, in the twelfth century, his bones were translated to a black marble sarcophagus beside the tomb of King Æthelred II 'the Unready' (r.978–1016) in the north aisle of the choir. Sæbbi was revered as a saint, and for five centuries more his body rested secure, a lure to pilgrims who made the journey to the ancient church at the heart of England's greatest city. And there his bones would have remained had not his tomb – along with the tomb of King Æthelred and many more besides – been destroyed in 1666 by the Great Fire that claimed old St Paul's and most of medieval London with it.

* King Æthelred of Mercia, who succeeded Wulfhere in 675 and reigned until 704.

Sæbbi has the honour of being the first English king to be buried in London. A Latin epitaph inscribed over his tomb remembered him as:

King of the East-Saxons, who was converted to the faith of Christ by that Holy Man Erkenwald Bishop of London, in the year of our Lord, 677. This good King was a person frequent in his daily duty and devotion towards God, and seriously intentive on religious exercises, and continual prayers, with the visible fruits of daily alms-deeds, he preferring a monastic and solitary retirement before all the treasures and pleasures of a whole kingdom. The which King, after he had swayed the sceptre for the space of thirty years, put off the world, and put on a religious habit by the benediction of Walter, then Bishop of London, who succeeded Erkenwald in that Sacred Function. Of whom Venerable Bede writes many things in his History of the English Nation.[40]

This rather free translation by the poet Payne Fisher in his *The tombes, monuments, and sepulchral inscriptions, lately visible in St. Pauls cathedral &c.* (1684) was published while the author was confined in the Fleet Prison. He was able to make this translation because an engraving of the tomb by the Bohemian artist Wenceslaus Hollar was used to illustrate Sir William Dugdale's *History of St. Paul's Cathedral*, first published in 1658 – eight years before the fire.[41] The original Latin of the inscription, however, is largely cribbed from Bede's *Ecclesiastical History*. Bede himself claimed – with uncharacteristic imprecision – to have got most of his information about Sæbbi from 'a little book', a statement that makes it rather hard to evaluate Bede's assessment of Sæbbi's life and death.[42]

Nevertheless, Bede leaves us with a final anecdote – a story of how the king was visited by dire illness in his old age (quite possibly the same plague that had so afflicted his kingdom). Wishing to die in the service of God, Sæbbi became a monk in the final months of his life.* When the hour came (as Bede recounts it) the once-king, in the company of Waldhere the Bishop of London, 'seemed suddenly to fall into a light sleep and breathed out his spirit without any feeling of pain'. He was laid to rest in a stone sarcophagus that – having initially been found too short for the body – miraculously extended to accommodate the former king. It was claimed by Bede's mysterious source (the 'little book') that this all occurred in the presence of the bishop and Sæbbi's son Sigeheard, the new joint-king of the East Saxon realm (with his brother Swæfred).†[43] Total bunk, but revealing nonetheless: Saebbi had died only a century after the cemetery at Mucking went out of use and the cremation of the dead came to an end in Essex. But the story told about his end reveals that the world he inhabited was a vastly changed one: a world of Christian mausolea set within Roman city walls, of power-ful bishops and metropolitan churches, of monasteries and kings who ended their lives as monks.‡

Yet unlike his royal peers in neighbouring realms – kings whose ancestors had guided their people through similarly traumatic transitions and mutations – Saebbi bequeathed to his heirs a king-

---

*   In taking religious vows and relinquishing power in his twilight years, Sæbbi had joined a small but distinct group of seventh-century kings that included the Mercian King Æthelred who ended his life as abbot of Bardney in Lindsey. The most famous of their number was King Sigeberht of East Anglia (reigned *c.*629–*c.*634) – not be confused with King Sigeberht of Essex – who, having renounced his throne and retired to the monastery at *Beodricesworth* (Bury St Edmunds), was forced against his will to ride with the East Anglian army against the invading Mercian forces of King Penda. Refusing to bear arms, he carried only a staff into battle, escorted as an unwilling living talisman by the East Anglian warband. It proved as futile as it was cruel: the East Anglians were routed by the Mercian charge and Sigeberht was cut down along with his kinsman King Egric (reigned *c.*629–636).

†   One has to wonder whether this story was put about to spare the thought of Sigeheard squashing his father's saintly corpse into an ill-fitting coffin.

‡   Eorcanwald [Erkanwald], the bishop of London who had baptised Saebbi in 677, had founded the substantial monastery of St Mary's at Barking in the years before 666.

dom that remained fatally hobbled by internal division and foreign meddling.

Sæbbi had owed his dominance in Essex to the Mercian kings Wulfhere (r.658–675) and Æthelred (r.675–704).* His alignment with these men had ensured the survival of his dynasty, but left his sons, Sigeheard and Swæfred, in possession of a throne that was dependent on Mercian power and a realm that was being eaten alive by it. King Æthelred, for example, owned land outright in Middlesex and was able to appoint his own officials in London. And in Hertfordshire and Middlesex, though they retained their royal titles, Sigeheard and Swæfred were forced to acknowledge Æthelred as their overlord when making grants of territory.[44] By the time of the Mercian kings Æthelbald (r.716–757) and Offa (r.757–796), all pretence at East Saxon rule in London and Middlesex had evaporated, these kings doing as they wished with land they clearly now considered their own. Writing in the 730s, Bede referred to '… the province of the East Saxons […] separated from Kent by the river Thames, and bounded on the east by the sea. Its metropolis is the city of London, which stands on the banks of the Thames, and is a trading centre for many nations who visit it by land and sea.' But by then London was only the ecclesiastical centre of East Saxon authority. Political power over the Middle Saxon lands had long slipped from the grasp of the Essex kings.[45]

Within the bounds of Essex proper, however, the East Saxon kings at least remained masters of their own house. They did so for most of the remaining history of the kingdom and dynasty, although the precise doings of its kings and the relationships between them are opaque. They seem to have continued to practise a particular tradition of splitting power among a number of joint

---

* Both of whom were sons of the great Penda (r.625–655). They were re-established as Mercian kings after a gap following Penda's defeat and death at the hands of Oswy of Northumbria at the battle of the Winwaed in 655.

kings – at least until 738 – though the exact terms of these co-rulerships and their spheres of authority are unknown. By the later eighth century, however, the East Saxon kingdom had become – like so many others – a subordinate vassal to the swollen Mercian empire. Sigeric, who abdicated in 798, and his son, Sigered, appear as witnesses to numerous charters of the Mercian kings Ecgfrith (r.796) and Coenwulf (r.796–821). Sigered – like the kings of Hwicce on the other side of the Mercian sphere – found himself progressively demoted, first to *subregulus* (from 812) and finally, from 814, to the rank of *dux*. It was, to all intents and purposes, the end of an independent East Saxon kingdom. The final act, however, came not at the hands of the Mercians, but the West Saxons. In 825, after the defeat of Mercia at the battle of Ellendun, the West Saxon King Ecgberht rolled the former Mercian protectorates of Kent, Sussex, Essex and Surrey into a fiefdom ruled by his son Æthelwulf.*

The kingdom of Essex was over. And yet the East Saxon dynasty had endured longer than many, its kings succeeding each other until the ninth century – an alliterative litany that carried their heritage back through the royal mausolea of old St Paul's and the burial mounds of Essex, past the cremation fields and the abandoned fora of forlorn Roman towns, over the sea to the forests of Germania – to strange forgotten gods once worshipped in flickering groves beneath the moon.

---

* There was a brief coda, a blink-and-you'd-miss-him appearance from a man named as 'King' Sigeric of the East Saxons in a charter of the Mercian King Wiglaf (r.827–839) detailing a Hertfordshire land lease. It is possible that this Sigeric was a dispossessed prince in exile.

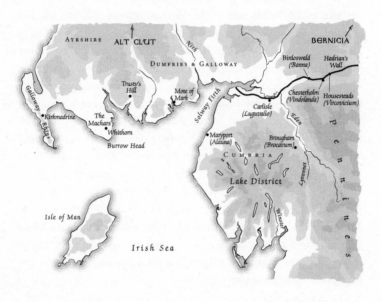

AYRSHIRE   ALT CLUT

BERNICIA

Nith

DUMFRIES & GALLOWAY

Birdoswald
(*Banna*)

Hadrian's
Wall

Trusty's
Hill

Mote of
Mark

Solway Firth

Chesterholm
(*Vindolanda*)

Housesteads
(*Vircovicium*)

Carlisle
(*Luguvalio*)

Galloway

Rhins

Kirkmadrine

The
Machars

Whithorn

Maryport
(*Alauna*)

Eden

Brougham
(*Brocavum*)

Burrow Head

CUMBRIA

P e n n i n e s

Lake District

Lyvennet

Isle of Man

Winster

Irish Sea

RHEGED

– *Cumbria, Dumfries and Galloway* –

And until I fail in old age,
In the sore necessity of death,
May I not be smiling,
If I praise not Urien

(Anon., *Llyfr Taliesin*, fourteenth century)[1]

I n an island filled with the shades of forgotten realms, Rheged is
perhaps the most mysterious of them all, a shimmering haze of
mountains and cataracts, of forested clefts and green sea-gulleys, of
ravens and spear-points and silver-haired kings, and blood-stained
rivers running under a pale grey sky. At its most generous, a reconstruction of Rheged's extent describes a land that swept from the
southern Lake District to the hills of Galloway, spreading eastward
to the Pennines and the Roman forts of Hadrian's Wall. Optimists
read the strange and difficult clues to Rheged's existence and find a
kingdom of the lakes and the high hills, of ruins and ragged coastline – a land split by the Solway Firth and stitched back together by
the Wall, haunted by the cries of sea eagles hunting the salmon that

thronged its silver rivers and the lambs that grazed its fells. And they find a kingdom inextricably bound to one of Welsh literature's most celebrated but enigmatic figures: 'Urien of the cultivated plain … the splendid prince of the North'.[2] Yet despite the confidence with which its name is sometimes written across a broad swathe of the map – in letters whose size and wide spacing hint at scale but never commit to borders – the fact remains that every brick from which Rheged's wide estate has been built is made of sand, an edifice liable to crumble in the face of the slightest breeze. For those who seek its elusive shadow, the possibility must always be seriously entertained that the kingdom of Rheged never existed at all.

Anyone who has spent time at Hadrian's Wall will know the melancholy of the place, the epic loneliness of it all – grey stone and undulating earthworks stretching away to east and west into the thinning distance, yellow grass bending in a hard breeze beside the hollowed-out footings of abandoned mile castles; the robbed and tumbled and – in places – restored limits of the Empire's farthest frontier strung in mute desolation across the humped back of Britain. For much of its length, the Wall passes through country that is largely empty of human habitation, its skies dark, its farmsteads isolated. The people may have left the Wall, but the wrinkled land remains saturated with patient vigilance. The landscape has the aspect of a storm-roiled sea suspended in the agonizing crawl of geological time, grey-green waves surging to the limits of vision, crested with foams of black woodland and the spray of strewn boulders.

The central portion of the Wall – its most famous and photographed section – skirts the southern edge of the Northumberland National Park to the north and the North Pennines AONB to the south. There the ridge of grey stone rides the Whin Sill above the dark rippling surface of Crag Lough to the north, making a rampart of the earth's grey bones where they have torn themselves free, rising as monstrous battlements of living rock. At the eastern end of the Lough, a dark rash of woodland overhangs the water, vivid moss clinging to the trunks of trees and tumbled boughs, colouring the stones of the Wall an acid green: a place that recalls the monster-haunted pool of the Old English poem *Beowulf* where 'on windswept crags […] a frost-stiffened wood waits and keeps watch above a mere; the overhanging bank is a maze of tree-roots mirrored in its surface'.[3]

To the south, the sun still makes its daily progress from Newcastle to Carlisle, sometimes breaking the fathomless cloudscape to send probing fingers of gold though the clouds, illuminating patches of hillside and scatters of grazing sheep, briefly selecting them – like the tractor beam of some alien spacecraft – before moving on. The receding ranks of hills vanish into a haze of blue, as though they go on for ever: the threshold of a boundless Empire that once rolled unbroken to the Red Sea. But to the north the horizon is nearer and the sky darker. Framed in the shattered arch of Milecastle 37 a line of hills, its long ridge smeared with woodland, casts a screen against the horizon. Whatever lies beyond, in that world outside the protective embrace of Roman frontiers, dwells unseen, unknown. And so the ghosts of the Wall remain.

To wait.

To keep watch.

At the end of the fourth century, in places like London, Lincoln and Cirencester, the economic underpinnings of Roman life collapsed. Civilian populations drifted away from cities that they were neither equipped nor motivated to defend; the wealthiest citizens lost the ability to maintain and protect the social distinctions they had formerly boasted of, losing access to imported and domestic lux-uries and ultimately abandoning their country villas (and, in some cases, probably the island altogether). By contrast, however, north-ern Britain was a militarized zone, and there different conditions gave rise to different phenomena. The defining infrastructure of the north was – to use Bede's phrase – the 'famous and still conspicuous' Roman Wall, an architectural statement of such unique magnitude that it remains both famous and conspicuous despite the passage of a further thirteen centuries since Bede's assessment. To his mind, the Romans had 'built a strong wall of stone directly from sea to sea in a straight line between the towns that had been built as strong points'.[4] Bede actually got this the wrong way round – though it was quite a reasonable assumption from his point of view. Modern archaeologists agree that the Wall was built first, and its forts – what Bede describes as towns (as they effectively became by the fourth century) – were added to the plan after the construction of the Wall had already begun. They were named (from west to east):

Mais (Bowness-on-Solway, Cumbria)
Coggabata (Drumburgh, Cumbria)
Aballava (Burgh by Sands, Cumbria)
Uxelodunum/Petriana (Stanwix, Cumbria)
Camboglanna (Castlesteads, Cumbria)
Banna (Birdoswald, Cumbria)
Aesica (Great Chesters, Northumberland)
Vercovicium (Housesteads, Northumberland)
Cilurnum (Chesters, Northumberland)
Hunnum (Halton Chesters, Northumberland)
Vindobala (Rudchester, Northumberland)
Condercum (Benwell, Tyne and Wear)
Pons Aelius (Newcastle, Tyne and Wear)
Segedunum (Wallsend, Tyne and Wear)

In addition, a number of fortified towns and 'supply forts' were built to the rear of the Wall, along the line of 'Stanegate', the medieval name for the Roman road that was constructed to service the Wall and facilitate the movement of troops and supplies up and down its length: places like *Luguvalio* (Carlisle), *Alauna* (Maryport, Cumbria), *Magnis* (Carvoran, Northumberland), *Brocolitia* (Carrawburgh, Northumberland), *Coria* (Corbridge, Northumberland), *Vindolanda*

(Chesterholm, Northumberland) and *Arbeia* (South Shields, Tyne and Wear). Along with the Wall, these forts formed part of an extensive network of roads, garrisons and watchtowers north of the Humber, all supplied, maintained and manned by a military occupying force that taxed and administered, as well as defended, these northern marches of the Roman Empire. This huge militarized zone was governed in the fourth century by an official known as the *Dux Britanniarum* – the 'Commander of the Britains' – a senior general in the Roman army with responsibility for the border. It was a post with wide jurisdiction, significant muscle and a great deal of latitude to flex it – particularly given the physical distance from Imperial oversight that the *Dux* enjoyed.

In many parts of the late Empire, military recruitment had become increasingly local, embedded within the communities that had grown up around fortresses and garrison towns. This was a characteristic of the *limitanei* – the border forces – whose lives and service were essentially sedentary (unlike the *comitatenses* – the mobile field armies who were moved around for whatever strategic purposes they were required). The garrisons of the Wall fell very much into the former category. In many cases they were people who, however much they identified with Roman military institutions, were thoroughly British by birth and deeply rooted in their localities. Although it is certain that many professional soldiers were removed from their garrisons during the upheavals of the late fourth and early fifth centuries (culminating in Constantine III's withdrawal of the British legions to support his doomed bid for the Imperial throne in 407), it is likely that the majority of the soldiers withdrawn from Britain were *comitatenses*, or otherwise those stationed closest to Imperial Gaul in the forts of the south and east coast (the Saxon Shore).* It is therefore probable that many of the *limitanei* stationed at the Wall never left Britain, and this is what the archaeology of its forts and supply garrisons strongly implies.

---

* And therefore easiest to transfer to new theatres of conflict on the continent.

Evidence of continued occupation at places like *Alauna* (Maryport), *Vircovicium* (Housesteads), *Vindolanda* (Chesterholm) and, especially, *Banna* (Birdoswald), indicate that life in many places continued into the late fifth century and beyond without interruption. During the late 1980s and 1990s, excavations at *Banna* led by the archaeologist Tony Wilmott revealed the degradation and remodelling of the fort's granaries at some time after the middle of the fourth century. This was followed, at some point between 388 and the early fifth century, by the construction of new timber buildings that included a large structure on the site of the former north granary. This was superseded – after an unknown amount of time had elapsed – by a yet more impressive timber hall that measured seventy-five feet in length and twenty-eight feet across. It was supported on wooden pillars that rested on stone footings and was carefully aligned with the southern edge of the western portal through the outer wall of the fort. By any measure, this was an imposing building, but it was utterly unlike the masonry structures of the Imperial past. The excavators estimated that it fell out of use around AD 520, the termination of a period of continuous occupation that spanned the total collapse of the Roman Empire in the west.[5]

The sequence of adaptation, reuse and rebuilding at *Banna* lasted for perhaps a century and a half, maybe more. It was complex and gradual – there was no moment of shattering change. But the material and cultural world inhabited by its last occupants was radically different from that enjoyed by the men who started remodelling the fort's granaries in the late fourth century. They at least could probably have still expected to receive the benefits of Imperial service and could feel reasonably secure and assured of their status within Britain as the only citizens with a legal right to bear arms. After Constantine III's bid for Imperial mastery collapsed in 409, however, the situation in Britain changed irrevocably. According to the Byzantine historian Zosimus, the Britons 'revolted from the Roman empire, no longer submitted to Roman law, and reverted to their native customs. The Britons therefore armed themselves and ran many risks to ensure their own safety and free their cities from the attacking barbarians.'[6]

For the soldiers of the Wall, things would at first have seemed much the same as they always had – by the late fourth century, only a quarter of a soldier's pay was made in coin. The rest was paid in food and other services. When the supply of coins dried up, the survival of professional fighting men could still be ensured by extracting produce from the local population – grain and cattle exchanged for security. Soldiers and commanders probably attempted to maintain as best they could the rituals and structures of the late Roman army, expecting that normal service might some-day be resumed. Like the Japanese holdouts who continued fighting the Second World War in the jungles of South East Asia, they waited for orders, reinforcements, supplies, pay. None of it ever came, of course, but no one could have known then that the Empire was never going to strike back. After all, the northern command had seen its ups and downs over the fourth century and witnessed the withdrawal and reinstatement of Imperial forces on a number of occasions.

But as months turned to years, and years turned to decades, expectations must slowly have changed. As garbled news arrived of distant wars and the depredations of Visigoths and Vandals, as the new normal crystallized and the Imperial twilight set in, there must have come a palpable sense that horizons had narrowed and that the certainties of the past had slipped away for ever. The means – and the incentive – to enforce laws written in faraway lands evaporated. Gone, too, were the foreign goods, the security provided by the might of the Imperial army, the opportunities for travel and advancement within a vast civil and military administration. From a continent-spanning institution, the Roman military system in northern Britain had broken down into individual cells of operation – self-reliant, vulnerable and in competition with each other, with the barbarian, and with anyone else who wished to take up arms for control of territory and resources. Now each fortress, each garrison, had to operate alone. None of them could expect any help from down the road or up the Wall, and the formerly pliant civilian population would suddenly have appeared more threatening than it ever had before. There can have been few rural communities who still felt inclined to respect old Imperial rules restricting weapon-bearing – not since the army's capacity and willingness to shield them from Angles, Saxons, Picts and each other had dissolved.

As memories were fogged by time and the turning of the generations, garrisons that were already knitted into local communities would have become indivisible from them as even their commanding officers no longer parachuted in from elsewhere. In many places, command may have become hereditary or elective or settled on the most capable, ruthless, assertive, strong or violent. These men would have continued to exercise their authority from the Wall's forts and other military compounds which, unlike the villas and cities of the south, were both well defended and small enough to manage and maintain. As their needs changed and their skills became less specialized, new types of buildings rose – buildings that more closely resembled the halls of native warlords north of the Wall, designed to accommodate warriors and mead-benches rather than the circumscribed routines of army life. These people may have continued to think of themselves as Romans and soldiers of Empire, but their culture was – even if they weren't aware of it – becoming ever more divergent from Empire-wide norms and even from their local neighbours, ever more embedded in the particularities of place and community.

Whoever ruled from the timber hall of *Banna*'s final phase had no expectation of relief or pay or fresh recruits or promotion. There was no longer any expectation of orders from above: he was on his own, and his people had been on their own for a generation or several. They had had to find new ways to support themselves, and a new outlet for inherited militarism, exploiting the local populations for food and other services, bringing the warriors of tribal elites and civilian populations into their retinues, their warbands. It is the Mad Max view of Dark Age Britain, a world of local clans all looking, in the famous words of Emperor Honorius, 'to their own defences', and competing with each other for resources.[7] At *Vindolanda*, an inscribed stone marks the resting place of a man named Brigomaglos, a British name that means 'high chief'.*[8] Based on the letter forms, a date between 500 and 600 is likely, and it is tempting to imagine him as exactly the sort of hard-bitten geezer who might have done well in the uncompromising conditions of the sub-Roman Wall. The north might have been filled with such characters, tin-pot warlords backed by a gang of local toughs, raiding their neighbours from the relative safety of their patched-up strongholds. It would not have taken much for such men to start calling themselves *dux* or *arbennig*, *rex* or *gwledig*.† In the violent and turbulent post-Roman world, men like these were looked to for protection. At the same time, it was from them that others needed protecting.

At some point in the fifth century, a man called Patrick, a British native, wrote his *Confessio* after many years of apparently successful work as a missionary among the heathen Irish. He began with a description of his early life with his father, Calpornius. 'He was a deacon,' Patrick explains, and 'his father was Potitus, a priest, who lived at *Bannavem Taburniae*. His home was near there, and that is where I was taken prisoner. I was about sixteen at the time. At that time, I did not know the true God. I was taken into captivity in Ireland, along with thousands of others.'[9] Patrick's *Confessio* paints a brief portrait of fifth-century Britain as an essentially Christian and Roman world with an apparently functioning church hierarchy that chimes with what Gildas had to say about Britain in *c*.500. (The fact that Patrick, in hindsight, regarded his 16-year-old self to have been lacking theological sophistication should not be taken as a comment on the essentially Christian environment in which he

---

* BRIGOMAGLOS HIC IACIT [–]CUS ('Brigomaglos lies here [*illegible word*]).

† Latin 'Commander'; Brittonic 'Headman'; Latin 'King'; Brittonic 'Supreme Ruler'.

evidently grew up.) A number of places have been proposed as *Bannavem Taburniae*, including Carlisle, Birdoswald (*Banna*) and Ravenglass in Cumbria. There is little prospect of the problem ever being resolved, but – given Patrick's unhappy fate at the hands of Irish slave-raiders – it has generally been assumed to lie along the Irish Sea coastline of Britain. It is very possible, therefore, that Patrick was a native of northwest England or southwest Scotland.

Plenty of evidence for functioning Christianity and vestigial *Romanitas* has survived across the north. Possible fifth- or sixth-century inscriptions on stone – like the Brigomaglos inscription at *Vindolanda* – are also known from the towns and forts of *Camboglanna* (Castlesteads), *Alauna* (Maryport), *Luguvalio* (Carlisle) and, further south in Cumbria, *Brocavum* (Brougham).[10] They are part of a long continuity of inscription that originated firmly in Roman tradition and the language, alphabet and many of the names are Latin ones. Some are more contentious in their dating than others, but a stone from Carlisle remembering a woman named Tancorix (a British Celtic name) dates to the mid–late fifth century, judging by the spellings used in the inscription. It commemorates her long life of sixty years: an impressive run for the time.*[11] Carlisle in fact seems to have retained a surprising amount of functioning Roman infrastructure. The anonymous *Vita Sancti Cuthberti* ('Life of Saint Cuthbert') tells how St Cuthbert went to visit the Northumbrian queen at Carlisle and was introduced to a functioning Roman fountain – a civic wonder that presumably required a working aqueduct to supply it as late as 685.† It is reasonable to assume that even more of the city was still in functioning order two hundred years earlier, despite otherwise typical evidence for urban decay.

---

* TANCORIX MULIER VIGSIT ANNOS SEGSAGINTA ('Tancorix, a woman, lived sixty years').

† Cuthbert was shown around by a man called Waga who bore the title *civitatis praepositus* ('city overseer'), a title analogous to the *praefectus* who was in charge at Lincoln a few decades earlier.

Elsewhere, the remains of buildings interpreted as possible churches are known from a number of fifth- and sixth-century contexts. Roman forts at *Banna*, *Vercovicium* and *Arbeia* have all yielded evidence for buildings interpreted as possible churches dating to the late fourth century and later. In 2020, investigation of an apsidal structure of the fifth or sixth century at *Vindolanda* revealed that the building had collapsed in on itself, sealing the remains of a lead chalice within the ruins. Fourteen broken fragments of this staggeringly rare object were recovered, all of them smothered in Christian graffiti: crosses and Chi-Rho monograms, fish and whales, Latin and Greek letters, an angel and a bishop, a ship … all sort of doodles and scribbling, possibly even some ogham. It is probably as close as anyone will come to a smoking gun (or smoking censer) for formal Christian worship on the post-Roman Wall – and incredibly compelling evidence that other 'apsidal structures' of the Roman north were indeed early churches.[12] Some of the most dramatic evidence for Christianity in the region, however, comes not from the enclosures of the northern Roman military command, but from its northern hinterland beyond the border.

A ragged axe-rent in Britain's western flank, the Solway Firth today forms part of the border between England and Scotland, between Cumbria and Dumfries/Galloway, disgorging the island's ichors out towards the Isle of Man and the Irish Sea. Its long northern edge is veined with waterways, rivers carrying water from the Galloway hills and further afield down towards the Firth. Between the outlets of streams and rivers, dozens of islands and peninsulas stand out into the wider flood, nubbins of flat land skirted by wide, sandy beaches, backed by rising hills and distant mountains. It is a landscape of astonishing quiet beauty, only slightly unsettled by its role as the fictional Summerisle of director Robin Hardy's 1973 classic *The Wicker Man*. In a way, the coastline of Dumfries and Galloway makes sense as a locus for atavistic pagan rites and hidden bucolic terror. The history of its people is plunged into a penumbra unusually dark, even for an island riddled with shadowed nooks and crannies. Nevertheless, the religious rites of its

Dark Age inhabitants have left their mark, and these traces suggest that – rather than a weird attachment to the depraved rituals of an imagined Iron Age – the people who dwelt here sixteen hundred years ago were already Christians of some sophistication.

The Machars is one of the larger masses that projects south into the Solway's stream. Its craggy southern tip, Burrow Head, is forever immortalized as the setting for the *The Wicker Man*'s horrifying gut-punch of an ending. A little further inland – around five miles to the north – is the site of Whithorn Priory. Ruined now, it was for hundreds of years an important centre of medieval Christianity, placed on firm institutional footings in the twelfth century. Its origins, however, are much older. Bede, writing in the eighth century, attributed its foundation to St Ninian, who – according to the Northumbrian monk – converted the southern Picts and established an episcopal see dedicated to St Martin of Tours at a place that Bede called *Candida Casa* (the 'White House'), supposedly 'because he built the church from stone, which was unusual among the Britons'.[13] At the time that Bede wrote, Whithorn had been subsumed into the Bernician kingdom, and the name 'Whithorn' (from OE *whit* + *ærn*) is a straightforward English translation of the Latin *candida casa*. It was, in Bede's day and since early in the seventh century, a monastic centre and a major cemetery, with evidence of impressive timber structures and high-status accommodation.

Ninian, if he ever existed, probably lived in the fifth century, although the details of his life are largely unknowable and mired in later embellishment. What is certain, however, is that Christianity in the Machars dates back just as far. The 'Latinus stone' commemorates a 35-year-old man of that name and his 4-year-old daughter, noting that he was the grandson or ancestor of someone called Barrovadus and that he had, presumably by raising the stone, made his mark here (his *signum*). The inscription dates to the mid-fifth century.[14] At the same time, huge quantities of coloured glassware, wine and spices were being imported to the Machars from the Mediterranean and the Loire Valley. What for, however, remains something of a mystery – recent research has been attempting to refine the chronology of the site and understand its early history as a Christian centre, but so far no evidence of this date for church buildings or burials has emerged. That it was a place occupied by Christians with high status and far-flung connections is not in doubt, but whether Whithorn was the religious engine of the north Solway coast is much less clear. Another stone found in the environs of Whithorn Priory, dedicating the place to Peter the Apostle (LOCI/PETRI APU/STOLI), dates to the beginning of the seventh century.[15] It did not originate there, however. The block was quarried from the stone of a peninsula several miles to the west.

The north Solway coast terminates at the hammer-shaped Rhins of Galloway. There, in the ancient parish of Kirkmadrine, in an upland landscape of arable grassland overlooking the distant sea, a little disused chapel of reddish-brown stone houses twelve carved stones dating to the early Middle Ages. Most date to the period between 800 and 1100, but three of them – pillars inscribed in Latin and bearing neatly and expertly incised cruciform versions of the Chi-Rho monogram – date to the sixth century. The stones were found between the early nineteenth and early twentieth centuries in contexts that strongly imply that they were part of an early ecclesiastical foundation on the site of the existing chapel. The apparently oldest of the stones, 'Kirkmadrine 1', carries the longest inscription. Inscribed in Latin, it translates as 'Here lie the holy and outstanding priests [i.e. bishops] Viventius and Mavorius'. It also includes a rendering (broken and thus incomplete) of the Christian formula A E[T Ω] – Alpha and Omega, the first and last. 'Kirkmadrine 2' commemorates someone called Florentius, along with someone else whose name is missing (*[—]s et Florentius*). The last of the trio, 'Kirkmadrine 3', is the latest and probably dates to around AD 600. Its inscription echoes the Alpha and Omega of 'Kirkmadrine 1' with the words *initium et finis* – 'the beginning and the end'.[16]

The names (a mixture of Latin and Celtic), the use of Greek characters and indications of biblical learning, the continental influence of the Chi-Rho imagery, the evidence of a functioning church hierarchy – all these elements situate the people who died here within a cultured and connected ecclesiastical world, the same world that finds expression in the writings of Patrick and Gildas and on the inscribed stones of Wales and Dumnonia.* The quality of the carving and calligraphy – on 'Kirkmadrine 1' in particular – speaks to a community with access to masons of some skill, possibly even a school of craftsmen whose work was fostered and commissioned by a monastic foundation of some significance. On current evidence, it seems very plausible that Kirkmadrine – not Whithorn – was the premier religious site in Galloway until the political winds changed after the year 600. Whatever the true relationship of the two sites, between them they demonstrate very clearly that literate, well-connected, Latinate Christian culture was thriving north of the Solway during the fifth and sixth centuries. Such culture, however, depended for its wealth, security and survival on protection, and there is ample evidence that the land beyond the Wall threw up men just as hard as their southern neighbours.

The wide belt of territory that extended between Hadrian's Wall and the Antonine rampart (that spanned the narrow waist of land between the Forth and Clyde) had been lost to direct Roman authority since the early third century. It nevertheless remained part of a world that was ordered in accordance with Imperial priorities, its tribes bound to the Empire by trade, political interference and the threat of military intervention. Roman diplomacy at the frontiers had long been focused on encouraging divisions among tribal groups – pitting them against each other by building and breaking alliances through access to the wealth and military backing of Empire. Without the carrot of Imperial bribes (diplomatic 'gifts') and the stick of the Roman legions, the barbarian warlords of northern Britain may well have seen opportunities to expand their authority at the same time as experiencing heightened competition for the prestige goods and natural resources on which tribal power had come to depend.

---

* The name Mavorius may be a Latinized version of a possible Celtic *Magurix*.

Kirkmadrine stones 1 and 2.

The Empire had also provided opportunities for trade that brought the remote regions of northern Britain into contact with goods from all over the Empire. When that infrastructure collapsed and access to foreign goods was restricted, new trade routes and partnerships were sought by those whose position in society depended on conspicuous consumption and the material signifiers of wealth and powerful connections. The region was – and remains – rich in copper and lead, commodities that may have been a powerful draw for merchants and middlemen dealing across Britain, Ireland and continental Europe. Evidence from hill-forts in Galloway – as elsewhere in western and northern Britain – bears witness to both the foreign trade and specialized crafts that were being cultivated by a new elite from at least the middle of the sixth century. At Mote of Mark, a hill-top site overlooking the estuary of the River Urr, substantial evidence for the skilled working of gold, silver and copper-alloys (brass and bronze) has been excavated: tools, crucibles, moulds, cast-offs, by-products – the detritus of smithcraft on an industrial scale, all protected by a massive timber-laced stone rampart. There were also considerable quantities of imported glass and pottery from Gaul and evidence for the consumption of animals on a conspicuous scale. This sort of wealth and these far-reaching contacts are surprising at a site which is small by the standards of other hill-top settlements in Britain. If not the fortress of a warlord, however, the Mote may have been the fortified workshop of a highly valued specialist, no doubt under the protection of a powerful ruler.[17]

Trusty's Hill, a rounded nub of granite overlooking the Water of Fleet, a couple of miles north of where the river empties itself out into the Solway, has recently been proposed as the seat of just such a ruler. Reinvestigation of the site, despite targeting only around one per cent of the total area of the fort, has revealed a substantial settlement in which a (probable) central hall complex came by $c.600$ to be surrounded by multiple concentric stone-walled ramparts: what, in archaeological jargon, is known as a 'nucleated fort'. As at the Mote, Trusty's Hill revealed evidence of metalworking, feasting and more continental imports. Most eye-catching of all, however, is the presence of a basin cut into the rock – about thirty inches deep and nearly six feet across – that was discovered in a demarcated area beside an elaborate gateway, opposite a stone carved with Pictish symbols.* By analogy with the features and layout of the fortress of Dunadd in the northern kingdom of Dál Riata, which also includes a basin cut into the rock and Pictish symbol-stone, Trusty's Hill has been interpreted as a royal stronghold, perhaps one in which rituals of inauguration once took place at the height of its importance.[18] This seems like rather a lot of weight for the hard evidence to bear. But what is certainly clear – even from the limited scope of the investigation – is that Trusty's Hill was once home to someone who

* See **FORTRIU**.

wielded considerable power around the close of the sixth century. There is no history, no chronicle to provide a sure guide to the identities of the men and women who lived as kings and queens of bastions such as these, beneficiaries of an expansive European trading network, patrons of craftsmen and protectors of the Church, contending with the heirs to the degenerate Roman commands of northern England and the English-speaking warlords of the east. No one now can trace their fortunes; their names are lost.

All but one.

'Wait! I, Uryens, will try!'

With these words, the actor Keith Buckley barges into the action of John Boorman's movie *Excalibur* (1981), seizing hold of the sword in the stone and humiliating himself in exhausting failure before the impatient crowd makes its feelings known: 'Let the boy try!' The boy, of course, is Arthur – the true king in waiting and the secret son of the late Uther Pendragon, kept in hiding by Merlin and unwittingly fostered to the good knight Sir Ector. The sword is drawn – 'We have our king!' exclaims the curious druidic character who seems to be presiding – and the assembled throng, for the most part, falls to its collective knee to the strains of 'Siegfried's Death and Funeral March' from Richard Wagner's *Götterdämmerung*. Uryens, however, is having none of it: 'Do you want a bastard as a king!' he bellows.

We next encounter Uryens, the crown denied to him, literally mired in his error, wading waist-high in the moat of Castle Camelyarde, searching for enemies upon whom to vent his rage, his sense of injustice. It is there, deep in the freezing water, that he is surprised and unmanned by the boy king. Stubborn and prideful, however, Uryens will not yield to a mere squire. And so Arthur hands over the sword and asks that his enemy knight him. Uryens thus finds himself suddenly in possession of the means by which he can exercise his will to power: a terrible weapon, the source of royal legitimacy, given freely into his hand. Before him stands an unarmoured boy, utterly vulnerable. And yet Uryens does not strike.

Overpowered by Excalibur and the spirit it possesses (or is it by his subconscious recognition of Arthur's moral right?), the warlord finds himself compelled, struggling against the sword and himself, to perform the ritual. Finally, his rage dispelled by revelation, he falls at last to his knees in the water, kissing Arthur's hands and gushing: 'Rise, King Arthur. I am your humble knight [...] I doubt you no more.'[19]

In *Excalibur*, Uryens is an angry man, violent and impulsive, blinded by his own sense of entitlement and the strictures of class. Until his revelation in the moat, he fails to see the rightful king in the boy Arthur, instead taking up arms against him, the darkness of his armour reflecting the corruption of his heart. For Boorman, Uryens serves a useful purpose: he is a personification of the challenges faced by the new king in unifying his realm and a foil against which Arthur can prove his moral and military quality. He is, in other words, dramatically useful in the early stages of the film. The choice by Boorman and scriptwriter Rospo Pallenberg to use the character of Uryens to perform this role, however, was not an innovation. His most obvious prototype is the 'Uriens' who appears in Thomas Malory's *Le Morte d'Arthur*, a fifteenth-century retelling of the Arthur story that has won an enormous readership since it was first printed by William Caxton in 1485, becoming – for English readers at least – the definitive codification of the Arthurian cycle, a distinction won largely through its dissemination as one of England's earliest printed books.

Malory's 'Uriens' is introduced as 'King of the land of Gore' – one of a number of kings who reject Arthur, 'a beardless boy that was come of low blood, and sent him word that they would [have] none of his gifts, but that they were come to give him gifts with hard swords betwixt the neck and the shoulders'.[20] He begins as a potentially sinister figure, wedded to Arthur's sister, Morgan le Fay (who, Malory informs us, 'was a great clerk of necromancy').[21] Arthur is eventually forced to bring him to heel over the course of a number of frankly confusing military episodes. Malory, however, was not the inventor of this rebellious Urien: the thirteenth-century French 'Vulgate Cycle', which Malory translated and retold, likewise depicts the king of 'Gorre' as a refusenik in Arthur's project of national unification.

'Gore' or 'Gorre' seems to have been an invention of French writers, and it reflects a general geographical vagueness about Urien's dominions that pervades the Arthurian tradition. Geoffrey of Monmouth, writing in the twelfth century, had 'Urian' pegged as a king of 'Mureif' whose lands were restored to him by the beneficence of Arthur. Mureif seems to have been somewhere in Scotland – either Moray in the north or Monreith in Galloway. There is no trace here of the mysterious land of Gorre, or of Urien's rebellious nature. Instead it seems that Geoffrey's idea of Urien and his homeland was – as one might expect – closely related to traditional Welsh lore: a body of disparate and interwoven matter from which a very different Urien emerged. Unlike the quasi-villain of courtly French Arthuriana, the Welsh Urien was remembered as a hero – one of the 'three bull-protectors', the 'three battle-rulers' and the 'three fair womb-burdens' of the island of Britain (in the Triads), an ancestor worth bragging about (in the genealogies) and the subject of a medieval cycle of short narrative poems (known as *englynion*) contained in the 'Red Book of Hergest'.[22]

This Welsh material built upon the earliest securely datable reference to Urien, a passage contained in the early ninth-century *Historia Brittonum* that describes resistance to the sixth-century kings of Bernicia, the northern province of what later became (with Deira) the kingdom of Northumbria:

Four kings fought against them, *Urbgen* [Urien], and *Riderch Hen* [Rhydderch Hen], and *Guallauc* [Gwallawg] and *Morcant*. *Deodric* [Theoderic, king of Bernicia] fought vigorously against Urien and his sons. During that time, sometimes enemies, sometimes citizens [i.e. the Britons] were victorious, and he [Urien] besieged them for three days and three nights in the island of *Metcaut* [Lindisfarne]. But during that campaign, he was murdered on the instigation of Morcant, from jealousy, because in him, beyond all other kings, was the greatest skill in war-making.[23]

It is chiefly from this brief and tantalizing story that the Welsh sense of Urien as a mighty and implacable foe of the English developed – an Arthur of the north who briefly seemed capable of turning the tide of fate against the invaders, a hero whose untimely death through treachery dealt a mortal blow to British resistance. In particular he was seen as the leader of an alliance of famous heroes – the *gwyr hen ogledd* (the 'men of the old north') – a unified front of British kingdoms against the hated English.*

In truth, all the passage really reveals is that in ninth-century Wales it was believed that there were four kings in the north who fought at some time or another against the Bernicians, that Urien was the best of them, and that he was murdered by Morcant during a siege of Lindisfarne. It does not actually suggest that the four kings fought in concert with each other, or at the same time, or even whether all the individuals referred to were contemporary with each other. Nevertheless, it indicates that already by the 820s there was a legend of Urien in circulation, a legend that would lead later generations of poets to pen laments for his demise and propel him into the upper echelons of honoured ancestors. And by naming him as a contemporary of Theoderic of Bernicia – a figure whose rule is conjecturally dated to the late sixth century – the *Historia*

---

* 'Gwallawg' is the same Gwallog ap Lleenog, law-giver of Elmet, who preferred piles of the slain to subterfuge (see **ELMET**). Rhydderch *Hen* ('the Old') – or Rhydderch *Hael* ('the Generous') as he is known in other texts – was a king of Alt Clut, the western realm whose fortress clung like a barnacle to the summit of Dumbarton Rock, rising impregnable from the cold waters of the Clyde until its destruction by Vikings in 871. According to later legend, Rhydderch was the owner of a famous sword named *Dyrnwyn* ('white hilt') which, when unsheathed, burned with a savage fire. Of the infamous Morcant, there is little to say. His realm – if he ever ruled one – is unknown and unknowable, although two men of that name appear in a late genealogy of northern kings, one of them bearing the epithet *Bulc* ('Gap'). There is also a faint possibility that he might be the character referred to in the life of St Kentigern as 'King Morken' of Strathclyde (i.e. Alt Clut), but this sits rather uneasily with his supposed contemporaneity with Rhydderch Hen/Hael who was also supposed to be king of the same place; although being called 'king' need not imply much more than very local authority.

Britonnum also established a chronological niche into which a 'historical' Urien could be inserted.*

The existence of this Urien is apparently corroborated by a manuscript that dates to the fourteenth century, a famous volume known as the *Llyfr Taliesin* (the 'Book of Taliesin') that preserves fifty-six poems of varying antiquity. In particular, eleven of these poems were considered by the great scholar of Welsh literature, Sir Ifor Williams, to be the work of a poet (or poets) who was a contemporary of his or her subjects, and this opinion continues to carry enormous weight.† Whether or not a 'real' Taliesin ever existed cannot be proved either way (there is no independent corroboration for his existence that can be dated earlier than the ninth-century *Historia Brittonum*), but these eleven 'old' poems are frequently accepted to be at least consistent with a sixth-century milieu: compositions written to entertain kings as they feasted and held court, basking in the glory of bloody-handed exploits and

---

* Theoderic is recorded in a genealogy of Bernician kings that appears in both the *Historia Brittonum* and among the genealogies of the Anglian collection (see **LINDSEY**). In the *Historia Brittonum* he is said to be a son of the great king Ida who conquered *Dun Guoaroy* (Bamburgh) for Bernicia and there founded a dynasty known as 'Idings' (the people of Ida). Theoderic Iding supposedly reigned for seven years and his brother Freodwald for six after him. It was apparently in Freodwald's time – and almost certainly right at the end of his reign – that 'the kingdom of the Kentishmen received baptism, from the mission of Gregory'. King Æthelberht of Kent was probably converted in 597 immediately on Gregory's arrival. This would mean that Theoderic's reign in Bernicia began thirteen years earlier in around 584 and lasted until *c.*591. This dates the death of Urien to sometime in the same span of years.

† Sometimes the poet is imagined to be the legendary Taliesin himself, a bard who was supposed in the Middle Ages to be the author of the entire *Llyfr Taliesin* (though that has long been recognized to be impossible). The rest of the poems collected in the Book of Taliesin are of ninth-century date or later and present Taliesin as a quasi-supernatural figure or an archetype for future poets (they are, in other words, the work of several other, later, writers).

revelling in the remembered groans of vanquished foes.* The figure that looms largest in these poems is Urien, and it is in them that his kingdom is named as a place called Rheged. Thus, at base, the most ancient poems of the *Llyfr Taliesin* are the foundations on which the whole conjectured realm of Rheged must stand or fall.

The Urien poems in the *Llyfr Taliesin* are eight in number, plus one which is an elegy for Urien's son Owain.†[24] Leaving aside for a moment the question of their antiquity (and thus whether they present a truly contemporary portrait of their subject), the Urien who emerges from them is not a particularly well-rounded figure. So far as the poet was concerned, he was a man whose character could be painted with an extremely limited palette of qualities. The first, and most important, was his ability to successfully enact violence upon his neighbours. In this arena, the king's capability to rain death and despair down upon his enemies, to trample their corpses and terrorize their communities, was particularly praise-worthy ('I saw valiant men assembled in armies – after a morning's fighting, mangled flesh!').[25] This was the Urien whose name, according to the poet, was well known to the English – to those who: 'Had death at his hands, And many afflictions: Their houses burning, Their chattels stolen, With frequent losses, And bitter distress.'[26] He was also a steadfast defender: 'From summer to winter, weapons in hand, He's kept his watch at ford and rampart,

---

* In the *Historia Brittonum*, Taliesin (whose name means literally 'radiant brow') appears in the company of four other famous British bards: Talhearn Tad Aen ('Ironbrow the Father of Inspiration'), Bluchbard ('bald poet'), Cian 'Gueinth Guaut' ('grain of song') and Aneirin, the supposed author of *Y Gododdin*. Taliesin is in fact mentioned in *Y Gododdin*, but there is no way to know when the reference to the poet was inserted into the text and therefore no reason to believe it significantly predates the thirteenth-century manuscript in which it appears.

† Not all of them are provided with titles in *Llyfr Taliesin*, though some of them are. The most recent translators of these poems – the poet Gwyneth Lewis and former Archbishop of Canterbury Dr Rowan Williams – refer to the untitled poems by their first lines (as in standard poetic convention) and I have followed their lead.

Sleeping stretched out in trenches.' This was probably an important quality given the number of people he must have inspired to try dealing out some reciprocal death and affliction. Overall, in the poet's assessment, Urien of Rheged was good at doing war. 'Till the end of the world,' the poet insists, 'all accounts will agree: He sweeps aside enemies; he deserves the image, "Lightning-destroyer".'[27]

In fact, all the poems emphasize warlike themes with the exception of *Here at My Rest*, and even this contrives to address the king with martial flattery. ('Great men snort and groan, For fear of your onslaught, Stirrer of battle, Buttress of the land!')[28] Otherwise, however, *Here at My Rest* is chiefly concerned with the second of Urien's qualities. This, an attribute no doubt emphasized with healthy regard to self-interest, was the king's great generosity as provider – to the poet, to poets in general and to others of his court – of 'Wealth in plenty, Of glittering gold, Golden good times, And glowing esteem'. It is an exuberant poem, overflowing with booze ('Mead for me […], And beer for drinking, beer to drink') and all the other joys of the Dark Age highlife: feasting and poetry, horses, land and fine gifts of gold.[29]

The open-handedness of Urien, and the 'great respect rendered to the world's great poets', is also stressed in three other poems: *Taliesin's Plunder*, *All Through One Year* and *Urien of Erechwydd*. The last of these, however, introduces an otherwise underplayed aspect of Urien's persona, opening with a direct address to 'Urien of Erechwydd, Most generous Christian'.[30] If generosity and warmongering were essential skills in the royal job description, however, piety was merely desirable. Only three other of the Urien praise-poems have any reference to religion at all, and none of these relate to the king's own faith (*Here at My Rest* suggests that Urien's quality was God-given;[31] *Taliesin's Plunder* contains a reference to the 'paschal blaze of candles and foliage' – presumably a reference to Easter festivities;[32] *To Pacify Urien* describes the poet's devotion to Urien as a bond unbreakable save only by 'God in Heaven', i.e. by death).[33] For anyone seeking radiant images of sacral kingship and holy Christian warlords of Arthurian splendour, this is thin gruel.

Nevertheless, it is pretty consistent with what all other evidence indicates about the religion of post-Roman British kings: i.e. that they considered themselves Christians, even if they often weren't very good at it, and generally seemed more enthused by the brutality of the Old Testament than by any notional blessings that might be conferred upon the meek.*

Sometimes, the poet's sycophantic ejaculations run to the silly end of the spectrum. Taken out of context, pronouncements like – 'You're my delight [...] There's no competition'; 'You are the best [...] my leader for life'; 'I'll sing the praises, Of all you've done'; 'No leader can compare' – share the cadences of state-controlled media in autocratic states.[34] At its best, however, Taliesin's praise rises to levels that would exceed the expectations of even the most insatiably narcissistic dictator:

> His delight is great in his poets and his deer,
> His anger is great against his enemies.
> His power is great over the clans of the Britons.
> Like a wheel of fire across the earth,
> Like a river in spate is Llwyfennydd's true lord;
> Like a hymn or a battle-song known to all,
> Like the great-souled sea is Urien.[35]

Clearly, Urien was imagined to be an important guy. Among the many epithets bestowed upon him by the poet was *gwledig*, which seems to have been reserved for only the most exulted of overlords and means something like 'supreme leader'. If Urien was truly as powerful as the poems suggest, he must have been able to project his authority widely and engage in diplomatic relations with other powerful realms. The development of power in this period was – as the experience of many other kingdoms demonstrates – often founded on personal relationships between kings

---

* The complaints levelled by Gildas and Patrick demonstrate that these issues were not lost on contemporaries.

and sub-kings, with the loyalties of groups and control over territory dependent on a complicated web of family loyalty, religious affiliation, political opportunism and economic imperative. A sense that Urien's kingdom maintained an elevated diplomatic status in its dealings with neighbouring realms is implied by a tradition, recorded in the *Historia Brittonum*, that one of Urien's sons – Rhun – was the bishop who baptized King Edwin of Northumbria.* It is quite possible, therefore, that the ruling dynasty of Rheged was a major player in northern politics at the end of the sixth century and maybe even later.† Exactly where the heart of Rheged lay, however, and precisely how far Urien's reach may have extended, is a question that only the poetry can hope to answer.

Urien and Rheged are inextricably bound by and to the Taliesin poems. Urien is both the 'defender of Rheged' (*Reget diffreidyat*) and the 'lord of Rheged' (*glyv reget*), as is his other son, Owain.‡[36] All reconstructions of the extent of his realm are founded in the mention of places where his writ ran or his sword was bloodied, where the mountains trembled at the mention of his coming. And if the corpus of poems is taken to reflect a genuine picture of

* The reference is hard to assess, as by the time it was recorded it was probably already influenced by the developing legend of Urien and the Old North. It also directly contradicts Bede, who doesn't mention Rhun and states that Edwin was baptized by Bishop Paulinus (see **LINDSEY**).

† It is worth noting that the same source also suggests that Rhun's granddaughter Rieinmelth, daughter of Royth, was married to Oswy of Northumbria (r.642–670) and this is apparently confirmed by a Northumbrian source from Durham (also of the ninth century) that identifies the woman as 'Raegnmaeld' (an anglicized version of the same name). If this marriage reflects any sort of genuine connection to Urien, it might imply that Rheged's power lasted through several generations – long enough, at any rate, to make an alliance with the line of Urien politically appealing as late as the mid-seventh century.

‡ Owain (as Ewain, Yvain etc.) also became a figure of Arthurian legend.

northern British geography (however much some of the details may have reflected wishful thinking over practical reality), it becomes possible to sketch the conjectural limits of this most forgotten kingdom – to glimpse a shadow, spread upon the wrinkled face of northern Britain, that marks the blurry outline of his realm.

A number of specific places – all bearing British (that is to say Brittonic Celtic) place-names – are explicitly described by the poet as being territory over which Urien wielded authority. These are *Catraeth*, *Llwyfennydd*, *Erechwydd* and *Aeron*. In addition, the poems also name a number of places at which Urien's warriors are said to have fought: *Gwen Ystrad* and *Llech Wen*, *Argoed Llwyfain*, *Alclud* ford, *Brewyn*'s cells, *Clutuein* and *Pencoed*. Then there are a number of regions, mostly unfriendly, that filled out the wider geography of the *Hen Ogledd* and which help to narrow down where Rheged could conceivably fit. These are *Manaw*, *Goddeu*, *Mathry*, *Powys*, *Gododdin* and *Alclud*.

The regions are relatively straightforward to identify, although attempts to map them with precision are attended by their own challenges. *Alclud* is the British kingdom of Alt Clut – the 'rock of the Clyde' – and its territory comprised modern Renfrewshire and probably parts of Ayrshire and Lanarkshire as well. *Gododdin* refers to the eastern kingdom that had its fortress at *Dun Eidyn* (Edinburgh) and whose territory ran south through Lothian on the eastern side of Britain, and whose identity and name originated in the tribal territory of the Roman and pre-Roman Iron Age *Votadini*. *Manaw* refers to an adjacent and perhaps allied territory (sometimes referred to as 'Manaw Gododdin') in the region of Stirlingshire and Clackmannanshire (Clackmannan means 'stone of Manaw') and which may have included a fortress at Stirling where the Castle Rock commands the head of the Forth. *Powys* was a post-Roman kingdom in what is now central Wales and the Welsh marches that extended north towards the Roman city of *Deva Victrix* (Chester). *Mathry* is more of an enigma. Since so little is known about the context in which the poems were written, it is possible that Mathry in Pembrokeshire, despite its geographical distance from the general setting of the *Hen Ogledd*, was intended.* That leaves *Goddeu* – a word in medieval Welsh (*goddau*) that refers to trees or woodland. Many suggestions for the location of this place have been advanced, none of them susceptible to proof, and it may well be that it was never really a place-name at all.†[37]

Despite the many uncertainties, this exercise at least sets some parameters by roughly establishing where Urien's kingdom wasn't. And, after taking into account the fledgling 'Northumbrian' kingdoms in the coastal regions east of the Pennines, there is only one area unaccounted for in the crowded geography of northern Britain: a broad swathe of northwest England and southern Scotland that roughly corresponds to the modern counties of Cumbria, Dumfries and Galloway, extending south into Lancashire and west towards Northumberland, Durham and the Borders. This is a massive area, however, and its limits are vague in the extreme. Any attempt at greater precision relies on the correct identification of the specific places over which Urien claimed lordship and the battles that he fought. That, however, has proved easier said than done.

---

* The relevant passage – an allusion to the hapless foes of Urien 'Wailing like greedy white gulls in Mathry' – might well have made sense to whomever the poem was originally composed, adapted or performed for. It could, in fact, constitute evidence for the late composition of the poem (*Rheged, Arise, its Lords Are its Glory*) in a Welsh court setting far from the imagined borders of Rheged (Mathry is a seaside settlement in Pembrokeshire).

† The term appears in a line from *The Battle of Argoed Llwyfain* referring to Urien laying 'waste the lands of Goddeu and Rheged'. This is followed by the line: 'From *Argoed* to *Arfynydd* the muster was summoned'. *Argoed* and *Arfynydd* can be translated as 'by the woods' and 'by the mountains' respectively, and it may be that these terms were introduced as an explanation or amplification of the foregoing pair of place-names: *Goddeu-Argoed*, 'Goddeu of the forests' and *Rheged-Arfynydd*, 'Rheged of the mountains'. (Where exactly Goddeu was, however, apart from being somewhere presumably close to Rheged, remains essentially unknowable.)

The author of the Urien poems apparently considered Urien to be master of *Catraeth*, *Llwyfennydd*, *Erechwydd* and *Aeron*. Of these places, *Aeron* can plausibly be associated with Ayrshire, a region of southwest Scotland north of the Galloway uplands and south of the Clyde, a territory likely contested by the lords of Alt Clut to the north.* By contrast, *Erechwydd* (or *Yrechwydd*) is rather less easy to interpret. It means something like 'at the clear (or fresh) water' and, if it was ever really intended as a specific place-name, could be pretty much anywhere. The name *Llwyfennydd*, however, is generally considered to be preserved by the Lyvennet, a river that rises in the fells near Crosby Ravensworth in Cumbria, and later Welsh tradition also associated Rheged with the same part of northwest England. A twelfth-century poem – *Gorhoffedd Hywel ab Owain Gwynedd* ('the boasting of Hywel son of Owain of Gwynedd') – linked Rheged with the old Roman town of *Luguvalium* (Carlisle or *Caer Lliwelydd* in Welsh). In addition, a reference in one of the 'prophetic poems' included in the 'Book of Taliesin' (and which probably dates to the early thirteenth century) alludes to campaigns fought *tra merin reget* – 'Beyond Rheged's Firth' according to the poem's most recent translators, but more literally 'over the sea of Rheged'. The poem in which this line appears envisages the destruction of the English and the southern Welsh in campaigns waged by Cadwalladr, the seventh-century king of Gwynedd.[38] From the perspective of its intended audience in North Wales, the parts of Britain most obviously 'over the sea' were the coastal regions of Cumbria and Galloway.†

Catraeth, however, is the most eye-catching of the claims made for Urien's power. At first sight it seems to be a reference to the same place at which the famous battle described in Aneirin's *Y*

---

* Airedale – far to the south of Catterick and west of Leeds in what otherwise might be imagined as Elmetian territory – has also been proposed, but requires an unseemly degree of special pleading to make much sense in a wider context.

† The sea in question has often been assumed to refer specifically to the Solway Firth, though not for any particularly good reason that I can make out.

Gododdin was fought, and has generally been identified with the former Roman fortress town of *Cataractonium* (modern Catterick). Catterick, however, is situated considerably further east and south than the region normally associated with Rheged. While there is no particular reason to doubt that Urien's dominion was territorially impressive, if Catterick was ever part of his kingdom it must have been at its most extreme limits. Archaeology, meanwhile, has not provided any evidence for late fifth- or sixth-century occupation at Catterick, and although excavations have revealed an extensive cemetery, it seems to have fallen out of use by the mid-fifth century – facts that sit a little awkwardly beside the grand claims made by poets for its importance in the schemes of kings and the doom of heroes. And in any case, the etymological argument in favour of the equation of Catterick with *Catraeth* is convoluted and not entirely convincing.* On the other hand, the place-name has a perfectly good Celtic meaning that avoids the whole argument altogether. In Old Welsh *Catraeth* means 'battle-shore', a simple compound of the terms *cat/cad* ('battle) + *traeth* ('shore, bank').[39]

---

* The Roman name for Catterick, *Cataractonium*, means place of waterfalls. Since Catterick is not known for its cataracts, it has been assumed that this was a Latinized form of a Celtic place-name that sounded a bit like – to Roman ears – the Greek-derived Latin word *cataracta*. The native British place-name that it superseded has been assumed to be something like *caturatis, meaning 'battle ramparts'. By the end of the Roman period a new place-name, derived from the Latin name, is assumed to have developed among speakers of native Celtic languages. This name – something like *Cadarachta – thereafter mutated into newer, shortened forms like *Cadracht or *Catracht and from there to the Old English version of the name – *Cetrecht* or *Cetreht* (from whence Catterick) – and an Old Welsh form: *Catraeth*. It is a clever and persuasive thesis. Indeed, there is a feeling that the very cleverness of the argument has distracted from the fact that it proves nothing at all. While it is true that the Roman place-name that eventually became Catterick could, hypothetically, have spawned a pair of meaningless syllables that in Old Welsh were written down as *Catraeth*, there is no evidence that it actually did.

Rivers wound incessantly through the imaginations of early poets, coursing beside the fluttering standards of kings and heaving ghastly with the dead. Throughout the early medieval period, named rivers and river crossings were one of the topographical features most commonly associated with warfare. They are an iconic part of the battlescape, a red ribbon that runs through the writing of Gildas, Bede and Taliesin alike, a thread that binds the conflict narratives of the *Historia Brittonum* and the *Anglo-Saxon Chronicle*. They were, of course, in many ways, obvious places for battles to be fought. Rivers often formed boundaries between territories and their crossings were the points at which enemies could be most easily brought to battle. These were places where defending militias might seek to halt incursions or where returning raiders might be cut off and forced to fight, the river at their backs sealing off easy retreat. The threat of drowning was all too real for those who fled. At the battle of the Winwaed in 655, the army of King Penda of Mercia was destroyed by the Northumbrian king Oswy; Bede explained how the river, 'owing to heavy rains, had overflowed its channels and its banks to such an extent that many more were drowned in flight than were destroyed by the sword in battle'.[40]

Rivers, however, also had symbolic associations, representing boundaries of the most permanent and archaic kind – lines scored deeply into the face of the earth by the ever-flowing water. Control of them could therefore signify authority over much wider territory and reflect a warlord's authority and efficacy, the ability to hold his own. Defeat at the river's edge could therefore undermine the prestige of a ruler in a fundamental way. Urien's *Catraeth* – his 'battle-shore' – was evidently a place worth boasting of, the rise-and-shine vigour of its inhabitants a source of kudos: 'The men of Catraeth are up with the sun, Around their commander, the triumphant cattle-thief.'[41] But there is really no reason to think of it as a specific fortress or a discrete territory. A 'battle-shore', in a poetic sense, could have referred to any militarized frontier – not even, necessarily, one defined by water. To be called Lord of Catraeth, 'the lord of the battle-shore', emphasized Urien's belligerence, his preparedness and his control: an ability to hold what was his and a willingness to lead the warriors of the borderlands in cattle-raids across the frontier. It could have been anywhere, or nowhere.*[42]

The central role that riverine borders played in the dramatization of conflict and the defence of territory is encapsulated by *The Men of Catraeth*, another of the supposedly ancient compositions contained in the Book of Taliesin. The poem, recalling Urien's triumph in battle at a place called *Gwen Ystrad* (the 'white valley'), is awash with fluvial imagery that emphasizes the sense of riverine borders as a critical psychological component of the conflict land-scape. Urien's 'men of Catraeth', the defenders of the battle-shore, find themselves locked in a struggle against a people 'from over the border' – a menace that crashed upon Rheged 'likes waves roaring savagely over the land.'†[43] A cogent case has been for locating the battle of *Gwen Ystrad* at the River Winster in Cumbria, at the southern end of the Lake District.‡[44] Crucial to this identification is an etymological argument that relates the name 'Winster' to the Celtic place-name *Gwensteri* (from which *Gwen Ystrad* probably derives).§ The poem also refers to a feature of the battlefield named as *Llech Wen* – the 'White Crag' – which is very plausibly the same geological feature that came later to be known in English as

* The Catraeth of Aneirin's poem (*Y Gododdin*) may likewise have referred to a more generalized border location; the poem makes reference to a number of topographical and man-made features, including a ford.

† Whether this was intended to imply that the invaders had arrived from across the sea – as Pictish raiders are known to have done – is unclear; it is certainly not necessarily so.

‡ If correct, the association of *Gwen Ystrad* with the Winster would imply that Urien's lordship, and perhaps the bounds of Rheged, included the whole of the Lake District within its compass.

§ *Gwensteri* probably derives from the Brittonic words for 'white' (*gwen*) and 'streams' (*steri*). This relies on an otherwise unattested occurrence of the Breton word *steri* in an insular context. Since Breton is so closely related to Cornish, however, this not at all implausible.

Whitbarrow (the 'white barrow/hill'), a substantial outcrop of lime-stone cliff that overlooks the Winster Valley from the east. It was here, perhaps, as the afternoon sun lit the face of the pale crags, that the poet saw the vanquished foes of Urien Rheged 'Laying their swords at the grey-haired king's feet, They sue for peace, finding no way out, Pale-faced, hands crossed, on the ford's gravel, […] Waves washing through their dead horses' hair.'[45]

Most of the other battles that apparently punctuated Urien's career and illumined his poetic aura cannot be located with any great degree of confidence, but none of them significantly interfere with the developing geographical sense of where Rheged lay. Several of the apparently specific places referred to occur in a single poem, *Rheged, Arise, its Lords Are its Glory*:

A fight for the crown at *Alclud* ford:
Battle for *Brewyn*'s cells, a battle long famed,
Battle in a wood, battle in an estuary,
There was fighting with clamorous steel:
Battle at *Clutuein*, fighting at *Pencoed*,
Drawing wolves to gorge on cascading blood.
Fierce men are brought to their knees;
The Angles' plans are defeated,
Made bloody by steadfast Ulph at the ford.[46]

The precise location of *Alclud* ford is not known, but it implies a location bordering on the kingdom of Alt Clut. *Clutuein* also contains a place-name element (Clut) that links it to the Clyde. This fits well with Urien's supposed lordship in Ayrshire (*Aeron*), and – assuming that Cumbria was at Rheged's core – would make it very hard to imagine how Galloway (south of Ayrshire and north of Cumbria) could also have avoided falling under Urien's sway.*

* It is possible that the place-name Dunragit (a village in the historic county of Wigtownshire) might be derived from something like *Din Reghed* – the 'fortress of Rheged'. However, there is actually no real evidence to suggest that it is.

Brewyn's cells could be a reference to the abandoned Roman fort and vicus at *Bremeniun* in Redesdale (Northumberland) and would be a notably eastward extension of Urien's reach, but the association is very far from solid. *Pencoed* ('head of the forest') is uselessly vague. Another battle poem – *The Battle of Argoed Llywfain* – seems to suggest a specific location. But *Argoed Llwyfain* in fact simply means 'at the elm wood' and is of no geographic help whatsoever. In any case, battles, though they might very often be fought at the borders of a realm, could well occur deep inside friendly or hostile territory. In themselves they are therefore no sure guide to the limits of a ruler's authority. Indeed, in the context of the effulgent praise-poetry in which they appear, notices of successful military entanglements – like assertions of lordship – could emphasize the widest conceivable (or even downright fantastical) reach of a king's arm, however ineffectual the grip at the end of it may have been in reality.*

Ultimately, the Rheged that emerges from the Taliesin poetry (and from a few crumbs of other evidence) is a realm centred on Cumbria, with an extension of its power into Galloway and, possibly, further east. There is no way of knowing where or when its borders were inscribed and, in truth, looking for them too hard is to misunderstand the nature of Dark Age power. As the experience of Essex demonstrates, kingdoms could gain and lose influence, prestige and authority over territory with bewildering speed and regularity. Nevertheless, by taking the eight relevant poems at face value, the broad shape of 'Greater Rheged' outlined here seems on balance to be the best fit for the preserved place-names – at least during Urien's exalted reign. The problem, of course, is that the poems should probably not be taken at face value at all.

The most obvious objection to treating the supposedly early Taliesin poetry as a source for the sixth century is that the poems

---

* Consider, for example, Arthur's infamous 'battle list' in the *Historia Brittonum*; see **LINDSEY**.

exist only in a single manuscript (*Llyfr Taliesin*) that was written (copied from its source text) in the fourteenth century. This makes it impossible for any analysis to be made of the textual history of the poems and very difficult to assess the antiquity of their language. While much of the material the manuscript contains must, for formal, stylistic and linguistic reasons, be older (and in some cases probably considerably so) than its date of transcription, proving the age of any single composition and disentangling the 'original' poetry from the accretions of later minds and hands is next to impossible.[47] The only things of apparent solidity that can be clung to, in fact, are Urien and his named contemporaries. But, as we have already seen, no source earlier than the ninth-century *Historia Brittonum* makes any reference to Urien, and it is well established that Welsh poets remained attached to producing deliberately archaicizing work for centuries. Thus the supposedly ancient poems could be the work of ninth-century (or later) poets fabricating authentic sounding eulogies to the heroes of a lost golden age. At its base, this is a circular problem with no real solution: the historicity of Urien and Rheged are bound to the poems, and the age of the poetry is bound to the reign of Urien.

With these facts before us, it is necessary to accept that Rheged may be no more than an imaginative projection onto a blank region of space and time, an illusion to satisfy the tastes and political aspirations of later generations of Welsh princes – no more real than the 'land of Gorre'. On the other hand, however, one might well object that a deliberate work of the imagination would probably be more elaborate and less abstruse than the material preserved in *Llyfr Taliesin*. At the same time, the transmission of place-names far from Wales (where the manuscript versions of these poems were written down) suggests that a tradition of northern British geography and history was accessible to Welsh poets by the beginning of the ninth century (and must therefore have been in existence for some time prior). Although it seems very likely that much of the surviving poetry is irredeemably confused – with the identity of some individuals conflated, time-lines collapsed and the precise shape of kingdoms distorted – the idea that a real British kingdom of Rheged lies behind the poems remains an inherently plausible one. And while few would now argue that the early poems sprung from the lips and lyre of a single sixth-century bard, there are many who would admit the possibility – even the likelihood – that they contain elements of real tradition and ancient lore, the echoes of sixth-century verses that once thrummed through the halls of the warlords of wall-fort and hill-fort in the wrack of Roman Britain.*

Doubt will always cling to Urien and his kingdom, no matter the reality. But whatever the lands between the Rhins of Galloway and the Cumbrian fells were called, and whatever role the kin of Urien played in governing them, the people who inhabited those lands have left traces of their lives that cannot be argued away. Some – including the most recent excavators of Trusty's Hill – have seen in the hill-forts and Christian sites of Galloway the material proof of Rheged's existence, even of Urien himself, suggesting that this 'archaeological kingdom without a historical record in Galloway, and Rheged, a historical kingdom without an archaeological record, may in fact be one and the same.'[48] Others are less convinced.[49] What is certain, however, is that whatever name is applied to that once formidable and well-connected cluster of settlements, it died in the early seventh century. These were the years of Northumbrian expansion, when that kingdom was able to flex its muscles deep into the lowlands of Scotland, bringing Bernician kings into conflict with realms – Dál Riata and Fortriu – whose borders lay further to the north than Roman power had ever effectively reached. The material culture of Cumbria and the north Solway coast became ever more Anglian, ever more 'English'. Great crosses in the Anglian

---

* If the poems were indeed sixth-century compositions, they would have been composed in a Cumbric Brittonic dialect before transmission through Old Welsh (c.800–c.1100) to Middle Welsh (c.1100–c.1400). Mangling and garbling of the text of some poems suggests that the fourteenth-century scribe who committed them to parchment didn't understand everything he was copying/adapting.

tradition rose at Hoddom (Dumfries and Galloway), Ruthwell and Bewcastle (both Cumbria) and the buildings and paraphernalia and – ultimately – personnel of Whithorn became ever more English. It was not a peaceful transition. The hill-forts at both the Mote of Mark and Trusty's Hill were destroyed by burning in the first few decades of the seventh century. The heat was so overwhelming, so obliterating, that it melted the stone of the ramparts, turning them to glass.* Whatever that land was called, it perished in flame.

But in the dust and the heat and the pall of the burning, the trace of a shadow remains, the shadow of a people, and perhaps of a king, who – even if only for a moment – knitted the lands of the northwest together into a mighty realm. Whether that land was Rheged, and whether that king was Urien, will never truly be known.

The questions, however, will ever echo.

> If there is a cry on the hill,
> Is it not Urien that terrifies?
> If there is a cry in the valley,
> Is it not Urien that pierces?
> If there is a cry in the mountain,
> Is it not Urien that conquers?
> If there is a cry on the slope,
> Is it not Urien that wounds?[50]

---

* A process known as vitrification.

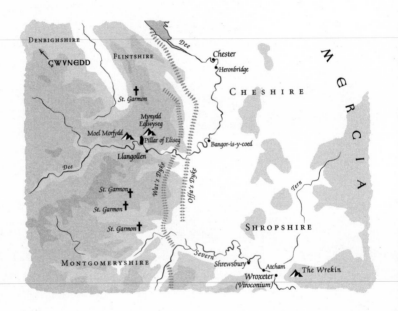

POWYS

– Montgomeryshire, Denbighshire, Flintshire, Cheshire, Shropshire –

The gale, it plies the saplings double,
It blows so hard, 'twill soon be gone:
To-day the Roman and his trouble
Are ashes under Uricon.

A. E. Housman, 'On Wenlock Edge the wood's in trouble',
A Shropshire Lad (1896)[1]

I n a field a few miles from Llangollen, among the steep, wooded slopes of the Nant Eglwyseg Valley in the parish of Llantysilio-yn-Iâl, stands an eight-foot-tall pillar of stone known as the Pillar of Eliseg. Once upon a time it stood taller – probably at least thirteen feet and possibly more – and was almost certainly topped by a cross. Hefted upright onto a dry-stone plinth atop a Bronze Age cairn, the pillar rises mute and broken; an Ozymandian phallus of the Welsh borders. Its history as a cross is not entirely forgotten. From its mound the pillar gazes sightlessly down upon the ruins of a medieval monastery named after the land and its headless sentinel: Valle

Crucis, the 'valley of the cross' – a place known in Welsh as *y Nol yr Hen Groes yn Iâl* ('the Meadow of the Ancient Cross in Iâl'). Around it swirl the high hills and sheer-sided slopes of mountainous border country, hiding and swaddling the pillar in rugged contours of land and sprays of dark woodland until found by the pilgrim or the wanderer, the merchant or the warrior – each time to be discovered anew by travellers taking the roads that led north and west into the interior of the highland zone, or the route that led east along the valley of the Dee, out to the wide plains of the lowland country.

To this one object the history of the ancient kingdom of Powys is inextricably bound – a monument that acts as a lightning rod for the folklore and sense of belonging constructed by the people of Powys and its kings in the early decades of the ninth century, shortly before a veil fell over the realm for centuries.

To look at a modern map of Wales, one might imagine that the Pillar of Eliseg stands in the wrong place altogether. Llangollen and Valle Crucis lie near the Anglo-Welsh border in the county of Denbighshire. Modern Denbighshire (post-1996) has very different borders from historic Denbighshire (pre-1972). Neither, however, has ever been part of the preserved county of Powys. Even more than England, Wales has suffered an egregious degree of bureaucratic meddling with the boundaries of its subdivisions, with tremendously confusing results. The 'historic' shires of Wales date in the most part either to the aftermath of Edward I's conquest of Wales in 1282, or to the 'Laws in Wales Act' of 1535. These replaced a hodgepodge of ancient principalities, Welsh cantrefs, Norman lordships and other arrangements that had developed over the preceding centuries. The historic shires, however, as a result of the 1972 Local Government Act, were replaced by a much smaller number of what are now referred to as 'preserved' counties, many (but not all) of which bear the names (but not really the outlines) of ancient Welsh kingdoms: Clywd, Dyfed, Gwent, Gwynedd, Mid Glamorgan, South Glamorgan, West Glamorgan and Powys. These, in turn, were largely set aside in 1996 but retained for ceremonial purposes – an unfortunate convention which applies a gloss of tradition and antiquity to what are in fact very modern geographical entities. The demise of the preserved counties for administrative purposes was a result of the 'Local Government (Wales) Act 1994' which created new 'Principal Areas' (counties by any other name), some of which used the names of the old 'preserved' counties and some the names of the older 'historic' counties. Some retained their former boundaries, others not so much.

Since 1972, modern Powys has occupied the central portion of eastern Wales, the border country that abuts the English counties of Herefordshire, Shropshire and Cheshire. It encompasses the historic shires of Montgomery, Radnor and Brecknock and retains the shape of the preserved county that preceded it. The kingdom of Powys, however, was something else entirely.* The southern part of the modern county – historic Brecknockshire and Radnorshire – was, in the centuries following the withdrawal of Roman authority, a patchwork of tribal groups and territories – Maelienydd, Elfael, Gwrtheyrnion, Buellt – that have little or no known connection to the old kingdom of Powys.† The kingdom seems instead to have lain further to the north, spanning the modern border between England and Wales and taking in parts of the historic counties of Montgomeryshire, Denbighshire, Flintshire (Wales), Shropshire and Cheshire (England), but even the most diligent of historical geographers would be hard pressed to map its precise boundaries. For all that the name has endured down the centuries, and for all

* The name Powys is thought to derive from the Latin term *paganses*, 'country-folk', and may have been a label applied by others rather than by the people themselves: perhaps by the urban populations of late Roman western Britain. If so, it could have been pejorative – perhaps better translated as 'bumpkins' or 'yokels' – a name that was gradually adopted by the people themselves, a claimed identity or a label that stuck and lost its sting as the centuries passed. On the other hand, the name is unattested before the early ninth century, so whether anybody actually called themselves or anyone else 'Powysians' before that date is moot.

† Not that there is a lot of evidence to the contrary either. A king named Ffernfael ap Tewdwr ruled the territories of Buellt and Gwrtheyrnion in the early ninth century and his relation to the kings of Powys is unknown.

The Pillar of Eliseg, as drawn by Alfred Clint in 1838
(© The Trustees of the British Museum).

the pride invested in its elusive heritage, the history of the kingdom is largely a created one – an accretion of disparate matter around a people whose identity may always have been ephemeral, ever-shifting, their sense of themselves and their past moulded and reshaped by the lines drawn by their neighbours.

By the time the first description of the Pillar of Eliseg was written down, by the English antiquary John Aubrey in 1682, the pillar-cross had fallen. Fourteen years later, in the year before he died, it was visited by the Welsh scholar Edward Lhuyd (1626–97). He found it broken in pieces upon the mound it had once surmounted, thrown down and mutilated – so he believed – by Cromwell's puritanical soldiers during the Civil War, its head struck off in an iconoclastic foreshadowing of the fate of the doomed Stuart monarch.* Lhuyd's chief interest in visiting the remains of the pillar was to see what yet survived of an inscription that covered the curved surface of the lower trunk, an inscription that had already withstood the battering of perhaps 850 years of Welsh weather. What he managed to record of that inscription constitutes the best surviving evidence for the letters that a further three centuries and more have effectively erased.[2]

The inscription, written in Latin and already in the seventeenth century badly damaged and hard to decipher, was recorded by Lhuyd with – so far as can be established – admirable fidelity. It is as well that he took the trouble; when the writer Thomas Pennant visited the site in 1773 the inscription was already illegible. The late eighteenth century occasioned a flurry of antiquarian interest in the Pillar of Eliseg; according to Pennant the mound on which it had stood had been opened in the years prior to his excursion and in the same year as his visit a paper regarding the toppled pillar was read to the Society of Antiquaries of London by the lawyer, naturalist and antiquary Daines Barrington (1727/8–1800). Six years later, in 1779, what remained of the pillar was re-erected by the local squire – Trevor Lloyd of Trevor Hall in Llangollen parish. (Lloyd, in a self-conscious assertion of ownership and status, had a new Latin inscription cut onto the opposite side of the pillar (now missing its lower portion as well as its cross) to commemorate the event and to permanently associate his own name with the physical remains and dramatis personae of Welsh antiquity: an impulse which, as we shall see, he shared with the inscription's original patron.†[3])

Lhuyd's handwritten 1686 transcript of the original ninth-century inscription records thirty-one lines of what was once a longer text, carefully cut in a conservative half-uncial style that evoked the

* There is no corroborating evidence for this, and no indication where Lhuyd had gained this impression: it may well be surmise on his part.

† *Quod hujus veteris Monumenti/Superest/Diu ex oculis remotum/Et neglectum/Tandem restituit T. LLOYD/de/TREVOR HALL/A. D./ MDCCLXXIX* ('That which remains of this old monument, long removed from eyes and neglected, T Lloyd of Trevor Hall finally restored AD 1779').

insular manuscript traditions of the eighth century. The content, however, dates the inscription to the lengthy reign of Cyngen ap Cadell, king of Powys, which lasted from 808 until his death in 854/5. It consists of a number of statements regarding the ancestry of Cyngen (whose name is rendered 'Concenn' in the inscription) and, in particular, his forebear Elise ('Eliseg'). It is in honour of the latter figure that the monument has come lastingly to be known as the Pillar of Eliseg.

In translation, the inscription reads as follows. It is difficult, fragmentary and extremely hard to interpret. It is also one of the only documents to deal with the early history of Powys and is by far the most important:

+ Concenn son of Cattell, Cattell son of Brohcmail, Brohcmail son of Eliseg, Eliseg son of Guoillauc.

+ Concenn therefore, great-grandson of Eliseg, erected this stone for his great-grandfather Eliseg.

+ It was Eliseg who united the inheritance of Powys ... however through force ... from the power of the English ... land with his sword by fire(?).

[+] Whosoever shall read out loud this hand-inscribed ... let him give a blessing [on the soul of] Eliseg.

+ It is Concenn ... with his hand ... his own kingdom of Powys ... and which ... the mountain.

... monarchy ... Maximus of Britain ... Pascent ... Maun Annan ... Britu moreover [was] the son of Guarthigirn whom Germanus blessed [and whom] Sevira bore to him, the daughter of Maximus the king, who killed the king of the Romans.

+ Conmarch represented pictorially this writing at the demand of his king, Concenn.

+ The blessing of the Lord upon Concenn and likewise(?) on all of his household and upon all the province of Powys until …[4]

This sort of stuff is what historians will euphemistically describe as 'difficult'. Nevertheless, and despite the difficulties, the pillar reveals more than its broken Latin sentences might at first glance imply. In particular it speaks of the royal dynasty of Powys and its relationship to their Mercian neighbours and – crucially – how it saw itself in relation to the past, a past that is referred to not only in the names of ancestors near and distant, but also in the physicality of the monument itself and the temporal references it invoked. Its columnar form was not at all typical of ninth-century monuments. The only analogues are the round-shafted crosses of Northumbria, but these are probably too remote in time and space from ninth-century Powys to have exerted a direct influence. It seems more likely that its shape was a deliberate summoning of past ghosts. The round pillar was an enduring symbol of classical antiquity. Inscribed in Latin to record the triumphs of Powysian kings, it consciously resembled the victory columns raised by Roman emperors, a thrusting symbol of military virility and Christian *Romanitas*. But it was also more than that, an antenna drawing down vibrations from the lore of its makers to meet the upwelling tremors of a deeper past.

The pillar surmounted a mound that is now known to have been a Bronze Age cairn, a mound that once contained a barrow-dweller of some antiquity.[5] In a book describing the parish of Llangollen published in 1827, the writer W. T. Simpson recalled how he had met two old fellows who had 'assisted in opening the tumulus before the pillar was re-erected'; they described to him how 'on digging below the flat pedestal in which the base of the Pillar had been inserted, they came to a layer of pebble stones; and after having removed them, to a large flat slab, on which it seems the body had been laid, as they now found the remains of it, guarded round with large flat blue stones, and covered at the top with the same; the whole forming a sort of stone box or coffin. The bones were entire, and of very large dimensions. The skull and teeth, which were very white and perfect, were particularly sound. My informants said they believed the skull was sent to Trevor Hall, but it was returned, and again deposited, with the rest of the bones, in its former sepulchre. [...] One of the persons who assisted at the exhumation is now a very old man, and was huntsman to Mr. Lloyd when the tumulus was opened. He says there was a large piece of silver coin found in the coffin, which was kept; but that the skull was gilded to preserve it, and was then again deposited with its kindred bones. I asked if the bones were sound; and he answered (I give his own words), "O, no, sir; they broke like gingerbread."[6]

The account raises rather more questions than it answers – it is sad to say that the location of the gilded skull is now unknown – but it does at least imply (as modern excavation has confirmed) that the mound itself was indeed a tomb and that the position of the pillar directly above it was probably not accidental. Whoever raised the monument presumably knew – or, more likely, guessed – that someone was down there. With its roots sunk into the summit of a burial mound the pillar co-opted the folk of deeper ages, anchoring the achievements of the kings of Powys in a landscape that had been turned over for millennia to construct loam houses for the dead. It is unknowable whom the people of the ninth century imagined to slumber under the multitudes of turf-grown mounds that swell like molehills from Britain's hillsides and valleys; unlikely, perhaps, that they ever imagined the depth of time into which the barrow-dead truly receded. But it is entirely likely that they imagined ancient tumuli to house the people of their own legends and half-remembered history, investing an ancient landscape with their own created sense of the past, rooting it in soil and crumbling bone. That, at its heart, is what the pillar seems most eager to articulate – stability in time, a claim to territory founded in a pedigree claimed by Cyngen for himself and for Powys: a technology of legitimacy and invented heritage.

The Pillar of Eliseg was, on its face, a celebration of Cyngen's own achievements and a memorial to his great-grandfather Eliseg whose deeds prefigured his own. The very general gist of it all seems to be that Eliseg had, in his own time (probably in the eighth century), brought the lands which Cyngen regarded to be the rightful inheritance of the kings of Powys 'back together' under his rule after fighting 'the English' (*Anglo[rum]*). Cyngen himself, meanwhile, seems to have regarded his own achievements in the ninth century in a similar light: 'It is Concenn ... with his hand ... his own kingdom of Powys ...' These statements, when seen in their historical context, shine a valuable light on the last flourish of the kingdom, even if – from our current perspective – what the extent of that kingdom looked like remains fuzzy and indistinct. But much of the material that the pillar sets out is not concerned with the present, or even with the recent past. Like the setting of the monument itself, it is instead preoccupied with situating Cyngen and Powys in relation to a deeper antiquity, to anchor the realm while the shifting currents of time and politics broke around it.

To that end, Cyngen sought to position himself as heir to an ancestral past, and he did so in two ways. The first, more prosaic, was effected by the straightforward business of dynastic genealogy, a favoured tactic of rulers throughout Britain's myriad realms: 'Concenn [i.e. Cyngen]' was the 'son of Cattell, Cattell son of Brohcmail, Brohcmail son of Eliseg, Eliseg son of Guoillauc.' Of these men, only Cattel (or 'Cadell') is referred to anywhere else. The tenth-century *Annales Cambriae* (Welsh Annals) records the death of *Catel Pouis* ('Cadell of Powys') in 808, providing one of the few chronological anchors for the line of Cyngen. The second, more imaginative, way that Cyngen sought to shore up his legitimacy, however, was by associating himself with a host of legendary figures who peopled a world that had long drifted out of clear recollection: the world of Pascent, Maun Annan, Britu, Guarthigirn, Germanus, Sevira and, paramount among them, 'Maximus of Britain […] Maximus the king, who killed the king of the Romans.'

Maximus of Britain was a foundational figure to the British dynasties of the post-Roman west. Magnus Maximus, to give him his proper name, was a high-ranking Roman career soldier of Spanish origin based in Britain at the beginning of the 380s. In 383, having been proclaimed Emperor by his men, Maximus mounted an expedition into Gaul with the goal of usurping the authority of the western Roman Emperor, Gratian. He withdrew a substantial proportion – if not all – of the legions stationed in Britain, including the troops who had lately proclaimed him Emperor. He achieved swift success in fighting around Paris, and Gratian was murdered by Maximus' general Andragathius near Lyons in the same year. After a round of Imperial negotiation, Maximus was formally recognized as Emperor in the provinces of Spain, Gaul and Britain. A subsequent invasion of Italy to depose Gratian's younger brother (and junior co-emperor) Valentinian II, however, resulted in a counter-offensive by the eastern Roman Emperor Theodosius which ultimately led to Maximus' execution in 388.

Maximus was remembered in two contrasting ways in later British sources. Gildas, for one, was not impressed at all by his memory. To him Maximus was a tyrant and usurper who 'turned the neighbouring lands and provinces against Rome, and attached them to his own kingdom of wickedness with the nets of perjury and lying' and who had emptied Britain of 'her whole army, her military resources, her governors, brutal as they were, and her sturdy youth', setting the stage for all the calamities that followed.[7] Even the pillar seems to equivocate a little, drawing attention to the role of Maximus in killing 'the king of the Romans'.* But here and elsewhere, a legend seems to have developed that cast the usurper

---

* i.e. the Emperor Gratian.

as the wellspring of native British power, the progenitor of dynasties. In genealogies and medieval legends, Maximus – in the Welsh guise of Maxen Gwledig ('supreme ruler') – literally fathered British kings.*[8]

Leaving Maximus to one side, there is something to be said about all the other personae with whom Cyngen seems to have wished to demonstrate an association. Most notable among them, however, are Germanus and Guarthigirn, the former best understood as a fictionalized shadow to the historical St Germanus, bishop of Auxerre, who is famous for the journey (or possibly journeys) that he undertook to Britain at the end of the 420s to combat the heresy of Pelagianism.†[9]

The reasons why the 'historical' Germanus would inspire legends and folklore in western Britain is readily apparent from the *Vita Germani* that was written by Constantius of Lyon in the fifth century. According to Constantius, Germanus had little trouble in convincing the Britons to abandon Pelagianism.‡ He was also able

---

* The most famous expression of this legend can be found in the 'Dream of Macsen Wledig', a tale contained in the medieval Welsh compendium of stories known as the *Mabinogion*.

† It is sometimes thought that the Germanus of the pillar is a different figure from the bishop of Auxerre – that he should instead be identified with a 'St Garmon', fragments of whose otherwise lost *vita* were preserved in the *Historia Brittonum*, a local saint associated with the dynastic and territorial claims of Powys. I find this argument unnecessary. If the lives of St Garmon and the historical Germanus are hard to reconcile, that is surely because the former is a fictionalized outgrowth of the latter's outsized reputation in Britain: there is no need to invent an entirely different Germanus to explain discrepancies of chronology or career trajectory.

‡ In the late fourth to early fifth century, the British theologian Pelagius – in association with the Roman aristocrat Caelestius – developed a set of beliefs that challenged developing doctrines relating to original sin and free will. It was Pelagius' view that humans could, by their own choices and actions, avoid sin and thus attain salvation. He also rejected the notion that the sins of Adam and Eve constituted a stain on all humanity that could only be erased through divine grace. To many modern eyes, Pelagianism seems to offer a humane, rational and liberal view of the world that

to visit the shrine of St Alban (providing important support to the longevity of this proto-martyr's cult in Britain) and, more dramatically, to defeat an army of pagan Saxons and Picts by encouraging his men to shout 'Hallelujah' very loudly at them. This was quite enough for the pagans (who in hagiographic literature are always either stupid or cruel, and frequently both). They 'were panic-stricken, thinking that the surrounding rocks and the very sky itself were falling on them. Such was their terror that no effort of their feet seemed enough to save them. They fled in every direction, throwing away their weapons and thankful if they could save at least their skins. Many threw themselves into the river which they had just crossed at their ease, and were drowned in it.'[10] It was a bloodless victory for the Britons and St Germanus, and a good story. A story that, crucially from a later Welsh perspective, placed Germanus among the ranks of those who had fought on the side of the Britons against the hated Saxon invader. By the ninth century when the *Historia Brittonum* was being compiled, the memory of the late bishop of Auxerre had transmuted into local religious celebrity, with much of his literary existence devoted to harassing the British king named on the Pillar of Eliseg as *Guarthigirn*, a man better known in Arthurian lore as Vortigern.

expresses optimism in the human capacity to do good and emphasizes personal responsibility over arbitrary God-centric caprice. This was not, however, the view of Christian morality that Pelagius' chief critic, St Augustine, embraced. Instead the Church – under Augustine's influence and with enormous implications for the development of western civilization – turned towards a more pessimistic vision of human nature. This would come to regard humans as fallen, corrupted and incapable of escaping damnation other than by the grace of God – an uncompromising and unforgiving religion that consigned unbaptized infants to hell (thanks to their unexpunged original sin). The views of Pelagius were condemned at the Council of Carthage in 418, and Pelagius and his colleague Caelestius were excommunicated. That didn't mean, however, that his way of thinking was eradicated overnight, and clearly it seems that it had some purchase in Britain – enough to motivate Bishop Germanus to make a personal effort to stamp it out.

Vortigern has a special place in Arthuriana. Put simply, he is a baddy – a tyrant and a lecher who invited the pagan English into Britain, precipitating the ruin of civilization and the need for a saviour (Arthur) to rise among the beleaguered Britons.* The roots of Vortigern's unwholesome persona run deep. In the oldest manuscript of Gildas' *De Excidio Britanniae*, a person described only and anonymously as a *superbus tyrannus* ('proud tyrant') is held responsible for decisions that led – in Gildas' view – to a dire reckoning for the people of Britain.[11] When Bede came to retell the same story in his own eighth-century writing, he added a name – *Vortigernus* – securing for it enduring infamy. As Bede tells it, in the years after 449, at some point during the reign of the eastern Roman Emperor Marcian (r.450–457), 'the Angles or Saxons came to Britain at the invitation of King Vortigern in three long-ships, and were granted lands in the eastern part of the island on condition that they protected the country: nevertheless, their real intention was to subdue it'. Having defeated an army sent (plausibly enough) from the north to deal with their unruly ways, the Angles/Saxons sent word back to their compatriots in continental northern Europe that 'the country was fertile and the Britons cowardly'.[12] The conditions were thus set for the atrocities and mayhem that Gildas, and later Bede, described as the result of the ensuing conquests and depredations.

Bede must have got the name *Vortigernus* from somewhere, and it is very possible that the version of *De Excidio* that he had access to did include the name.† That does not mean, however, that his identity as a real historical figure is straightforwardly accepted. It has been suggested, for example, that 'Vortigern' (from Brittonic *Wortigernos*, 'over-lord') may have been the same person as Magnus Maximus (whose name means 'great biggest').[13] It has also been suggested that 'Vortigern' was a title and not a name at all,

---

* This is the light in which he appears in, for example, Geoffrey of Monmouth's *Historia Regum Britanniae* (see **DUMNONIA**).

† Indeed, it does appear in later manuscripts of *De Excidio*.

even though it can be found as a personal name in both Ireland and Brittany and *tigernos* ('lord', 'king', 'ruler') is a perfectly acceptable and fairly common Brittonic name element found in, for example, the names Catigern (*Cat* + *tigernos*: 'battle lord') and Kentigern (from *Cuno* + *tigernos*: 'dog lord').[14] More generally, when set aside other Brittonic names like Brigomaglos ('mighty prince') and Maglocunus ('top dog'), Vortigern hardly seems out of place.* (Even Biggus Dickus might feel at home in this sort of company.[15])

As for Arthur himself, it was the *Historia Brittonum* that put flesh on the bones of Vortigern's reputation. There he is presented as an essentially rotten egg, a man who – quite apart from his errors regarding the English – fathered a child on his own daughter, consorted with murderous pagan wizards and plotted human sacrifice. He was, apparently, 'hated […] by all men of his own nation, mighty and humble, slave and free, monk and layman, poor and great'.[16] His doom was supposedly ushered in by the great Hallelujah-inspiring Germanus who, incensed at the king's incestuous habits, determined to harangue him into recognizing his errors. Driven by the saint's unwanted attention (which included forty days and forty nights of incessant preaching from the top of a rock) to *Caer Gwrtheyrn* ('the fortress of Vortigern') in Dyfed, he was ultimately immolated by a fusillade of heavenly fire conjured by the prayers and fasting of the saint and his gang of priests. 'Vortigern', the *Historia Brittonum* recounts, 'was destroyed with all who were with him, and all his wives'.[17] (Some, the author concedes, had different ideas about what happened to him. Some imagined that he wandered hither and thither, pursued by opprobrium so universal that 'at last his heart broke, and he died without honour'. Others, however, maintained that 'the earth opened and swallowed him up'.[18])

Why, one might ask, would a king like Cyngen want to include such a stinker of an ancestor in what was very plainly a made-up genealogy? This puzzle has led to suspicions that traditions about

* See **RHEGED**; Maglocunus literally means 'noble hound'.

Vortigern – which only appear in the ninth century – were distorted for political purposes by whoever was doing the telling. The compiler of the *Historia Brittonum*, working probably at the behest of the rulers of Gwynedd in northwest Wales, seem to have been keen to emphasize a negative version of Vortigern's legend that blackened the reputation of those who claimed him as their ancestor. It also seems probable that the source used to draw this unflattering portrait was composed during a period when Powys was ruled by a different dynasty altogether – as we shall see. [19] The inscriber of the Pillar of Eliseg, by contrast, may have had a more wholesome version of the legend in mind. But whatever the stories that people told of him, Vortigern remained a pivotal character in the British imagination: a powerful over-king who stood at the wellspring of tension between the 'English' and the 'Welsh'. As such, and whatever his perceived faults may have been, he was seen in the ninth century as an instrumental actor in the development of the post-Roman kingdoms of Britain. For Cyngen that alone might have made Vortigern a name worth conjuring with.

By associating his family with Magnus Maximus, St Germanus, Vortigern and others, Cyngen seems to have been implying that the roots of his own family – and, by extension, the kingdom of Powys over which he claimed dominion – lay in the dying days of Empire, a heritage that could lay claim to the tattered mantle of Roman authority, to upholding a vision of an old order against the benighted barbarian tide that had swept in from the east. And as will become clearer, he probably had very good political reasons for emphasizing those notions. The fact remains, however, that none of these individuals had specific connections to Powys. They were towering figures of island-wide significance, whose legends had been co-opted by a provincial dynasty. The true roots of Powys are buried deeper, in the Roman civitas of the Cornovii. Digging them out requires a special effort.

* * *

Viroconium Cornoviorum – A. E. Housman's 'Uricon' – was once one of the largest and most important Roman towns in Britain. As the second part of its name indicates, it was the civitas capital of the Cornovii tribe, whose territory spread across the lowland plains of Shropshire and Cheshire, bounded by the Welsh uplands to the west. Their original power base is presumed to have been focused on the summit of the Wrekin, a whacking great lump of geologically complex volcanic rock that protrudes from the spreading lowlands that surround it like Tolkien's Lonely Mountain. An Iron Age stronghold once commanded the reaches of the River Tern and the upper Severn from its summit.* Unlike other Roman cities of comparable scale and significance – *Corinium* (Cirencester), *Lindum Colonia* (Lincoln), *Londinium* (London), *Eboracum* (York) – *Viroconium* never recovered its status as a major settlement in later centuries. The village of Wroxeter that grew up later near the city's southwest perimeter was always small potatoes by comparison (Dickens called it 'a puny little changeling'), although it had a church (St Andrew's) that was originally constructed between the ninth and eleventh centuries and which, by the time of the Domesday survey in 1085, had an impressive complement of four priests.[20] (The oldest parts of the church were constructed from Roman masonry, but also incorporated part of an eighth-century standing cross, an indication that the remains of *Viroconium* may

---

* Like many of Britain's lumps and bumps, the Wrekin has inspired several folk tales. The most popular – at least in the nineteenth century when it was recorded – involved a Welsh giant with a grudge against Shrewsbury. His plan was to block the Severn with a huge clod of earth that he had dug up for the purpose and was carrying with him in a sack. As he roamed around looking for his destination, the giant met a cobbler and asked him for directions. The cobbler, not keen to be party to the giant's destructive mission, told him he had no hope of reaching the city any time soon. Tired and dismayed, the giant set down his sack of earth where he stood and tramped back home. Where the orphaned pile of earth was abandoned, the Wrekin stands today. The giant would have done better had he been less precipitate about digging up his clod and instead waited until he arrived at his destination. But giants are notoriously dim.

have held an enduring religious significance despite their general neglect.)

Most of the city, however, was simply abandoned, its carcass stripped for building material, a few old bones left jutting from the Shropshire Plain. Some still remain visible in the landscape, stumps of walls and broken buildings in an otherwise empty landscape, the brittle brick flank of the Roman baths basilica standing against the sky like a slab of crumbling pastry-crust while behind it, to the east, the Wrekin looms black on the horizon – the Vesuvius of the Welsh borders.* This lonely hunk of Roman masonry has been remarked upon by visitors for many centuries. William Camden (1551–1623) drew notice to it in *Britannia*, his monumental survey of British antiquities, describing a place that 'presenteth often times to those that aire the ground Roman coines, to testifie in some sort the antiquity thereof [...] I saw nothing of antiquitie but in one place some few parcels of broken walles (which the common people cal the Old Worke of Wroxceter).'[21] The first to 'aire the ground' in any sort of systemic way was the antiquary Thomas Wright, whose excavations in 1859 caused a sensation and led Dickens to write about the place in the essay 'Rome and Turnips'. What to Camden was the 'Old Worke' was to Dickens the 'Old Wall' and he saw it as 'a sort of colossal ruined headstone' for the city buried beneath, a city which, in his day, was finally yielding its secrets to bedazzled antiquarian excitement:

That heap of earth, on the old Roman town concealing all its skeletons, except, as it may be, a bony index finger represented by the stones of the Old Wall, is resolute to speak. In spite of all the efforts made to stop its mouth with turnip-crops and corn for it is arable land upon the surface it cries out, 'Look into me. Pay the men for their turnips, and away with them. Dig me, I say, for the knowledge I contain.'[22]

* Despite appearances to the contrary, the Wrekin is not an extinct volcano, although much of its rock is volcanic in origin.

Dig they did. For a century, interest in the site of this provincial Pompeii continued unabated. Even Wilfred Owen, the celebrated poet of the First World War, wrote 227 lines celebrating the 'ancient glories suddenly overcast, And treasures flung to fire and rabble wrath […] under Wrekin's shade' that were now seeing the light of day once more.[23] Treasures were unearthed, archaeologists honed their skills and the timelines of Roman Britain were refined. And for many, the most remarkable revelations came latest of all.

Beginning in 1966, University of Birmingham archaeologist Philip Barker undertook a new phase of investigation that pioneered the use of 'open-area' excavation, then a departure from the cellular grid-type excavations that had been popularized by Mortimer Wheeler and Kathleen Kenyon in the 1930s and 1940s, and which would continue for twenty-four years. The enhanced sensitivity to ephemeral phenomena that was provided by open-area excavation enabled Barker to identify features that would otherwise have been overlooked and allowed him to propose a chronology for post-Roman *Viroconium* that would radically upend received wisdom regarding the nature of life in the so-called Dark Ages. In brief, Barker's interpretation of his evidence envisaged a phase of occupation in the ruins of the baths basilica complex that lasted from some point during the fifth century for around a century. This then gave way to a massive programme of clearance and wholesale urban regeneration that saw the construction of multi-storey timber structures in the old Roman town centre, including a colossal three-storey tower-fronted building of imposing classical proportions. This new timber town was erected between 530 and 580 and remained in use until its systematic dismantling between 650 and 700.

If this were to be accepted in its entirety, it would be staggering evidence for a type of urban life and economy without parallel in Britain in the sixth and seventh centuries. But the passage of time has not been kind to post-Roman *Viroconium*, and the doubts have begun to stack up, finding particular voice in a piercing critique by Cardiff University archaeologist Alan Lane in 2014.[24] Without getting into the weeds, the conclusion now seems unavoidable that the evidence is just too subtle, the traces of life too ambiguous, to bear the weight of the remarkable town that was conjured to rest upon them. Almost every plank of evidence has been tested and found fragile. The slender archaeomagnetic dating evidence has been revisited and effectively dismissed. Assumptions around the stratigraphy have been undermined. The hypothetical reconstruction drawings were always entirely imaginative beyond their ground plans, but now even those outlines have been seriously called into question. Most troubling of all, however, is the lack of artefactual evidence that would concretely date the phases of the post-Roman town. Other important economic centres of the sixth century – Tintagel (Cornwall), Mote of Mark (Galloway), Dinas Powys (South Glamorgan), South Cadbury and Cadbury Congresbury (Somerset) – positively groan with dateable objects from the Mediterranean, continental western Europe and the 'Anglo-Saxon' parts of Britain. Similar material has also been found in the near vicinity of *Viroconium* – at an early medieval settlement at New Pieces to the west and at Wenlock Priory to the southeast. Nothing comparable, nothing much at all in fact, was found at *Viroconium* itself; certainly nothing to suggest a pulsating new wooden metropolis.

This is not to say that nothing was going on in fifth- and sixth-century *Viroconium* – just that whatever it may have been was almost certainly less elaborate, extensive, enduring and impressive than was once imagined. Timber buildings, some seemingly quite substantial, were apparently erected among the ruins in the late fifth/early sixth centuries. This is consistent with the situation in other Roman towns and forts in Britain around the same time. The presence of an eighth-century Christian monument in the recycled building material of St Andrew's church in Wroxeter, alongside the ephemeral traces of timber structures close to the centre of the Roman city, could suggest the presence of an early and long-lived religious centre. It could be that post-Roman religious life at *Viroconium* mirrored that at *Lindum Colonia* (Lincoln),

Verulamium (St Albans) or the forts of Hadrian's Wall and the Saxon Shore. On the other hand, the evidence for wooden buildings might suggest the halls of post-Roman warlords like the hill-forts of the north and west or the repurposed compounds of somewhere like *Banna* (Birdoswald).*

It remains, therefore, entirely possible to see in the intriguing remains of *Viroconium* a place that could have served as the seat of a bishop or Dark Age chieftain, a base whence the heirs to the Cornovii might have laid the foundations of a realm that their royal descendants recognized as the germ of Powys. It is possible, even, that warlords of island-straddling influence once flexed their muscles from the throne of long-forgotten Uricon – men like Vortigern, or the real-life lords whose deeds his legend aped. An inscribed stone found just outside the town walls – almost certainly a grave marker – was erected in the late fifth century to the memory of a man named *Cunorix*, an Irish (Goidelic) name meaning something like 'hound-king'.[25]

Possible, but unknowable: a considerable amount of research is still required to make sense of all the archaeological material turned up by a century and a half of digging. And the humbling fact remains that even now only around 10 per cent of the 190-acre town – the fourth largest by area in Roman Britain – has been excavated at all.† But whether or not *Viroconium* played a major role in the developing politics of the area, it appears certain that regional identities were strong. The names 'Viroconium', 'Wrekin' and 'Wroxeter' all share the same origin: 'V' and 'U' are interchangeable in Roman orthography, and 'W' in Celtic languages approximates a

---

* *Lindum Colonia* (Lincoln), see **LINDSEY**; *Verulamium* (St Albans), see **ESSEX**; the forts of Hadrian's Wall, see **RHEGED**; the Saxon Shore, see **SUSSEX**; hill-forts of the north and west, see **HWICCE**; **DUMNONIA**; **RHEGED**; **FORTRIU**; *Banna* (Birdoswald), see **RHEGED**.

† After *Londinium* (London), *Corinium* (Cirencester) and *Verulamium* (St Albans); much more of the stone city has been plotted with remote sensing technology – ground-penetrating radar and the like – than has been physically excavated.

long vowel sound like the 'oo' in 'food' or the 'u' in 'dude'. Thus 'Virocon(ium)' and 'Wrekin' are essentially the same word, the 'Uricon' of Owen and Housman.*[26] 'Wroxeter' is essentially a portmanteau of this word plus *caester*, the Old English term for a Roman fortified settlement: the fortress-town of Uricon. This name would ultimately be attached to an entire people, a tribal group inhabiting the western marches of Mercia at the time the Tribal Hidage was compiled (probably in the seventh century): the *Wreocansaete* – the 'Uricon-dwellers'. An 'Anglo-Saxon Great Hall' complex – dated to the middle of the seventh century – was recently confirmed through excavation at Atcham, less than two miles from Wroxeter. It is this place – and later the town of Shrewsbury that grew up nearby – that should be seen perhaps as the true successor to faded Viroconium; a home, perhaps, to new lords of the Shropshire plain.[27] What the Wreocansaete had to do with the Cornovii, however, and what either had to do with the kingdom of Powys, is the central mystery at the heart of this region's history. Any attempt to unravel it requires an excursion into the intractable undergrowth of Welsh literature.

The family of Eliseg was not the only dynasty to have exercised claims to rule in the developing kingdom of Powys. There are other figures whose words and deeds were remembered for centuries in Welsh literature, braided into the genealogies and sagas of bards and dynasts in ways which are almost impossible to disentangle from fantasy. Three kings in particular – three generations of the same family: Brochfael, Cynan and Selyf – made their presence felt in this part of Britain. They were believed in later Welsh genealogies to be descended from a legendary character called *Cadell*

* Or as Dickens put it: 'The Romans had no W or K, they were obliged to write down Wrekin Urecin; ium is only the addendum, which says there's the name of a place. Vowels are pronounced and altered in all sorts of ways: so ancient Uriconium is old Wrekinium.'

Ddyrnllug ('Cadell of the Gleaming Hilt') by the *Historia Brittonum*. This figure, like Vortigern, was associated in the *Historia* with St Germanus – albeit, unlike Vortigern, in an entirely positive way. The miraculous narrative that the compiler incorporated has the saint bestowing royal status on Cadell and his sons, thus establishing a sanctified legitimacy to the notion that 'from their seed the whole country of Powys is ruled'.[28] This, on the face of it, contradicts the Pillar of Eliseg and the claims of Cyngen to Powysian lordship in the early ninth century, but the source from which the Cadell story is derived – a lost life of St. Germanus, the *Liber Beati Germani* – may well predate the rise of Eliseg's family to royal power.*[29]

The earliest of the Cadelling kings of whom anything is known at all was named Brochfael (*Brochfael Ysgithrawg* as he later became known – 'Brochfael of the Tusks') who, if he lived at all, did so around the middle of the sixth century. Unsurprisingly, not much can be said about Brochfael, except that, by the later Middle Ages, he was remembered specifically as a king of Powys and the father of *Kynan Garwyn* ('Cynan of the White Chariot').[30]

Cynan, like Urien of Rheged and Gwallog ap Leenog, was immortalized in the small corpus of early poems attributed to Taliesin. *Trawsganu Kynan Garwyn mab Brochfael* ('In Praise of Cynan Garwyn, son of Brochfael') is not a poem that deviates from the conventions of its genre. According to the poet, Cynan is a

---

* There is, in fact, a suspiciously tidy parallel between the Germanus-blessed Cadellings and the Vortigern-sprung family of Eliseg who – according to the pillar inscription – had their own tradition of blessing by the saint. These equivalences have the appearance of duelling traditions between separate dynasties vying for control or legitimacy within the same territory. The particular emphasis on Germanus seems to suggest that the saint represented both a religious and geographical centre of gravity for the kingdom of Powys, regardless of which dynasty co-opted his legendary blessings. Early church dedications to him focus on the upper Dee valley where the pillar of Eliseg was ultimately raised, and the major church most local to the Pillar of Eliseg – Llanarmon yn Iâl – is itself dedicated to Garmon (Germanus).

king 'who's hated by no one'. It is a statement that is hard to reconcile with Cynan's other 'qualities' which – as might by now be expected – largely coalesce around themes of bloody mayhem and genocidal xenophobia. It is hard to imagine that the people of Gwent bore him no ill feeling ('Attacking the Wye, With numberless spears, Gwentmen are killed, By his blood-drenched blades'). The ruler of Dyfed was forced to watch 'his realm raided, Foes leading his herds' – a turn of events that seems likely to have dented any enthusiasm he felt for Cynan. Nor can the inhabitants of Anglesey ('War waged in fair Môn') or Brecon ('[Cynan] Takes war to Brecon, Heights molehills to him') or the Cornovii ('Bad luck is their fate, He gives them distress, Till they sue for peace') have felt any more warmly.*[31]

The Taliesin poems, it bears repeating, are not a sound guide to their subjects. Even if they do date to the period of their purported composition in the sixth century, the events and achievements they describe may have had only a very loose relationship with the truth. In any case, the poem in praise of Cynan represents the barest toehold for the early history of the kingdom later known as Powys; if it does in fact reflect anything resembling reality, then all it tells us is that Cynan was a warlord at odds with many of the kingdoms bordering his own – Gwynedd (of which Anglesey was part), Brecon and Gwent to the south, Dyfed in the southwest. It does not even specify that Cynan was king of Powys, although later generations of medieval Welsh poets assumed this to be the case.

Cynan's son, Selyf (an early Welsh form of the name Solomon), is better attested. Although he is only directly associated with Powys in much later Welsh genealogies, where he appears as *Selyf Sarffgadeu* ('Solomon Battle-snake'), he is mentioned by name in two early medieval sources that put him in the right place, with the proper title and the correct parentage. The oldest is the possibly

---

* Cornovii is possibly a reference to Cornwall (see **DUMNONIA**) but is more likely to refer to the people who occupied lands in Cheshire and Shropshire later settled by the Wreocansaete (see **LITTLE KINGDOMS**).

contemporary notice in the *Chronicle of Ireland*, whose annalist – probably writing at Iona – recorded the 'battle of Caer Legion [Chester], in which holy men were slain, and Solon [Selyf] son of Conaen [Cynan], king of the Britons fell'.[32] The Welsh Annals (*Annales Cambriae*) repeat a summary of the same information and may well be derived directly from the Irish account. The most famous and detailed account of the battle of Chester/Caer Legion, however, is that provided by Bede.* Although he does not mention Selyf at all, he does provide a wealth of narrative detail that helps to illuminate his own prejudices as well as the course of the fighting.†
He begins his narrative with the blunt assessment that 'Æthelfrith, whom we have already spoken of, collected a great army against the City of the Legions […] and made a great slaughter of that nation of heretics [the Britons]'.‡[33]

Legacæstir or *Caer Legion* – formerly the Roman city of *Deva Victrix*, or Chester as it is known in modern English – lay at the centre of a network of major Roman roads that led into North Wales to the west, across the Pennines towards York and south to

---

* Dating the battle is problematic as all the major sources give different dates. It is most commonly supposed to have taken place in 616, but could well have been earlier in the seventh century.

† Although Selyf is not mentioned by Bede, the one Briton whom he does name – Brocmail – appears in a later Welsh genealogy as another son of Cynan. The genealogies are late, hopelessly confused and plainly political documents of the time they were written. Nevertheless, it remains quite possible that Selyf and Brocmail were both a part of the same dynasty.

‡ *Legacæstir* 'city of the legions' is a direct translation of the Brittonic name for Chester: *Caer Legion*; Æthelfrith was the king of Northumbria, the first to unite the realms of Bernicia and Deira into a single kingdom. Although Æthelfrith was a heathen (his successor, Edwin, became a Christian in 627), Bede apparently regarded him as an instrument of divine retribution, a sort of noble savage 'who ravaged the Britons more cruelly than all other leaders of the English.' As we have seen, Bede was full of approval for that sort of thing, and there are good reasons to believe that Chester was a place of considerable importance – a meeting site located, like Augustine's Oak, at the interface between cultural, religious and political communities: part of the Anglo-British fault-line of the early seventh century.

Viroconium. Although Chester's post-Roman archaeology is unspectacular, it is entirely possible that the city retained a religious function – maybe even an episcopal church – and at very least the sort of symbolic heft that might have made it an attractive venue for gatherings of all kinds. (Excavations in the amphitheatre have revealed a post-Roman sequence that might imply the fortification of the site in a manner analogous to that at Cirencester; at any rate, the building seems plainly to have been repurposed in some way during the long post-Roman hangover.[34]) After the abortive meeting that Augustine had held with British bishops at Augustine's Oak in 602/3, the British delegation had 'asked that a second and fuller conference might be held' in order to reconcile their differences regarding the date of Easter and the monastic tonsure.* Although Bede does not specify where this happened, the Welsh Annals record that a synod was held at Chester in the early 600s and it is almost certainly here that the meeting took place: the seven British bishops who attended were accompanied by 'very many learned men [...] who had come mainly from their most famous monastery which the English call Bancornaburg'.[35] This was the monastery of Bangor-is-y-coed, or Bangor-by-Dee, near Wrexham in Flintshire. It is situated a little over fifteen miles from Chester: certainly close enough to be convenient.

The synod at Chester was an unmitigated disaster. After the meeting at Augustine's Oak, the British delegation had visited a wise hermit for guidance on how to deal with Augustine. He instructed them that 'if Augustine is meek and lowly in heart, it shows that he bears the yoke of Christ himself, and offers it to you. But if he is haughty and unbending, then he is not of God, and we should not listen to him.' The test was to be whether Augustine stood up in the presence of the British delegation at their next meeting. When the appointed hour came, however, stand up Augustine did not. Instead, he remained steadfastly 'seated in his chair'.[36] After this, things went predictably pear-shaped. The British became angry and shouted at

* See **HWICCE**.

Augustine; Augustine issued baleful prophecies of death and destruction. No reconciliation ever followed. If Bede is to be believed at all (the story has the glimmer of fable about it), Augustine's failure to shift his arse had done irrevocable damage to religious and political relationships in Britain with implications that have lasted centuries.

For Bede, however, the repercussions of crossing Augustine were more immediate. As he relates it, when Æthelfrith arrived at Chester around fifteen years later, the Northumbrian king found more than a thousand monks from Bancornaburg arrayed against him, all ready to deliver their weaponized prayers on behalf of the Britons – a sort of holy artillery deployed in the face of the pagan Northumbrian war machine. It was a tactic straight from the St Germanus playbook, one that finds a physical expression in the religious objects, including a massive processional cross, found among the enormous hoard of seventh-century sword fittings and other gear discovered in a field in Staffordshire in 2009. One strip of gold – an arm from another large cross – is inscribed with the words: *Surge domine et disepentur [dissipentur] inimici tui at fugent [fugiant] qui oderunt te a facie tua* ('Rise up, O Lord, and may thy enemies be dispersed and those who hate thee be driven from thy face'.[37] If the inscription did indeed adorn a battlefield cross – or even, as has been mooted, some sort of portable war-altar – it would be hard to conceive of a less ambiguous convergence of spiritual and military invective.

But if this sort of thing was indeed in the minds of the monks from Bangor, they had placed their trust in the wrong weapons, believed in the wrong stories.

When he [Æthelfrith] was about to give battle and saw their priests, who had assembled to pray to God on behalf of the soldiers taking part in the fight, standing apart in a safer place, he asked who they were and for what purpose they had gathered there. [...] When Æthelfrith heard why they had come he said, 'If they are praying to their God against us, then, even if they do not bear arms, they are fighting against us, assailing us as they do with prayers for our defeat.' So he ordered them to be attacked first and then he destroyed the remainder of their wicked host, though not without heavy losses.*

According to Bede, 1,200 monks died on English swords and only fifty fled with their lives.[38]

The specific site of the battle of Chester is not known. However, in 2004, excavations at Heronbridge (Cheshire) uncovered a mass grave containing the remains of twelve people tightly packed into an area measuring only nine feet by six, part of a cemetery that may have contained well over a hundred individuals.[39] Carbon dates obtained from two of the skeletons suggest that they died during the late sixth or early seventh centuries, consistent with the date of the battle. And even though the dead cannot be said with certainty to have died in that specific conflict, the Heronbridge bodies nevertheless bring us face to face with the violence of the period. Many of the bones – both those excavated in 2004 and the remains of around twenty skeletons excavated at what was probably the same location in the early 1930s – displayed evidence of brutal injuries inflicted in the moments immediately prior to death. Triangular punctures were found in the skull of one individual where the bite of spear-points had driven through bone to penetrate the brain. Another victim was battered with sword blows that rained down from every angle, leaving behind a web of trauma across his cranium. A third man was struck in the face with a sword, a blow landed with such force that the edge of the blade sheared through the orbital socket of the eye, destroying internal bones of the skull and smashing into brain tissue. Some of the dead, to judge from the pattern of cranial trauma, seem to have worn helmets, but not all of them. One of the two men whose remains have been dated – a young man, in apparent good health on the day he left for battle –

---

* This was the harsh judgement that – in Bede's eyes – God had ordained for the Britons on account of their obdurate attachment to practices disapproved of by Augustine.

was killed by a sword blow from above that split his head in half. His attacker continued to rain down blows, slicing off the back of the skull, hacking at the forehead, slashing the face. When early medieval battles got down to business it was sharp-edged implements – not religious invective – that put men into the ground.

The battle tied things up nicely from Bede's point of view. The first time the monks of Bancornaburg came to Chester they had come in peace, but had sown discord within the Church. The second time they came in anger and found only death; the pagan Northumbrians had been wielded like a divine scourge, delivering God's judgement and the fulfilment of Augustine's prophecy. The parallels are so clearly drawn by Bede that the whole story resembles a moralizing sermon more than it does faithful historical reportage.* Nevertheless, the whole business does throw a little light on the occluded kingdom of Powys (or whatever the kingdom ruled by Selyf – son of Cynan – was called at the time). Firstly, it is evident that the people attacked by Æthelfrith in the early seventh century regarded the Roman legionary city *Deva Victrix* (Chester) as part of – or at least proximate to – their own territory. That would mean that territories presumably ruled by Selyf extended considerably further north and east than the Powys of later ages.

Secondly, the monastery of Bancornaburg/Bangor-is-y-coed must also have lain within Selyf's sphere of influence, with implications for the cultural assets and inclinations of his realm. The scale of the monastery as Bede reports it seems improbable, and he is careful to frame his knowledge as hearsay ('it is said that …'), but the monastery was evidently a well-known and significant foundation. Its presence also indicates that Christianity was well entrenched in the region, and implies a degree of learning and Latinity that was not matched among the pagan Northumbrians who had descended upon it. No amount of Anglocentric spin can

---

* And yet, apart from Æthelfrith's allotted role as scourge of God, neither Bede nor any other credible source provides any explanation for what he was actually doing so far from home (apart from ravaging); some elaborate and ingenious theories have been advanced, none of them provable.

disguise who, in this encounter, were the 'barbarians' and who the 'Romans'. And, in fact, Bede is actually fairly candid, mentioning that the monks 'had a guard named Brocmail, whose duty it was to protect them against the barbarians' swords while they were praying'. (He didn't do a very good job of it – 'Brocmail and his men at the first enemy attack turned their backs on those whom they should have defended, leaving them unarmed and helpless before the swords of their foes'.)[40] None of this is very much to go on, but it at least gives a flavour of the realm that would become Powys (or at least part of it), a hint of its origins in the lands abutting the highlands of northern Wales, already at loggerheads with its neighbours, already under pressure, clinging to the dwindling currency of Roman civilization.

Selyf 'Battle-Snake' was not the only figure of Welsh legend supposed to have fought and died at the battle of Chester. A man named Gwiawn son of Cyndrwyn (a character associated in a later Welsh genealogy with the cantref of Caereinion in Montgomeryshire) is remembered in the Triads as one of the 'Three Gate-Keepers at the Contest of Bangor Orchard' – probably an oblique reference to the battle.[41] More significant than Gwiawn, however, was his brother. Cynddylan son of Cyndrwyn was a man of big reputation, and a record of both his deeds and his undoing is preserved in two poetic sources of unequal authority. The most 'reliable' is a poetic elegy called *Marwnad Cynddylan* that laments the hero's death in battle.[42] It is entirely possible that it was composed in the mid-seventh century, and that it was roughly contemporary with the death of its subject. Sadly, it is somewhat difficult to interpret, but it does describe a battle fought at Lichfield (*Caer Lwytgoed*) by the kindred of Cyndrwyn, and it may have been here that Cynddylan met his untimely end.

Before Lichfield they fought,

There was gore under ravens and keen attack.

Limed shields broke before the sons of the Cyndrwynyn [the
    kin of Cyndrwyn].

I shall lament until I would be in the land of my resting place
for the slaying of Cynddylan, famed among chieftains.[43]

The problem, however, is that no other source mentions a battle
fought at Lichfield, and it isn't even clear who the Cyndrwynyn
were fighting. (Lichfield was central to the early kingdom of Mercia,
but it is entirely possible that Cynddylan was fighting on behalf of,
rather than against, the Mercian king against Northumbrian or
other invaders.) Apparently more promising for details of political
geography and historical narrative is a cycle of poetry known as
Canu Heledd, an epic which purports to lament the conquest and
destruction of Cynddylan's ancestral lands from the perspective of
his sister Heledd.[44] From place-names in the poetry, Cynddylan's
kingdom can be localized in the Shropshire Plain and bounded by
the River Tern that flows from the northeast corner of Shropshire
to join the Severn near Shrewsbury. At one point, Heledd even
recalls gazing out from *dinlleu ureconn* – the 'City of Uricon' –
presumably a reference to the Wrekin and Uriconium. And of her
brother, the narrator recalls, 'Cynddylan Powys, you had a splendid
purple cloak, a storehouse to feed guests, like a lord'.[45]

Cynddylan Powys. Land and king – in the poet's eyes – were one
and the same.

Canu Heledd is a fascinating work of literature, poignant and
powerful and distinguished for the rarity of its female narrator. Its
undoubted strength as literature, however, has seduced some into
accepting it as an essentially accurate preserved tradition of
Powysian decline and dispossession. Taken alongside the
conjectured realm of Selyf Battle-snake and the little that is known
of Cynddylan's father Cyndrwyn, the poems of *Canu Heledd* seem
to preserve the memory of a kingdom that once included all the
land west of the Tern: a Powys that ran from Chester to Shrewsbury

and from Bangor-on-Dee to Caereinion (Montgomeryshire) – ruled, perhaps, from the mighty citadel of Uricon in splendid timber halls fit for glorious princes, a refitted civitas of the Cornovii draped in Roman purple. One can propose any number of arrangements of kinship, alliance or overlordship that might have connected the family of Cyndrwyn with the descendants of Cadell – Brochfael, Cynan and Selyf 'Battle-Snake'. And one can envisage a whole saga of Mercian conquest that carved the eastern half of Powys from its highland rump, a conquest that settled the Shropshire Plain with English speakers who came, in time, to be known as 'Wreocansaete' after the mighty hill that dominated their landscape.

But if that is how it went, then only the Welsh of later centuries remembered it. *Canu Heledd* was probably composed during the ninth century, but could have been written later still. No other source anywhere recalls the devastating war of conquest it describes: not Bede, not the *Anglo-Saxon Chronicle*, not even the Welsh Annals or the *Historia Brittonum*. In the end, all that can be said for certain is that a lingering sense of a lost 'greater Powys', of aggrieved dispossession, is what generations of later Welsh writers clung to. That idea obscured a situation of much greater complexity – and quite possibly lesser drama – than can ever be recovered. But the mighty fallen kingdom it conjured sustained an enduring sense of group identity and regional pride.

If *Canu Heledd* is a dirge for a lost realm, then the Pillar of Eliseg is by contrast animated by a sense of restoration – of wrongs made right, of repossession. 'It was Eliseg', the relevant part of the inscription promisingly begins, 'who united the inheritance of Powys'. Both pillar inscription and poem were probably composed in the ninth century. It is even possible that the legends that informed the poems also inspired the tenor of the inscription. But if that is so, there is no way to really understand the pillar-scribe's frame of reference. Nestled between the massive limestone bulwark of the

Eglwyseg Mountain and the towering peak of Moel Morfydd, the secluded spur on which the pillar stands controlled access into and through these dramatic and forbidding folds of Britain. It was a place that had to be confronted on any journey deeper into the western highlands or east along the valley of the Dee towards the wide plains of Shropshire and Cheshire to which Cynddylan might once have laid claim. That lowland region, however, by the time that the pillar was inscribed, lay under the shadow of another power, gouged and turned over in a working of the earth that incised domination into the belly of the land. If that great sweep of territory had ever been part of Powys, it is hard to imagine how it can ever have been reunited with the Valley of the Cross.

The pillar's text suggests that Eliseg had, in his own day (i.e. at some point probably in the late eighth century), brought the lands which Cyngen regarded to be the rightful inheritance of the kings of Powys back together under his rule following some some argy-bargy with the *Angli* ('English' or 'Anglians') that involved 'force' and 'fire' and 'swords'. These particular 'Angli', it seems reasonable to assume, were the Anglian people of Mercia – the kingdom that lay directly to the east.* What remains curious, however, is that these apparently dramatic and triumphant events of Eliseg's reign in the eighth century, like those of Cynddylan's doomed reign in the seventh, are not referred to in the Welsh Annals or anywhere else. In fact, although the Annals do make reference to a number of Welsh altercations with the kingdom of Mercia in the eighth and ninth centuries, they seem largely to have been to the disadvantage of Britons near and far.† The Mercian king Offa (r.757–796) was responsible for the 'devastation of the South Britons' in 778 and then, with unhelpful generality, the 'devastation of the Britons' in

---

* It is notable that the scribe uses the word *Angli* instead of *Saxones*, the more common term in British sources; Mercia, as we have seen, was a self-consciously 'Anglian' realm.

† Probably drawing on contemporary Irish chronicles.

784.* Later references to conflict in Wales, all occurring during the reign of Coenwulf (r.796-821), successor to Offa's short-lived son Ecgfrith (d.796), can be located more closely: to Rheinwg, a region in south Wales in 796, at Rhuddlan on the north coast in 797, in Snowdonia and Rhufoniog in Gwynedd in 816, at Llanfaes on Anglesey in 817, in the kingdom of Dyfed in 818.

What is notable about this list of targets for Mercian aggression is that, in Coenwulf's reign, conflict with the Britons of the west was concentrated in the southern and northern regions. The parts of central Wales that lay directly adjacent to Mercian territory seem never to have been the main targets of aggression. And although it is certain that we do not possess an exhaustive account of major events in this region, the apparent absence of conflict along the line of the Mercian border (if one sets aside the generalities of Offa's reign) is striking. Part of the answer may lie in the defining legacy of Mercia in the Welsh borders and the most impressive civil engineering programme of early medieval Britain.

Bishop Asser of Sherborne, writing towards the end of the ninth century, described how 'Offa, terrifying to all the neighbouring kings and provinces around him [...] ordered a great ditch to be built between Wales and Mercia from sea to sea'.[46] That ditch has been known ever after as 'Offa's Dyke'. In truth, the Dyke does not stretch quite the entire distance and nor is it entirely continuous; it is, in fact, rather more complex than the image its name, Asser's assessment and popular imagination tend to project (often forgotten and marginalized are the stretches of secondary dyke to the east – known as Wat's Dyke – that mirror substantial sections of Offa's Dyke, albeit with slightly different characteristics and a still poorly understood chronological relationship to it). Whether the Dyke was truly constructed during the reign of Offa can be disputed –

* Although it is generally assumed that 'South Britons' is intended to imply the kingdoms of southern Wales, there is no particularly good reason to assume this is what the chronicler meant (it could simply mean that Offa attacked the Britons of 'Wales' rather than the northern Britons of 'Scotland').

despite repeated archaeological intervention no firm evidence has ever been found that would date its construction more precisely than post-Roman. But even without Asser's word for it, there would be good reason to think that the most likely context for its construction was during the belligerent reign of Offa. What is not in any doubt, however, is that the Dyke was constructed to the general disadvantage – whether psychological, practical, economic or military – of the people of central Wales whom it faced; at its most monumental it presented a ditch and bank that rose more than 26 feet from trough to peak, in places its outer face lined in stone to steepen, reinforce and intimidate. There can be no serious doubt that Offa's Dyke was, in the form it took, intended to be recognized as a means to control and surveil the landscape over vast distances, to stamp Mercian dominion across a wide frontier zone, to deter or delay the movement of people from the western side of the structure to its eastern side, to shut the door on land that may once have been freely theirs to roam.[47]

The sources for Mercia during the late eighth century paint a picture of a kingdom and a king incontinent with violent ambition (Asser used the euphemism 'vigorous').[48] In the early part of Offa's reign the king imposed his authority on the Hwicce and the Magonsaete and in 760 his armies were fighting the Britons near Hereford. By 772 the king had conquered the region around Hastings (East Sussex) and demoted the South Saxon kings to the rank of *duces*; by 764 he was in control of Kent and in 776 was fighting the resurgent Kentish kings at Otford (where he seems to have suffered a rare defeat); in 778 he was harassing the Welsh and in the following year defeated the West Saxon king at Bensington (Oxfordshire). In 784 he was at it again with the Welsh and back in charge in Kent. He was also busy expropriating land from the diocese of Worcester, a habit that led the Archbishop of Canterbury to mutter darkly about 'the rapacity of a certain king'.[49] In the 790s he conspired to exile one of the contenders for the West Saxon throne – Ecgberht – to the court of Charlemagne; there he was joined by Eadberht Præn, the exiled king of Kent. In 794 he had the East Anglian king Æthelberht beheaded for not respecting his authority. The so-called Mercian Supremacy was really an exercise in early medieval gangsterism, and the Mercian king was an Offa you couldn't refuse.

If, as Asser claimed, it was indeed Offa who built the Dyke, then it is easy to see it – like other military and self-aggrandizing projects of his reign – as a statement of his majesty and might, an irrefutable and permanent reminder of the men and resources at his command. Just as the Pillar of Eliseg proclaimed the *Romanitas* of Powysian kings through its form and Latinity, so the Dyke in cruder terms reminded those who beheld it, or who toiled upon its construction, that Mercia was ruled by a king whose raw power matched that of Caesar; that Offa was a new Hadrian, a warlord with Imperial aspirations and the same Roman disdain for barbarian outlanders. Walls, however, also speak of fear, something often forgotten in discussion of the Dyke. And while there is little to suggest that Offa himself was easily rattled, it may have been the fears of others that the Dyke was intended to address.

Authoritarian rule, wherever it is found, typically depends on stoking a fear of others. Building walls is an easy way to divide insiders from outsiders, to project the anxieties of a community onto whatever lies beyond. In this way, wall-builders transform erstwhile neighbours into existential threats – the wolves that stalk the sheepfold, the monsters that stalk the hall. At the same time, the wall-builder presents himself as a bulwark against impending doom. Seen as a protector and a saviour, he develops a powerful grip on the labour, the obedience, even the devotion, of his people. For any ruler who wishes to be seen in heroic terms, and who depends on unprecedented support for his projects, the political benefit of such a large public work may be incalculable. Whether the threat is entirely invented or simply magnified out of all proportion, whether the wall itself 'works' or is ever used as advertised – indeed, whether it is even finished at all – is all largely beside the point.

Perhaps the warriors of Powys really were so terrible that the Mercians needed a massive earthwork to cower behind, but it seems unlikely. Its message and its greater purpose were social and political, and it helped to cement Offa's reputation in the eyes of those who remembered him: a conqueror, a builder, a Great King.

The apparent lack of conflict in the central stretch of the Mercian frontier may well be related to the presence of the Dyke, not because it was an impregnable barrier that left the Welsh barbarians howling on the other side, but because the ability to construct such a sustained feat of civil engineering unmolested implies that the region it faced had already been effectively pacified. The descendants of Eliseg used the pillar to commemorate their former king for uniting 'the inheritance of Powys […] through force', but this may well be a post-rationalization of a more complex, and less heroic, reality. Eliseg's reign probably coincided with the beginning of Offa's and, whatever the violent backdrop to it (Eliseg's swords and fire, Offa's devastation of the 'South Britons'), it is entirely possible that any consolidation of Powys was made possible by political arrangements of some sort (Mercian overlordship on the Hwicce pattern being the most likely). The fact that all remained quiet along the border for most of Offa's and Coenwulf's reigns (plus the fact of the Dyke's very existence) suggests that a negotiated settlement between Mercia and Powys may well have governed relationships between the two kingdoms; a settlement that, from a Mercian perspective, had transformed a potentially troublesome neighbour into a controlled and managed hinterland.

This arrangement did not last. After languishing for perhaps half a century in the shadow of Mercian power, the kingdom of Powys fell to Mercia in 822 during the reign of Cyngen, the king who raised the Pillar of Eliseg. The Mercian campaign in Powys took place during the reign of King Ceolwulf (r.821–823), his brother Coenwulf's successor. Ceolwulf's reign, however, was a short-lived affair. He was deposed in 823 by a man named Beornwulf (r.823–826) who was installed as king in his stead and who spent his own short reign presiding over the spectacular collapse of the empire his predecessors had built. The critical blow came early in his reign. Ecgberht, the man whom Offa had driven into Frankish exile in the 790s, had recovered the throne of Wessex in 802, possibly with the help of Charlemagne. It may have been a self-fulfilling prophecy, but Ecgberht proved to be every bit as dangerous to Mercian interests as Offa's pre-emptive actions had marked him out to be. In 825, at a place called Ellendun ('elder-tree down') – somewhere beneath the western suburbs of Swindon (Wiltshire) – the Mercians and the West Saxons met in battle 'and [Ecgberht] had the victory and a great slaughter was made there'.[50]

The battle of Ellendun is one of the pivotal moments in English history. Although it is rarely now afforded the same status as other major battles of the early Middle Ages, its significance at the time was well understood and celebrated in verse: a probable fragment of Old English poetry, translated into Latin and incorporated into an Anglo-Norman chronicle in the twelfth century, recalls that 'Ellendun's stream ran red with blood, was stuffed up with corpses, filled with stink'.[51] Beornwulf's defeat triggered the terminal decline of Mercian power and the rise of the West Saxon dynasty, a dynasty that was destined in time to forge and rule over a unified English nation. It also, however, shook a number of previously subordinated realms, including (perhaps) Powys, loose from the shackles of Mercian dominance.*

It is in this period of Mercian weakness that the Pillar of Eliseg was most likely raised (or at least inscribed), a commemoration of independence regained – snatched by Cyngen of Powys as he watched the fortunes of his once mighty neighbour ebb. The inscription suggests that Cyngen wished it remembered that these were deeds of his own doing, that it was he – like his grandfather Eliseg – who had Made Powys Great Again ('It is Concenn ... with his hand ... his own kingdom of Powys ...). But it was not on Mercia's western

---

* Although most of them simply exchanged Mercian for West Saxon overlordship, the kingdom of East Anglia asserted its independence by rebelling against Mercian rule. When the unlucky Beornwulf turned up to pacify them in 826, the East Angles killed him in battle.

marches that the independence of Powys had been restored, not in blood spilled over the walls of dyke and rampart. It had happened far away, on elder-grown slopes, under West Saxon swords.

The text of the Pillar of Eliseg ends with a typical, if truncated, Christian coda:

+ The blessing of the Lord upon Concenn and likewise(?) on all of his household and upon all the province of Powys until …

'Until …' the broken end of the inscription hangs with prophetic uncertainty. And for all real purposes, it marks the end of the kingdom of Powys, a provisional epitaph. For his own part, Cyngen (Concenn) does seem to have actively pursued the blessing of the Lord. Not that it did him much good in the material world: he died in 854/5, apparently on a pilgrimage to Rome.[52] As for his kingdom, the Lord seems to have looked elsewhere when dispensing his blessings. No source mentions Powys at all in a contemporary context between the middle of the ninth century and the second half of the eleventh.* When, in 1069, the kingdom finally reappeared in the historical record, its independence had already evaporated, reduced to a province ruled by the kings of Gwynedd.

What happened to Powys during its long dormancy is unknown. It might have limped on, subject to the waxing and waning dominance of mightier neighbours and the upheavals of the Viking Age, struggling to regain the sense of self it had once known.

Or maybe it died with Cyngen, only to be reborn two centuries later: an old brand-name revived under new ownership, cashing in on the glamour and the mystery of a time that had already receded deep into legend.

---

* Note that Powys does appear in literary works that may date to this interval, but these are all texts that look backward to a lost age.

MERCIA

SURREY

Wey

Mole

North   Downs

Medway

KENT

The Weald
(Andredesweald)

Rother

WEST SUSSEX

Apple Down

South

Arun

Harrow
Hill

Adur

Thundersbarrow
Slonk Hill

EAST SUSSEX

Ouse

Cuckmere

Camber
Sands

Downs

Beddingham

Hastings

Westhampnett

Bosham
Chichester

Highdown

Alfriston

Pevensey Castle
(Andredesceaster)

Eastbourne

Selsey

English Channel

SUSSEX

– *East Sussex, West Sussex* –

They were always landing in those days, or being driven back
to their ships, and they always brought their Gods with
them. England is a bad country for Gods.

Rudyard Kipling, *Puck of Pook's Hill* (1906)

I t was in the year 666 that Bishop Wilfrid of Northumbria and his
companions arrived on the Sussex coast, driven on the teeth of a
storm. 'The wind,' wrote Wilfrid's biographer Stephen of Ripon (or
'Eddius Stephanus' as he is also known), 'howled from the southeast, and white crested waves drove them towards the land of the
South Saxons' depositing them on the beach before the tide withdrew 'laying bare the shores, and receded far out to sea'.[1] No one
knows exactly where Wilfrid found himself washed up – the shape
of the coastline has changed a lot since his day – but the conditions
that stranded him are familiar to anyone who knows the dynamics
of England's southern coastline.

When I was a very young child I was taken to Camber Sands
(East Sussex) by my parents and grandparents. It was a strange day

– a thick fog had rolled in from the sea, blanketing the beach as far as the sand dunes and obscuring the view in all directions. Through even thicker clouds of fogged recollection I can remember walking for what felt like hours in a bewildering ghostlight, surrounded by pale scraps of mist and the endless desert of dull yellow sand below. We quickly became lost in that dreamscape, all sense of direction melting away as we wandered towards where we imagined the horizon might be. No sea, no sky; we never found the water.

Camber Sands is a more dangerous place than I think any of us were aware. The land shelves away very gradually at Camber, and when the tide goes out it goes out fast and far – exposing more than three thousand feet of open sand. It comes back just as suddenly. In 2016 five young men drowned on the beach, caught by the returning tide and trapped by the deep water that pools in troughs between the sandbars. If Wilfrid had any concerns about natural hazards in 666, however, he had little opportunity to register them. Waiting for him on the Sussex strand was 'a great horde of pagans [...] intending to seize the vessel, loot it, carry off captives, and slay without more ado all that resisted.'[2]

Wilfrid was uncommonly robust, even by the uncompromising standards of his age. His career was defined by an almost pathological truculence and a limitless capacity for exhausting self-aggrandizement. He held grudges, he feuded with kings and fellow prelates, he maintained a paramilitary following and he went to great lengths to defend what he felt were his rights and prerogatives. When in 678 he was deprived of the Northumbrian bishopric by King Ecgfrith and Archbishop Theodore of Canterbury – who were apparently disturbed (and perhaps made a little jealous) by 'the number of his monasteries, the vastness of the buildings, his countless followers arrayed and armed like a king's retinue' – he travelled all the way to Rome in order to canvas Pope Agatho for the restoration of his power and possessions (with mixed results).*[3]

---

* According to Stephen of Ripon, Wilfrid was pursued by his enemies abroad; they were apparently not the sharpest of assassins and mistakenly

When later imprisoned by King Ecgfrith, Wilfrid is alleged to have claimed that he would 'rather lose his head' than acquiesce to the king's desires.[4] Confronted with the mob of murderous South Saxons in 666, however, Wilfrid adopted a more pragmatic stance: 'anxious to save his friends' lives' (and especially mindful, one suspects, of his own), the bishop 'tried to pacify them with soothing words, and promised a large sum of money'.[5]

According to Stephen of Ripon, the Saxons were not at all impressed, and the situation quickly got away from Wilfrid. In a heathen counterpoint to the Christian invective of St Germanus or the weaponized prayers of the Bangor monks, 'the chief priest of their idolatry set himself up on a high mound like Balaam and started to curse God's people, trying to bind their hands with his magical art'.* Luckily for the Christians, they had the example of the Old Testament to draw upon: one of Wilfrid's companions brained the offending sorcerer with a well-aimed rock and 'death took him as it took Goliath, unawares'. This seems to have injected some steel into the beleaguered landing party and the words that Stephen puts into their mouths represents one of the oldest articulations of heroic sentiment in any literature produced in England: 'stout-hearted and well-armed, they formed a pact – that no one should turn his back and flee in battle but that each should either die with honour or live in triumph.' Meanwhile St Wilfrid and the other clergy who were present, in a pious riposte to the dark Saxon sorceries that had been levelled against them, 'fell to their knees, raised their hands to heaven, and gained God's help'.[6]

With their backs to the sea and their weapons towards the enemy the Christians supposedly repelled three waves of assault ('with no mean slaughter') for the loss of only five of their number. They had

set out after Bishop Winfrid of Lichfield. The unlucky Winfrid 'fell into their hands and may as well have fallen into the lion's jaws, for they seized him, took all his money, killed many of his friends, and inflicted the extremes of misery on him by leaving him naked. Luckily for our bishop [Wilfrid] they had mistaken the first syllable of Winfrid's name.'

* See **POWYS**.

managed, as Stephen tells it, to 'vanquish a fierce and untamed pagan host' (although, since he doesn't relate how big or well-armed this 'great horde' actually was, this may not have been all that impressive an achievement).*[7] Whatever happened, however, Wilfrid and his party must have been relieved when the tide returned, lifting their vessel and returning them to the comparative safety of the sea just as South Saxon reinforcements, led by their king, hoved into view. Deliverance had arrived, a timely *deus ex machina*.

Stephen's *Vita Wilfrithi* ('Life of Wilfrid'), composed between 709 and 720, is the earliest source to mention the land of the South Saxons. The picture it presents is of a strange and barbarous realm, populated by heathen wizards and murderous plunderers with an instinctively homicidal attitude towards outsiders. This, perhaps, is to be expected: the life of St Wilfrid was a work of hagiography designed to stress the ungodly obstacles to its subject's career, and the blessings and miracles that were generated to overcome them. Its depiction of non-Christian people was always unlikely to be generous. It is, moreover, padded with large wads of biblical stuffing that engender a healthy scepticism about many of the details. It seems unlikely, for example, that Wilfrid's companions numbered exactly 120 ('one for each year of Moses' life').[8] But, true or not, the story that Stephen tells reflects a view of the South Saxon lands as seen by outsiders, a place that 'dense forests and rocky coasts had saved from conquest by other kingdoms', and which as a result 'had remained persistently heathen'.[9]

Writing ten to twenty years after Stephen, Bede painted his own dark vignette of South Saxon heathendom. He recalls a period of the late 670s when the realm was on the brink of conversion, a time when 'no rain had fallen in the province for three years [...] and a terrible famine ensued, which reduced many to an awful

---

* Stephen compares it to the slaughter of 120,000 Midianiates by Gideon and his three hundred companions in the Old Testament, a story which frankly has its own credibility issues.

death. It is said that frequently forty or fifty emaciated and starving people would go to a precipice, or to the edge of the sea, where they would join hands and leap over, to die by the fall or by drowning.'[10] It is a vision of a forsaken land struggling in the grip of dark and unforgiving gods – a place benighted by death and despair. Though Bede is not explicit, perhaps unwilling to undermine the pathos of his story, there is an unspoken shadow that lingers – a sense that the gods might be placated, that crops might be restored, if people would only toss their bodies freely into the sea, shatter them upon the shoreline. The Old English word for sacrifice is *Blot*, a term that shares its roots with the word for blood (OE *Blod*). Bede himself explained that the old name for November was *Blot-monath* – 'sacrifice month' – and was the time when cattle were slaughtered and given to the gods as burned offerings. It is not beyond the realms of possibility that, *in extremis*, a more dreadful sacrifice might be called for. To quote *The Wicker Man*'s Lord Summerisle, 'animals are fine, but their acceptability is limited. A little child is even better, but not *nearly* as effective as the right kind of adult.'[11]

Bede's story of heathen tragedy and barbarism is, of course, a moralizing Christian parable, and not a sober historical anecdote. It was driven by didactic impulses, distorted by religious and political biases. Like Stephen's tale of pagan wizards it was constructed to paint an image of the South Saxons as tragically ignorant and backward.*[12] This does not change the fact, however, that of all the early English-speaking realms of Britain, Sussex remains one of the strangest and most impenetrable. It emerges as a land defined by its isolation and its persistent heathenry: cut off from the mainstream religious and political life of Britain, its migrant people

---

* The story also preserves a sense of the central role that fertility and fecundity played in agrarian communities, and the way in which these became a prime focus for supernatural interventions of all kinds. As Bede concludes, 'on the very day that the nation received the baptism of faith a soft but ample rainfall refreshed the earth, restoring greenness to the cornfields and giving a happy and fruitful season.'

sundered from their ancestors beyond the sea, its natives sundered from their past – embowered and tide-locked and, ultimately, doomed.

The 'province of the South Saxons', as Bede knew it, 'stretches west and south from Kent as far as the land of the West Saxons'.[13] It occupied, give or take a little round the edges, the region now covered by the modern counties of East and West Sussex. The coastline is not as it once was. Now the silting up of rivers and estuaries has narrowed the coastal plain, filling creeks and obliterating salt marshes, smoothing and rationalizing the edges of the land. It is no longer the dangerous and difficult littoral that Wilfrid encountered. The white cliffs at Beachy Head in the east – the place where it is easiest to imagine the starving and desperate South Saxons plunging to their doom – are the hardest edge that the former kingdom possessed. They are the snapped end of the South Downs, a chalk ridge that rises sharply from the narrow coastal plain and ends in a shallow diagonal sweep towards the west. From up on the chalk the rivers run, from north to south, in tidy parallels, carving their valleys to the sea: the Arun, Adur, Ouse and Cuckmere – each one a channel linking uplands to coastline, an ecological wiring system.

Beyond the South Downs, to the east and north, lay the Weald – *Andredesweald* or *Andredesleah*, 'the forest of Andred', as it was known in Old English – an arc of ancient woodland that once extended from the Kent coast east of Hastings to fill the space between the South Downs of Sussex and the North Downs of Kent and Surrey. According to the *Anglo-Saxon Chronicle*, the Weald in the 890s measured 120 miles long and 30 miles wide, a vast forested zone in which the persecuted could hide themselves and entire armies travel unseen.[14] It formed the northern and eastern boundary to the South Saxon realm, a great forbidding screen of shadows and beast-haunted glades that remained largely undisturbed by human settlement for centuries: no trace of farmstead, church or cemetery dating between the fifth and eighth centuries has ever been discovered in the Weald. Apart from a brief period in the seventh century, when it encompassed the Isle of Wight and the valley of the Meon in east Hampshire, the South Saxon kingdom never broke out of those boundaries. It was self-contained, constrained by its environment. Nearly all of the archaeology of the region – not only in the period of the old kingdom but for centuries after its demise – is confined to a narrow belt of settlement along the coast and up onto the Downs.

Andredesweald gained its name due to its apparent coastal terminus at the Roman fortress of *Anderitum*, known in Old English as *Andredesceaster* ('Castle of Andred') and today as Pevensey Castle. It was one of several imposing Roman garrison forts that were constructed during the third century as part of a chain of fortifications along the southern and eastern coasts of Britain, from the Isle of Wight to the Wash. Nine of these fortresses are listed in a document called the *Notitia Dignitatum* ('List of Offices') originally compiled in the late fourth century and preserved in manuscripts of the fifteenth and sixteenth centuries:

Portus Adurni (Portchester Castle, Hampshire)
Anderitum (Pevensey Castle, East Sussex)
Portus Lemanis (Lympne, Kent)
Dubris (Dover Castle, Kent)
Rutupiae (Richborough, Kent)
Regulbium (Reculver, Kent)
Othona (Bradwell-on-Sea, Essex)
Gariannonum (Burgh Castle, Norfolk)
Branodunum (Brancaster, Norfolk)[15]

As its name implies, the *Notitia* is a breakdown of job titles held by late Roman administrators and military officials across the Empire. One of these is the *Comes Litoris Saxonici per Britanniam* – the 'Count of the Saxon Shore for Britain' – and the list of forts provides a view of the real estate (as well as the garrison units) under his command. It is not exhaustive – a number of other fortresses along these coastlines are now thought almost certainly to have formed part of this system and to have fallen under the Count's authority, including the original defences at Walton Castle (Suffolk) and Caistor-on-Sea (Norfolk). Carisbrooke Castle, on the Isle of Wight, may have been another.* In fact it seems fairly clear that the 'Saxon Shore' was really an extensive network of sites that had been evolving since the third century, not all of which were massive stone installation like Pevensey Castle. It formed a part of an interconnected network of military bases that included logistical centres and roads and a string of coastal watchtowers extending up Britain's eastern seaboard as far as the Humber.

What exactly the Saxon Shore was intended to achieve, however, is not entirely clear and may have changed considerably over time. The most common interpretation is that it was a defensive system designed to ward off barbarian attacks on stretches of Britain's coastline. The Roman historian Ammianus Marcellinus describes how, in 364, Britain was battered by assaults from Picts, Scots, Saxons and 'Attacotti'.† Three years later, in 367, he notes that 'a concerted attack by the barbarians had reduced the province of Britain to the verge of ruin', and that 'Nectaridus, the count of the coastal region, had been killed, and the general Fullofaudes surprised and cut off'.‡[16] This 'count of the coastal region' may well be a reference to the 'Count of the Saxon Shore' referred to in the *Notitia Dignitatum* or, if not, at least someone with a similar portfolio.

---

* In truth, popular perception of Saxon shore forts has been rather distorted by the *Notitia* and the impression it gives of a canonical list of important centres.

† 'Attacotti' are presumed to be some flavour of northern Britons.

‡ The Roman general Theodosius subsequently arrived (at Richborough in Kent) and swept up the marauders that he discovered around London before mounting a larger, and successful, expedition into northern Britain. Although Ammianus is not very clear about this, it seems likely that the trouble Theodosius encountered in southern Britain came from the Continent rather than from Ireland or the north. Ammianus in this section only specifically mentions Scots, Picts and Attacotti; Saxons are mentioned, but only as a menace to Gaul – although it is possible that Ammianus conflated Gaul with southeast Britain.

It is also possible that the 'Saxon Shore' actually referred to a region deliberately settled by groups of friendly Saxon mercenaries for the purpose of deterring and repelling other barbarians. That, of course, is precisely how Gildas explained the presence of English-speaking people in Britain. His story, of how a 'proud tyrant' (named Vortigern, according to Bede) invited Saxon mercenaries into Britain to defend the island from the Picts and Scots (with disastrous results), took place – depending on how the organization of Gildas' material is read – in either the 380s or in the middle of the fifth century. That obviously leaves some fairly wide latitude regarding the date that these particular Saxon mercenaries were deliberately settled, but it could conceivably have occurred before the *Notitia* was compiled. And it remains possible, of course, that soldiers from Germania were deliberately settled by Roman administrators along the south coast of Britain at various different times. If Saxon mercenaries were brought to Britain, however, there can be very little confidence that their presence would be archaeologically distinguishable from other late Roman military graves in the majority of cases.

There is plenty of other evidence, however, that has been taken to support the presence of continental migrants in Sussex from at least the early to mid-fifth century. Cemeteries at Westhampnett near Chichester (*Noviomagus Reginorum*, the civitas capital of the *Regnenses*), Highdown, Alfriston and Eastbourne all appear to have originated in the mid-fifth century, dated by the same sort of high-status, late Roman artefacts that characterize the earliest phases of cemeteries in Essex. Elsewhere, traces of occupation – sunken-featured buildings in the Adur Valley, secondary occupation of a desolate villa at Beddingham – have been seen as the signs of settlement by a migrant people. But, as everywhere in southern and eastern Britain, the actual mechanisms that might explain these phenomena remain opaque. As in Essex, there is nothing much about the earliest burials in these cemeteries that is not consistent with late Roman burial practice.* And, although

* Several contain quoit-brooch style artefacts; see **ESSEX**.

these burial grounds were established on new plots in the early to mid-fifth century, discontinuity with late Roman cemetery locations is not a phenomenon that requires overseas migration to explain it.[17]

The picture is complicated further by the presence of communities whose dead, from the later fifth and sixth centuries, were buried with material attributes and customs that tie them to the 'Frankish' culture of northern Gaul rather than conforming to any Romano-British or 'Saxon' pattern. From the fifth century onwards, a number of graves – particularly between Eastbourne and the Ouse, but also at Highdown and near Chichester – contained distinctively 'Frankish' material: bird-shaped brooches and throwing axes among the most eye-catching.[18] In some ways, this is remarkably unsurprising. If these continental fashions and artefacts – and, indeed, people – were going to turn up anywhere, it was always most likely to be along the south coast of Britain. And in any case, the social and political entanglements of the neighbouring kingdom of Kent were long bound up with the religious and political interests of the Kingdom of the Franks.* It does, however, add a further layer of complexity to understanding who the South Saxons were, or who they thought themselves to be.

Recent scientific investigation of the cemetery at Eastbourne, however, has shed some light on these issues.[19] Examination of the strontium isotopes present in tooth enamel was conducted on the remains of nineteen individuals, all of whom were buried between 375 and 600 (dated on the basis of accompanying grave goods) and who were selected by the researchers to represent a diversity of age, sex and generosity of grave furnishing. The results, though based on only a sample of graves, have significant and potentially wide-ranging implications. Of all the people tested, only one can be said with any confidence to have grown up in continental Europe. Six others

---

* It is notable that the areas of Sussex that show the strongest influence are those closest to the Kentish border, and otherwise cluster along major routes of communication.

Typically 'Frankish' brooches from cemeteries at Eastbourne (left)
and Highdown (right) (© Gilli Allan 2022).

might also have originated in western Europe, but just as likely came
from somewhere else in Britain. Two others came from communities outside the immediate area, but not from very far away (probably
Kent). All the others – ten in total – grew up locally. These findings
alone are enough to raise serious questions about any migration
narrative that one might want to propose. What is most arresting
about the results of this study, however, is that the ten individuals
who grew up locally are also those whose graves were the most
lavishly furnished. They include one woman who was buried with a
quoit-brooch and a man buried with a 'Frankish' throwing axe.

Apparently wealthy local people were buried at Eastbourne from
the earliest phase of the cemetery, findings which neither support a
sudden all-conquering Saxon migration nor a continuous steady
flow of migrants. Rejecting all the established narratives, the
authors of the study conclude that the formation of these communities must instead have been the result of 'diverse migratory and
demographic processes'.[20] In other words, it was complicated – far
more complicated than the people of southern Britain themselves
in later ages cared to imagine.

* * *

The traditional narrative explaining how heathen Saxons came to Sussex is preserved in the *Anglo-Saxon Chronicle*. In 477, so the story goes, 'Ælle and his three sons, Cymen and Wlencing and Cissa, came to the land of Britain [*Bretenlond*; i.e. 'Briton-land'] with three ships at the place which is named *Cymenesora* ['Cymen's Shore'], and there slaughtered many *wealas* [i.e. 'Welsh/foreigners' – native Britons in this context] and drove some to flight into the wood which is named *Andredesleag* ['Wood of Andred'; the Weald)]'.[21] Eight years later, in 485, 'Ælle fought against the Britons near the bank of *Mearcredesburna* ['Mearcred's Stream']'.[22] Finally in 491, in what was presumably imagined to be a decisive victory, 'Ælle and Cissa besieged *Andredesceaster* ['the (Roman) fortress of Andred'; *Anderitum*; Pevensey Castle], and slaughtered all who lived therein; there was not even one Briton left.'[23]

The archaeology of *Anderitum* (Pevensey Castle), the Saxon Shore fort that was supposed to have borne the brunt of Ælle's murderous campaign, presents a mixed and fascinating picture. Excavations that took place there between the 1930s and 1960s reveal a site that appears to have remained sporadically occupied from the late Roman period until the late seventh or early eighth century – a sequence of occupation that presents numerous challenges to interpretation. Fragments of 'DSP' ('Dérivée Sigillée Paléochrétienne' – fancy tableware manufactured in southern Gaul) dated to the late fourth or early fifth century were discovered there, as was a 'Kempston-style' glass cone beaker (a typically 'Anglo-Saxon' object type) dated to the fifth/sixth century, alongside fifth-century pottery of a variety that developed in continental Saxony. Later excavations in the 1990s revealed fragments of African Red Slip Ware and a sherd of what may well be an amphora from the eastern Mediterranean: exactly the sort of stuff (though in much smaller quantities) that was arriving in bulk at Tintagel between 475 and 550.

These later finds caused considerable excitement among archaeologists because they represent the first discovery in southeastern Britain of the sort of exotic imports that characterize places like

Tintagel, bringing parts of what has traditionally been seen as the 'Anglo-Saxon' coastline into wider networks of Atlantic and Mediterranean commerce. Taken alongside the other finds from *Anderitum*, these artefacts – few and fragmentary though they are – present an image of a site settled by people wealthy and organized enough to acquire a broad range of imported luxuries. No excavations comparable in extent to the archaeological work undertaken at Tintagel has ever been attempted, but the nature of the artefacts and their diverse geographical origins – coupled with the sheer monumentality of the enclosed fortress – allow for the possibility that, at some point between the late fourth and early eighth centuries, *Anderitum* was a power centre to rival any of the better known hill-forts and citadels of western Britain.[24]

It is easy to imagine Pevensey Castle as the fortress of a Dark Age potentate of some magnitude. Its still-standing Roman perimeter walls, with their distinctive red-tile lines sandwiched between courses of pale flinty masonry and Roman concrete, still stand to an impressive height, reinforced with mighty drum tower bastions. From their tops the view once extended widely over the surrounding sea – now distant, but once an enclosing presence – that isolated the fortress on its own peninsula, projecting from a chaotic landscape of wetlands and tidal channels. It was, and remains, a massive compound, the later medieval castle tucked into one end of the site, dwarfed by the vast oval circuit of the Roman walls. However, establishing who exactly occupied this site in the post-Roman period and when and how they used it is extraordinarily difficult. Partly this is complicated by the presence – alongside the fine imported glass and pottery – of dark earth, rubbish, building detritus and evidence of burning. Far from clarifying the situation, the evidence admits a huge variety of scenarios. Almost any sequence of invasion, displacement, continuity, resettlement and abandonment can be accommodated, so long as all the material evidence is accounted for somehow. Even the *Anglo-Saxon Chronicle*'s tale of Ælle's genocidal conquest in 477 can – with a lot of imagination and a willingness to massage the approximate date ranges – be made to fit the archaeology: which is not to say that it should be.

The origins of the South Saxon kingdom as presented in the *Anglo-Saxon Chronicle* are very similar to a number of other 'Anglo-Saxon' origin stories. The kingdom of Kent, for example, was supposedly founded by the brothers Hengest and Horsa (and Hengest's son Æsc) who arrived at *Ypwinesfleot* (probably Ebbsfleet in Thanet) with three ships in 449. Similarly, the territories west of the South Saxon lands (which later became part of the kingdom of Wessex) were allegedly founded in a sequence of landings: by Cerdic and Cynric who arrived at *Cerdicesora* ('Cerdic's Shore') with five ships in 495, by Port and his sons Bieda and Mægla who arrived at *Portesmuþa* ('Portsmouth') with two ships in 501 and by the three ships that arrived at Cerdic's Shore in 514 bearing Stuf and Wihtgar. In each case the new arrivals supposedly set about defeating native kings and nobles, seizing land and driving the Britons into flight. This narrative of invasion and conquest continues throughout the sixth century and into the seventh with a litany of battles – many fought at prominent and dramatic locations – charting the inexorable expansion of Anglo-Saxondom into southern Britain.*[25]

On the face of it, this story of post-Roman conquest and upheaval chimes with the picture that Gildas (and Bede) painted, an epic ethnic struggle that erased the Romano-British populations of lowland Britain, driving them into the highlands of Wales, Dumnonia and the north. It also appears to offer what those broad-brush narratives did not: the names and dates and places from

---

* For what it's worth, the *Historia Brittonum* has its own (dubious) version of how southern England was 'lost' to Saxon interlopers. In this version of things, Vortigern convened an unarmed council of peace with Hengest and his barbarian cohorts. The latter deceitfully stashed knives in their shoes and, at a word from their leader, slaughtered 300 British delegates; Vortigern was captured and, to save his own life, 'Essex and Sussex, together with Middlesex and other districts that they chose and designated' were ceded to Hengest.

which historians might construct elaborate narratives of the progress of armies and the fate of the Britons. From the early Middle Ages onwards, generations of writers repeated and elaborated this story of 'Anglo-Saxon' conquest until it became enshrined as an enduring national myth; not only for the English but also for those inhabitants of Britain for whom it served as a legend of ancestral dispossession and a wellspring of Anglophobic resentment. Up until the middle of the twentieth century, its hold remained strong in histories of post-Roman Britain, the movements of migrant warbands through Britain charted by cemeteries and battlefields: an inexorable pinking of the British map behind an expanding 'Anglo-Saxon' front that spread from east to west and south to north (oftentimes illustrated with maps complete with little pointy arrows of the *Dad's Army* variety).

No competent scholar of the period would now support this view of the fifth, sixth and seventh centuries. As the example of the Eastbourne cemetery demonstrates, data drawn from graves can no longer be relied upon to identify 'peoples' or demonstrate the migration of human beings instead of fashions and objects. Evidence for widespread violence and mayhem in the fifth century is largely absent.*[26] Evidence for mixed communities is growing, as other chapters in this book have touched upon. However, it is only because the traditional narrative of Anglo-Saxon conquest is so entrenched that it is necessary to debate these issues at all. Taken on its own merits, the *Anglo-Saxon Chronicle* presents such deeply, and obviously, flawed evidence for the fifth and sixth centuries that there is really no reason to trust it in the first place, let alone rest so much weight on it.

The earliest manuscript of the *Chronicle* – the so-called 'A' or 'Winchester' chronicle – was written in the late ninth century and

* Although I would add that there is no consensus as to what the archaeological footprint of fifth–seventh century warfare should actually look like; the skeletal remains from Heronbridge (see **POWYS**) are to date the only credible evidence for warfare of this period (as opposed to evidence of militarized culture, for which the evidence is plentiful).

is associated with the grand project of self-promotion that occupied the court of King Alfred of Wessex (r. 871–899). None of the information it contains can be securely dated any earlier than the ninth century, apart from those bits that were obviously cribbed from Gildas and Bede. While it might be fair to assume that it *does* contain elements of older written or oral tradition that have not survived elsewhere, there is no way of knowing whether it reproduces that material faithfully and what it deliberately excludes. In any case, even if the *Chronicle* does contain traces of older sources, there is no way of evaluating whether those hypothetical sources themselves ever preserved an accurate record of the past.

What *can* be said with confidence, however, is that a number of assertions in the annals for the fifth and sixth centuries are demonstrably false, that a good deal more are highly questionable and that the vast bulk of them are suspiciously compatible with, if not downright supportive of, Alfred's political aspirations, territorial claims and sense of dynastic entitlement.*[27]

* By the late ninth century, when the *Anglo-Saxon Chronicle* was compiled, Alfred's Wessex was the only 'Anglo-Saxon' kingdom to have survived the Viking wars with its original dynasty still in charge. Mercia, Northumbria and East Anglia had all fallen to Viking warlords or been dismantled. Alfred – drawing his lineage all the way back to Cerdic (and beyond) – was positioning himself as the natural inheritor of all the realms of southern Britain: the last man standing. While the *Chronicle* was one of Alfred's main vehicles for articulating those claims, the process of co-opting the royal pedigrees of the Kentish and South Saxon kingdoms had begun before Alfred's time. (Alfred's grandfather Ecgberht (r.802–839) had won a victory over the Mercians in 825 at *Ellendun* (near Swindon) that changed the balance of power in southern Britain, bringing the southeastern realms under West Saxon domination; Alfred's father Æthelwulf (r.839–858) had initiated the policy of installing his sons as 'sub-kings' of Surrey, Sussex, Essex and Kent.) The creation of a linked history for these places – embedded in a landscape that served as a constant reminder of dynastic rights – was a deliberate strategy of the West Saxon royal house, one that was designed to solidify their right to rule and mythologize their expansive ambitions. All of which is a long way of saying that the early history of Sussex – as we have received it – was a product not of the South Saxons but of the West Saxons and that it was a history that served the interests of the latter.

The origin stories in particular are dubious for a number of reasons, not least their formulaic similarity to each other. The martial exploits that were ascribed to men like Hengest, Cerdic and Ælle – killing the natives, seizing their land, settling down – were precisely the sort of myths that later kings could use to legitimize their claims to territorial rule. The conspicuous use of personal names provided later genealogists with the legendary personae who could be inserted into the family trees of their royal patrons (e.g. Cerdic in the West Saxon genealogy, Hengest in the Kentish genealogy).* Moreover, by locating the events of conquest with reference to specific places, the territorial claims of kings could be rooted in real geography. The landscape thus effectively became a storybook of conquest, where landmarks – many of them named after (or supposed to be named after) the victorious warlords who had fought there – acted as a continuous reminder of the past, and a statement of the pedigree of contemporary royal authority. The power of kings, in other words, was entrenched in the landscapes they laid claim to and the stories told about them. Many of those stories, however, were never true at all.

In its earliest annals, the *Anglo-Saxon Chronicle* repeatedly insinuates that the origin of place-names can be explained by reference to the doings of legendary individuals. So, for example, 'Cerdic's Shore' was the place where Cerdic arrived by sea; Portsmouth the place where Port turned up. Wihtgar was put in charge of the Isle of Wight (*Wiht*) after Cerdic and Cynric pitched up there in 530 and killed some of the locals. This supposedly happened at a place called *Wihtgarasbyrg* ('Wihtgar's Stronghold'). The implication is that these places were (re)named in Old English in honour of the heroes who had ruled, conquered or made landfall at them, and on the face of it this seems perfectly plausible. (This sort of land-naming is actually a fairly unremarkable and seemingly universal method of claim-staking that came as naturally to Viking settlers

---

* No South Saxon royal genealogy has survived, but if it did ever exist then it almost certainly contained Ælle.

around the north Atlantic in the ninth century as it did to British explorers and colonial administrators in the nineteenth.) Several of the *Chronicle*'s implied etymologies, however, simply do not stand up to scrutiny. *Wiht*, for example, is an Anglicized form of *Vectis*, the Latin name for the Isle of Wight, and *Portesmuþa* (Portsmouth) is an English name that described the *muþa* 'mouth of the harbour' at *Portus Adurni* (the Latin name for the Roman fortress of Portchester). It would be a surprising coincidence indeed if two separate men were to have crossed the sea to a new land only to stumble upon places that already possessed names identical to their own. Wihtgar and Port, we can be fairly sure, were made up.*[28]

Even setting aside all the other problems, this sort of evidence for flagrant falsehood (and these are not the only examples) means that there are good grounds for distrusting pretty much every detail that the *Anglo-Saxon Chronicle* has to offer regarding the origins of the southern kingdoms of Britain. Ultimately, the best that can be said of the *Chronicle* in its account of the fifth and sixth centuries is that it presents a fascinating digest of folklore, invention and warped memory. But it is not history. That, however, doesn't make it useless. By the late ninth century it is evident that a body of lore relating to Britain's most southerly realms either already existed or was in the process of being created. The specific elements of that corpus which Alfred's scribes saw fit to repeat in their chronicle represented the origins of southern 'Anglo-Saxon' kingdoms in very specific ways. In particular, the process was seen in explicitly military terms, with violence against the Romano-British as the decisive arbiter of the right to land and rulership. It also saw migrant status – what we might call 'authentic Saxon-ness' – as more valuable than native origins, and it also bound specific places in the landscape into a founding mythology for the West Saxon dynasty. All of this says something powerful about how West Saxon kings viewed the

---

* Also made up was the British king 'Natanleod' who was killed by the homicidal duo Cerdic and Cynric in 508. This unfortunate fellow supposedly gave his name to the land around Netley in Hampshire. Netley, however, means 'wet wood' or 'marshy clearing' (from OE *naet + leah).

basis for their power and their place in history, even if it says nothing much about how the South Saxons viewed themselves.*[29] With no surviving chronicles of their own, however, discovering what animated the minds and souls of the rulers of Sussex and their people is an uphill battle that may never be won.

According to Bede, the kingdom of the South Saxons was, with the exception of the Isle of Wight, the last of the 'Anglo-Saxon' kingdoms to abandon heathen practices. Bede was very clear that he believed the South Saxons – like the East Saxons – to be descended from the Old Saxons of continental northern Europe, and broad artefactual correlations between the cemeteries of Sussex and the Elbe–Weser region can be drawn (Frankish influences notwithstanding). And whatever doubts now exist about the scale of human migration, there are hints that, as in Essex, the gods of the Old Saxons managed the crossing: at least one recorded place-name in Sussex – *Þunorslege* – preserves the name of a grove dedicated to Thunor, and a burial mound known as Thundersbarrow, on the South Downs above Shoreham-by-Sea, may also have been named after the god.†[30]

The wider beliefs of the Old Saxons, as they were encountered by missionaries in the eighth century, are hard to recover. A flavour of them can be gleaned from a list preserved in the Vatican entitled the *Indiculus Superstitionum et Paganiarum* – a 'little index' of thirty superstitious and pagan practices.[31] Though the exact context

* None of this means that Ælle and his three sons did not exist at all; Bede, writing in the early eighth century, refers to King Ælle of the South Saxons by name, crediting him as the first English king to have claimed overlordship over his peers (though without specifying exactly when). This, however, seems to have been the limit of his knowledge on the matter.

† *Þunorslege* means Thunor's *leah* ('woodland clearing/grove') and appears in the Old English boundary clause of a charter dated 772 concerning Barnhorne Manor near Bexhill. Unfortunately, no early forms of the name Thundersbarrow have survived to prove its age and derivation.

of its compilation remains uncertain, it is thought to have originated in the same period and circumstances that produced the Old Saxon baptismal vow: that is to say the Christianization of pagan Germania – and particularly Saxondom – by the missionaries that both preceded and followed Charlemagne's armies in the late eighth century. Although it is not at all certain, it appears to have been intended as a contents page for a longer treatise dealing with practices that were to be condemned and eradicated. It provides a glimpse, occluded though it is by all the many things left unsaid and unexplained, of the way the recently repressed people of northern Germany were imagined to conduct themselves: a primer, perhaps, for what the missionary priest might encounter amongst unconverted heathens and backsliding converts. These worrisome behaviours included such apparent abominations as 'sacrilege at the graves of the dead', 'swinish feasts in February', 'the sacred rites of Mercury [Woden] and of Jupiter [Thunor]', 'an idol which they carry through the fields', 'undetermined places which they celebrate as holy', 'amulets and knots', women who command the moon 'so that they can steal the hearts of men' and, most sinister of all, 'those things which they do upon the stones'.[32]

Evocative though it is, however, the *Indiculus* is not really very useful for understanding the beliefs of the South Saxons in Britain two centuries earlier. Thunor may have crossed the sea, but there is little else that seems to connect the pre-Christian praxis of these widely sundered 'Saxon' worlds. The *Indiculus*, for example, makes specific reference to 'little houses, that is sanctuaries', and such structures do indeed find form in Britain. But the early medieval remains identified by British archaeologists as pagan sanctuaries have no clear parallel in northern Europe and there is no way that they can be straightforwardly accepted as evidence for an intrusive 'Germanic' paganism. On the contrary, these 'sanctuaries' most closely parallel the rectilinear temple structures of pre-Christian Roman and Iron Age Britain and fit within an island-wide tradition of reusing the remains of the prehistoric and Romano-British past for new – or perhaps sometimes not so new – purposes.

Slonk Hill in West Sussex is a low prominence on the southern edge of the South Downs commanding views of the sea and the valley of the River Adur to the west. It was the location of a Bronze Age barrow that was repurposed in the post-Roman period with the addition of a rectilinear enclosure, each side fifty feet long, that was superimposed on top of the circular ring-ditch of the barrow, squaring the circle. This secondary enclosure was defined by holes that once supported upright timber posts – the evidence for walls – and at the northwest corner, the perimeter was broken by a grave, dated to the seventh century, which contained the body of a woman buried with an iron knife. The position of the burial suggests that she was deliberately interred in what was probably a gateway – a guardian perhaps, or a sacrifice, or a place of honour at the threshold of another world.

Slonk Hill is just one of a number of structures across Britain that are interpreted as post-Roman pagan sanctuaries. Bede refers quite explicitly to temples, altars and shrines complete with enclosures – albeit specifically in relation to Northumbria – and English speakers also had their own word for temple: *hearg*, the origin of the place-name element 'harrow'.[33] A place called Harrow Hill, further west on the South Downs close to Findon and Patching, is a site with considerable evidence of Neolithic mining and a substantial Bronze Age enclosure. There are no known early forms of the name, so it remains unclear how old it really is, but it is in the vicinity of a lost place-name – *stanherie* – which is derived from Old English *stan* + *hearg*: 'the stone temple'.*[34] Although no trace of a stone structure has been found in the vicinity, four cemeteries – dated to the fifth to eighth centuries – were all established in sight of Harrow Hill, leading to the suggestion that the Hill may have had a ritual connection to the communities that surrounded it.[35] Evidence of butchered cattle – especially skull remnants – were

---

* *Stanherie* is recorded in a thirteenth-century charter describing the bounds of 'Clapham and Findon'.

discovered within the Bronze Age enclosure and date to a period later than its construction.*

This relationship between places of apparently elevated religious or supernatural significance, prominent landscape features (frequently of ancient construction) and the world of the dead seems to be a defining quality of the pre-Christian landscape. A mile to the north of Slonk Hill (and a little east) lies the aforementioned Thundersbarrow, a prehistoric burial mound (another Bronze Age round barrow to be precise) of significant size that may have been named after the god Thunor. Situated near the summit of Thundersbarrow Hill and beside a substantial circular Iron Age or Romano-British enclosure, the barrow remains a prominent landmark and would have been even more conspicuous 1,500 years ago. From its summit, the hill and barrow encompass views that command the horizon, the gun-metal waters of the Channel and the long, broken edge of the land that extends on either hand. It would have been clearly visible to anyone approaching from the sea. In the fifth or sixth century, it attracted the attention of local people who chose it as a suitable place for interring the charred remnants of their cremated dead, making it one of a number of ancient monuments in Sussex and across Britain that were (re)used in this way.[36]

It may be that conspicuous and memorable landmarks like Thundersbarrow or Slonk Hill suggested something outside the normal social world of the communities who interacted with them – places where gods, dead ancestors and supernatural entities could be communicated with, included in rituals, summoned or simply remembered; places where other realms could be entered, or where other entities could break through. Certainly in later days the remains of the past were explicitly recognized as home to unearthly denizens: *draca sceal on hlawe* ('dragon belongs in barrow') as the Old English *Maxims II* has it – a theme visited with far greater elaboration in *Beowulf*:

---

* Whether Iron Age, Romano-British or post-Roman is sadly unknown.

Then an old harrower of the dark
Happened to find the hoard open,
The burning one who hunts out barrows,
The slick-skinned dragon, threatening the night sky
With streamers of fire. People on the farms
Are in dread of him. He is driven to hunt out
Hoards underground, to guard heathen gold
Through age-long vigils, though to little avail.[37]

It is possible that these poems captured residual memories of the supernatural forces once invested in the landscape: dark echoes in a Christian age of phenomena that had once been more complex and less sinister. Certainly, large earthworks and ancient monuments must have been recognized as the products of beings no longer obviously manifest, though who or what those beings were imagined to be – ancestors, gods, giants, Romans – is difficult to establish. In some cases, the names that were attached to ancient monuments and landscape features can offer clues. Occasionally those names were the names of gods or monsters (as, perhaps, at Thundersbarrow in Sussex and more convincingly elsewhere in Britain). Sometimes they were the names of legendary figures associated with stories recorded in the *Anglo-Saxon Chronicle*. More commonly they were the names of individuals about whom we know nothing whatsoever but which must have had special significance to whatever community was doing the naming. And while it is often impossible to date the coining of a new place-name, it is certain that many names are older than their first attestation in the written record and so reflect something of the mindset of very early English-speakers.

It was not, however, only through the appropriation of older forms and structures that the pagan people of Sussex mediated between different worlds or states of being. Apple Down cemetery near the village of Compton in West Sussex is a mixed inhumation and cremation cemetery that was in use from the late fifth/early sixth century to the eighth.* It is one of the most important burial grounds of its period to be fully excavated, not least because of the quantity of evidence it yielded for the above ground structures that marked and shielded the interred bodies and cremated remains of the dead: posts, ditched mounds that recalled (and may have been intended to mimic) the larger and older barrows that studded the landscape and, most striking of all, little houses or shrines that may once have housed human remains, objects and images.[38] These traces of elaborate commemoration transform the default notion of how a grave-field – so often visualized exclusively from the perspective of the subterranean world of the dead – may actually have appeared to the living. Far from a level field of submerged graves, Apple Down was a place of significant – if ephemeral – upstanding structures, studded with mounds and pillars and little buildings: a timber necropolis, its posts and surfaces most likely carved and painted, hung – perhaps – with flags and fetishes, flapping and chiming in the wind off the Channel, bustling with the traffic of the living come to visit the departed, come to commune with the shades drifting between the shingled roofs and gabled houses of the dead.[39]

The communities whose cemeteries and cult sites stud the narrow inhabited band of Sussex territory have no history that can be easily written. The topography of the region and the distribution of its archaeology have been used to hypothesize a fragmented political map of multiple micro-kingdoms or tribal territories, focussed around river valleys and able to exploit the full range of natural resources available – from woodland in the north to coastline in the south – all making use of the landscape and its monuments in expressions of communal identity.[40] Certainly the people who dwelt

---

* Apple Down actually comprises two cemeteries, one a large mixed-rite burial ground of around 115 graves, the other a slightly later (but overlapping) cemetery of thirteen inhumations.

around Hastings – the *Hæstingas*, 'the people of Hæsting' – retained a distinct identity within Sussex for a long time and may originally have been more Kentish than Saxon in their affinities. It is very hard, of course, to be certain about any of this and it is only with the arrival of Wilfrid on the South Saxon strand in 666 that any sort of conventional history can be unravelled. By that point there seems to have been a single dominant dynasty, although it is very likely that the two writers whose words we rely on – Stephen of Ripon and Bede – simplified or overlooked or were just plain ignorant about the complexities of South Saxon politics. It was probably more convenient for them to imagine that Sussex was a unified territory with a single ruler: it allowed for simple narratives of conversion and political domination to be written.

After his terrifying encounter of 666, Wilfrid – according to Stephen – returned to Northumbria, but came back to the land of the South Saxons later in life, at the beginning of the 680s. Stephen was keen to emphasize the kingdom's isolation, depicting it as a place cut off from the rest of Britain by sea and forest, a strange and backward realm of superstition and idolatry whose gloomy thickets the light of Christ was yet to penetrate. He had an agenda, of course. Stephen wanted to present Sussex as virgin territory for conversion, a land whose salvation could be attributed solely to Wilfrid, the hero of his book. The bishop, so the story goes, befriended the first South Saxon king of whom anything is known, Æthelwealh, and then set about converting the rest of the royal family. He then embarked upon the task of convincing the South Saxon people, a challenge which Wilfrid supposedly found remarkably easy. 'Hosts of pagans,' Stephen claims, 'some freely and some at the king's command, left their idolatry and acknowledged the Almighty God, and many thousands were baptized in one day.'[41]

Bede gives the lie to some of this, although what he was able to relate was limited by his access to reliable information. Most of his knowledge of the South Saxons came from Bishop Daniel of Wessex (d.745) who was based in Winchester and who was, himself, an outsider whose own sources of information are unknown. What

Bede's history does suggest, however, is that the conversion of the realm was not simply a superhuman effort on the part of Wilfrid alone – Bede names the members of a small gang of priests who assisted in the mission: Eappa, Padda, Burghelm and Oiddi. But he otherwise concurs with Stephen that 'the whole South Saxon province' was – 180 years after St Augustine had arrived on the shores of neighbouring Kent – 'ignorant of the Name and Faith of Christ'.[42] This was not entirely for lack of Christian effort. According to Bede (presumably channelling Bishop Daniel) an Irish monk called Dicul 'had a very small monastery at a place called Bosham [West Sussex], surrounded by woods and the sea, where five or six brothers served the Lord in a life of humility and poverty: but none of the natives was willing to follow their way of life or listen to their preaching'.[43]

Unlike his people, Æthelwealh was probably already a Christian, at least outwardly, when Wilfrid turned up. In 661 he had apparently entered into an alliance with the Mercian king Wulfhere, a political arrangement designed to turn up the heat on the West Saxon kingdom which, at the time, was centred on the Upper Thames Valley. As part of the settlement, Æthelwealh travelled to Mercia to be baptized, with Wulfhere standing as his godfather. It was an arrangement that implies the South Saxon king was willing to accept a degree of protective overlordship – recognition, perhaps, of the influence that Mercian power now wielded in southern Britain (and possibly also the role that Mercian power had in elevating the prospects of what might have been one South Saxon king among several). In return, Æthelwealh received the Isle of Wight and the territory of the *Meonwara* (the people of the Meon Valley in southeast Hampshire) from Wulfhere as a gift – territories that the Mercian king had conquered earlier in the same year. The arrangement was sealed by the South Saxon king's marriage to Eafe, the Christian princess of Hwicce.

Wilfrid stayed in Sussex for five years. He was granted eighty-seven hides of land at Selsey – the end of a triangle of land at the western end of the kingdom that sticks out into the Channel like the tip of a flint arrowhead – to found a monastery and continue the work of conversion as bishop of the South Saxons. His stay in the kingdom, however, came to an abrupt end in 686, precipitated by a meeting with 'an exile of noble birth [who] came to him from the desert places of the Weald. His name was Cædwalla'.[44]

Stephen of Ripon presents Cædwalla's visit to Wilfrid as one of student to teacher, the young prince 'vowing that if Wilfrid would be his spiritual father and loyal helper he in turn would be an obedient son', a Luke Skywalker to Wilfrid's Master Yoda. As a result of Wilfrid's guidance, Stephen suggests, Cædwalla – an exile from the West Saxon court – was able to 'quell his enemies and establish his sway over the whole area of the West Saxons'.[45] What Stephen glosses over, however, is the manner in which the young West Saxon fugitive came to Sussex in the first place. As Bede tells it, Cædwalla swept south into Sussex with an army, killing King Æthelwealh and 'wasting the province with slaughtering and plunder' – rather more Darth Vader than young Jedi.[46] The South Saxons responded: two *duces* – Berthun and Andhun – drove him out and assumed control of the kingdom. But Cædwalla, after returning home to claim the throne of Wessex, came back to Sussex, killed Berthun and, in Bede's words, left the province 'reduced to a worse state of subjection', a situation that persisted into the reign of Cædwalla's son, Ine (r.689–726).[47]

Wilfrid may have been left with little option but to be a 'loyal helper' to the usurping West Saxons. But in any case, he left Selsey and Sussex behind shortly afterwards, recalled home to make mischief in his native Northumbria. No bishop replaced him. The newly converted South Saxons, beaten down by West Saxon aggression, were forced to make do with spiritual oversight from the West Saxon see at Winchester. Sussex was finally granted its own bishop when Eadberht, abbot of Selsey, was named bishop at some point after 709 and was succeeded by Eolla at his death in c.716. When the latter died, however, he was not replaced and at the time Bede was writing the South Saxons still lacked a bishop of their own.

By the eighth century Sussex had found its faith but lost its soul, absorbed into the body of greater realms. Bishops Eadberht and

Eolla were among those who witnessed charters issued by some of the last known kings of Sussex: Noðhelm (also known as Nunna) and his co-rulers Wattus and Æðelstan (more evidence, perhaps, of a more crowded royal playing field than the narrative sources allow). Noðhelm, however, was described as a kinsman of Ine, and it may well be that he was installed as ruler of Sussex by the West Saxon royal family. A restored bishop of Selsey, Sigeferth, was invested in the early 730s and he was succeeded by Aluberht whose tenure lasted into the 780s. By then the bishopric had stabilized, but the bishops of Selsey no longer ministered to an independent realm. In the early 770s, Offa of Mercia first annexed the territory of the *Haestingas*, and the rest of Sussex shortly afterwards. A group of South Saxon joint-rulers – Oswald, Osmund, Oslac and Ælfwald – were the last to be named as kings in charters. After the Mercian conquest they found themselves – just like many of their fellow kings all over Britain – demoted to *duces*.

Finally, in 825, after the Mercian kingdom was defeated at the battle of Ellendun by King Ecgberht of Wessex, the people of Sussex were absorbed into the greater West Saxon realm.*[48] With that, the transylvanian kingdom of the South Saxons was dead.

There is no genealogy of the South Saxon kings. Perhaps, like their East Saxon cousins, they traced their lineage back to Seaxnot. Or perhaps, like their West Saxon neighbours, they imagined themselves descendants of Woden. They might have had different traditions all their own. Whatever the case, no one saw fit to make note of them – or, if they did, those records have not survived. The absence of the South Saxons from the mainstream of British culture and politics also meant that the scribes of other kingdoms took

---

* The *Anglo-Saxon Chronicle* notes that Ecgberht, as a result of his spectacular victory, became the eighth king to be distinguished in the *Chronicle* by the label *Bretwalda* – 'wide-wielder' – an Old English term that was used to translate Bede's use of *imperium* to describe the island-wide power of certain 'English' kings. It is worth nothing that the first of those kings to whom Bede applied this honorific, though sadly without explaining why, was Ælle of Sussex.

barely any notice of what they were getting up to. All that can be said is that, for the most part, whatever it was didn't concern anyone else. The South Saxons remained a mystery and a law unto themselves until Wilfrid rocked up on the Sussex shore and into the teeth of heathen sorceries. Like a mist before the dawn, the shadows and the magic of the South Saxon realm dissipated and fled, creeping back into the river valleys, retreating to the forest, seeping into the earth; gone forever.

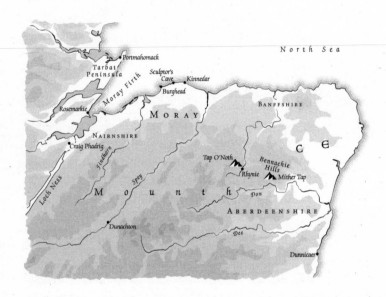

North Sea

Portmahomack

Tarbat
Peninsula

Sculptor's
Cave
Kinnedar
Burghead

Rosemarkie

MORAY

BANFFSHIRE

NAIRNSHIRE

Craig Phadrig

Findhorn

Tap O'Noth
Bennachie
Hills
Rhynie
Mither Tap

Loch Ness

M o u n t h

Spey

Don

ABERDEENSHIRE

Dunachton

Dee

Dunnicaer

Moray Firth

FORTRIU

– *Nairnshire, Moray, Banffshire, Aberdeenshire* –

Picts – what were they? Stunted dwarfs whose day had passed.

Robert E. Howard, *Men of the Shadows* (1926)[1]

Fortriu, the land of the *Verturiones*, was once the mightiest realm of northern Britain, a kingdom whose power ranged widely from its origins around the Moray Firth over grey rock and purple heather, bringing multitudes of subject peoples under its sway, crushing the aspirations of the Northumbrians, raising fortresses among the peaks and inscribing symbols on stone. But at some point in the ninth century, these mountain-kings vanished from Britain, their power crumbling in the red dawn of the Viking Age; with them vanished the culture of the Picts, a people who had shaped the destiny of northern Britain since the third century – a people distinct, so those who documented their deeds seem to have believed, from all the other peoples of Britain. And while the supposed mysteries of the Picts have been determinedly down-played within academia, their popular image remains stubbornly saturated in primordial glamour and otherness; their traces seen as the vestiges not merely of a lost realm but of a lost civilization: of mountain-fastnesses and inscrutable pictograms, of tide-beaten promontories and lonely monasteries, of buried treasures and forgotten tongues.

Savage and simian, high, sloping foreheads and wild, dark hair, heavy brows and gaping mouths, swarming over rocks, a dirty and unkept horde, bestial and barbarian. On their spears ride the heads of butchered foes, bobbing on the surging tide of filthy bodies as wild ululations rise into a red and riven sky. This image – painted by the celebrated fantasy artist Frank Frazetta (1928–2010) – was commissioned for a collection of stories entitled *Bran Mak Morn*, published by Dell Publishing in 1969. The book is a pulp paperback collection of short tales by the American author Robert E. Howard, the pioneer of Sword'n'Sorcery fiction, which mostly concern the eponymous hero but which also include a number of other tales that are thematically linked by their setting in a fictionalized British past. More specifically, the stories are all connected by the inclusion of characters – including Bran Mak Morn himself – that are identified as Picts: 'a race that was very old, which had spread over western Europe in one vast Dark Empire, before the flood of Aryan conquest. Only the Picts of Caledonia had remained free, and they had been scattered into small feuding tribes.'[2]

Robert E. Howard, most famous as the creator of Conan the Barbarian, was a virulent racist. There is no sugar-coating this; anyone who doubts it should (if they can stomach it) read the Conan tale 'Vale of Lost Women', the racial bigotry of which is matched only by its misogyny. It is partly Howard's attitude to race, however, that makes his writing interesting: interesting, that is, in that his depiction of the rise and fall of peoples and civilizations demonstrates how deeply a racialized model of human evolution had permeated popular culture in the 1920s and 1930s when Howard wrote – ideas which were entirely within the mainstream of early twentieth-century anthropological and archaeological thought. Of all the people who interested him, the Picts loomed large, appearing in stories concerning not only Bran Mak Morn, but also Conan and the proto-Conan barbarian Kull the Conqueror. In Howard's stories the Picts were the archetypal savages of the western imagination – one part offensive Native American caricature, one part troglodytic caveman. 'Short, stocky, with thick, gnarled limbs, beady black eyes, a low, retreating forehead, heavy jaw, and straight, coarse black hair' was how Howard described his 'conception of a typical Pict'.[3]

Howard encountered the Picts in the 1920s in books that, insofar as they can be judged by his descriptions of them, embodied nine-teenth- and early twentieth-century racial attitudes and simplistic, credulous readings of classical and medieval sources: 'The fullest description of this race that I read at that time was a brief remark by an English historian that the Picts were brutish savages, living in mud huts.'[4] This view of the Picts, formed in the minds of others, had been developing since the moment they entered the written record. The first mention of Picts appeared in an anonymous pane-gyric to the Roman Emperor Constantius Chlorus (d.306) in 297. It describes how the Britons were easy to conquer because they were 'primitive and used only to foes as yet half-naked, like the Picts [*Picti*] and Irish [*Hiberni*].'[5] The nakedness of Rome's enemies was a standard trope that implied barbarism and shouldn't be taken too literally, but the panegyric sets a precedent for how the Picts were seen while also introducing a term (*Picti*) to documented history that must already have been in currency before the end of the third century. Earlier writers had made no reference to Picts in their descriptions of Britain's most northerly parts. Tacitus, writing in the first century, had identified the lands beyond the Forth–Clyde isthmus as 'Caledonia', and the geographer Ptolemy, writing in the second century, had identified the Caledonians as one of a number of tribes who inhabited the region that lay beyond Rome's northernmost frontier.*[6] In 310, however, another anonymous panegyric referred to the 'forests and marshes of the Caledonians and *other* Picts', firmly locating Pictdom beyond the Antonine Wall and implying that the term had become a catch-all for a variety of peoples.[7]

It was another hundred years before the specific deeds of Picts received any attention from writers. The Roman historian Ammianus Marcellinus, writing in the 380s, described how the Picts – along with the Scots and another group of presumably northern barbarians that Ammianus calls 'Attacotti' – were at large in Roman Britain, 'ranging widely and causing great devastation' during the troubles of 367–8.† After this active irruption into Romano-British history, the Picts fell silent once again until St Patrick, in his letter to the British warlord Coroticus, described northern Britain in the fifth century as 'a land where sin abounds, openly, wickedly, impudently; there freeborn men are sold, Christians are reduced to slavery, and worst of all among the most worthless and vilest apostates, the Picts'.‡ Likewise Gildas, writing probably in the late fifth or early sixth century, described them as a people possessed of a 'greed for bloodshed' who were 'readier to cover their villainous faces with hair than their private parts and neighbouring regions with clothes'.[8] Not a flattering portrait and one that compounded the already rather compromised image of Pictdom.

The very name that Roman writers used carried connotations of savagery and otherness. *Picti* is a Latin term meaning 'painted ones', leading naturally to the assumption that the Picts painted or tattooed their bodies. Although some debate persists about the original etymology, this straightforward interpretation is certainly

* *Cornovii, Caereni, Smertae, Lugi, Vacomagi, Taexali, Epidii, Venicones, Decantae, Carnonacae, Creones, Caledonii.*

† See **SUSSEX**.

‡ This should not be taken as implying that the Picts had formerly been Christian.

how the term was understood by writers in the early Middle Ages.*
Isidore of Seville, writing in around 600, was convinced that 'the
Picts, whose name is taken from their bodies', were so called
'because an artisan, with the tiny point of a pin and the juice
squeezed from a native plant, tricks them out with scars to serve as
identifying marks, and their nobility are distinguished by their
tattooed limbs'.[9] While tattoos and body paint were by no means
unheard of among contemporary peoples – even among other
inhabitants of Britain – the pigmentation of the Picts became literally the essential aspect of their ethnicity, a people defined by
personal appearances that flew in the face of Roman norms and
which recalled the words of Caesar on first encountering the
Britons in 55 and 54 BC.†[10] The Picts were a throwback to a time of
unreconstructed barbarism in a world untouched by the civilizing
hand of Rome.

This, then, was how the Picts entered history and how they
appeared in the writing that informed Howard: a naked, painted,
menace from beyond the Roman *limes* – a people whose only relevant deeds were of violence and whose later days were spent in the
abuse of Christian slaves and the despoliation of civilization. And
yet, while their raids on Britain in the fourth century were afforded
a role in triggering larger events – the Roman military expedition
to Britain of the fourth century and the increasing role of Saxon
migrants in the defence of Britain – their longer-term presence in
the north was largely regarded as vestigial and decadent. They were
a savage barbarian people doomed to annihilation, destined to be
swept aside by the Gaelic-speaking Scots whose contributions to
the formation of Scotland were more easily reconciled with the
tastes and agenda of Scottish nationalism. The Picts were instead
seen as living fossils, shouldering the baggage of deep time and the

---

* An alternative interpretation is that the term was a Latin rationalization
of a similar sounding Pictish word.

† 'All the Britons, indeed, dye themselves with woad, which occasions a
bluish colour, and thereby have a more terrible appearance in the fight'.

inherited memories of prehistoric Europe: 'men of another age', in Howard's words, 'in very truth, the last of the Stone Age peoples, whom the Celts and the Nordics had driven before them when they came down from the North'.[11]

These sorts of narratives imagined 'peoples' – a term used interchangeably with 'races' – as discrete blocs of humanity that moved through space and time essentially unchanged, carrying with them their traditions, languages and physical attributes. It was an idea that assumed that the people of the past exhibited an extraordinary degree of insularity, conservatism and resistance to external influence (despite abundant evidence that human societies have very rarely functioned in this way over even short periods of time). The Picts were naturally assumed to conform to this model, representing an ancient human tribe whose origins could be traced indefinitely backwards into the deep shadows of pre-Indo-European antiquity. The problem, for those who were wedded to this idea of the immutable, antediluvian Pict, was that the prehistoric archaeology of Scotland did not provide the sort of unambiguous commonalities that this paradigm demanded. Wherever archaeologists looked, they found groups of people who apparently expressed themselves culturally in very different ways – some constructed massive and enigmatic round towers of stone ('brochs'), others raised hill-forts; some built subterranean chambers ('souterrains') that apparently served as storage for the surface dwellers. Some raised great square barrows for the dead, others stone-lined graves ('cists'); still others did no such thing and their dead can hardly be found at all. It just didn't add up.

This, famously, was 'The Problem of the Picts' – a problem that a group of eminent scholars sought to solve in the 1950s, and which provided the title of a book shepherded to publication by the historian and archaeologist Frederick Threlfall Wainwright. A strange and contradictory book in many ways, the contributions of its authors both brought together a great deal of pioneering historical, linguistic and archaeological data and also singularly failed to solve the self-imposed dilemma. Ultimately, as modern re-evaluation of

Wainwright's work has emphasized, he and those who worked alongside him were simply prisoners of a false paradigm. It is now well established that ethnicity and identity – let alone genetic heritage – cannot be tied in any simple or homogenous way to outward material manifestations. Thus the fact that no archaeologically identifiable ancient Pictish 'culture' readily presents itself is not really a problem at all. Nevertheless, the impression of mysterious and occluded origins added to a number of other supposed traits that together produced an image of the Pict as weird, outlandish and other: a lost language, a monumental architecture, a repertoire of inscrutable hieroglyphs, a proclivity for matrilineal succession, an irretrievable religion, an unusual proclivity for body art.[12]

The earliest suggestion of exotic Pictish origins is found in the writings of Gildas. With his usual maddening lack of specificity he describes with pungent ethnic animus how, emerging from 'the coracles that had carried them across the sea-valleys, the foul horde of Scots and Picts, like dark throngs of worms who wriggle out of narrow fissures in the rock when the sun is high and the weather grows warm [...] seized the whole of the extreme north of the island from its inhabitants, right up to the wall'.[13] Bede, writing centuries later, had a slightly more complex story to tell – one which seems likely to have derived from Pictish or Gaelic sources. In his *Ecclesiastical History*, he told how 'some Picts from Scythia put to sea in a few longships, and were driven by storms around the coasts of Britain, arriving at length on the north coast of Ireland'. These pioneers negotiated with the Irish who, having first explained that there was no room for them on their own island, pointed out that 'there is another island not far to the east, which we often see in the distance on clear days'. Not needing much further prompting, these Scythian Picts were given Irish wives, 'crossed into Britain, and began to settle in the north of the island'.[14]

In Irish versions of the legend the Picts came from Thrace (in the southeastern Balkans on the southwestern shores of the Black Sea) and the Irish women were taken by force. These stories exist in versions written down later than Bede's *Ecclesiastical History*, although they could conceivably derive from versions that predate it. Either way, they do little to solve the problem of Pictish origins. Whatever the truth of prehistoric population movements into and around northern Britain, the mass migration theory is no longer considered credible. In its specifics it seems ultimately to stem from an over-interpretation of Vergil, who wrote in the *Aeneid* of a tribe called *picti Agathyrsi* ('painted Agathyrsi') who were later identified in the fourth century as a Scythian people and thus easily conflated by learned authors with the *Picti* of northern Britain.[15] More generally, however, the story fits a pattern by which people of the early Middle Ages assigned themselves (or were assigned) exotic classical or boreal origins.*

Quite what Bede and other early medieval writers pictured when they thought of Scythia is a little hard to pin down. Insofar as it was imagined to be anywhere real, Scythia was generally thought to be a land north of the Black Sea and east of the Baltic. Classical writers thought of it as a realm of intolerable cold haunted by monsters – Herodotus (*c*.485 BC–425 BC) has its people living alongside one-eyed men and griffons – and its outlandish reputation was exceptionally tenacious. In the tenth century, for example, the French monk Abbo of Fleury reported Scythia to be a land inhabited by cannibals who worshipped the Antichrist.[16] What these mythical origins conferred to the Picts was an aura of sinister mystery that, for outsiders, reinforced images of wild barbarism and outlandish monstrosity. What the Picts thought of their own origins, however, is utterly obscure: they left practically nothing in writing to speak of how they saw themselves or their relationships with the other people of Britain. The result has been that their image was and remains defined by others – firstly by those whose writings and culture survived for longer, and secondly by those who have used the few surviving traces of the Picts to shape perceptions of the past and the identity

---

* The Pictish origin story is in fact closely mirrored by Irish origin legends which posit that the *Scotti* (the Gaelic Irish) also travelled from Scythia.

of modern nations. Real 'Pictishness' – whatever that was – has been lost along the way: all that endures is a confected sense of savagery and otherness that continues to colour the way that the Picts are understood.

According to Bede, when making arrangements for the handover of women to the Scythian Pictish migrants, 'the Irish consented on condition that, where there is any doubt, they should choose a king from the female royal line rather than the male'.[17] Although the Pictish origin story as a whole is no longer given much credence, it is responsible for contributing a critical plank of evidence to the idea that the Picts, unlike almost all other European peoples, organized the transfer of royal power through the matrilineal line. This supposed facet of Pictish culture, along with the many extrapolations that flow from it, has long excited the imaginations of scholars and the public and the issue can be organized into what one might term 'weak' and 'strong' theses. The weak thesis posits that the Picts placed an emphasis on royal power as transmitted through the maternal line, creating a system in which, in theory, sons would never succeed their fathers to the throne. The strong thesis proceeds further, assuming that in such a society the feminine principle would be held in higher regard than it might otherwise, with implications for the nature of spiritual observance and other aspects of social organization. The evidence for both (and in particular the latter) is, however, pretty meagre.

There is a critical caveat in Bede's passage: *ubi res veniret in dubium* ('where there is any doubt'). On the face of it, this doesn't seem to support a matrilineal system so much as a model for genealogical dispute resolution. This line, however, is missing from Irish versions of the legend, and without knowing for certain which version is the more authoritative it is very difficult to assess how old the idea was at the time it was recorded or the particular political or dynastic context in which the story first circulated.* Even without this crucial subordinate clause, it remains possible that, for example, the whole idea may have been dreamed up to imply a controlling Irish interest in the Pictish royal dynasty at some point or other. Other evidence in support of Pictish matriliny is no less difficult to wrangle. The 'Pictish King-list' is the name given to a number of related lists that catalogue 60 or so consecutive kings of the Picts alongside the lengths of their reigns, covering a period of over a thousand years up to the mid ninth century. They survive in two main versions contained in a number of medieval manuscripts, but ultimately derive from a Pictish tradition that may have been maintained and added to from as early as the mid seventh century. These lists do indeed seem to reveal some unusual features of the Pictish succession. In particular, no king on the list appears to be the son of any previous royal ruler before the late eighth century. Several, however, seem to be the sons of foreign kings, implying that their claim to rule had passed down through their (presumably Pictish) mothers. This has been interpreted as demonstrating a general presumption of matrilineal succession in operation. On the other hand, the absence of royal fathers in the king-list can be explained in a number of other ways. In particular, there are many examples that can be drawn from Britain, Ireland and beyond, of systems of succession that were non-lineal and instead favoured the siblings of ruling kings (agnatic succession) or alternated between branches of a dominant clan or family. In any case, in the absence of corroborating evidence, the accuracy of the king-list (particularly for the sixth century and earlier) and the political intentions that informed it, remain hard to fathom.

It would be wrong to suggest that a true consensus has been reached on the matter, but it would be fair to say that most scholars no longer believe that the evidence should be expected to support

---

* It is worth noting that Bede's version is the oldest extant to survive. That does not necessarily mean, however, that his is the most accurate – being certainly based on second-hand accounts.

too much weight. Although it is generally accepted that some aspects of matriliny *could* have been a part of Pictish royal succession, this is not, in itself, particularly unusual or revealing. The fact that the subject has been debated so vigorously is in some ways more interesting than the underlying issue itself and reflects the novelty felt by earlier generations of historians at encountering manifestations of female power. In the decades after the 1960s, the supposedly feminine orientation of Pictish society became implicated in developing theories of a pan-European cult of the mother goddess – itself an outgrowth of feminist scholarship that moved in synergy with new-age religious movements. Marija Gimbutas (1921–94), arguably the most important academic influence on the goddess movement, ventured the observation that 'present-day Scotland was inhabited by a tribe known as the Picts, who spoke a non-Indo European language and who escaped Indo-Europeanization until quite late because the Roman Empire never extended farther north than Hadrian's Wall.* The Picts also preserved matrilineal laws and the goddess religion and its symbols. In this culture, transmission of property was matrilineal.'[18] This is an effective encapsulation of the 'strong thesis' of Pictish matriliny, none of which would now find any serious academic support.

The book in which these lines appear was published posthumously in 1999, and represented work that had kept its author occupied right up until the end of her life in 1994. Gimbutas was an archaeologist of European prehistory and can perhaps be forgiven for having a shaky grip on Romano-British geopolitics. What is striking, however, is the degree to which the outsider status of the Picts had become taken for granted and how this related in large measure to ideas about their language. So far as Bede was concerned, the Picts possessed a language that was clearly distinct from that of their neighbours: 'At the present time there are in Britain [...] five languages and four nations – English, British, Irish

---

* An error. The Empire had briefly in the second century extended to the Antonine Wall between the Firths of Forth and Clyde.

and Picts. Each of these have their own language; but all are united in their study of God's truth by the fifth – Latin.'[19] Bede, we can be certain, knew more about the Picts of his own time than we do, and we should therefore be inclined to trust him. However, what sounded to Bede like a distinct language may not – to the trained modern linguist – have been more divergent than a regional dialect; how can anyone be certain that the Picts weren't simply speaking Gaelic or Brittonic in (from an outsider's perspective) a funny accent? Unfortunately, the evidence to assess this is very limited indeed.

The Picts left almost no written records in their own tongue. All that survives is the aforementioned king-list which uses apparently Pictish orthography for the rendering of Pictish names and also 'Picticizes' a number of Gaelic names as well (which is very useful for understanding how Pictish names were meant to be pronounced). Beyond that the evidence consists of: 1) a number of written inscriptions (mostly in ogham) that include Pictish personal names, some of which feature Gaelic spellings and some of which are indecipherable; 2) place-names (which are extremely difficult to accurately date); 3) the fact that, according to Adomnán the abbot of Iona (d.704), the Irish-born St Columba (*Colum Cille*) needed an interpreter when he went to visit the Picts in the 560s (although, as above, that doesn't necessarily mean that the Picts weren't speaking a language that Columba knew – just that they were speaking it in a way that he couldn't understand – and since we don't know what languages Columba *did* know, apart from Latin and Gaelic, this isn't very helpful anyway).[20]

To simplify what is an extremely complex and technical argument, it has been shown that many of the place-name elements, as well as the personal names and spellings in the king-list, are consistent with a Brittonic (or 'P-Celtic') language. This would suggest that the Picts spoke a version of the language spoken by the Britons – though the degree of divergence is impossible to establish. Conversely, the indecipherable elements of the ogham inscriptions and a number of inexplicable place-name elements have been taken to suggest that a stratum of the language is, indeed, non-Indo-European.* If this is true, it would make the Pictish language extremely unusual in Europe and would carry with it profound historical implications: that somehow the Picts, uniquely among the people of Britain, had clung on to an identity that predated the advent of Celtic (and therefore Indo-European) culture and language, a heritage that reached back into an abyss of prehistoric time.

This, of course, is precisely the sort of thing that resonates strongly with romantic nationalist sentiment. The sense among some modern inhabitants of Scotland that their place in the world is founded in a uniquely deep antiquity – even aboriginality – is an appealing one that carries with it misleading implications of primacy. As such, Pictish 'otherness' has been readily adopted as an important (even if not the most important) stratum in various constructions of Scottish national identity. This has made it, like matriliny, extremely tenacious despite serious doubts having been raised over the last twenty-five years.[21] In general, most now agree that Pictish is more similar to other Celtic languages in Britain and Ireland than once thought and that many of its apparent inscrutabilities can be explained without recourse to a surviving non-Indo-European language community.

---

* The Indo-European (I-E) family of languages comprises nearly all of the major linguistic sub-groups spoken in Europe: Italic (including the Romance languages), Germanic, Celtic, Balto-Slavic and a number of individual languages including Greek. Finno-Ugric (F-U)– a group of languages spoken primarily in Hungary, Estonia, Finland and other northern regions of Fennoscandia and Russia – is the main non-Indo-European exception to this rule. Otherwise, the only other non-I-E language in Europe is Basque. Whereas the relative ages and early distribution of I-E and F-U languages remain uncertain, Basque is confined to a small region isolated among I-E speaking areas. The implication is that the Basque language is a holdout from a period that predates the spread of I-E speakers or their language. Genetic studies have recently demonstrated that the people of the Basque region remained physically isolated from contact with other groups between c.1000 BC and relatively recent times.

Bull

Crescent and V-rod

Comb and mirror

Fish

Serpent and Z-rod

Double disc and Z-rod

Pictish Beast

Rhynie Man

A selection of Pictish symbols.

Of course, even if the Picts did indeed retain elements in their culture and language of great antiquity, this did not make them unusual. Every people, every language community, has its antecedents. All of them recede to an equal depth in time – all of them produce their own echoes. What the Picts did have to set them apart, however, was a class of quasi-linguistic motifs that have resisted all attempts at adequate explication – a lexis of symbols and animal images that were used to adorn the surfaces of monoliths and cave walls, metal objects and scraps of bone and, very likely, an irretrievable corpus of perishable objects. 'Serpent and Z-rod',

'Crescent and V-rod', 'Double disc', 'Mirror and comb', 'Bull', 'Fish', 'Pictish beast' … these, among others, were the hieroglyphs of the north, an iconographic repertoire that represented the unique vocabulary of lost Pictdom. They provide one of the only native clues to the political and dynastic reach of Pictish power and speak to a world, and a way of seeing that world, that is confounding and irretrievable but also profoundly rooted in the geology and land-scape of the north. Their beauty and their mystery confer an aura that few other cultural artefacts of early medieval Europe can match.[22]

Pictish symbols are most famously found carved into monumental stones. These 'symbol stones' have long been classified by a tripartite system that groups them by style and imagery in a loose chronolog-ical framework. Class I comprises the oldest group of stones – incised symbols devoid of Christian symbolism, carved into upright, often undressed rock surfaces, and which date roughly to the fifth–seventh centuries. Class II stones, generally dated to the later seventh and eighth centuries, combine the symbolic vocabulary of the former with Christian motifs and are typically more finely carved and elaborately worked. Class III stones (late eighth and ninth centuries) are very different and are chiefly distinguished by the absence of distinctively 'Pictish' symbology. Like all classification systems, however, there is a great deal of argument and overlap at the margins and a number of stones fit only uncomfortably into the scheme. Leaving aside the Class III stones, it is acknowledged that the symbol stones represent the clearest indicator of a distinctively Pictish identity – albeit one that is probably narrowly dynastic, aris-tocratic and, later, religious – and that their distribution throughout Scotland provides an indication of what we might call 'political Pictishness'. In this spirit, the map of Class I and II stones can be taken as a crude proxy for those territories under Pictish political or cultural influence and, when combined with emerging evidence for the settlements and fortifications of early medieval northern Britain, help to build up a picture of the scale and scope of developing Pictish power that supports such meagre historical records as survive.

The Pictish King-list opens with a section that states that 'Cruithne the son of Cinge, father of the Picts living in this island, ruled for a hundred years. He had seven sons. These are their names: Fib, Fidach, Floclaid/Foltlaid, Fortrenn, Got/Cat, Cé, Circinn.'[23] According to the same list, each of these sons also then reigned as king (though whether the compiler intended their reigns to be understood as concurrent or consecutive is uncertain). This preamble to the king-list is very plainly of no value as straightforward history: 'Cruithne' is the Gaelic word for Picts (a literal translation of 'painted ones') and the seven sons bear names which each correspond to a region of the Pictish north. Like the early annals of the *Anglo-Saxon Chronicle* or the mythological figures in the lower reaches of early 'Anglo-Saxon' genealogies, the inclusion of these spurious kings represented the deployment of dynastic myth to explain and legitimate the claims of kings over territory. In a manner similar to other invented ancestral figures, the seven sons of Cruithne were probably intended to embody the building blocks from which the Pictish confederation was assembled at the height of its power in the ninth century and at face value are of little worth to the political historian. For the picture of geographical organization they imply, however, the sons of Cruithne provide a useful measure of Pictdom and its constituent territories. Pre-eminent among them, to judge by the length of his spurious reign, was *Fortrenn*, a conjugation of the Gaelic place-name **Fortriu*.

The first mention of the people who gave their name to Fortriu came in the late fourth century when Ammianus Marcellinus made reference to the *Verturiones* as one of two peoples (along with the *Dicalydones* – a people related, presumably, to the 'Caledonians') involved in the barbarian rampage into Roman Britannia of 367/8. It is from 'Verturiones' that the term Fortriu is ultimately derived. As a place, however, Fortriu is not mentioned before an Irish chronicle entry for the year 664, and as a kingdom it first appears in an entry for 693 that recorded the death of Bridei son of Beli, *rex Fortrenn*, the 'king of Fortriu'.[24] Working out where Fortriu actually was, however, has been a vexed issue. Until 2006 it was generally believed to have lain south of the Mounth in Fife and the valley of the Rive Earn. This was turned on its head by the historian Alex Woolf who revisited the evidence – patchy and difficult though it is – to convincingly situate the kingdom north of the Mounth in a region originally centred on the valley of the River Findhorn and the land to the south and east of the Moray Firth.*[25]

Since then, consensus has hardened around Woolf's thesis, and both circumstantial historical details and the developing archaeology of the northern Picts seem to bear it out. Nevertheless, the actual extent of the core of the kingdom and its borders at any given time are impossible to reconstruct with any precision. Indeed, as a geographical term, the extent of 'Fortriu' appears to have shifted with the political success of its rulers – in Irish chronicles, the term *Fortrenn* (lit. 'of the Fortrius') is deployed as a synonym for the Pictish territories in general and as such could be applied to an extremely broad swathe of what is now eastern Scotland. The area encompassed by modern Aberdeenshire, for example, seems originally to have been the province or kingdom of Cé (one of Cruithne's mythical sons). This region is referred to twice in a list of Irish legends dating to the tenth–eleventh centuries, one of which mentions the mountain or peak of Cé – most probably a reference to the Bennachie Hills, an impressive range near Inverurie.†
Fortifications on Mither Tap – a prominent peak of the range –

---

* It satisfying to note that the 'Caledonians' (Ammianus' *Dicalydones*) left a trace of their ethnonym in a number of place-names south of the Mounth, most notably at Dunkeld *(Dúin Chaillden* as it appears in the *Annals of Ulster)*, the 'fortress of the Caledonians', raising the possibility that kingdoms of the northern and southern Picts, separated by the Mounth, traced their origins back to the bifurcated Pictdom described by Ammianus.

† *Orgain Benne Cé* (the ravaging of Mount Cé) and *Orgain Maige Cé la Galo mac Febail* ('The Ravaging of the Plain of Ce by Galo son of Febal'); the stories themselves, alas, have not survived.

were occupied during the seventh and eighth centuries of the Pictish period. As well as extensive evidence of settlement and craftwork, a carefully crafted stone staircase, descending into a hand-cut well, was discovered there during fieldwork conducted in 2019.[26] These remains date, however, to a period when – so far as the evidence will allow – the northern Picts were governed solely by the kings of Fortriu. No kings of Cé are referred to in any Irish, English or Latin text and – if they ever existed – it seems likely that their territory had already by the seventh century been absorbed into the greater Verturian realm.*

That the kings of Fortriu were, from the moment they were first documented, expanding their authority to incorporate their neighbours and subordinate their fellow rulers is implied by the scant references that do exist to the politics of northern Britain in the sixth century. In the life of St Columba, written in the late 690s by Abbot Adomnán of Iona, but describing events of the 560s, the saint visits the Pictish king Bridei son of Mailcon (reigned *c.*554–*c.*585) at his fortress near the shores of the River Ness – quite possibly the Iron Age hill-fort of Craig Phadrig near Inverness which can be shown archaeologically to have been renovated and inhabited at around this time.[27] Given other evidence for the likely location of the Verturian heartland, this would make Bridei (*rex potentissimus* – 'most powerful king') very probably a king of Fortriu. In one incident, he is found accompanied by the *sub-regulus* ('little under-king') of Orkney, implying that Bridei was overlord of the northern island realm.

Adomnán, it should be noted, wrote a century later than the events he describes and, confusingly, did so during the reign of another Pictish king named Bridei – Bridei son of Beli (r.672–693) – whose explicit identification as 'king of Fortriu' in Irish annals represents the earliest mention of such a title. Given that Bridei son of Beli was also a determined botherer of the Orkney Islands, it

* 'Verturian' (derived from the Latin ethnonym Verturiones) is used here as the adjectival form for 'things pertaining to the kingdom of Fortriu'.

may well be that Adomnán's characterization of royal power-dynamics was coloured by the contemporary political situation; and certainly not everything the abbot had to say about goings-on around Loch Ness should be taken at face value.*[28] Nevertheless, it at least raises the possibility that pretensions to Verturian hegemony had their origins as early as the sixth century.

One of the earliest centres that can be associated with burgeoning royal aspirations in northern Pictland is Rhynie in Aberdeenshire.[29] The place-name, though its earliest attestation is late (thirteenth century), probably derives from the Celtic word *rīg ('king') and the archaeology certainly seems to indicate a region set aside as special in some way. Most famously, the Rhynie landscape has yielded an important group of eight Class I symbol stones, including one – the Craw Stane – that very likely stands at the place where it was originally erected.† The most striking of these – breaking radically from the usual repertoire of symbols – is the so-called 'Rhynie Man', a vivid depiction of a bearded, trollish humanoid figure, an axe-hammer resting casually on his stooping shoulder. Whom, or what, he represents is impossible to determine, but his peculiarity contributes to the sense of Rhynie as an exceptional place. It had been known since the late 1970s that the Craw Stane

---

* Most famously, Columba was on one occasion said to have encountered a group of locals burying one of their people who 'said they had seen a water beast snatch him and maul him savagely as he was swimming' in the Ness. The saint, using one of his companions as bait, drew out the beast which 'swam up to the surface, rushing open-mouthed with a great roar towards the man'. Columba made the sign of the cross, invoked the name of God and commanded that the creature clear off immediately with dramatically successful results: 'the beast fled in terror so fast one might have thought it was pulled back with ropes.' While Columba may have been temporarily successful in banishing the monster from Loch Ness, its memory has troubled the deep and haunted waters ever since.

† The Craw Stane is a standing stone incised with an image of a fish set above a so-called 'Pictish Beast' – a frequently depicted dolphin/sea-horse/water-monster that has long defied any attempt at identification or explanation.

and the findspot of the Rhynie Man had lain within a series of man-made enclosures, but more recent archaeology has refined the picture considerably. Two substantial semi-circular ditches, dug around AD 400, were superseded around a century or more later by at least two buildings – one rectangular and the other ovoid, and both around thirty feet in length – erected inside the area described by the two ditched enclosures which, by c.500–550, had been filled in.* Both the buildings and the line of the ditches lay within the bounds of a large enclosure (around two hundred feet in diameter) that surrounded the entire site with a continuous wall of timber planks and supporting pillars. This wall may have stood up to around fifteen feet in height, and possibly incorporated a wall-walk on the inside, allowing occupants to patrol the perimeter behind a wooden parapet.

Nearby, in the environs of the modern village of Rhynie, where other symbol stones and evidence of burials had earlier been discovered, two large square enclosures were revealed in association with square barrows, one of which contained the remains of a woman who lived sometime between 400 and 570. The development of ostentatious burial is paralleled elsewhere in northern Pictland during the fifth and sixth centuries. Monumental cemeteries including cairns and round and square barrows sprung up widely in what is now Moray, Inverness and Aberdeenshire. They can only ever have catered for a small subset of the population, but their appearance in the fifth and sixth centuries is perhaps indicative of increasing social stratification within Pictish society, reflecting the development of local ruling dynasties whose most

---

* The ovoid building is particularly intriguing: one side of its entrance apparently lay adjacent to where the Craw Stane still stands. On the other side of the entrance was found evidence for a substantial socket-hole for a missing monolith, and it seems very likely that twin standing stones once flanked the entrance to the building. The most likely candidate for the absent stone is the Rhynie Man – the only carved stone to have been discovered in the vicinity of the Craw Stane; he certainly has the attributes one might seek in a portal guardian.

prominent members came to be treated in death in ways that set them apart from the rest of the population. In this they parallel the development of burial traditions in southern Britain, where high-status barrow graves in the years before 600 indicate the growing insistence of local elites on visible displays of power – a reflection, perhaps, of increasing competition between regional rulers and the insecurity generated by mutual ambition.

Although symbol stones are not a normal feature of these cemeteries, their coincidence at Rhynie points to a complex use of space that drew together multiple different strands from which the northern Pictish elite drew legitimacy and expressed their authority. The carved stones found in the vicinity of the square barrow – including one which depicts an armed warrior, another unusual subject for a Class I stone – suggest an association between the dead and other sources of political or even supernatural power. Stunning recent discoveries, however, have revealed other more imposing and tangible expressions of dominion in the wider Rhynie landscape.

To the north of the Craw Stane, the hills rise ominously above the plain, topped by the dark peak of Tap O'Noth a little to the west. Its dark summit is dominated by a vitrified Iron Age hill-fort, the rusting crown on a dirty balding crest of rock that commands the territory around it. A grim sentinel, the fort overlooks the Rhynie complex below and was clearly visible from it. It was believed until as recently as 2019 that the hill-fort represented to the Rhynie builders nothing more than a relic of a bygone age – that, like the occupants of Crickley Hill in Gloucestershire, the northern Picts were raising new buildings in sight of the dwellings of those who came before them, drawing down the legitimating presence that inhabited them, reminding themselves of the transience of power, associating their presence in the landscape with older, deeper roots. Sophisticated scanning and radiocarbon dating techniques deployed by the University of Aberdeen, however, have revealed that the massive outer fortress that enclosed the vitrified summit fort may actually have been constructed in the sixth century. The results have not yet been published, but if this is so – and if indications that the wider hillside of house platforms was occupied in the same period (and not only in the Bronze Age as previously suspected) are also confirmed – Tap O'Noth may prove to be the mightiest fortified settlement yet found anywhere in Dark Age Britain, a mountain fastness to make Tintagel look like a pillbox.[30]

Who exactly the people were who built and inhabited the settlements around Rhynie and Tap O'Noth is unknowable, but the use of space at Rhynie recalls the construction of complex aristocratic and cult sites in Britain, Ireland and Scandinavia. It suggests, alongside the growth of monumental cemeteries, the spread of symbol carving and the construction of massive defensive works, the beginnings and development of – if not necessarily kingship – aristocratic chiefdoms in northern Pictdom that mirrored in many ways similar contemporary phenomena elsewhere in Britain. Artefactual finds from Rhynie bear out the comparison – evidence of metalworking points to the production of prestige goods and the resources to acquire raw materials and organize expertise and acquire craft-specialists. More surprising, perhaps, is the evidence for long-distance trade: late Roman amphorae of the same type that characterize finds from southern locations like Tintagel and Pevensey have been found at Rhynie, as has continental glassware. And so, even here, far beyond the old Roman frontier in a distant province of the barbarian northlands, the products of the Mediterranean wended their way, into the hands of tribal leaders whose tastes ran to the expensive and whose status – one must imagine – was only improved by access to them. These were the individuals who laid the groundwork for the kings to come, though their days were numbered, their way of life drawing to an end.

Rhynie was abandoned in the late sixth century, dying out as an active settlement at much the same time as a number of other northern Pictish sites went into decline. Monumental burial mounds came to an end in the seventh century, and, while the dating evidence is often slight, there appears to have been little investment in many defended sites after the mid-sixth century, implying that they were already in terminal decline as major centres as the seventh century dawned. Instead, resources across Pictland – north and south – seem increasingly to have been concentrated at a smaller number of locations, and it is to these that one must turn for the evidence of enduring Verturian power. The most compelling of all lies on the south shore of the Moray Firth, at Burghead.

Past the tatty edgeland fringe that bleeds into the funnel mouth of dwindling coastline; past squatting steel and concrete industry to walk down rail-straight roads from which – to left and right – a glimpse of bullet-grey, the waters of the Firth, appear on either side of low-rise buildings. Drawn by rectilinear logic, walking the plank to where it ends: a grass-grown moundland by a graveyard and the termination of the land.

Modern Burghead is an unexpectedly eerie town, a bubble of regularity whose soothing grid plan and architectural uniformity betray its origins as a planned village of the early nineteenth century. But the anodyne townscape of Burghead belies the violent context of its genesis. Laid out in the years after 1805, the new town levelled and obliterated much of the largest and most impressive Pictish promontory fort in Britain.

The extent of the fort at Burghead can be gauged from a detailed plan and elevation drawn by William Roy in 1793 that depicts in detail the lines and contours of the promontory, the site revealed as a stubby phallus projecting into the Firth.[31] All that remains now is the tip of the fortress, the undeveloped land beyond church, town and harbour where the visitor centre now lies among low mounds that indicate where massive stone-faced and timber-strengthened walls – well over thirty feet wide and twenty feet high – once surrounded and bisected the fortress behind a further three massive ramparts on the landward side. Enclosing nearly fourteen acres, the fortress at Burghead was an exceptionally large and well-defended site for its day. Although the precise dating of the ramparts is fraught with difficulties, the surviving sections are no earlier than the fourth century and probably later, with evidence of occupation accumulating from the seventh century.[32]

The most remarkable finds from Burghead – finds which help to date and contextualize the fortress in its heyday – are a series of carvings which all depict naturalistic outline images of bulls, retrieved from the destruction visited upon the fortress by town-planners and archaeologists alike. Of the twenty-five to thirty bull carvings that were apparently recovered, only six have survived to be housed in museum collections. Their precision and naturalism are startling, as is the singularity of vision that produced them. Nowhere else in Scotland does a symbol carver seem to have possessed such monomaniacal dedication to replicating images of the same animal. It is, perhaps, inevitable that interpretations of this bovine proclivity should have tended towards the religious, and it has been suggested that Burghead began as (or became) an important pre-Christian cult site involving the particular veneration of a bull-avatar or in connection with a bull-focused fertility cult.

Other northern Pictish sites could equally be invested with numinous connotations – the much smaller promontory fort at Dunnicaer (near Stonehaven), for example, was replete with symbol carvings. Sculptor's Cave, just five miles east of Burghead, is filled with rough and ready iterations of Pictish symbology, etched into the living rock. Rhynie, of course, could well have incorporated cultic functions within its richly symbolic topography and aristocratic display. That these were places of significance is clear, and that this significance was otherworldly in nature is very possible. It bears stressing, however, that there is no explanation for inexplicable behaviour that is easier to offer and harder to disprove than that mysterious 'rituals' might be involved; which is not to say that they weren't, but considering that knowledge of pre-Christian Pictish belief is effectively null, speculation is unlikely to take anyone very far. Whatever its religious meaning to the Picts, however, the bull is an obvious symbol of authority. As a formidably aggressive and dangerous beast, and as an animal whose ownership marked status and wealth in the societies of early medieval Britain and Ireland, the bull was naturally synonymous with aristocratic power. It is easier to justify an association between the Burghead bulls and the presumably impressive authority wielded by the settlement's paramount inhabitants than it is to find a straightforwardly religious dimension to the carvings.*

Whatever interpretation is favoured, conjecture of this sort inevitably forces a confrontation with what Pictish symbols actually meant. For many who work on symbol stones, their weird beauty and resistance to definitive explanation present an obstacle rather than a thrill; much of the recent scholarship has focused on demystifying the symbol stones, their normality stressed above their strangeness. Efforts have been made to reintegrate them into the mainstream of European monumental art, with stress laid on their similarity to the symbol stones of Gotland, to the standing crosses of Northumbria, to the inscribed stones of Wales. For all that, however, the intent behind them remains as opaque as ever. Did they symbolize individuals? Their apparent occasional use as grave markers might imply that they did, though not necessarily. Or were they more general indicators of identity or allegiance – 'heraldic' devices or tribal emblems, their combinations signifying marriage and alliance, the interconnections of families and power relationships, of clientage and overlordship? Or were they a system of writing, with symbols standing in for syllabic sounds or individual words – the building blocks from which names or simple concepts could be built?† It seems likely that, as in other symbolic systems,

* Not that these are mutually exclusive concerns; evidence from pre-Christian Scandinavia – in many ways a better comparison for northern Scotland than southern Britain – suggests that chieftains held many of the religious functions that, in a monotheistic context, might be associated with a priesthood.

† Taking Germanic names as an example, these were frequently compounds of two words which were intelligible in their own right, and

they had multiple meanings that were dependent on context; like runes or Egyptian hieroglyphs, they may have functioned as ideograms (symbolic depictions of concepts or objects) but could also have a phonetic function when required to do so. No doubt their purpose and their meaning changed over time and space. The one thing that seems not to be in doubt, however, is their association with places that were important to the exercise of political power, their presence forming – along with fortifications, ostentatious burial, relation to prehistoric monuments, evidence for metalworking and long-distance trade – one of a number of indicators of status and, perhaps, control.

Burghead remained an active settlement until at least the ninth century, when its defences were destroyed by burning. In the years between the carving of the bulls and the final abandonment of the citadel radical change was to break over northern Britain – upheavals that would profoundly affect the whole of Pictish society as well as the symbolic repertoire of its stonemasons. New symbols – Christian symbols – would be added to the carved stones of Pictland. At Burghead, a number of fragmentary relief-carved stones, some of which may originally have formed part of a shrine, were discovered in the area of the nineteenth-century graveyard, beneath which the foundations of a chapel and a mysterious subterranean well-house were also found. The stones bear decoration – knotwork and a finely realized hunting scene – that is reminiscent of the Christian cross-slab monuments (often combined with Pictish symbols to form the so-called Class II stones) that were increasingly being raised across the north. Their iconography was no less tied to the articulation of power than the symbols of the pagan past had been, but it was now a conception of power that drew legitimacy from a different source – a source that conferred new mechanics and ideologies of royal authority on the warlords of Fortriu.

often included animal terms (e.g. Wulfstan = OE *wulf* + *stan* = 'wolf-stone'); it is conceivable that Pictish names operated in a similar way.

If Abbot Adomnán is to be believed, Christianity came to the northern Picts with St Columba in the 560s. What he apparently discovered was a society in which the Pictish king, Bridei, was served by a caste of sorcerors (*magi*) led by a chief wizard named Broichan (also the king's foster-son). One tale – particularly interesting for the efficacy that Adomnán attributes to the powers of pagan wizards – recounts how Broichan (for reasons not entirely clear) determined to prevent the saint from leaving by boat up the River Ness by bringing to bear (in his own words) the 'power to produce an adverse wind and to bring down a thick mist'. Sure enough, on the day of Columba's departure, 'a great mist covered the loch and a stormy wind was blowing against them', causing the Pictish wizards to rejoice at the successful realization of their cunning plan.[33] Unsurprisingly, however, Columba – through the power of prayer – turned the wind in his favour and effected an exit from the wicked bounds of pagan Pictland. This doesn't tell us a great deal about Pictish pre-Christian religion. Even if Adomnán, writing a hundred years after the event in a genre not noted for its fact-based reportage, managed to accurately transmit knowledge of Bridei's court, all we would be able to say is that a magico-priestly class was well integrated in the higher reaches of the northern Pictish hierarchy. This in itself would not be hugely revelatory, although it might at least suggest that there was a distinction between those who exercised political and magical/religious functions.

Elsewhere Adomnán refers to multiple gods – including one who lived in (or personified) a well, a story that brings to mind the significant investment in wells that are observed archaeologically at sites such as Mither Tap and Burghead with its enigmatic wellhouse – but he provides no indication of their identities or fields of interest. Aside from speculation regarding the landscape situation of monuments, analogy with broadly comparable and better documented cultures, and speculation about the meaning of animal or human-animal hybrid imagery, there is little that can be said about the nature of pre-Christian belief in northern Britain. Nor is there, to be frank, a great deal more which can be said about how the Picts became Christian. That they did so, however, is not at all in doubt.

Adomnán, writing more than a century after the event, clearly wanted Columba to be seen as the instigator of Pictish Christianity. His account of the saint's life, though not exclusively concerned with the evangelization of the Picts, is nevertheless peppered with conversions and miracles intended to demonstrate the errors of Pictish paganism. Bede, for one, had a relatively straightforward understanding of these events, writing (probably with Adomnán's *Vita Columbae* to hand) that 'Columba arrived in Britain [from Ireland] in the ninth year of the reign of the powerful Pictish king Bride son of Meilochon [Bridei son of Mailcon]; he converted that people to the Faith of Christ by his preaching and example, and received from them the island of Iona on which to found a monastery'.[34]

In truth, one suspects that Columba's role in the conversion was played up by Adomnán. It served as a useful foundational narrative for northern Christianity – one that cast the father of Adomnán's own monastery, Iona, as the wellspring of Pictish enlightenment. Whoever exactly was responsible for the conversion process – and it is very likely that several monks from Iona as well as other Christian territories in Britain and Ireland were involved – the mechanics remain opaque. What is not in doubt, however, is that by the time outsiders were writing about the Picts in the seventh century the question of their religion was not at issue – they were assumed, like all the other peoples of Britain, to be Christians, and the evidence of their faith constitutes one of the great artistic legacies of early medieval Britain.

Although written evidence for Pictish Christianity is extremely thin, what there is seems to suggest that the Picts were remarkably normal in the structures and institutions of their faith. They had bishops, one of whom is even known by name – Curetán, who may have had his seat at Rosemarkie on the Black Isle peninsula in Ross and was active at the end of the seventh century. They also had monasteries, the archaeological evidence for which has accumulated over the last quarter century. The most dramatic discoveries came with a series of digs between 1994 and 2007 led by Professor Martin Carver on the Tarbat peninsula at Portmahomack. These revealed a place of considerable wealth and industry, engaged in the production of vellum for manuscripts, the working of precious metals, the carving of elaborate standing and recumbent cross-incised stone slabs, and the manufacture of glass. Numerous early medieval graves – overwhelmingly of men – indicate a monastic settlement that developed in the mid sixth century before destruction around the year 800, probably at the hands of Viking raiders. It is a remarkable site not only because of its evidence for the sophistication of Pictish religious life and the implication that the monks of Portmahomack may have been engaged in the production of illuminated books, but also because – despite being a place of obvious significance – it had left no trace whatsoever in the historical record.[35]

Other important ecclesiastical sites in Fortriu can be inferred from clusters of monuments and the presence of enclosing earthworks (the 'monastic vallum'), even where large scale archaeological campaigns have not been possible. Rosemarkie – where, to judge by local place-name evidence, the aforementioned Bishop Curetán may have had particular significance – is home to a cluster of sculptural fragments adorned with unambiguous Christian imagery, including the famous Rosemarkie cross-slab: one of the most celebrated of all Class-II Pictish carved stones. A characteristically eclectic appropriation and repurposing of imagery and decorative traditions, the Rosemarkie stone combines vine-scrolls and geometric patterns, elaborated Pictish symbols loaded with decorative infill (Crescent-and-V-rod, Double-disc-and-Z-rod) and crosses embedded in square panels of decoration that recall the carpet pages of insular manuscripts from Kells, Lindisfarne and Durrow.[36] The distinctively Pictish elements were being diluted, but the artistic vocabulary was expanding at a fierce rate.

At Kinnedar in Moray, where traces of a vallum have recently been detected, a substantial assemblage of sculpture has survived

The Rosemarkie Stone.

which runs the gamut from Class-I symbol stone to Class-II cross slabs and carved box-shrines of which one fragment features a remarkable three-dimensional relief carving depicting the biblical King David rending a lion's jaw. Sites like these, as well as a number of other locations across the territory of Fortriu that boast individual cross-slabs and smaller collections of carvings, speak not only to the presence of organized Christianity but also substantial investment from a wealthy and powerful stratum of Pictish society. Images of King David, in particular, have been taken to imply a vested royal interest in ecclesiastical patronage, and the Pictish symbols may well perpetuate dynastic or personal involvement in the fortunes of monastic houses. Elsewhere in Britain, flourishing monasticism and the development of increasingly sophisticated art and culture were marching hand in hand with the growth and expansion of royal power. For all that the details remain obscure, Fortriu was evidently no exception: the fortunes of the Pictish kings were rising.[37]

The political history of the Pictish kings is notoriously difficult to decipher from the limited sources. Most of the kings recorded are just names, registered in the Pictish King-list, their deaths notarized in Irish chronicles. It is impossible to understand their relationship to each other – as already noted, their fathers were never, until the eighth century, king before them – and though it is sometimes assumed that the kings of Fortriu were identical with the kings of the Picts, this is very far from certain and probably unlikely. Of those who reigned after Bridei son of Mailcon, the likes of Garnait II (584–595), Nechtan II (595–616) and Cinioch (616–631) may well have emerged from any one of a number of rival factions and provinces throughout the wider Pictish lands. Not until the reign of Talorgan I (653–657) does any greater clarity of family and dynastic arrangements present itself, and then it comes with the intrusion of foreign powers into Pictish affairs: Talorgan was the son of the exiled Bernician prince (and later briefly king) Eanfrith by a Pictish princess whose name and dynastic connections are unknown. His rise to prominence as over-king of the Picts could be taken to imply the potency of matrilineal descent, but probably more significant was the fact that Talorgan's uncle was the Northumbrian king Oswy, a man who, according to Bede, had 'subjugated most of the Picts to English rule'.[38]

English power in southern Scotland was not new to Talorgan's reign. It seems to have arrived earlier, with the expansion of Northumbrian power first into the British territories of Goddodin, and then to the southern Pictish lands north of the Forth. Though it may well be rhetorical flourish, Bede claimed that Oswy's father,

Oswald, had brought all the peoples of Britain under his rule – 'British, Pictish, Irish and English'.[39] But it was the aggressive expansion of Northumbrian power in Oswy's reign that seems to have chafed the most in Pictland. On Talorgan's death in 657, two brothers succeeded in turn to the Pictish throne – Garnait IV and Drest VI, both sons of a certain Dungal. Whatever their relationship to Talorgan, they were evidently not content with subordination to Northumbria. This came to a head in 671, when Drest led a Pictish revolt against the Northumbrian king, Ecgfrith. The account of the battle that followed was given in Stephen of Ripon's life of St Wilfrid and is an obviously partisan account, triumphalist in tone and dehumanizing in a manner that recalls Gildas' description of the Picts two centuries earlier: 'the vicious tribes of the Picts,' Stephen wrote, 'began to stir up revolt. Swarms of them gathered from every cranny of the north, like ants in summer sweeping up an earthwork to prevent their home from ruin.' Ecgfrith 'quickly mustered a troop of cavalry' and set off northward with a 'little band of God's people against a vast army hidden in the hills'.[40]

In the short-term the outcome was a disaster for the Picts. 'Host upon host of the enemy fell before him [Ecgfrith]. He filled two rivers with the slain and his men crossed dry-shod over the corpses to slay the fugitives. Thus,' Stephen concludes, 'the Picts were reduced to slavery.'[41] For Drest the battle was undoubtedly a calamity: he was deposed in 672 in the aftermath of the battle and replaced by Bridei son of Beli. But for Ecgfrith the triumph was short-lived. It is generally assumed that Bridei, who was a son of the British king Beli of Alt Clut and whose grandfather, Nechtan, had been Pictish king before him, was initially installed with the blessing of Ecgfrith and acted in a subservient role – as had become customary during much of the seventh century. But Bridei revealed himself to be an aggressive and ambitious ruler. He attacked the fortress at Dunottar in southern Aberdeenshire in 680/81 (implying that his rule north of the Mounth was not entirely secure) and assaulted the kingdom of Orkney in 682, leaving it – in the words of the Annals of Ulster – 'destroyed'.[42] The following year, war broke out between Bridei and the Gaelic kingdom of Dál Riata in the west. The general impression was of a king fighting to dominate all the lands over which the kings of the Picts had ever had a claim, and some that they hadn't. It was a strategy that was inevitably to bring him into conflict with the Northumbrians in the south, and in 685 that tension exploded once again into war with King Ecgfrith.

According to Bede, in 685 Ecgfrith – apparently enraged by the growing ambition and independence of his neighbour to the north – ignored the advice of his friends and counsellors and 'rashly led an army to ravage the province of the Picts. The enemy pretended to retreat, and lured the [Northumbrian] king into narrow mountain passes, where he was killed with the greater part of his forces on the twentieth of May in his fortieth year and the fifteenth of his reign.'[43] The battle was fought at a place called, in English, *Nechtansmere* – 'the pool of Nechtan'. In Irish it was called *Dun Nechtan* – 'Nechtan's fortress'. The Britons had a different name for it: *Linn Garan*, the 'lake of cranes'.[44] But the fact that it received so much attention from so many different quarters is an indication of how significant the battle was. It was a terminal defeat for Ecgfrith and a pivotal moment for both the Pictish realm and the future of Northumbrian rule in northern Britain. As Bede saw it, 'henceforward the hopes and strength of the English realm began to waver and slip backward ever lower. The Picts recovered their own lands that had been occupied by the English, while the Irish living in Britain and a proportion of the Britons themselves regained their freedom [...] Many of the English at this time were killed, enslaved or forced to flee from Pictish territory.'[45]

When Bridei died in 693 he was the first to be described as king of Fortriu.[46] But it is plain that the meaning of Fortriu had, already by the end of the seventh century, come to mean more than the northern region that it had once described. The aggression and ambition of its kings had transformed it from one province among many to a synonym for Pictdom writ large and it was in this way that the term continued to be used by Irish chroniclers for several centuries. And while it is often assumed that the power base of these kings remained in Moray, there is little evidence to suggest that this was so – several later Pictish kings were well connected with neighbouring realms; Bridei himself was a scion of the British kingdom of Alt Clut with little obvious connection to the Verturian heartlands. Other kings followed Bridei, men whose vision of Pictish kingship was just as expansive as his had been. Their wars and frequently homicidal relationships with their rivals can be traced in growing detail through the eighth century, their role in the political and ecclesiastical politics of the north becoming increasingly tangled. But Pictdom had by then become a greater entity than the sum of its provinces, a realm that had thoroughly outgrown its original core, stretching from Shetland in the north to Lothian in the south.

In that sense, Fortriu stands alone among the lost realms described in this book. It was a kingdom that vanished not because it dwindled into insignificance or was subsumed by its neighbours, but because it outgrew its cradle, losing the singular identity it had once possessed. One could say that after *Nechtansmere*, and probably long before, Pictland was as much 'Fortriu' as England in the eleventh century was 'Wessex'. Which is to say that, despite whatever traditional associations still survived, it really wasn't. Unlike England, however, Pictdom was not destined for longevity. It faced a bitter unravelling in Viking fire, a calamity that would affect the region of Fortriu more directly perhaps than any other. It was to be an end from which the kingdom of Alba – the kingdom of the Scots – would ultimately be born, delivered in blood by the most brutal of midwives.

But that, as they say, is another story.

A NOTE ON TERMINOLOGY

I n the autumn of 2019, when the writing of this book was already well under way, a controversy exploded over the use of the term 'Anglo-Saxon' to describe the cultural artefacts, identities, kingdoms and time periods (early, middle and late) associated with the English-speaking inhabitants of early medieval Britain. In a call to rename the 'International Society of Anglo-Saxonists' (ISAS), it was forcefully argued that the terms 'Anglo-Saxon' and more particularly 'Anglo-Saxonist' and 'Anglo-Saxonism' are irrevocably tarnished by association with white supremacy and racist imperial/colonial attitudes, attitudes associated with both the traditional historical narrative alluded to at the beginning of this book and the construction of race (through archaeology, linguistics and the racist science of eugenics) in the nineteenth and twentieth centuries.* In addition, it was stressed that the term 'Anglo-Saxon' exists as a synonym for 'whiteness' in modern (particularly, but not exclusively, American) usage and is prevalent in the construction of white supremacist identities. It was suggested therefore that the continued uncritical use of these

---

* The strength of these associations is amply demonstrated in the pages of the short-lived magazine *The Anglo-Saxon* (1849–50), which confidently assured its readers that 'the whole earth may be called the Fatherland of the Anglo-Saxon. He is a native of every clime – a messenger of heaven to every corner of this Planet.'

terms across a range of associated disciplines sustains the implication that 'Anglo-Saxon studies' are the sole preserve of white scholars, and that this is a major barrier to non-white academics, researchers and members of the public engaging with this period of British history and culture.[1]

It is hard not to agree with this on its face. The idea that Anglo-Saxon history is white history for white people is widely and intuitively felt by large segments of society, and in England this feeling has been explicitly and deliberately exploited by the far right. Large numbers of weird, cross-pollinating and dysfunctional organizations with close links to white nationalist ideologies infest the English re-enactment and heathen neo-pagan scenes: groups like English Shieldwall, Anglo-Saxon Foundation, Steadfast Trust and Woden's Folk have all been abundantly clear about their devotion to preserving an explicitly white 'Anglo-Saxon' construction of Englishness from any number of perceived 'enemies'.*[2] While many of the individuals and groups that promote ethnic 'Anglo-Saxonism' exist at the margins, however, their use of language and imagery blends seamlessly with much wider public understandings of early medieval history and, sometimes, bleeds into more academic circles. The fact that many established scholars have failed to acknowledge these issues, or even to recognize them when they present themselves in plain sight, speaks volumes about the unconscious biases that infest the field.

Nevertheless, it is much easier to identify problems than it is to implement solutions. Although ISAS ultimately decided to change its name (to the International Society for the Study of Early Medieval England), strenuous efforts to defend and perpetuate the use of the term 'Anglo-Saxon' have subsequently been made, mainly within British archaeology where it is deeply embedded in the

---

* The Steadfast Trust was deregistered by the Charities Commission in 2015 after an investigation by ITV. Members and supporters of the Trust attending a commemoration of the battle of Maldon (991) were observed giving Nazi salutes, bellowing 'white power' and suggesting that an affiliated Essex group should be called 'Burn the Mosques'.

scholarly literature.[3] Some of the points advanced in favour of retaining the term 'Anglo-Saxon' are stronger than others. While it is hard to disagree with the statement that 'alternative constructions involving "Early Medieval" with "England" or "English"' are 'stylistically clumsy in the adjectival construction', this is a pretty flimsy barricade against accusations of systemic racism and the marginalization of minorities within the academy. Defenders of 'Anglo-Saxon' are on stronger ground when they argue that any attempt to reformulate this terminology throws up formidable challenges for educating the public, contextualizing older scholarship and reconciling popular with academic discourse. There certainly seems to be little to no prospect of the term 'Anglo-Saxon' falling out of widespread popular use, and it would be deeply counterproductive for scholars and their public audiences to start using increasingly divergent vocabularies.*

No simple solution is likely to present itself, and certainly the idea that the term 'Anglo-Saxon' can be simply swapped out for something like 'early English' is itself deeply problematic (and not merely for stylistic reasons). Modern English nationalism draws much of its strength from narratives that conflate the past and present (white) inhabitants of England to create an illusion of unbroken continuity and racial belonging – a fantasy that supports dreams of a racially 'pure' ethno-state with ancient origins. Unlike the words 'English' and 'England', the hyphenated term 'Anglo-Saxon' does, at the very least, imply that the people to whom it is applied were not a primordial monolithic group – that they were, in some sense, possessed of a negotiated and mixed identity. It also suggests that

---

* There is also a legitimate concern that to abandon 'Anglo-Saxon' as a term cedes territory to racists who will continue to use it to engage a public already primed to understand and respond to it by major museum exhibitions, popular and academic literature and the English National Curriculum. Given that the stated aims of groups like the Steadfast Trust are to provide educational resources to schools and community groups, the danger of allowing racists to control public understanding of the early medieval past is very real.

some sort of significant transformation occurred between the first millennium and the third – that the 'Anglo-Saxon' people of the fifth to eleventh centuries are not identical to modern white 'English' populations. Conversely, referring to the inhabitants of early medieval England as 'English' ignores the fact that large areas of what is now modern England were then populated by people who would never have thought of themselves as 'English' (or 'Anglo-Saxon' for that matter) during the early Middle Ages (Cornwall, Cumbria and many areas of later Scandinavian settlement, for example). At the same time, it also runs afoul of the fact that some parts of England that were culturally 'Anglo-Saxon' *then* are no longer part of England *now* (southeast Scotland in particular).

This is not to say, however, that the term 'Anglo-Saxon' is in itself a particularly useful one. For much of the history of archaeological scholarship, it was widely assumed that the ethnic identity of past peoples – conflated with biological notions of race and heredity – could be determined from the style of the weapons they used, the clothes they wore, the cups they drank from, the floor plans of their homes. This meant that certain types of brooch, for example, could be confidently ascribed to ethnic groups: they became 'Anglian' or 'Frankish' or 'Saxon' or 'Pictish' based largely on where the objects were found and uncritical readings of late and often compromised written sources. By circular argumentation, the discovery of such objects could then be used to 'prove' the presence of, say, Angles or Picts at a given place and time. By extension, it became possible to build narratives of migration, conquest and even genocide based on the appearance, disappearance or development of particular styles of object. Thus the appearance of new funerary rites has frequently been taken to indicate the penetration of newcomers into Britain, cemeteries used as an index to the extent of territory conquered by foreign migrants.

The problems with this way of thinking – the 'culture-historical paradigm' – have been pointed out many times, and simple thought experiments are sufficient to undermine it.* But although the flaws in this sort of reasoning seem obvious, it has nevertheless been extremely influential in shaping the way that both archaeologists and historians have thought about ethnicity and the material traces of the past. So influential, in fact – despite its unfortunate and troubled history, particularly in the first half of the twentieth century when eugenicists and Nazis used it to 'prove' the historical superiority and past territorial possessions of their supposed ancestors – that it is sometimes hard to break free of it altogether: it infects the very words we use to talk about past people, sometimes to the point of linguistic gridlock.

In particular, the use of adjectival ethnonyms to describe things, people, languages, places and time periods has confused a great deal of early medieval scholarship by implying a spurious relationship between all of these variables: it encourages, for example, the notion that 'Anglo-Saxon' brooches were worn by 'Anglo-Saxons' who spoke 'Anglo-Saxon' and lived in 'Anglo-Saxon' kingdoms during the 'Anglo-Saxon' period. This might have been broadly true of some people (though none of them at the time would have identified themselves, their home, their possessions, their language or the time they lived in as 'Anglo-Saxon') but clearly it was always possible for people to use their considerable agency to behave and think in contrary ways.

All of which prompts the question: what is it that defines ethnicity if not material culture, or language, or geography? A large part of the answer is to do with self-identification – about who, or what, people saw themselves as being. Another part is group acceptance (i.e. other people who also identify the same way need to agree with

---

* There are few, for example, who would argue that the ability to produce a competent croissant implies that the baker was born in France or even of French ancestry. Nor does a surfeit of croissant producers in a particular town imply a wave of French migration. Even if the popularity of croissants had resulted in a dramatic decline in, say, scone production, none would seek to explain the phenomenon by postulating a genocidal French invasion that wiped out everyone with ancestral knowledge of English baking.

an individual's right to assume that identity). Some of it may be to do with language and dress, but not necessarily in a straightforward way. Objects of diverse origin, when combined in a particular way, may have signified identities of various kinds that we can no longer easily perceive: age, gender, status, role in society, local affiliation. The person buried under Mound 1 at Sutton Hoo, for example, was buried with (among other things) 'Celtic' hanging bowls, Byzantine silverwear, 'Frankish' coins, Scandinavian-style militaria and locally crafted brooches that incorporated garnets from India. The symbolism and iconography of the objects chosen encompassed the Roman and the barbarian, the Christian and the pagan, the local and the far-flung. It was a curated assemblage of things both unique and meaningful – a confection that said something about the individual's wealth, status, purpose in life, perceived role in the wider world, aspirations, cultural horizons and sense of self; all, of course, as seen through the eyes of others – through the eyes of the still-living. And so, while the East Anglian location of the Sutton Hoo burial ground is instructive, it is not definitive, and to call it 'Anglo-Saxon' is reductive to the point of meaninglessness.[4]

I have discussed this matter at some length, not because I have any obvious or immediate solutions, but because it is vitally important to recognize the problems inherent in discussing past ethnicity. At every stage it is necessary to ask what exactly is meant when a writer refers to 'Celtic' craftspeople or 'Anglo-Saxon' warriors or 'Germanic' migrants because, despite their casual ubiquity in vast tranches of academic and popular writing, these are labels that tell us nothing about how people self-identified, from whom they were descended, or where they were born. What these terms can very easily do, however, is foster spurious divisions between past communities, spurious commonalities among others and spurious associations between the inmates of modern nation states and the inhabitants of long lost kingdoms. In short, they have caused, and continue to cause, a lot of trouble.

In this book I have tried to avoid ethnonyms – and 'Anglo-Saxon' in particular – wherever possible. Where they inevitably crop up, I have tried to be clear about what exactly I mean or else indicate that their meaning is contestable with the use of single quote marks. Where they appear without qualification it is generally in relation to standard systems of classification (e.g. 'Anglo-Saxon sculpture'). In these contexts I am referring to things that are widely categorized by the use of these terms in (mostly) archaeological typologies – it does not imply any judgement on my part regarding ethnic provenance. There are some exceptions. Unlike 'Anglo-Saxon', the terms 'Briton', 'British', 'Welsh' and 'English' were used in early medieval sources, and were clearly meaningful categories in certain contexts even if their implications were primarily linguistic. Nevertheless, if applied incautiously these terms suffer from the same problems as all ethnonyms, and for that reason they are also sometimes placed within quotation marks if the context of their use is not sufficiently clear. The same considerations apply to 'Pict', 'Pictish' and any other broad ethno-linguistic term. 'Celtic' and 'Germanic' are avoided entirely except when referring to language groups or to the historiographical uses of such terms. The terms 'Briton' and 'British' are used to describe the inhabitants of Britain where it is necessary to make a distinction between them and people identified differently in the contemporary record.

A few other terminological issues bear mentioning. 'Britain' is used in an exclusively geographical sense to mean the mainland of Britain and its smaller, most proximate islands. Except where context suggests otherwise, 'England' refers to the land area contained within the boundaries of the modern nation state. The same is true of 'Wales' and 'Scotland'. 'English', however, is used in a broader sense as a simple adjective to describe things pertaining to the geography of 'England' specifically (as in 'English countryside'), but also to the language spoken by various groups in Britain during the period that the book covers. Technical linguistic terms such as 'Old English' and 'Old Welsh' are capitalized throughout. Where 'Empire' and related terms ('Emperor', 'Imperial') are capitalized they should be taken as pertaining specifically to the Roman Empire.

This book is intended for a general readership and I haven't felt it necessary or desirable to include the full academic apparatus that would be expected of a scholarly work. Nevertheless, the endnotes provide references to all primary sources and direct citations in the text, as well as archaeological reports and, on occasion, particularly salient analyses. (Each reference contains a full bibliographical citation at its first mention in any given chapter, and in truncated form thereafter.) In addition, for each chapter I have listed a selection of what are, in my opinion, the most important works that are directly relevant to the region in question. These are the books and articles that I have relied on most heavily in my research. I also include a section of general reading that includes the works that I have found most useful for the period overall.

Finally, and briefly, the names of individuals during this period present a particular challenge as they are frequently recorded using a variety of divergent forms and spellings. I have tried to be consistent by using a single standardized spelling for each name, while providing original spellings or variant forms in direct citations from primary sources. In such cases, where it may be unclear to whom the name belongs, I have provided the standardized form in square brackets for clarity. While most names are based on original spellings, in a few cases I have used normalized modern versions where they are already in common currency: e.g. Patrick rather than Latin *Patricius* or Old Irish *Pátraic* and Alfred rather than Old English *Ælfred*.

Written Welsh can present something of a barrier to these unfamiliar with its orthography. There is not the space (and I am not the right person) to attempt a comprehensive guide. However, knowing that 'dd' represents a 'th' sound, 'w' is generally pronounced 'oo', 'll' approximates to a 'hl' sound and that 'ch' is a hard consonant (as in 'loch') can smooth the path considerably.

FURTHER READING

ELMET

Breeze, A., 'The Kingdom and name of Elmet', *Northern History* 39 (2002), pp. 157–71

Geraint Gruffydd, R., 'In Search of Elmet', *Studia Celtica* 28 (1994), pp. 63–79

Jones, G. R. J., 'Early territorial organization in Gwynedd and Elmet', *Northern History* 10.1 (1975), pp. 3–27

Roberts, I., 'Rethinking the Archaeology of Elmet', in F. K. Haarer et al. (eds), *AD 410: The History and Archaeology of Late and Post-Roman Britain* (Society for the Promotion of Roman Studies, 2014), pp. 182–94

Taylor, C. M., 'ELMET: boundaries and Celtic survival in the post-Roman period', *Medieval History* 2.1 (1992), pp. 111–29

HWICCE

Bassett, S., 'In Search of the Origins of Anglo-Saxon Kingdoms', in Bassett, S. (ed.), *The Origins of Anglo-Saxon Kingdoms* (Leicester University Press, 1989), pp. 3–27

Coates, R., 'The name of the Hwicce: a discussion', *Anglo-Saxon England* 42 (2012), pp. 51–61

Holbrook, N., 'The Roman Period', in N. Holbrook and J. Jurica (eds) *Twenty-Five Years of Archaeology in Gloucestershire. A*

Review of New Discoveries and New Thinking in Gloucestershire South Gloucestershire and Bristol 1979–2004, Bristol & Gloucestershire Arch. Reports 3 (Cotswold Archaeology, 2013)

Hooke, D., *The Anglo-Saxon Landscape: The Kingdom of the Hwicce* (Manchester University Press, 2009)

Reynolds, A., 'The Early Medieval Period', in N. Holbrook and J. Jurica (eds) *Twenty-Five Years of Archaeology in Gloucestershire* (2013)

Sims-Williams, P., *'Religion and Literature in Western England, 600–800* (Cambridge University Press, 1990)

LINDSEY

Eagles, B., 'Lindsey', in Bassett, S. (ed.), *The Origins of Anglo-Saxon Kingdoms* (Leicester University Press, 1989)

Vince, A. (ed.), *Pre-Viking Lindsey* (City of Lincoln Archaeology Unit, 1996)

Green, C., *Britons and Anglo-Saxons: Lincolnshire AD 400–600* ([2nd edn], History of Lincolnshire Committee, 2020)

Leahy, K., *The Anglo-Saxon Kingdom of Lindsey* (Tempus Publishing, 2007)

DUMNONIA

Dark, K., 'Western Britain in Late Antiquity' in F. K. Haarer et al. (eds), *AD 410: The History and Archaeology of Late and Post-Roman Britain* (Society for the Promotion of Roman Studies, 2014), pp. 23–35

Padel, O. J., 'Place-Names and the Saxon Conquest of Devon and Cornwall', in Higham, N. J. (ed.), *Britons in Anglo-Saxon England*, Publications of the Manchester Centre for Anglo-Saxon Studies 7 (2007, Woodbridge), pp. 215–30

Pearce, S., 'Early Medieval Ecclesiastical Sites in South-western Britain: Their dates, characters and significance', *The Antiquaries Journal* 92 (2012), pp. 81–108

Reed, S. A. et al., 'Excavation at Bantham, South Devon, and Post-Roman Trade in South-West England', *Medieval Archaeology* 55 (2011), pp. 138–82

Barrowman, R. C., Batey, C. E. and Morris, C. D., *Excavations at Tintagel Castle, Cornwall, 1990–1999* (Reports of the Research Committee of the Society of Antiquaries of London, 2007)

ESSEX

Blackmore, L., Blair, I., Hirst, S. and Scull, C., *The Prittlewell Princely Burial: Excavations at Priory Crescent, Southend-on-Sea, Essex, 2003* (Museum of London Archaeology, 2019)

Baker, J. T., *Cultural Transition in the Chilterns and Essex Region, 350 AD to 650 AD* (University of Hertfordshire Press, 2006).

Cowie, R. and Blackmore, L., *Early and Middle Saxon rural settlement in the London region* (Museum of London Archaeology, 2008)

Dumville, D., 'Essex, Middle Anglia and the expansion of Mercia in the South-East Midlands', in Bassett, S. (ed.), *The Origins of Anglo-Saxon Kingdoms* (Leicester University Press, 1989), pp. 123–40

Hamerow, H., *Excavations at Mucking*: Volume 2, *The Anglo-Saxon Settlement* (English Heritage, 1993)

Hirst, S. and Clark, D. *Excavations at Mucking*: Volume 3, *The Anglo-Saxon Cemeteries* (Museum of London Archaeology, 2009)

Yorke, B., 'The kingdom of the East Saxons', *Anglo-Saxon England* 14 (1985), pp. 1–36

RHEGED

Breeze, A., 'Urien Rheged and Battle at Gwen Ystrad', *Northern History* 52:1 (2015), pp. 9–19

Clarkson, T., *The Men of the North: The Britons of Southern Scotland* (Birlinn, 2010)

McCarthy, M. R., 'Rheged: An Early Historic Kingdom near the Solway', *Proceedings of the Society of Antiquaries of Scotland* 132 (2002), pp. 357–81

Toolis, R. and Bowles, C., *The Lost Dark Age Kingdom of Rheged: The Discovery of a Royal Stronghold at Trusty's Hill, Galloway* (Oxbow, 2017)

Woolf, A. (ed.), *Beyond the Gododdin: Dark Age Scotland in Medieval Wales* (University of St Andrews, 2013)

POWYS

Edwards, N., 'Rethinking the Pillar of Eliseg', *The Antiquaries Journal* 89 (2009), pp. 143–77

Jones, O., 'Hereditas Pouoisi: the Pillar of Eliseg and the History of Early Powys', in *Welsh History Review* 24.4 (2009), pp. 41–80

Lane, A., 'Wroxeter and the end of Roman Britain', *Antiquity* 88, pp. 501–15

Murrieta-Flores, P. and Williams, H., 'Placing the Pillar of Eliseg: Movement, Visibility and Memory in the Early Medieval Landscape', *Medieval Archaeology* 61.1 (2017), pp. 69–103

Ray, K. and Bapty, I., *Offa's Dyke: Landscape & Hegemony in Eighth-Century Britain* (Oxbow, 2016)

SUSSEX

Harrington, S. and Welch, M., *The Early Anglo-Saxon Kingdoms of Southern Britain AD 450–650: Beneath the Tribal Hidage* (Oxbow, 2014)

Fulford, M. and Rippon, S., *Pevensey Castle, Sussex. Excavations on the Roman Fort and Medieval Keep, 1993–95*, Wessex Archaeology Report (26) (Trust for Wessex Archaeology Ltd, 2011)

Semple, S., 'Polities and princes AD 400–800: New perspectives on the funerary landscape of the South Saxon kingdom', *Oxford Journal of Archaeology* 27 (2008), pp. 407–29

Welch, M., 'The kingdom of the South Saxons: the origins', in Bassett, S. (ed.), *The Origins of Anglo-Saxon Kingdoms* (Leicester University Press, 1989), pp. 75–83

FORTRIU

Driscoll, S. T., Geddes, J. and Hall, M. A. (eds), *Pictish Progress: New Studies on Northern Britain in the Early Middle Ages* (Brill, 2011)

Fraser, J. E., *From Caledonia to Pictland: Scotland to 795* (Edinburgh University Press, 2009)

Henderson, G. and Henderson, I., *The Art of the Picts* (Thames & Hudson, 2004)

Noble, G. and Evans, N., *The King in the North: The Pictish Realms of Fortriu and Ce* (Birlinn, 2020)

General Reference

Bassett, S. (ed.), *The Origins of Anglo-Saxon Kingdoms* (Leicester University Press, 1989)

Charles-Edwards, T., *Wales and the Britons 350–1064* (Oxford University Press, 2012)

Dark, K., *Britain and the End of the Roman Empire* (Tempus, 2000)

Esmonde-Cleary, A. S., *The Ending of Roman Britain* (B. T. Batsford, 1989)

Halsall, G., *Worlds of Arthur* (Oxford University Press, 2013)

Hamerow, H., Hinton, D. A. and Crawford, S. (eds), *The Oxford Handbook of Anglo-Saxon Archaeology* (Oxford University Press, 2011)

Yorke, B., *Kings and Kingdoms of Early Anglo-Saxon England* (Seaby, 1990)

ACKNOWLEDGEMENTS

There were times over the last few years when it felt as though this book would never be completed. Though in many ways the pandemic was easier to navigate for a writer than it was for many, many others, the shutdown of libraries, museums and of opportunities to travel presented obstacles that only time has allowed me to circumvent. As a result, this book has taken longer to write than anyone would have wished and was completed in an unwonted (and unwanted) spirit of self-reliance and atmosphere of professional isolation. That said, there remain a number of debts of gratitude. Tim Clarkson and Howard Williams read several chapters between them in draft and made a number of valuable suggestions, pointing me in the direction of recent research that circumstances might otherwise have obscured. The library of the Society of Antiquaries of London – and in particular the society's electronic resources – provided a lifeline without which this book could not have been written. I am grateful to my editor, Arabella Pike, and the rest of the team at William Collins, for their patience, professionalism and enthusiasm for this project, and to my agent Julian Alexander for keeping me on course and getting the stone rolling in the first place. I hope that any moss that did accumulate over the last few years has finally been dislodged.

This book is dedicated to my parents, Gilli and Geoff, for everything they have done for me in so many different ways – not least for instilling in me an enduring love of books and writing and a sense of magic in the world. More specifically, my father read the entire book multiple times in draft and saved me from innumerable errors and infelicities, and my mother provided several wonderful illustrations at absurdly short notice; all of this at a time when much of their energy was being consumed by a shadow closer to home.

Finally, to Caspar, whose arrival has shown me just how much I really owe them; and to Zeena who has shared with me all the joy and pain of recent times whilst bearing burdens I will never know. My love for them both is deeper than the great-souled sea.

ABBREVIATIONS USED
IN THE NOTES

AC – *Annales Cambriae*; Morris, J. (ed.), *Nennius, British History and the Welsh Annals* (Phillimore, 1980)

ASC – *Anglo-Saxon Chronicle*; Bately, J. M. (ed.), *The Anglo-Saxon Chronicle: A Collaborative Edition*, vol. 3. *MS. A* (Brewer, 1986)

ASPR – *Anglo-Saxon Poetic Records*; Krapp, G. P. and Dobbie, E.V (eds), *The Anglo-Saxon poetic records: a collective edition*, 6 volumes (New York: Columbia University Press, 1931–1953)

AU – *Annals of Ulster*; Charles-Edwards, T. (ed. and trans.), *The Chronicles of Ireland* (2006 Liverpool University Press)

Beo. – *Beowulf*; Heaney, S., *Beowulf: A New Translation* (Faber and Faber, 1999)

CISP – Celtic Inscribed Stones Project: ucl.ac.uk/archaeology/cisp/database

Ex – Gildas, *De Excidio Britanniae*; Winterbottom, M. (ed. and trans.), *Gildas: The Ruin of Britain and Other Works* (Phillimore, 1978)

Gododdin – Aneirin, *Y Gododdin*; Clancy, J. P. (trans.), *The Earliest Welsh Poetry* (Macmillan, 1970)

HB – *Historia Brittonum*; J. Morris (ed. and trans.), *Nennius, British History and the Welsh Annals* (Phillimore, 1980)

HE – Bede, *Historia Ecclesiastica Gentis Anglorum*; Sherley-Price, L. and Farmer, D. H. (ed. and trans.), *Bede: Ecclesiastical History of the English People* (Penguin, 1990 [1955])

*__HE__ – Bede, *Historia Ecclesiastica Gentis Anglorum* (alternative translation); Colgrave, B. and Mynors, R. A. B. (eds), *Bede's Ecclesiastical History of the English People* (Clarendon Press, 1991)

__HRB__ – Geoffrey of Monmouth, *Historia Regum Brittaniae*; Thorpe, L. (ed. and trans.), *The History of the Kings of Britain* (Penguin, 1966)

__LT__ – *Llyfr Taliesin*; Lewis, G. and Williams, R. (eds and trans.), *The Book of Taliesin* (Penguin, 2019)

*__LT__ – *Llyfr Taliesin* (alternative translation); Skene, W. F. (ed. and trans.), *The Four Ancient Books of Wales*, 2 volumes (Edmonston and Douglas, 1868)

__S__ – Charter number in Sawyer, P. H., *Anglo-Saxon Charters: An Annotated List and Bibliography* (Royal Historical Society Guides and Handbooks, 1968); see also esawyer.org.uk

__TYP__ – *Trioedd Ynys Prydein*; Bromwich, R. (ed. and trans.), *Trioedd Ynys Prydein: The Triads of the Island of Britain* ([4th edn], University of Wales Press, 2014)

__VC__ – Adomnán, *Vita Columbae*; Sharpe, R. (trans.), *Adomnán of Iona: Life of St Columba* (Penguin, 1995)

__VSG__ – Felix, *Vita Sancti Guthlaci*; Colgrave, B. (ed. and trans.), *Felix's Life of Saint Guthlac* (Cambridge University Press, 1956)

__VSW__ – Stephen of Ripon, *Vita Sancti Wilfrithi*; Webb, J. F. (trans.) and Farmer, D. H. (ed.), *The Age of Bede* (Penguin, 1998 [1965]), pp. 105–84

A note on primary sources

Unless otherwise indicated, all translations from Old English prose and poetry are my own. It should be noted that not all of the translations cited in this book are those most widely relied upon for scholarly purposes, and on occasion I have used more than one version of a particular text. This has mainly been driven by necessity (in a time of curtailed library access), partly by a desire to point readers to accessible editions and occasionally by literary or poetic preference.

NOTES

Epigraphs

1. Tolkien, J. R. R., *Farmer Giles of Ham*, illustrated by Pauline Baynes; edited by Christina Scull and Wayne G. Hammond (HarperCollins, 2014 [1949]), p. 34
2. Campbell, J., *The Anglo-Saxons* (Penguin, 1982), p. 20
3. *ASPR* 3, lines 92–6
4. Gilliam, T. (Director), *Jabberwocky* (Python Films/Umbrella Films, 1977)

A JOURNEY IN THE DARK – *Prologue*

1. Rudkin, D. 'Penda's Fen' [1974 screenplay], in Harle, M. and Machin, J. (eds) *Of Mud & Flame: The Penda's Fen Sourcebook* (MIT Press, 2019)

LITTLE KINGDOMS – *Introduction*

1. Tolkien, *Farmer Giles*, p. 133
2. *HRB*
3. Carpenter, H. (ed.), *The Letters of J. R. R. Tolkien* (HarperCollins, 2006 [8th edn]), letter 116, p. 130
4. Carpenter, H., *J. R. R. Tolkien: A Biography* (HarperCollins, 2002 [1977]), p. 212
5. Carpenter, *Letters*, letter 122, p. 133
6. Tolkien, *Farmer Giles*, p. 34
7. Hamerow, H., Ferguson, C. and Naylor, J. 'The Origins of Wessex Pilot Project', *Oxoniensia* 78 (2013), pp. 49–69
8. Yorke, B., *Wessex in the Early Middle Ages* (Continuum International, 1995)
9. Carpenter, *Letters*, letter 95, p. 108
10. Stenton, F., *Anglo-Saxon England* (Clarendon Press, 1943 [1st edn])
11. Shippey, T., *The Road to Middle-Earth: How J. R. R. Tolkien Created a New Mythology* (Harper Collins, 2005 [2nd edn]), p. 111
12. Freeman, E. A., *The History of the Norman Conquest of England*, 6 volumes (Clarendon Press, 1867–1879), vol. I (1870 [2nd edn]), p. 48
13. Horsman, R., 'Origins of Racial Anglo-Saxonism in Great Britain Before 1850', *Journal of the History of Ideas* 37: 3 (1976); Parker, J., *England's Darling: The Victorian Cult of Alfred the Great* (Manchester University Press, 2007)

14. Stephens, W. R. W., *The Life and Letters of Edward A. Freeman, D.C.L., LL. D.*, 2 vols (Macmillan, 1895), vol. II
15. Horsman, R., *Race and Manifest Destiny: The Origins of American Racial Anglo-Saxonism* (Harvard University Press, 1981)
16. The Tribal Hidage exists in a number of versions, the oldest being an eleventh-century manuscript – *Harley MS 3271* – held by the British Library; Dumville, D., 'The Tribal Hidage: An introduction to its texts and their history', in Bassett, S. (ed.), *The Origins of Anglo-Saxon Kingdoms* (Leicester University Press, 1989), pp. 225–30
17. *Beowulf*, line 2195
18. Davies, N., *Vanished Kingdoms: The History of Half-Forgotten Europe* (Penguin, 2010)

ELMET – *West Yorkshire*
1. Hughes, T. (with Godwin, F.), *Remains of Elmet* (Faber and Faber, 1979), p. 63
2. Breeze, A., 'The Kingdom and Name of Elmet', *Northern History* 39 (2002), pp. 157–71
3. Hughes, *Remains*, p. 9
4. Ibid.
5. Roberts, I., 'Rethinking the Archaeology of Elmet', in Haarer, F. K. et al. (eds), *AD 410: The History and Archaeology of Late and Post-Roman Britain* (Society for the Promotion of Roman Studies, 2014), pp. 182–94
6. *TYP* 5, 6, 25; see also pp. 371–3
7. *Llyfr Taliesin* xi and xxxviii
8. 'Rhagoriaeth Gwallawc', *Llyfr Taliesin* xxxviii
9. 'Cadau Gwallawc', *Llyfr Taliesin* xi (trans. Breeze, 'The Kingdom', p. 167)
10. Ibid.
11. The translation of these lines, and discussion of them, is to be found in Gruffydd, R. G., 'In Search of Elmet', *Studia Celtica* 28 (1994), pp. 63–79, p. 72
12. For modern context, approaches to, and interpretations of, the poem see Woolf, A. (ed.), *Beyond the Gododdin: Dark Age Scotland in Medieval Wales* (University of St Andrews, 2013)
13. *Gododdin*, verse viii
14. Ibid., verse vi
15. Ibid., verse xcvi
16. Ibid., verses xviii, xxi, lxvi, lxvii, lxxx; xix, lxxiv; xxii; xcix
17. CISP: LAEL2/1
18. *TYP* 41; see also p. 312
19. *HE* 'Preface'
20. Ibid.
21. *HB* 63; *HE* V.24; details of the Bamburgh research project and its publications are available online at bamburghresearchproject.co.uk
22. *HE* IV.23; *ASC* s.a. 588 and 593
23. *HE* II.12, p. 128
24. *HE* II.12, p. 127
25. *HE* IV.23, p. 245
26. *HA* II.30, pp. 114–15

27. *HE* II.5
28. *AC*, pp. 46, 86
29. *HB*, pp. 38, 79
30. *HB*, pp. 9, 50.
31. Dumville, D., *The Historia Brittonum: The Vatican Recension*, vol. 3 (D. S. Brewer, 1985)
32. *HE* III.1, p. 144; II.20, p. 40
33. Hughes, *Remains of Elmet*, p. 11
34. *HE* II.15
35. Ibid.
36. Smith, A. H., *The Place-Names of the West Riding of Yorkshire*, Part 4. English Place-Name Society, vol. 33 (Cambridge University Press,1961)
37. Roberts, 'Rethinking', p. 189
38. Hughes, T., 'Wadsworth Moor', in Hughes and Godwin, *Remains of Elmet*, p. 83

HWICCE – *Gloucestershire and Worcestershire*

1. *ASPR* III
2. *ASC* s.a. 577
3. Gaimar, G., *Estoire des Engleis*, lines 855–72, in Short, I. (ed. and trans.), *Gaimar: Estoire des Engleis/History of the English* (Oxford University Press, 2009), pp. 48–9
4. Halsall, G., *Worlds of Arthur* (Oxford University Press, 2013), pp. 53–7
5. *Ex* 23.1–2, p. 26
6. *Ex* 24.3–4, p. 27
7. *Ex* 26.1, pp. 28, 98; *HB* 56, pp. 35, 76
8. *Ex* 26.2, pp. 28, 98
9. For a flavour of the various interpretations see Halsall, *Worlds of Arthur*, pp. 97–101.
10. The archaeology of Roman Cirencester has been published in seven volumes by Cotswold Archaeology between 1982 and 2017; all are available to download for free (cotswoldarchaeology.co.uk/community/publications)
11. Holbrook, N. (ed.), *Cirencester: The Roman Town Defences*, Public Buildings and Shops, *Cirencester Excavations*, V (Cotswold Archaeological Trust, 1998)
12. Faulkner, N., 'Urban Stratigraphy and Roman History', in Holbrook (ed.), *Cirencester*, V, pp. 371–88
13. Hurst, H., 'Excavations at Gloucester, 1968–1971: First Interim Report', *The Antiquaries Journal* 52.1 (1972), pp. 24–69, at p. 58; see also most recently Hurst, H., *Gloucester: The Roman Forum and Post-Roman Sequence at the City Centre*, Gloucester Archaeological Reports 3 (Gloucester Archaeological Publications, 2020)
14. Gerrard, J., 'The Temple of Sulis Minerva at Bath and the End of Roman Britain', *The Antiquaries Journal* 87 (2007), pp. 148–64
15. Woodward, A. and Leach, P. E., *The Uley Shrines: Excavation of a Ritual Complex on West Hill, Uley, Gloucestershire 1977–9* (English Heritage Archaeology Reports, 1993)
16. Faulkner, in 'Urban Stratigraphy'

17. Zosimus, *Historia Nova*, 6.5.3: Ridley, R. T. (ed. and trans.), *Zosimus, New History* (Australian Association for Byzantine Studies 1982)

18. Holbrook, N. and Wheeler, L., 'The Amphitheatre', in Holbrook (ed.), *Cirencester*, V, pp. 145–71

19. Jarrett, K., *A Summary of Roman and Early Medieval Activity at Crickley Hill, Gloucestershire* (self-published, 2011)

20. Davies, W., *Patterns of Power in Early Wales* (Oxford University Press, 1990), p. 13

21. Hills, C. and Hurst, H., 'A Goth at Gloucester?', *The Antiquaries Journal* 69.1 (1989), pp. 154–8

22. Chenery, C. and Evans, J., 'Results of oxygen, strontium, carbon and nitrogen isotope analysis for the "Kingsholm Goth"', trans. *Bristol & Gloucestershire Archaeological Society* 130 (2012), pp. 89–98

23. Reynolds, A., 'The Early Medieval Period', in Holbrook, N. and Jurica, J., (eds) *Twenty-Five Years of Archaeology in Gloucestershire. A Review of New Discoveries and New Thinking in Gloucestershire, South Gloucestershire and Bristol 1979–2004*, Bristol & Gloucestershire Arch. Reports 3 (Cotswold Archaeology, 2013)

24. Ibid.

25. Booth, T. J. and Madgwick, R., 'New evidence for diverse secondary burial practices in Iron Age Britain: A histological case study', *Journal of Archaeological Science* 67 (2016), pp. 14–24

26. Gerrard, J. F., 'Synthesis, Chronology, and "Late Roman" Cemeteries in Britain', *American Journal of Archaeology* 119.4 (2015), pp. 565–72

27. S 117

28. Gelling, M., 'The Place-Name Volumes for Worcestershire and Warwickshire: A New Look' in Slater, T. R. and Jarvis, P. J. (eds), *Field and Forest: An Historical Geography of Warwickshire and Worcestershire* (Geo Books, 1982), pp. 59–78, at p. 69

29. Coates, R., 'The name of the Hwicce: A discussion', *Anglo-Saxon England* 42 (2013), pp. 51–61

30. *HE* V.21 (own translation)

31. Mc Carthy, D. P., 'On the shape of the insular tonsure', *Celtica* 24 (2003), pp. 140–67.

32. *HE* V.21, pp. 318–19

33. *HE* V.22, pp. 321–32 and V.23, p. 324

34. *HE* II.2, p. 105

35. *HE* II.2, p. 104

36. *HE* IV.13, p. 226

37. *HE* II.2 (own translation)

38. *ASC* s.a. 628

39. *ASC* s.a. 800

40. Finberg, H.P.R., 'The Princes of the Hwicce' in Finberg, H.P.R., (ed.) *The Early Charters of the West Midlands* (Leicester University Press, 1972 [2nd edn]), pp. 167–80; however, cf. Bassett, S., 'In Search of the Origins of Anglo-Saxon Kingdoms', in Bassett, S. (ed.), *The Origins of Anglo-Saxon Kingdoms* (Leicester University Press, 1989), pp. 3–27

41. Whybra, J., *A Lost English County: Winchcombeshire in the Tenth and Eleventh Centuries* (Boydell Press, 1990)

42. S 51
43. *HB* 67, pp. 40, 81
44. S 70
45. S 76; S 77
46. As *rex*: S 53; as *comes/subregulus*: S 1429, S 1255
47. S 89
48. S 113
49. S 57
50. Sims-Williams, P., *Religion and Literature in Western England, 600–800* (Cambridge University Press, 1990), p. 88
51. Barker, P. A. (ed.), 'The Origins of Worcester', *Transactions of the Worcestershire Archaeological Society*, third series, vol. 2 (1968–9), pp. 1–116
52. The phrase *enta geweorc* appears several times in Old English poetry: in *Beowulf* at lines 1679, 2717 and 2774, *The Wanderer* (line 87), *The Ruin* (line 2), *Andreas* (lines 1235 and 1495) and *Maxims II* (line 2); see *ASPR*

LINDSEY – *North Lincolnshire*

1. *ASPR* 3, lines 57–62, 68–9, 79
2. *VSG* XXIV, pp. 86–9
3. *VSG* XVI, pp. 80–81
4. *VSG* XXV, pp. 88–9
5. Bradley, pp. 332–3; *ASPR* (lines 1–26; 33–47; 48–57)
6. *VSG* XXXV
7. Eagles, B., 'Lindsey', in Bassett, S. (ed.), *The Origins of Anglo-Saxon Kingdoms* (Leicester University Press, 1989), pp. 202–12
8. Jones, M. J., 'The Latter Days of Roman Lincoln', in Vince, A. (ed.), *Pre-Viking Lindsey* (City of Lincoln Archaeology Unit, 1996,), pp.14–28; Jones, M. J., *Roman Lincoln: Conquest, Colony & Capital* (The History Press, 2002)
9. Ibid.; Steane, K. and Vince, A., 'Post-Roman Lincoln: Archaeological Evidence for Activity in Lincoln in the 5th–9th Centuries', in Vince (ed.), *Pre-Viking Lindsey*, pp. 71–9; Leahy, K., *The Anglo-Saxon Kingdom of Lindsey* (Tempus Publishing, 2007), pp. 24–6; Leahy, K., *The Anglo-Saxon Kingdom of Lindsey* (Tempus Publishing, 2007), pp. 24–6
10. Steane and Vince, 'Post-Roman Lincoln', pp. 72–4
11. Leahy, *Kingdom of Lindsey*, pp. 35–6
12. *HE* I.15, p. 63
13. Green, C., *Britons and Anglo-Saxons: Lincolnshire AD 400–600* ([2nd edn], History of Lincolnshire Committee, 2020), pp. 57–60
14. Findell, M and Kopár, L., 'Runes and Commemoration in Anglo-Saxon England', *Fragments: Interdisciplinary Approaches to the Study of Ancient and Medieval Pasts* 6 (2017), pp. 110–137; Findell, M., Runes (The British Museum Press, 2014)
15. *Ex* 25, pp. 27–8
16. Though by no means the only, or even most likely one: Halsall, G., *Barbarian Migrations and the Roman West: 376–568* (Cambridge University Press, 2007). For an overview of the evidence and its interpretation over time see Hills, C., 'Frisia and England: The Archaeological Evidence for Connections', *Amsterdamer Beiträge zur älteren Germanistik*, 45.1, pp. 35–46

17. Procopius, *Bellum Gothicum*, 8.20.6: Dewing, H. B. (ed. and trans.), *Procopius, with an English Translation by H. B. Dewing*, 7 vols (1914–40, Harvard University Press), vol. 5

18. *HE* V.9, p. 278; *ASPR* 3

19. Bassett, S., 'Lincoln and the Anglo-Saxon See of Lindsey', *Anglo-Saxon England* 18 (1989), pp. 1–32

20. *HB* 56, pp. 35, 76

21. Ibid.

22. Green, C., B*ritons and Anglo-Saxons*, pp. 89–95

23. *Gododdin*, verse xv

24. Bruce-Mitford, R. L. S. and Raven, S., *A Corpus of Late Celtic Hanging Bowls with an Account of the Bowls Found in Scandinavia* (Oxford University Press, 2005)

25. Ibid.; Bruce-Mitford, R. L. S, 'Late Celtic Hanging-Bowls in Lincolnshire and South Humberside', in Vince (ed.), *Pre-Viking Lindsey*, pp. 45–70; Leahy, *Kingdom of Lindsey*, pp. 84–5

26. Leahy, *Kingdom of Lindsey*, pp. 83–4

27. Leahy, *Kingdom of Lindsey*, p. 111

28. Dumville, D., 'The Anglian collection of royal genealogies and regnal lists', *Anglo-Saxon England* 5 (1976), pp. 23–50

29. Tolkien, J.R.R., *Finn and Hengest: The Fragment and the Episode*, edited by Alan Bliss (HarperCollins, 2004 [1982])

30. Frank, R., 'Germanic legend in Old English literature', in Godden, M. And Lapidge, M. (eds.), *The Cambridge Companion to Old English Literature* (Cambridge University Press, 1986), pp. 88–106

31. Jarvis, Revd E., 'Account of the Discovery of Ornaments and Remains, Supposed to be of Danish Origin, in the Parish of Caenby', *Lincolnshire Archaeological Journal* 7 (1850), pp. 36–44

32. Leahy, *Kingdom of Lindsey*, pp. 93–6; Everson, P., 'Pre-Viking Settlement in Lindsey', in Vince (ed.), *Pre-Viking Lindsey*, pp. 91–8

33. *HE* II.16, p. 134

34. Ibid.

35. Ibid.

36. *HE* III.9, pp. 242–3; V.24, pp. 564–5

37. *HE* III.11, p. 160

38. *VSW* 20, pp. 128–9

39. *HE* IV.12

40. Ibid.

41. *HE* III.11, p. 160

DUMNONIA – *Devon and Cornwall*

1. Tennyson, A., 'The Coming of Arthur', *Idylls of the King* (Penguin, 2004 [1859–1873]), p. 31, lines 369–85

2. Allan, J. et al., 'The Early Medieval Period c. 410–900 and Urban Revival c. 900–1200' in Rippon, S. and Holbrook, N. (eds.), *Roman and Medieval Exeter and their Hinterlands: From Isca to Excester* (Oxbow Books, 2021), pp. 221–268

3. *Gododdin*, cii

4. *HRB*, 'Dedication', p. 51

5. Malory, T., *Le Morte d'Arthur*, volume 1 (Penguin, 2004 [1485])

6. Kalinke, M. E. (ed.), *The Arthur of the North: The Arthurian Legend in the Norse and Rus' Realms* (University of Wales Press, 2016)

7. *HRB*, vii.19, p. 206

8. Ibid.

9. *HRB*, vii.19, p. 207

10. Ibid.

11. *HRB*, vii.20, p. 208

12. Tolkien, J. R. R., *The Two Towers* (HarperCollins [1949])

13. Hearne, T. (ed.), *Joannis Lelandi Antiquarii De Rebus Britannicis Collectanea*, 6 vols (London, 1774 [3rd edn]), p. 115

14. Thomas, C., 'Tintagel Castle', *Antiquity* 62 (236), pp. 421–434; Nowakowski, J. A., 'Working in the shadows of the giants: Charles Thomas, Courtney Arthur Ralegh Radford (and King Arthur) – past and current fieldwork at Tintagel, Cornwall' in Jones, A.M. and Quinnell, H., (eds.), *An Intellectual Adventurer in Archaeology: Reflections on the Work of Charles Thomas* (Archaeopress, 2018), pp. 83–100

15. CISP: TNTIS/1/1

16. 'Fellows Reveal Second Inscribed Tintagel Stone', *Society of Antiquaries of London Online Newsletter (SALON)* 409 (19 June 2018)

17. *Ex* 66.4, pp. 52–3

18. *Ex* 66.6, pp. 53

19. *Ex* 27, p. 29

20. *Ex* 28.1, p. 29

21. *Ex* 28.1–2, p. 29

22. *HE* I.25, p. 75

23. Agate, A. et al., 'Early Medieval Settlement at Mothecombe, Devon: The Interaction of Local, Regional and Long-Distance Dynamics', *Archaeological Journal* 169 (2012), pp. 343–94; Reed, S. A. et al., 'Excavation at Bantham, South Devon, and Post-Roman Trade in South-West England', *Medieval Archaeology* 55 (2011), pp. 138–82

24. Quinnell, H., *Excavations at Trethurgy Round, St Austell: Community and Status in Roman and Post-Roman Cornwall* (Cornwall County Council, 2004,); Dark K., *Britain and the End of the Roman Empire* (The History Press, 2011 [2000]), pp. 150–70.

25. Green, C., 'St Ia of St Ives: A Byzantine saint in early medieval Cornwall?' (2018, caitlingreen.org) [caitlingreen.org/2018/01/st-ia-of-st-ives-byzantine-saint – URL inactive]

26. Procopius, On Buildings, I.ix; Dewing, H. B. and Downey, G. (trans.), Procopius. On Buildings. General Index: Loeb Classical Library 343 (Harvard University Press, 1940), I.ix, p. 79

27. Procopius, *De Aedificiis*, trans. Lethaby, W. and Swainson, H., *The Church of St. Sophia Constantinople* (Macmillan & Co. 1894), pp. 24–8

28. Ex 27, pp. 29, 99; Anon., *Vita Sancti Samsonis*; Taylor, T. (trans.) *The Life of St. Samson of Dol* (Society for Promoting Christian Knowledge, 1925)

29. CISP: MADR1/1/1

30. CISP: CSTLD/1

31. *TYP* 6; see also p. 325

32. Gregory of Tours, *Historia Francorum*, IV.4: Thorpe, L. (ed. and trans.), *The History of the Franks* (Penguin, 1974), pp. 198–9

33. Dash, M., 'The Breton Bluebeard' (mikedashhistory.com, 2015) [mikedashhistory.com/2015/12/28/the-breton-bluebeard]

34. Wrdestin (Vurdestinus), *Vita Sancti Wingualoei*: in Doble, G. H. (ed.), *The Saints of Cornwall*; Part 2: *Saints of the Lizard District* (Truro: Dean and Chapter, 1962), pp. 61–92

35. CISP: SHILL/1; MADR1/1; SOURT/1

36. *ASC* s.a. 658

37. *ASC* s.a. 661

38. *ASC* s.a. 682

39. Aldhelm, *Carmen Rhythmicum*, lines 9–12; Howlett, D. R., 'Aldhelmi Carmen Rhythmicum' in Archivum latinitatis medii aevi 53 (1995), pp. 119–140 at p. 125

40. *ASC* s.a. 722, p. 47; p. 87

41. *ASC* s.a. 823

42. *ASC* s.a. 835

43. Keynes, S. and Lapidge, M. (ed. and trans.), *Alfred the Great: Asser's 'Life of King Alfred' and Other Contemporary Sources* (Penguin, 1983), pp. 173–8

44. S 1451a; S 1296

45. S 1451a

46. Aldhelm, *Carmen Rhythmicum*, lines 93–96, 111–114; Howlett, 'Aldhelmi Carmen Rhythmicum', p. 127

ESSEX – *Essex and Middlesex*

1. Simek, R., 'Saxon Baptismal Vow', *Dictionary of Northern Mythology* (D. S. Brewer, 1993), p. 276 (own translation)

2. Blackwater Against New Nuclear Group (BANGG), 'The coming of Bradwell B. What once seemed incredible is now the "new normal"' (bangg.info, 2020) [bangg.info/news/the-coming-of-bradwell-b-what-once-seemed-incredible-is-now-the-new-normal]

3. Misler, A-R., *The Othona Community: 'A Strange Phenomenon'* (unpublished PhD thesis, 2017)

4. *Capitulatio de partibus Saxoniae*; Munro, D. C. (ed. and trans.), *Selections from the Laws of Charles the Great* (Kessinger Publishing, 2004)

5. *Royal Frankish Annals* s.a. 782: Scholz, B. W., *Carolingian Chronicles: Royal Frankish Annals and Nithard's Histories* (University of Michigan Press, 1970)

6. British Library Add. MS. 23211; see Yorke, B., 'The kingdom of the East Saxons', *Anglo-Saxon England* 14 (1985), pp. 1–36

7. Fn. 163: Bronnenkant, L. J., 'Thurstable revisited', *Journal of the English Place-Name Society* XV (1982–3), pp. 9–19

8. Scull, C. 'Approaches to material culture and social dynamics of the Migration Period in eastern England' in J. Bintliffe and H. Hamerow (eds.), *Europe between Late Antiquity and the Middle Ages: recent archaeological and historical research in western and southern Europe* (BAR Publishing, 1995) pp. 71–83

9. Hamerow, H., *Excavations at Mucking*: vol. 2, *The Anglo-Saxon Settlement* (English Heritage, 1993); Hirst, S. and Clark, D., *Excavations at Mucking*:

vol. 3, *The Anglo-Saxon Cemeteries* (Museum of London Archaeology, 2009)

10. Williams, H., *Death and Memory in Early Medieval Britain* (Cambridge University Press, 2006)

11. Lucy, S. et al., *The Romano-British Settlement and Cemeteries at Mucking: Excavations by Margaret and Tom Jones, 1965–1978* (Oxbow Books, 2016)

12. Halsall, G., *Cemeteries and Society in Merovingian Gaul: Selected Studies in History and Archaeology, 1992–2009* (Brill, 2009)

13. *HE*, I.7, p. 54

14. Ibid.

15. Constantius of Lyon, *Vita Germani* 12: Hoare, F. R. (trans.), 'Constantius of Lyon: The Life of St. Germanus of Auxerre', in Noble, T. and Head, T. (eds), *Soldiers of Christ: Saints' Lives from Late Antiquity and the Early Middle Ages* (Pennsylvania State University Press, 1994,), pp. 75–106

16. Frere, S., *Verulamium Excavations*, vol. 2 (Society of Antiquaries, 1983,); cf. Faulkner, N., 'Verulamium: Interpreting Decline', *Archaeological Journal* 153.1, pp. 79–103; also Frere, S. and Witts, P., 'The Saga of Verulamium Building XXVII 2', *Britannia* 42 (2011), pp. 263–74; Niblett, R., Manning, W. and Saunders, C., 'Verulamium: Excavations within the Roman Town 1986–88', *Britannia* 37 (2006), pp. 53–188

17. Baker, J. T., 'Cultural transition in the Chilterns and Essex region, 350 AD to 650 AD Hatfield' (University of Hertfordshire Press, 2006)

18. Crummy, P. (ed.), *Aspects of Anglo-Saxon and Norman Colchester* (CBA, 1981)

19. Evison, V., *An Anglo-Saxon Cemetery at Great Chesterford, Essex* (CBA, 1994)

20. Blackmore, L., Blair, I., Hirst, S. and Scull, C., *The Prittlewell Princely Burial: Excavations at Priory Crescent, Southend-on-Sea, Essex, 2003* (Museum of London Archaeology, 2019)

21. *Beo.* lines 36–40, p. 4

22. *HE* I.25, p. 75

23. *HE* II.3

24. Munier, C., *Concilia Galliae a.314-a.506* (Brepols, 1963)

25. *HE* I.29; fn.180: *HE* II.1, p. 103

26. Naismith, R., *Citadel of the Saxons: The Rise of Early London* (Bloomsbury, 2019)

27. *HE* II.5, p. 113

28. Ibid.

29. *HE* II.6, p. 114

30. *HE* III.22, p. 178

31. *HE* III.22, p. 180

32. **HE* III.27, pp. 310–12; **HE* III.13, pp. 252–3

33. Maddicott, J. R., 'Plague in Seventh-Century England', *Past & Present* 156 (1997), pp. 7–54

34. e.g. VC II.46i, pp. 203–204; Maddicott, J. R., 'Plague in Seventh-Century England', *Past & Present* 156:1 (1997), pp. 7–54

35. *HE* III.13, pp. 163–4

36. *HE* III.30, p. 200

37. Ibid.

38. S 233
39. *ASC* s.a. 686, 687 (S10)
40. Fisher, P., *The tombes, monuments, and sepulchral inscriptions, lately visible in St. Pauls cathedral &c.* (London, 1684)
41. Dugdale, W., *History of St. Paul's Cathedral* (Thomas Warren, 1658)
42. *HE* IV.11, p. 222
43. *HE* IV.11, p. 223
44. For the full complexity of the political situation, as revealed in surviving charters, see Yorke, B., 'The kingdom of the East Saxons', *Anglo-Saxon England* 14 (1985), pp. 1–36
45. *HE* II.3, pp. 107–108

RHEGED – *Cumbria, Dumfries and Galloway*

1. **LT* xxxii, lines 51–54
2. **LT* xxxii, line 49
3. *Beo.*, lines 58, 63–5, p. 45
4. *HE* I.12, pp. 59–60
5. Wilmott, T., Cool, H. and Evans, J., 'Excavations at the Hadrian's Wallfort of Birdoswald (Banna), Cumbria: 1996–2000', in Wilmott, T. (ed.), *Hadrian's Wall: Archaeological Research by English Heritage 1976–2000* (English Heritage, 2009,); Wilmott, T., *Birdoswald: Excavations of a Roman Fort on Hadrian's Wall and its Successor Settlements: 1987–92* (English Heritage, 1997)
6. Zosimus, *Historia Nova* VI.5.2–3: Ridley, R. T. (ed. and trans.), *Zosimus: New History* (University of Sydney, 1982)
7. Zosimus, *Historia Nova* VI.10.2: Ridley, *Zosimus*
8. CISP: CHOLM/1
9. St Patrick, *Confessio*: McCarthy, P. (trans.), *My Name is Patrick* (Royal Irish Academy, 2011)
10. CISP CASTL/1/1; MAPOR/1; MAPOR/2; OLCAR/1; BROUG/1
11. CISP: OLCAR/1
12. 'Unique Christian Artefact Uncovered at Vindolanda' (29 August 2020, vindolanda.com) [vindolanda.com/news/unique-christian-artefact-uncovered-at-vindolanda]
13. *HE* III.4, p. 148
14. CISP: WHIT1/1
15. CISP: WHIT2/1
16. *Statement of Significance: Kirkmadrine Stones* (Historic Environment Scotland, 2020); CISP: KMADR/1; KMADR/2; KMADR/3
17. Laing, L and Longley, D., *The Mote of Mark: A Dark Age Hillfort in South-West Scotland* (Oxbow Books, 2006)
18. Toolis, R. and Bowles, C., *The Lost Dark Age Kingdom of Rheged: The Discovery of a Royal Stronghold at Trusty's Hill, Galloway* (Oxbow, 2017)
19. Pallenberg, R. and Boorman, J., *Excalibur* (1981) [imsdb.com/scripts/Excalibur]
20. Malory, T., *Le Morte d'Arthur*, vol. 1 (Penguin, 2004 [1485]), 1.8, p. 21
21. Malory, *Le Morte d'Arthur* 1.2, p. 12
22. *TYP*, pp. 508–12
23. *HB* 63, pp. 38, 79

24. In the order that they appear in the manuscript, the relevant poems are as follows; the Arabic number indicates the number given to the poem in the Lewis and Williams translation; the Roman numeral indicates the number of the poem in its original manuscript order, and also corresponds to the influential Welsh edition prepared by Sir Ifor Williams): *The Men of Catraeth* (2; xxxi), *Urien of Erechwydd* (3; xxxii), *Here at My Rest* (4; xxxiii), *All Through One Year* (5; xxxiv), *The Battle of Argoed Llywfain* (6; xxxv), *Rheged, Arise, its Lords Are its Glory* (7; xxxvi), *Taliesin's Plunder* (8; xxxvii), *To Pacify Urien* (9; xxxix), *Lament for Owain, Son of Urien* (10; xliv).

25. *LT* 2 (xxxi)

26. *LT* 3 (xxxii)

27. *LT* 7 (xxxvi)

28. *LT* 4 (xxxiii), lines 27–30

29. *LT* 4 (xxxiii), lines 5, 34–5

30. *LT* 3 (xxxii), lines 1–4

31. *LT* 4 (xxxiii)

32. *LT* 8 (xxxvii), line 5

33. *LT* 9 (xxxix), line 7

34. 'You're my delight [...] There's no competition' (*LT* 3; xxxii), 'You are the best [...] my leader for life' (*LT* 5; xxxiv), 'I'll sing the praises Of all you've done' (*LT* 4; xxxiii), 'No leader can compare' (*LT* 7; xxxvi)

35. *LT* 8 (xxxvii)

36. *LT* xxxii, line 14; xxxi, line 27; xliv, line 3

37. On the identification of the place-names in the *LT*, see Clarkson, T., *The Men of the North: The Britons of Southern Scotland* (Birlinn, 2010), pp. 68–72; Clancy, T. O., 'The Kingdoms of the North: Poetry, Places, Politics', in Woolf, A. (ed.), *Beyond the Gododdin: Dark Age Scotland in Medieval Wales* (University of St Andrews, 2013,), pp. 153–76

38. **LT* 47 (liii)

39. Padel, O. J., 'A New Study of the Gododdin', *Cambrian Medieval Celtic Studies* 35 (1997), pp. 45–55

40. **HE* III.24

41. *LT* 2 (xxxi), lines 1–2

42. Dunshea, P. M., 'The Meaning of Catraeth: A Revised Early Context for Y Gododdin', in Woolf, *Beyond the Gododdin*, pp. 81–114; 'Ford roiled by his rush' (*Gododdin*, verse xvii); 'He stood firm at the ford' (*Gododdin*, verse xciii).

43. *LT* 2 (xxxi), line 10

44. Breeze, A., 'Urien Rheged and the Battle at Gwen Ystrad', *Northern History* 52:1 (2015), pp. 9–19

45. *LT* 2 (xxxi), lines 17–20, 22

46. *LT* 7 (xxxvi), lines 21–9

47. Padel, O. J. 'Aneirin and Taliesin: Sceptical Speculations', in Woolf, *Beyond the Gododdin*, pp. 115–52

48. Toolis and Bowles, *The Lost Dark Age Kingdom of Rheged*

49. Collins, R., review of Toolis and Bowles, *The Lost Dark Age Kingdom of Rheged* [socantscot.org/resource/the-lost-dark-age-kingdom-of-rheged-

the-discovery-of-a-royal-stronghold-at-trustys-hill-galloway-by-ronan-toolis-and-christopher-bowles]
50. *LT* xxxiv

POWYS – *Montgomeryshire, Denbighshire, Flintshire, Cheshire, Shropshire*

1. Housman, A. E., *A Shropshire Lad and Other Poems: The Collected Poems of A. E. Housman* (Penguin, 2010)
2. Edwards, N., 'Rethinking the Pillar of Eliseg', *The Antiquaries Journal* 89 (2009), pp. 143–77; Edwards N., *A Corpus of Early Medieval Inscribed Stones and Stone Sculptures in Wales: Volume 3, North Wales* (University of Wales Press, 2013)
3. Edwards, 'Rethinking the Pillar of Eliseg', p. 173
4. Ibid.
5. Edwards, N., Robinson, G. and Williams, H., *Excavations at the Pillar of Eliseg, Llangollen, 2010–2012*, Project Eliseg: final report prepared for CADW, February 2015 (Project Eliseg; Bangor University/University of Chester, 2015)
6. Simpson, W. T., *Some Account of Llangollen and its Vicinity, Including a Circuit of about Seven Miles* (London, 1927), p. 134
7. *Ex* 13–14, pp. 20–21, 93
8. *TYP*, pp. 441–4
9. Edwards, 'Rethinking', p. 166; Dumville, D. N. (1977), 'Sub-Roman Britain: History and Legend', *History* 62: 205 (1977), pp. 173–92
10. Constantius of Lyon, *Vita Germani* 3: Hoare, F. R., *The Western Fathers* (Sheed and Ward, 1954), p. 283
11. *Ex* 23, pp. 26, 96
12. *HE* 15, p. 62
13. Halsall, G., *Worlds of Arthur* (Oxford University Press, 2013)
14. *TYP*, pp. 386–90
15. Idle, E. (ed.), *The Life of Brian: Monty Python's Scrapbook* (Methuen, 1979)
16. *HB* 48, p. 33
17. *HB* 47, p. 33
18. *HB* 48, p. 33
19. Kirby, D. P. 'Vortigern', *Bulletin of the Board of Celtic Studies*, 23 (1968–72), pp. 50–2
20. Dickens, C., 'Rome and Turnips', *All the Year Round* (14 May 1859)
21. Camden, W., *Brittania*: Holland, P. (ed. and trans.), Britain: a Chorographicall description […] (1637, London) p. 593
22. Dickens, 'Rome and Turnips'
23. Owen, W., 'Uriconium' [1913], in Stallworthy, J. *The Complete Poems and Fragments of Wilfred Owen* (Chatto & Windus, 1983), lines 6–7
24. Lane, A., 'Wroxeter and the end of Roman Britain', *Antiquity* 88: 340 (2014), pp. 501–515
25. CISP: WRXTR/1
26. Dickens, 'Rome and Turnips'
27. White, R. H. and Young, J. 'Frogmore Hall, Atcham, Shropshire – Excavations June 2017', *Transactions of the Shropshire Archaeological and Historical Society* 95 (2020), pp. 103–132
28. *HB* 32, pp. 28, 68

29. Jones, O., 'Hereditas Pouoisi: the Pillar of Eliseg and the History of Early Powys', in *Welsh History Review* 24.4 (2009), pp. 41–80
30. *TYP*, pp. 321–2
31. *LT* 1 (xxiii)
32. *AU* s.a. 613
33. **HE* II.2, fn. 257: *HE* I.34, p. 97
34. Wilmott, T. and Gardner, G., Excavations on the Legionary Amphitheatres of Chester (Deva) in Wilmott, T. (ed.) *Roman Amphitheatres and Spectacula: a 21st-Century Perspective* (BAR Publishing, 2009), pp. 63–74
35. **HE* II.2
36. Ibid.
37. Psalm 68:1; Numbers 10:35; Leahy, K. and Bland, R., *The Staffordshire Hoard* (British Museum Press, 2009), pp. 38–9; Fern, C., Dickinson, T. and Webster, L. (eds.) *The Staffordshire Hoard: an Anglo-Saxon Treasure* (Society of Antiquaries of London, 2019)
38. **HE* II.2
39. Mason, D. J. P., *The Heronbridge Research Project: Third Interim Report on Archaeological Investigations at Heronbridge, Chester, Cheshire. Excavations and Survey 2004* (Chester Archaeological Society, 2004) [osteo report]
40. **HE* II.2
41. *TYP* 60; Tolley, C. 'Æthelfrith and the Battle of Chester', *Journal of the Chester Archaeological Society* 88 (2016), pp. 51–96
42. *Marwnad Cynddylan* [kmatthews.org.uk/history/marwnad_cynddylan/index]
43. Ibid.
44. *Canu Heledd* [kmatthews.org.uk/history/canu_heledd/index]
45. Ibid.
46. *Asser, Vita Ælfredi Regis Angul Saxonum* 14: Keynes, S. and Lapidge, M., *Alfred the Great: Asser's 'Life of King Alfred' and Other Contemporary Sources* (Penguin Classics, 1983)
47. Ray, K. and Bapty, I., *Offa's Dyke: Landscape & Hegemony in Eighth-Century Britain* (Oxbow, 2016)
48. *Asser, Vita Ælfredi Regis Angul Saxonum* 14: Keynes, S. and Lapidge, M., *Alfred the Great: Asser's 'Life of King Alfred' and Other Contemporary Sources* (1983, Penguin Classics), p. 71
49. Ibid.
50. *ASC* s.a. 823
51. Henry of Huntingdon, *Historia Anglorum*, IV.29; Greenway, D. (trans.), *Henry, Archdeacon of Huntingdon: Historia Anglorum/The History of the English People* (Oxford Medieval Texts, 1996)
52. *AC*, s.a. 854

SUSSEX – *East Sussex, West Sussex*

1. *VSW* 13, p. 121
2. Ibid.
3. *VSW* 24, p. 130; 25, p. 133
4. *VSW* 36, p. 146
5. Ibid.
6. *VSW* 13, p. 121

7. Ibid.
8. Ibid.
9. *VSW* 41, p. 150
10. *HE* IV.13, p. 226
11. Hardy, R. (Director), Shaffer, A. (Screenplay), *The Wicker Man* (British Lion Films, 1973)
12. *HE* IV.13, p. 226
13. *HE* IV.13, p. 225
14. *ASC* s.a. 894 [893]
15. *Notitia Dignitatum*; Fairley, W. (ed. and trans.) 'Notitia Dignitatum or Register of Dignitaries', in *Translations and Reprints from Original Sources of European History*, Vol. VI:4 (University of Pennsylvania Press, 1900)
16. Ammianus Marcellinus, *Res Gestae*, 27.6; Hamilton, W. (trans.), *The Later Roman Empire* (Penguin Books, 1986), pp. 342–43
17. Welch, M., *Early Anglo-Saxon Sussex*, Volumes 1–2 (BAR Publishing, 1983); Welch, M., 'The Kingdom of the South Saxons: The Origins', in Bassett, S. (ed.), *The Origins of Anglo-Saxon Kingdoms* (Leicester University Press, 1989), pp. 75–83; Harrington, S. and Welch, M., *The Early Anglo-Saxon Kingdoms of Southern Britain AD 450–650: Beneath the Tribal Hidage* (Oxbow, 2014)
18. Soulat, J. 'Between Frankish and Merovingian influences in Early Anglo-Saxon Sussex (fifth-seventh centuries)' in *Studies in Early Anglo-Saxon Art and Archaeology: Papers in Honour of Martin G. Welch*, (BAR Publishing, 2011), pp. 62–71; Bavuso, I., 'Balance of power across the Channel: reassessing Frankish hegemony in southern England (sixth–early seventh century), *Early Medieval Europe* 29:3 (2021), pp. 283–304
19. Hughes, S. S. et al., 'Isotopic analysis of burials from the early Anglo-Saxon cemetery at Eastbourne, Sussex, U.K.', *Journal of Archaeological Science: Reports* 19 (2018), pp. 513–25
20. Ibid., p. 523
21. *ASC* s.a.477
22. *ASC* s.a. 485
23. *ASC* s.a. 491
24. Fulford, M. and Rippon, S., P*evensey Castle, Sussex. Excavations on the Roman Fort and Medieval Keep, 1993–95*, Wessex Archaeology Report (26) (Trust for Wessex Archaeology Ltd, 2011)
25. *HB* 45–6, pp. 32, 72–73
26. Williams, T. J. T., 'Landscape and warfare in Anglo-Saxon England and the Viking Campaign of 1006', *Early Medieval Europe* 23, pp. 329–59
27. Yorke, B., 'The Representation of Early West Saxon History' in Jorgensen, A.D. (ed.), R*eading the Anglo-Saxon Chronicle: Language, Literature, History* (Brepols, 2010), pp. 141–159
28. *ASC* s.a. 530; 508; Sims-Williams, P., 'The Settlement of England in Bede and the Chronicle', *Anglo-Saxon England* 12 (1983), pp. 1–41; Yorke, B., *Kings and Kingdoms of Early Anglo-Saxon England* (Routledge, 1990)
29. Yorke, B., 'Anglo-Saxon Original Legends', in Barrow, J. and Wareham, A. (eds.), *Myth, Rulership, Church and Charters: Essays in Honour of Nicholas Brooks* (Ashgate, 2008), pp. 15–30; *HE* II.5
30. S 108

31. *Indiculus superstitionum et paganiarum*; Boretius, A. (ed.), *Capitularia Regum Francorum*, Vol 1 1 (Harrassowitz, 1886), pp. 222–23
32. Ibid.
33. *HE*
34. Mawer, A. and Stenton, F.M., *The Place-Names of Sussex, Parts I and II* (English Place-Name Society VI, 1929–30), p.165
35. Semple, S., 'Polities and princes AD 400–800: New perspectives on the funerary landscape of the South Saxon kingdom', *Oxford Journal of Archaeology* 27 (2008), pp. 407–29
36. Ibid.
37. *Beo.*, lines 2271–8, p. 72
38. Welch, *Anglo-Saxon Sussex*
39. Emery, K. M. and Williams, H., 'A Place to Rest Your (Burnt) Bones? Mortuary Houses in Early Anglo-Saxon England', *Archaeological Journal* 175.1 (2018), pp. 55–86
40. Semple, 'Polities and princes'
41. *VSW* 41, p. 151
42. *HE* IV.13, p. 226
43. Ibid.
44. *VSW* 42, p. 151
45. Ibid.
46. *HE* IV.15
47. Ibid.
48. *ASC* s.a. 829; HE II.5

FORTRIU – *Nairnshire, Moray, Banffshire, Aberdeenshire*

1. Howard, R. E., 'Men of the Shadows' [1926], *Bran Mak Morn* (Dell Publishing, 1969), p. 34
2. Howard, 'Worms of the Earth' [1932], *Bran Mak Morn*, p. 108
3. Howard, 'Foreword', *Bran Mak Morn*, p. 9
4. Ibid., p. 8
5. *Panegyrici Latini*, VIII: 'Incerti Panegyricus Constantio Caesari Dictus', Chapter 11; Mynors, R.A.B. *XII Panegyrici Latini* (Clarendon Press, 1964)
6. Tacitus, Agricola, Chapter 11; Huttin, M. and Peterson, W. (trans.), Agricola. Germania. Dialogus, revised by Ogilvie, R. M., Warmington, E. H. and Winterbottom, M., Loeb Classical Library 35 (Harvard University Press, 1914); Ptolomy, Geographike Hyphegesis II.2. There is no standard complete translation of Ptolemy's 'Geography' in English. The introductory material (Book I) is available in Berggren, J. L. and Jones, A. (eds. and trans.), Ptolemy's Geography: an annotated translation of the theoretical chapters (Princeton University Press, 2000); relevant parts of the Geography can be found widely online: e.g. at roman-britain.co.uk/classical-references/the-geography-of-ptolemy
7. *Panegyrici Latini*, VI: 'Incerti Panegyricus Constantino Augusto Dictus', Chapter 7; Mynors, *XII Panegyrici*
8. *Ex* 19, p. 23
9. Isidore of Seville, *Etymologiae*, 19.23.7: Barney, S. A. et al. (eds. and trans.), *The Etymologies of Isidore of Seville* (Cambridge University Press, 2006)

10. Julius Caesar, *Commentarii de Bello Gallico* 5.14; Edwards, H. J. (trans.), *The Gallic War* Loeb Classical Library 72 (Harvard University Press, 1917)
11. Howard, R. E., 'Men of the Shadows' [1926], *Bran Mak Morn*, p. 35
12. Wainwright, F. T. (ed.), *The Problem of the Picts*, (Thomas Nelson, 1955)
13. *Ex.* 19, p. 23
14. *HE* I.1, pp. 456
15. Virgil, *Aeneid* IV, line 136; Rushton Fairclough, H. (trans.) *Eclogues. Georgics. Aeneid: Books 1–6*, revised by Goold, G. P., Loeb Classical Library 63 (Harvard University Press, 1916)
16. Abbo of Fleury, *Passio Sancti Eadmundi*, V: Hervey, F. (ed. and trans.), *Corolla Sancti Eadmundi: The Garland of Saint Eadmund King and Martyr* (E. P. Dutton, 1907)
17. *HE* I.1, p. 46
18. Gimbutas, M., *The Living Goddesses* (University of California Press, 2001), p. 190
19. *HE* I.1, p. 45
20. *VC* I.33, II.32
21. Forsyth, K. Language in Pictland: the case against 'non-Indo-European Pictish' (De Keltiche Draak, 1997); Evans, N. 'Ideology, Literacy and Matriliny: Approaches to Medieval Texts on the Pictish Past' in Driscoll, S. T., Geddes, J. and Hall, M. A. (eds), Pictish Progress: New Studies on Northern Britain in the Early Middle Ages (Brill, 2011), pp. 45–65
22. Henderson, G. and Henderson, I., *The Art of the Picts* (Thames & Hudson, 2004)
23. Pictish King-list (*series longior*); Anderson, *Kings and Kingship*
24. *AU* s.a. 693
25. Woolf, A., 'Dún Nechtain, Fortriu and the Geography of the Picts', *The Scottish Historical Review* 85.2 (2006), pp. 182–201.
26. Noble, G., 'Fortified settlement in northern Pictland' in Noble, G. and Evans, N. (eds.), *The King in the North: The Pictish Realms of Fortriu and Ce* (Birlinn, 2020), pp. 39–57; discoveries made in 2019 at Mither Tap remain unpublished in 2022; for a short summary see digitscotland.com/finding-a-pictish-power-centre-bennachies-mither-tap
27. *VC* II.42, p. 196
28. *VC* II.27, pp. 175–76
29. Noble, G. et al. 'Rhynie A powerful place of Pictland' in Noble and Evans, *The King in the North*, pp. 58–80
30. Discoveries made in 2020 at Tap O'Noth remain unpublished in 2022; for summaries see theconversation.com/how-aerial-technology-helped-us-discoverthe-largest-pictish-settlement-in-scotland-139542 and abdn.ac.uk/news/14019
31. Roy, W., *The Military Antiquities of the Romans in Britain* (Society of Antiquaries of London, 1793)
32. Oram, R., 'Capital Tales or Burghead Bull?' in Arbuthnot, S. and Hollo, K. (eds.), *Fil súil nglais, A Grey Eye Looks Back: a Festschrift in Honour of Colm Ó Baoill* (Clann Tuirc, 2007), pp. 241–262; Ralston, I.B.M., The Hill-forts of Pictland since the Problem of the Picts (Groam House Museum, 2004)
33. *VC* II.34, p. 183
34. *HE* III.4, p. 148

35. Carver, M., *Portmahomack: Monastery of the Picts* (Edinburgh University Press, 2008)
36. Henderson and Henderson, *The Art of the Picts*
37. Evans, N. and Noble, G. 'The early Church in northern Pictland' in Noble and Evans, *The King in the North*, pp. 134–167
38. *HE* III.24, p. 185
39. *HE* III.6, p. 152
40. *VSW* 19, p. 128
41. Ibid.
42. *AU*, s.a. 682
43. *HE* IV.26, p. 254
44. Symeon of Durham, *Libellus de Exordio atque Procursuistius hoc est Dunhelmensis Ecclesie*; Rollason, D. (ed. & trans.), *Libellus [...]* (Oxford University Press, 2000), pp. 46–7; AU s.a. 686; HB 57
45. *HE* IV.26, p. 255
46. *AU* s.a. 693

A Note on Terminology

1. Rambaran-Olm, M. and Wade, E., 'The Many Myths of the Term "Anglo-Saxon"', *Smithsonian Magazine* (14 July 2021) [smithsonianmag.com/history/many-myths-term-anglo-saxon-180978169]
2. Collins, M., *The Steadfast Trust: Caught On Camera* (18 February 2015) [hopenothate.org.uk/2015/02/18/the-steadfast-trust-caught-on-camera]
3. Forum for Multidisciplinary Anglo-Saxon Studies, *The responsible use of the term 'Anglo-Saxon'* (updated 3 January 2020) [fmass.eu]; see also Williams, H. 'The fight for "Anglo-Saxon", *Aeon* (29 May 2020) [aeon.co/essays/why-we-should-keep-the-term-anglo-saxon-in-archaeology] and Wood, M. 'As a racism row rumbles on, is it time to retire the term "Anglo-Saxon"?', *History Extra* (4 November 2019) [historyextra.com/period/anglo-saxon/professor-michael-wood-anglo-saxon-name-debate-is-term-racist]

INDEX